AMERICAN STUDIES AS TRANSNATIONAL PRACTICE

RE-MAPPING THE TRANSNATIONAL
A Dartmouth Series in American Studies

SERIES EDITOR
Donald E. Pease
Avalon Foundation Chair of Humanities
Founding Director of the Futures of American Studies Institute
Dartmouth College

The emergence of Transnational American studies in the wake of the Cold War marks the most significant reconfiguration of American studies since its inception. The shock waves generated by a newly globalized world order demanded an understanding of America's embeddedness within global and local processes rather than scholarly reaffirmations of its splendid isolation. The series Re-Mapping the Transnational seeks to foster the crossnational dialogues needed to sustain the vitality of this emergent field. To advance a truly comparativist understanding of this scholarly endeavor, Dartmouth College Press welcomes monographs from scholars both inside and outside the United States.

For a complete list of books available in this series, see www.upne.com.

Yuan Shu and Donald E. Pease, editors, *American Studies as Transnational Practice: Turning toward the Transpacific*

Melissa M. Adams-Campbell, *New World Courtships: Transatlantic Alternatives to Companionate Marriage*

David LaRocca and Ricardo Miguel-Alfonso, editors, *A Power to Translate the World: New Essays on Emerson and International Culture*

Elèna Mortara, *Writing for Justice: Victor Séjour, the Mortara Case, and the Age of Transatlantic Emancipations*

Rob Kroes, *Prison Area, Independence Valley: American Paradoxes in Political Life and Popular Culture*

Etsuko Taketani, *The Black Pacific Narrative: Geographic Imaginings of Race and Empire between the World Wars*

William V. Spanos, *Shock and Awe: American Exceptionalism and the Imperatives of the Spectacle in Mark Twain's* A Connecticut Yankee in King Arthur's Court

Laura Bieger, Ramón Saldívar, and Johannes Voelz, editors, *The Imaginary and Its Worlds: American Studies after the Transnational Turn*

Paul A. Bové, *A More Conservative Place: Intellectual Culture in the Bush Era*

EDITED BY YUAN SHU AND
DONALD E. PEASE

AMERICAN STUDIES AS TRANSNATIONAL PRACTICE

Turning toward the Transpacific

DARTMOUTH COLLEGE PRESS
HANOVER, NEW HAMPSHIRE

Dartmouth College Press
An imprint of University Press of New England
www.upne.com
© 2015 Trustees of Dartmouth College

Manufactured in the United States of America
Typeset in Sabon by Integrated Publishing Solutions, Grand Rapids,
Michigan.

For permission to reproduce any of the material in this book,
contact Permissions, University Press of New England, One Court Street,
Suite 250, Lebanon NH 03766; or visit www.upne.com

Hardcover ISBN: 978-1-61168-846-7
Paperback ISBN: 978-1-61168-847-4
Ebook ISBN: 978-1-61168-848-1

Library of Congress Cataloging-in-Publication
Data available upon request

5 4 3 2 1

CONTENTS

YUAN SHU AND
DONALD E. PEASE

INTRODUCTION: TRANSNATIONAL AMERICAN STUDIES AND THE TRANSPACIFIC IMAGINARY

PREVIOUS CONTRIBUTORS TO THE series Re-Mapping the Transnational share the assumption that the significance and import of transnational practices depend on the contexts that articulate them to preexisting geopolitical formations. They have also indicated the difficulty in providing an agreed-on contextual focus for transnationalism's conflicted terrain. In an effort to provide such a focus, Donald Pease, a coeditor of the volume *Re-Framing the Transnational Turn in American Studies*, located the origins of transnational American studies in the 1960s, when transnational resistance to the Vietnam War supplied a cause that brought together disparate social movements demanding political and civil rights for women, ethnic and sexual minorities, political refugees, migrant laborers, stateless persons, and immigrants (Pease 2011, 12). Pease also remarked on the difficulties that contemporary practitioners of transnational American studies confronted in locating a coherent object of analysis for a field that was seemingly in perpetual transit and transition (ibid., 6–11; see also Jay 2010, 1–12). Transnationalism's definitional amorphousness rendered efforts at referential precision even more complicated.

The United States is perhaps the prototypical transnational state formation. Yet since World War II the United States has exhibited the uncanny ability to exercise military, economic, and geopolitical dominance across the planet while representing itself to its own population as a territorially bound nation-state. The Cold War sustained this nationalist orientation by creating the prospect of a seemingly permanent global war as the dominant framework for representing, interpreting, and evaluating US geopolitical and economic transactions and relationships. After 9/11, President George W. Bush established a continuum between Cold War nationalism and the global homeland state's transnational imperatives when he embedded US neoliberal political and economic policies in a twenty-first-century version of perpetual warfare.

Transnational American studies scholars who do not take the territorial United States as their primary object of analysis have had to reckon with challenges outside academe as well as within the field of American studies. In his response to Emory Elliott's 2006 presidential address to the American Studies Association, Winfried Fluck encouraged US practitioners of transnational American studies to return to the "task and interpretive challenge for which [the field American Studies] was created," namely, an "analysis of the cultural sources of American power" (Fluck 2007, 30). Robyn Wiegman has wondered whether transnational scholars' repeated expressions of a desire to "dis-identify with America" did not reveal the strength of a nation-state capable of soliciting such passionate acts of detachment (2011, 360).

Pace Fluck and Wiegman, contemporary American studies scholars cannot ignore the fact that the United States is itself a transnational circuit of physical, economic, and cultural exchanges whose dominion extends to regions that cannot be contained within the nation's geographical territory. Nor can they simply refuse to recognize the complex networks interconnecting regions (like the newly industrialized South), multinational corporations (like Google and General Electric), diasporic sites (such as Aztlan and Chinatown), and subnational formations (for example, the ecology and women's rights movements) within the territorial United States to processes that extend beyond its boundaries. While the twentieth century was a time when the nation and the idea of national culture predominated, the twenty-first century is marked by crossnational linkages and transnational processes.

Transnational American studies scholars who have devised frameworks with which to analyze geographical formations both beyond and below the level of the nation-state have extended the aims of their precursors in the 1960s. The critique that the American studies scholars who took part in the transnational resistance to the US war in the Asia-Pacific region in the 1960s mounted against the US imperial state contributed to the transnational public sphere's efforts to combat the nondemocratic decisions of the imperial state (Fraser 2014). The academic knowledge required to sustain these critical practices spurred the construction of African American, Asian American, ethnic, women's, and gender studies programs. The shift from anti-imperial and multicultural to transnational iterations of American studies was spurred on by transnational Americanists' construction of differently imagined relations with the US imperial state.

We have envisioned this volume as a sequel to *Re-Framing the Transnational Turn in American Studies*. Rather than affirming the 2012 representation of transnational American studies as a field in seemingly endless transition, however, we have solicited essays for this volume that would provide conceptual categories and modes of analysis for a broad range of transnational practices. In this introduction we intend to situate these practices as resources for understanding and critically engaging the so-called US pivot to Asia at this historical moment.

The grand-scale spatial restructuring and geoeconomic processes responsible for the US swerve to Asia constitute significant issues for transnational American studies scholars in the twenty-first century. State policies formulated to instigate, shape, and manage the geopolitical reconfigurations depend on tacit imaginaries that influence how we desire and feel about such changes and the sense we make of them. In this introduction we will explore the historical role that the Pacific and Asia have played in the construction of the US imperial state and examine the US role in bringing about the macropolitical restructuring of the region. Specifically, we will examine how contemporary efforts to subsume countries across the Pacific within the logics of neoliberal globalization are undergirded by colonial imperialism. Residual Cold War formations furnish lenses through which to begin to comprehend this pivotal moment in a region whose politics and culture remain saturated with traces of colonial imperialism.

The cessation of the Cold War in Europe brought about a significant shift in the geopolitical alignments throughout the Asia-Pacific region where the Cold War had not yet ended. However, 9/11 and the global war on terror distracted President Bush from attention to a region that was defined by China's spectacular economic growth. After the Bush administration turned Islamist fundamentalism into the global enemy of the United States, it elevated the Middle East into the political center of the world. But Bush's demand that countries throughout the Asia-Pacific region align themselves with his planetary crusade threatened to destabilize the region. It took the military fiascos in Iraq and Afghanistan and the 2008 collapse of global financial markets to persuade the United States to manage what Robert Kaplan has dubbed the "elegant decline" (2007, 104) of the US military intervention by downsizing its scale. In 2008, the last year of the Bush administration, the US trade deficit with China was about $250 billion annually. China owned about $1 trillion in debt guaranteed by the US government, a tenfold leap since 2001. Countries throughout the region were anxious about China's military spending, which had grown at a faster rate than its economy.[1] The 2011 announcement by the administration of President Barack Obama of a pivot to Asia was in part an effort to reassure countries that had been uneasy about the impact of China's economic and military build-up in the region.

Commentators have described this shift as the inauguration of a "cool war."[2] But the Obama administration's strategies for the so-called Pacific century drew on colonial and imperial imaginaries that originated in the nineteenth century and were resurrected in the inaugural years of the Cold War. The Pacific age, as we will explain in greater detail below, began when Admiral Alfred Thayer Mahan persuaded the administration of President Theodore Roosevelt to accept his conviction that maritime dominance in the Pacific was the key to US success in the great game of imperial expansion. Mahan's strategy, which based US imperial supremacy on the acquisition of markets and military bases, supplied the model for US control of the Asia Pacific throughout the Cold War.

The Cold War made the Asia Pacific important to the United States in ways it had never been before. Between 1945 and 1961, the United States expanded its political, military, and economic power along the crescent stretching from Korea through the Chinese mainland and Taiwan; then through the island chains of Japan, the Philippines, and Indonesia; and out into the Pacific, across the Southeast Asian peninsula, and up into the Indian subcontinent (Dirlik 1998a). The expansion of US power was in tension with the revolutionary processes of decolonization. Nationalists throughout the Asia-Pacific launched successful postwar decolonization movements: the Philippines gained independence from the United States in 1946; Indonesia won its independence from the Dutch in 1949; and Vietnam, Laos, and Cambodia gained nominal separation from the French in 1949 and actual independence in 1954. Although nations throughout the Asia-Pacific achieved formal independence, the United States repurposed the colonial apparatuses that Japan had installed in its imperial ventures across the region as infrastructures for the industrial, political, and military institutions through which the United States exercised postwar hegemony (Dirlik 1998b; Cumings 2010).

Resistance to the Vietnam War may have been site of origin for transnational American studies. But the Korean War was the transpacific event that coordinated the domestic and transnational aspects of the Cold War state. The three chief effects of the Korean War were the reincorporation of Japan into the world imperial system, the securing of US hegemony throughout the transpacific region, and the justification of Cold War ideological oppositions. It was the Korean War and not World War II that led to the establishment of a permanent standing US army, that authorized the formation of the national security state, and that transformed the United States into an empire of military bases abroad and a vast military-industrial complex at home to service that empire (Cumings 2010, 188–201).

US involvement in World War II began in 1941 and ended in 1945; the Korean War began in 1950 and has never really ended. Between 1945 and 1948, President Harry Truman's postwar demobilization program introduced drastic reductions across the US armed forces: the Army shrank from 11.0

million soldiers in 1945 to 554,000 soldiers; the Navy fell from 3.4 million men and 1,000 ships to 0.5 million men and 300 ships; and the Air Force underwent a comparable contraction. Defeats suffered by US-supported South Korean and allied troops at the hands of Chinese and Korean peasant armies in 1950 led Truman to declare a national emergency that quadrupled the national defense budget. In December 1950, US military expenditures exceeded the combined defense spending of the eighteen next highest spending military powers. After the movement of Chinese battalions caught the US intelligence community unawares, the Pentagon responded by consolidating its disparate intelligence services into the Central Intelligence Agency, whose surveillance networks have defined global power ever since. The United States derived its prerogative to act as policeman of the world from its response to the Korean War (Cumings 2010, 190–96).

The Cold War divided the planet into two distinct globally encompassing yet utterly contradictory historical realities. However, the Cold War's temporality, spatiality, and geopolitical import varied significantly according to where it was made to work and how people experienced its workings. For Europeans and Americans who thought of it in terms of a peaceful, balanced contest of power, the Cold War was a mostly imaginary military struggle. Much of Cold War history has been studied through this Euro-American lens. What is missing in this still dominant perspective is any account of the Cold War's on-the-ground violence in what the Korean anthropologist Heonik Kwon has called *The Other Cold War* (2010). Outside of Europe, the Cold War resulted in real wars and in the destruction of communities at the grass-roots level. The major difference in perspectives is that the Cold War that Europe and the United States experienced was a steady-state preliminary to war. But the Cold War that inhabitants of Korea, Vietnam, other countries in East Asia and the global South went through resulted in mass deaths (Kwon 2010). The perspective on the Cold War after 1989 ratified a Euro-American view of world history. The Cold War may have ended in Europe, but its colonial and imperialist dynamic continues to mediate colonial and postcolonial history throughout the Asia Pacific.

President Obama recalled Cold War governance structures when he modeled the Pacific Charter, his geopolitical strategy for the Asia-Pacific region in the twenty-first century, on multilateral principles spelled out in the Atlantic Charter (Patrick 2011). Issued in 1941 as a policy statement defining the Allied goals for the postwar world, the Atlantic Charter led to the founding of the chief transnational organizations—the North Atlantic Treaty Organization, the General Agreement on Tariffs and Trade, the World Bank, and the International Monetary Fund—responsible for maintaining the Cold War peace (ibid.). In January 2012 the Obama administration issued a strategic defense statement titled *Sustaining U.S. Global Leadership: Priorities for 21st Century Defense* that based the US pivot to Asia on the shift in the globe's strategic and economic epicenter from the North Atlantic to the Western Pacific. The document described the US strategic relationship with China in the Pacific century as involving two interdependent aspects—engagement and containment—that derived from an intractable contradiction: the US economy is inextricably integrated with that of its main international strategic competitor. The engagement component of the strategy would enmesh China's trade relations within the multilateral rules and regulations of the existing international system. The strategic containment dimension of the policy rebalanced military power in East Asia by deterring Chinese aggression.[3]

To enhance US standing in the East Asia region, Obama signed a memorandum of understanding on defense cooperation with Vietnam; strengthened military ties with India; renewed treaties with each of its Cold War regional allies, Japan, South Korea, Australia, New Zealand, the Philippines, and Thailand; attended the East Asia Summit; hosted leaders of the Asia-Pacific Economic Cooperation forum in Honolulu; secured a free trade agreement with Korea; forged an alliance to bring economies from across the Pacific into a single twenty-first century Trans-Pacific Partnership (US Trade Representative n.d.); and brokered an agreement at the Asian Regional Forum over the maritime rules regulating navigation in the South China Sea.

The transpacific attained significance as a zone of economic cooperation in 2005 when nine countries that border on the Pacific—Australia, Brunei Darussalam, Chile, Malaysia, New Zealand, Peru, Singapore, Vietnam, and the United States—entered into a Trans-Pacific Partnership. This partnership was to play a key role in the US effort to contain Chinese influence by building strategic collaborations across the Pacific. The participants in the partnership arrived at explicit agreements about free markets and transnational corporations that were tacitly underwritten by political, military, and strategic accords. Because the partnership was built on previously forged networks of power and domination—the Asia-Pacific Economic Cooperation forum and the Association of Southeast Asian Nations—and its members' economic, military, political, and cultural exchanges were codified in treaties and formal alliances, it suited the needs of US policymakers.

The Trans-Pacific Partnership induced the US State Department to recognize the transpacific as an official region. But transpacific history predates the partnership. Scholars deployed a transpacific framework decades before the formation of the partnership to explain how the three decades of war in Korea and Indochina that ostensibly were fought to contain communism were in fact undertaken to advance the development of capitalism, notably in Japan and South Korea. Japan, South Korea, Thailand, and the Philippines supported the US war in Vietnam by providing military bases, soldiers, contractors, and supplies. The US war in Indochina left a legacy of violence and displacement for the people of Vietnam, Laos, and Cambodia, many of whom fled across the Pacific to other countries. It also created sites of opposition and resistance and fostered crossregional collaborations, alliances, and friendships among subjugated and marginalized peoples who aspired to counter the hegemony of the United States, China, Japan, and other regional powers.

The transpacific cannot be reduced to the participants in the Trans-Pacific Partnership. Its areas of interaction include the extensive and continuing flows of people, goods, and ideas between Asian countries, across the Pacific, and between Asia and the Americas. Several benchmark academic studies have called attention to the contesting imaginings of the transpacific: it is a space of colonial exploration, conquest, exploitation, and expansion advanced by European, American, and Asian powers; it is also a contact zone, whose history is passed on by alternate narratives of translocalism, oppositional localism (Wilson 2000), and oppositional regionalism (Dirlik 1998b). There is nothing innocent about these spatial categorizations. How American studies scholars view the Pacific is a political as well as an academic question. East and Southeast Asia, Asia-Pacific, Pacific Asia, the Pacific rim and the Pacific are informed by multiple genealogies. These contesting topographies represent efforts to grasp conceptually a world in the process of being transformed by novel configurations of economic, social, and political forces that depend on regional and global institutions for their conceptual validation (Dirlik 1998a and 1998b; Yui 1930). Indeed, the transpacific is not a coherent region so much as a volatile space of interaction that contains overlapping contradictory forces and is defined by historical conflicts over geography, economy, and political spheres of influence. The end of the Cold War in Europe witnessed the elevation in the economic power of Japan and the so-called Asian Tigers—Singapore, South Korea, Taiwan, and Hong Kong. Created by unpredictable market forces that used this area to create new rules and regulations, the new networks of economic power throughout this region posed insuperable difficulties for policymakers accustomed to geographical entities supported by reliable institutional apparatuses. Yet these transpacific configurations of economic power have begun to vie with the transatlantic region for pride of place in contemporary discourses of globalization.

The formation of the Atlantic world depended on the emergence of what Walter Mignolo theorizes as "the Atlantic commercial circuit" in the sixteenth century (2002, 81) that culminated in the colonization of the Americas, the slave trade, and the founding of the American republic (Gulliver 2011, 89). The Atlantic world has occupied a privileged but settled space in constructing US history and narratives from the country's founding to the end of the so-called American century.

What role will the transpacific play in the US pivot to Asia? How do the historically complex and culturally diverse formations in the transpacific align with America's Pacific century? These are questions that transnational American studies scholars need to address in their efforts to explain the shift from the transatlantic to the transpacific organization of US geopolitical history and to delineate the differences between what historians and critics have described as the Atlantic world (Gulliver 2011, 89; Blank 1999, 265) and what former Secretary of State Hillary Clinton named America's Pacific century (Clinton 2011, 56).

One of the central contentions of this introduction is that a transpacific frame of reference for transnational American studies will enable the field's practitioners to look at US transatlantic activities from an inverted mirror. Practicing what Roger Daniels calls "looking at American history 'the wrong way'" (1988, 3)—that is, from west to east—would also facilitate what Mignolo calls "de-colonial thinking" (2007, 111). As heir to the contradictions, competitions, and uncertainties that continue to haunt and reshape the region (Dirlik 1998b), the Pacific century calls for transnational scholars' wholesale reimagining of the transpacific.

In the sections that follow, we intend to sketch the variations in the changing US practices of colonialism and imperialism in the transpacific—from their inception in the nineteenth century, through alternative formations during the Cold War, and into the American Pacific century. Framing the US pivot to Asia within the context of the transpacific as a site of economic integration and political, military, and cultural contentions, we will briefly spell out why and how the rise of China as a regional—if not a global—power is especially relevant to transnational American studies. We will conclude this introduction by situating transpacific studies within a genealogy that designates it as a possible future of transnational American studies.

Before turning to the transnational practices specific to these Pacific configurations, however, we need to paint the broad brushstrokes of a macropolitical sketch of the trajectory of global capitalism, from its origins in colonial imperialism to its present neoliberal adaptation.

In its five centuries of operation, colonial imperialism fundamentally transformed and linked together previously unconnected geographical spaces into a single measurable structure. According to James Blaut, prior to 1492 Europe, Asia, and Africa were more or less equally developed. Europe took the lead in capital formation through its imperial colonization of the Americas, beginning in 1492. Europe's proximity to North America accelerated the capital accumulation of European powers through the acquisition of colonies and the extraction of resources in the New World. Although European imperialists exported their institutions to the colonies, the basis of the interactions among the regions remained the local conditions formed in each region. Anibal Quijano and Immanuel Wallerstein have explained how colonial imperialist practices associated with transamericanity increased the efficacy of colonial imperialism by forcing New World regions to connect with the rest of the world. At the outset of the industrial revolution in 1800, European colonialism governed 35 percent of the earth's surface; that share rose to 67 percent in 1878 and reached 85 percent in 1914.[4]

Europe was at the epicenter of capitalism in the early sixteenth century. Economic dominance shifted to North America in the nineteenth and twentieth centuries. After World War II the hegemony that the United States exercised in the capitalist bloc extended worldwide. According to Paul Blank, the global economy reached a turning point in 1980 when the value of transpacific commerce outweighed that of transatlantic commerce for the first time (1999, 265). At the outset of the twenty-first century, the movement of capital from Western Europe across the Atlantic to North America had continued across the Pacific to Asia.

Why the Pacific? From the China Trade to America's Pacific Century

Arif Dirlik observed that from the beginning, it was "European (later Euro-American) concepts, visions, and fantasies" that invested the Asia-Pacific region with meaning (1998b, 4). After rehearsing the history of the European and American colonial influence on the region, Dirlik concluded that the discourse of the Asia-Pacific region defined the contours of a physical space that it purported to describe. To support this assertion, Dirlik implicitly engaged the work of the geographers Martin Lewis and Karen Wigen (1997), who explained that "Asia" was a term invented by the ancient Greeks to denote all lands to the east of them, in contrast to Europe to the north and west and Africa to the south. According to Lewis and Wigen, the Greeks invented these geographical spaces to locate the territorial landmasses out of which the network of interconnected trade routes surrounding the Mediterranean emanated. After explaining how the continental model for understanding the different regions of the globe mistakenly reified mutable geopolitical boundaries and thereby neglected the complex webs of capital and commodity exchange, Lewis and Wigen urged contemporary scholars to begin thinking in terms of oceans and bays rather than continents or cultural blocs.

Because of its immense expanse and the complexity of its borders, how-ever, the Pacific is far more difficult to conceptualize than the Mediterra-nean. Indeed, for many centuries the Pacific was portrayed as an insuper-able barrier to trade. American imaginings of the Pacific date back to the so-called period of the discovery, when Columbus searched for a passage that he hoped would link the Atlantic to the Pacific and so allow Europe to reach Asia through the Americas (Dirlik 1998a, 23). Dirlik explained the serial shifts in the names Euro-Americans attributed to the Pacific—from the Spanish Lake to the English Lake and then to the American Lake—as related to which imperial power exercised control over its trade routes. After draw-ing important distinctions between the Pacific as a concept within Euro-American cultural productions and its factual existence as the setting for myriad Asian economic practices and migrations, Dirlik showed how an affirmative American representation of the Pacific was shaped by the China trade between Salem, Massachusetts, and Canton (Guangzhou), which began with the journeys of the *Empress of China* in 1784 and the *Grand Turk* in 1785 and continued with the first entrance of New England whaling ships into the Pacific around Cape Horn in 1791 (Gulliver 2011, 89; Kuo 1930, 420; Leon W. 1994, 18).

President Thomas Jefferson, whose "vast geographical knowledge was augmented by political pragmaticism," fostered a change in the US govern-ment's perception of the Pacific from a vague place on the map to "one that demanded concrete government policies" protective of American interests (Leon W. 1994, 26). Jefferson believed the expedition by Meriwether Lewis and William Clark would open a pathway to the Pacific capable of stretch-ing the US republic from ocean to ocean, and of fulfilling his dual dreams of a property-owning democracy and a passage to India, opening up trade with East Asia.[5] Michael Hardt has correlated Jefferson's interest in the Pacific to "the Jeffersonian formula of democracy" (2007, 41). But Jefferson's early interest in East Asia and the commercial connection between New England and southern China did not translate into an equivalent interest in the peo-ples and cultures of the Asia Pacific (Kuo 1930, 439).

Indeed, the Pacific did not register in Euro-American consciousness as an American lake until the late nineteenth century, when Mahan described US sea power and presence in the Pacific as critical to the nation-state's rise as a global power. With the collaboration of Theodore Roosevelt, who as assistant secretary of the Navy played a key role in the 1898 conquest of the Philippines and the annexation of the Hawaiian Islands, Mahan success-fully advanced the policy of elevating the Pacific into an American sphere of influence to ensure US maritime dominance. Pekka Korhonen has ascribed the basis for Mahan's alliance with Roosevelt to their shared conviction that economic superiority was a function of race and civilization and to the fact that the "military background of both men pointed more to a world view of conflict than to one of harmony" (1996, 48). In keeping with this assessment, Christopher Connery has recently singled out Mahan's Pacific strategy as the foundation for the US imperial strategy across the American century: "Mahan is centrally responsible for the US posture of constant military preparedness and the posture of imminent global war, which has characterized so much of our century" (2001, 183).

The US rise to global power in the late nineteenth century turned the Pacific into what Bruce Cumings dubbed "a Euro-American name" for "measuring, delineating, and recognizing living space for the people who live there" (2009, 55). With the end of World War II in 1945 and the onset of the Cold War in 1946, countries throughout the Asia Pacific became crucial sites of Cold War contestation. According to Cumings, the region was painted red from 1945 to 1975, with China serving as a major threat at the center and with North Korea and North Vietnam as minor problems at the periphery. US policy reached a turning point in 1961, when Walt Rostow authored the Kennedy administration's "non-Communist manifesto" (Cumings 1998, 57), which defined capitalist growth by stages and repainted the Asia Pacific partly black by placing Japan at its center.

In *Dominion from Sea to Sea*, Cumings argues that Japan, as a non-Western imperial power, was the only country in the Asia Pacific that discovered how to thrive under British hegemony in the nineteenth century and then under US hegemony in the twentieth. During their occupation of Korea and Taiwan, the Japanese set up the colonial apparatuses that set the pace for their industrialization. Throughout the period of Japanese colonization of East Asia, the colonized used an admiration of US popular culture as a means of disidentification from Japanese domination. World War II military strategists imagined Pacific Asia as the theater of war operations where American and Japanese imperial interests in Asia collided.

But after World War II, Cold War administrators continued Japanese colonialism by military and commercial means. Overlaying Japan's colonial system of power with the Cold War structure, the United States instituted an empire of military bases centered in the Philippines, Okinawa, Guam, the Mariana Islands, Tokyo, Seoul, Taiwan, and the Bikini Atoll. The US government crafted a web of economic treaties that allied the United States with South Korea, Japan, Taiwan, the Philippines, Thailand, South Vietnam, Laos, Cambodia, Malaysia, and Pakistan. This increased US economic presence in Asia by pouring in billions in dollars in foreign aid, exporting American goods, importing Asia's raw materials, and encouraging the expansion in Asia of US private corporations. According to Cumings (2010), the

Cold War's military-industrial complex continues to flourish in this topsy-turvy world.

Japan's economic performance may have attracted interest in the transpacific in the twentieth century, but China's rise—together with the economic growth of Vietnam, South Korea, Malaysia, and Indonesia—has drawn scholarly interest in this upside-down region at the onset of the twenty-first century. Anticipating Lisa Lowe's argument concerning Asian unassimilability in *Immigrant Acts*,[6] Dirlik (1998a) has characterized the US construction of its archipelago of military bases across the Pacific as the geopolitical pretext for denying Americanness to Asian Americans. Dirlik has specifically argued that the history of US policymakers' relations with the Asia Pacific extended the doctrine of Manifest Destiny, representing this terrain as an alien geography occupied by exotic peoples with un-American cultures that was destined to be remade in the image of US democracy.

Rather than confirming the historical efficacy of Manifest Destiny, Patricia Nelson Limerick has supplanted conventional representations of westward expansion as a conquest of indigenous populations with an account of multidirectional movements of Mexicans, Indians, Canadians, and Asian Americans across the North American continent: "The east-to-west process of exploration now must compete with a recognition of Indian prior presence, as well as of northward movements from Mexico, southward movements from Canada, and eastward movements from Asia" (1992, 1022).

When Limerick rewrote Western histories "from the West" instead of from the East (1992, 1021)—the classic Eurocentric approach—she fundamentally altered our perception of the object in question. Limerick also added real Asian American gardens to the Jeffersonian dream of extending the boundaries of US agrarian democracy to the West Coast: "The gardens in the concentration camps, as well as the earlier Chinese and Japanese vegetable gardens and farms throughout California, offered a powerful statement that the term 'agrarian dream' could carry the adjectives 'Chinese' and 'Japanese' as well as 'Jeffersonian.' Originating in a very different set of historical and cultural circumstances, the Chinese agrarian dream and the Japanese agrarian dream joined up with the American version in bringing an ideal of order and productivity to bear on the 'wild' American landscape" (ibid., 1045).

By invoking Asian and Asian American material histories, Dirlik and Limerick have shown how Asian Pacific and Asian American experiences at once added to and complicated conventional accounts of US history. Changing the focus of Euro-American consciousness from the East Coast to the West Coast and from the North Atlantic to the Asia Pacific has made possible the construction of alternative epistemologies for understanding the transpacific. The repertoire of transnational practices that use the transpacific as their scholarly archive differs significantly from that of transnational scholarship drawing on the imperial rivalries and colonial topographies of the sixteenth-century European nation-states. The economic and human movements across the Asia Pacific have emboldened transnational American studies scholars not only to reevaluate the east-to-west narrative of US historical expansion but also to reconsider whether the Atlantic is the site of origin and the intellectual frame of reference for Euro-American consciousness.

According to Mignolo, modernity, coloniality, and capitalism were consolidated when the Atlantic commercial circuit emerged in the sixteenth century. Their convergence resulted in the production of two grand narratives. Mignolo named the first "the Western civilization macronarrative," (2002, 58) whose form of historiography and philosophy originated in Greece but emerged in Europe during the Renaissance and was codified into a grand narrative by German philosophers in the early nineteenth century. Mignolo called the second the "modern/colonial world-system narrative" (ibid.), which originated as an explanation of the transatlantic commercial circuit but came to fruition during the Cold War era across the Asia Pacific.

The founders of the US republic embraced the principles of Western epistemology undergirding both narratives. They looked backward to the Atlantic world for the origins of US history and philosophy, but they looked forward to the Pacific as the model for the economic and military expansions of American civilization. Mignolo, who believes that in remapping the Pacific, we should consider the epistemologies from indigenous and Third World cultures and societies as a decisive point of departure, pointedly criticized the Euro-American "observer" for situating himself "above" the earth and arrogating to himself the power to "map the world with the Atlantic, not the Pacific, at its center" (2011, 79). Building on this critique, Mignolo has prescribed a strategy of decolonial resistance: "Being where one thinks implies, first and foremost, recognizing and confronting both imperial categorization of being and universal principles of knowing; it means engaging in epistemic disobedience, in independent thoughts, in decolonial thinking" (ibid., 97). Mignolo's dual origin stories put us in a position to understand the pan-Asianism that emerged in the transpacific before and after the Cold War as a form of decolonial thinking designed to counter Euro-American imperial domination.

Reimagining the Asia Pacific: Japan, China, and Southeast Asia

The Obama administration did not invent the Pacific age. That phrase was first used by the Japanese political economist and historian Inagaki Manjiro in his 1892 study of British expansionism while he was studying under

John Robert Seeley at Cambridge University. Extending his British mentor's
conceptual understanding of the processes interconnecting the ocean, progress, economics, and the future, Inagaki concluded that in the twentieth
century the center of the world dynamics would shift from Europe to the
Pacific during "the railway-oceanic stage of civilization" (quoted in Korhonen 1996, 45) because of what Korhonen describes as "the diffusion of
European capital and trading experience, and the abundant resources" in
the region (ibid.).

Inagaki did not intend his proclamation of the Pacific age to represent
an Asia-Pacific region opposed to the European powers. Inagaki believed
that Japan could achieve regional dominance only through its adoption of
the European nation-state model to break with China-centered Confucian
imperialism. Inagaki's vision was closely related to the March 16, 1885,
editorial outlining Japan's grand strategy to "shed Asia and join Europe"
that was published in the Tokyo newspaper *Jiji Shinpo* and was presumed
to be the work of Fukuzawa Yukichi (Wang 2011, 13). In *The Politics of
Imagining Asia*, Wang Hui pointed out that Japan's Pacific Age strategy of
shedding Asia was embedded in an East Asian stance of self-negation. Wang
also observed that Europeans' orientalist understanding of world history
positioned East Asians' self-negation as at once Europe's starting point and
Europe's imaginary other.

If "shedding" Asia revealed Japan's understanding of modernization as
Westernization, joining Europe led Japan to adopt what Wang described as
an imperial "state rationality" linking modernity, colonialism, and capitalism as the motor of "world history" (2011, 21 and 58). With its integration
of Japan into the European economic system, the Pacific age designated the
moment at which Japan expanded Europe's nation-state system to include
countries across the Asia Pacific. The expansion began with Japan's 1895
annexation of Taiwan after the first Sino-Japanese War and continued in
1905, when Japan gained control of southern Manchuria after the Russo-
Japanese War and turned Korea into a protectorate.

The discourse of the Pacific age continued to evolve in the 1920s, at-
tracting attention and support from US and Japanese academics as well as
citizens of other nations in the region. The Chinese revolutionary leaders
Sun Yat-sen and Li Dazhao turned to Japan for inspiration before the 1911
revolution that overthrew the Qing dynasty in China. They later rejected Japan's expansionist "Greater East Asia" in favor of notions such as "Greater
Asianism" and "Pan-Asianism" that were rooted in the Confucian "kingly
way" that emphasized state relations of mutual recognition (Wang 2011,
31). US groups based in Hawaii and New York who were alarmed at Japan's
imperialist policies founded the Institute of Pacific Relations in 1925 to pro-

mote better relations among Asia Pacific countries. At a conference sponsored by the institute in Kyoto in 1929, the Chinese keynote speaker, David
Yui, challenged Japan's military occupation of northern China by criticizing
Japan's policy of "shedding Asia" in theory but "invading Asia" in practice (Yui 1930, 35; Wang 2011, 22). Invoking Yui's intervention implicitly,
Wang has proposed that residual traditions of the socialist and national
liberation movements of the twentieth century in East and Southeast Asia
should remain vital sources "for stimulating new ways of imagining Asia"
(Wang 2011, 62). Wang set the fragmented cultural forms and institutions
of the noncapitalist Confucian way in opposition to the global order that
the United States inaugurated after the tragic events of 9/11.

Before World War II, the critical issues for East Asia were related to the
contradictory relationship between modernity and colonialism. After World
War II, the Cold War opposition between democracy and totalitarianism
defined East Asia. Through an ideological sleight of hand, Cold War social
engineers represented the struggles between colonialism and anticolonialism and between imperialism and anti-imperialism as the confrontations
between totalitarian Iron Curtain communism and free democratic liberal
capitalism (Cumings 2010).

Drawing on Mignolo's theory of decolonization and extending Yoshimi
Takeuchi's critique of Japan, modernity, and coloniality (2005), Kuan-Hsing
Chen has recently presented a critique of colonial modernity that involves
both the colonized and the colonizers. For the colonized, decolonization
entailed the active critique of colonial legacies at the levels of ontology and
epistemology; for the colonizers, decolonization required the critical reflex-
ive understanding of colonial history and tradition and cautioned against
new forms of colonialism and imperialism, which Chen called "deimperialization."

Chen centered his thinking about decolonization on the insight that Cold
War administrators restored the infrastructures of Japanese colonialism
and imperialism to govern countries across East Asia. By reconfiguring the
region's postwar problems in terms of conflicts between good democracy
and evil totalitarian dictatorship, the United States undermined the energies needed to de-imperialize and decolonize East Asia, and it rechanneled
regional political activism into economic interests and developmental concerns in Japan, Okinawa, Taiwan, and South Korea. Chen shrewdly observed that, with the installation of the anticommunist and pro-American
structure in the capitalist zone of East Asia, "the United States has become
the inside of East Asia, and it is constitutive of a new East Asian subjectivity" (2010, 8).

The Cold War US state never offered any critical reflection on Japanese or

Western colonialism and imperialism in the Asia Pacific. By distinguishing US imperialism from its European iterations, US policymakers adapted what Donald Pease has critiqued as Cold War American exceptionalism throughout East Asia. In his case study of the symbolic role that Emperor Hirohito played during the US occupation of Japan, Naoki Sakai grounded his argument on an archive of documents spelling out the transpacific complicity between Japanese nationalism and US exceptionalism in sustaining Cold War governmentality in Japan and the Asia Pacific after World War II. The recently published "Memorandum on Policy towards Japan" (Reischauer 1942) dictated that Hirohito be forgiven all responsibility for World War II so that he could continue to perform the symbolic function of embodying the Japanese concept of national tradition and culture under postwar US hegemony (Sakai 2010, 247).

Worried that Asian communists would link the long history of US racial discrimination—from the enslavement of Africans to the exclusion of Chinese immigrants, and from genocide of indigenous populations to internment of Japanese Americans during World War II—to US neocolonial practices in Japan, administrators of the US occupation deliberately censored antiracist accounts of both Japanese and Western colonialisms and imperialisms in postwar Japan. As Sakai further notes, the International Military Tribunal for the Far East in 1946 was presented as a showcase, designed to exempt the emperor and the overwhelming majority of Japanese war criminals from further investigation into their crimes, ranging from their treatment of so-called comfort women to the Nanking Massacre (2010, 253). Edwin Reischauer, who authored the 1942 memorandum and masterminded the tribunal, would later become one of the founding fathers of area studies and serve as US ambassador to Japan from 1961 to 1966 (ibid., 247).

The Japanese Supplementary Police Forces introduced to protect US military bases in 1952 were renamed Security Forces and Self-Defense Forces in 1954. In January 2007, Japanese officials elevated the Self-Defense Agency to the status of Ministry of Defense without any change in the Japanese constitution but with the full support and endorsement of the Bush administration (Sakai 2010, 259). Sakai tellingly describes the postwar collaboration between Japanese colonialism and US Cold War neocolonialism as the agency responsible for the postponement in the Asia Pacific of "the process of decolonization, the process in which individuals gradually learn how to form new social relations that are not premised on the legacies and vanities of colonialism" (ibid., 261). Chen authored his account of the decolonization and de-imperialization tactics to break out of the residual effects of colonial imperialism (2010, 15).

North America's Decline, East Asia's Emergence,
and the New Global Order

In "America's Pacific Century," an essay that was featured in the November
2011 issue of *Foreign Policy*, Hillary Clinton asserted that "the future of
geopolitics will be decided in Asia, not in Afghanistan or Iraq," and that
"the United States should be right at the center of the action" (2011, 56).
Clinton also observed that by investing time and energy in Asia Pacific, "we
[Americans] put ourselves in the best position to sustain our leadership, secure our interests, and advance our values" (ibid., 57). While the investment
in the Asia Pacific that Clinton recommended was primarily economic, she
extended the arc of US interests to include diplomatic and military strategies.
When we inspect the assumptions informing Secretary of State Hillary Clinton's essay by means of the framework Chen recommends, we can discern
a neocolonial policy of transpacific complicity comparable to the target of
Sakai's case study.

Adapting US exceptionalist claims to her transpacific purposes, Clinton
represented the United States as "the only global power with a network of
strong alliances in the region, no territorial ambition, and a long record of
providing for the common good" (2011, 58), and she identified six key lines
of action that would prioritize strengthening bilateral security alliances with
US allies and advancing democracy and human rights. Representing Japan
as sharing with the United States "a common vision of a stable regional
order with clear rules of the road," Clinton singled out the US alliance with
Japan as "the cornerstone of peace and stability in the region" (ibid.). With
a nod to Mahan's model of sea power, Clinton reaffirmed the unique role of
the United States in what Chalmers Johnson called "the empire of military
bases" (2004, 151) and gestured at rearming Japan in the service of US imperial dominance of the region.

Clinton's foregrounding of Japan's position in twenty-first-century US
strategic culture has two important implications. First, the United States
expects Japan to shoulder much of the financial burden of the US military
bases in the Asia Pacific. Second, by representing Japan as the "Britain of
Asia"[7] Clinton reveals the US dependence on Japan's support to maintain
the military presence needed to sustain a divided East Asia and Asia Pacific. Cold War strategists designed this systematic division to prevent the
possible formation of a China-centered cultural world and an economically
integrated East Asia modeled after the European Union.

Clinton depicted China as a key beneficiary of the US-centered global
order. In stating that "we are asking these emerging partners to join us in
shaping and participating in a rules-based regional and global order" (2011,

59), Clinton turned the rise of China into the centerpiece of her essay. She also recommended taking precautions against possible Chinese trade or military policies that might pose threats to the United States. Like so many other countries in the past, Clinton remarked, China has prospered as part of the open and rules-based system that the United States helped to build and works to sustain.

In Clinton's view, its relations with China are the most challenging and consequential of the bilateral relationships that the United States has ever had to manage. Although Clinton considers China's increasing military power a potential threat to the us-centered global order, the European Union sees China as "a large developing country in the midst of multiple transitions, leading it away from state socialism and toward a market economy, a more open society, and a more representative and accountable government" (Shambaugh 2005, 14). Rather than attesting to us willingness to work with China as an equal partner, Clinton expresses her anxiety over how to manage and incorporate China's new position as the chief competitor to the United States in the region. Daniel Twining has cogently anticipated Clinton's position, writing: "In the face of the China challenge, the United States is encouraging the emergence of new centers of strength that will not erode U.S. power but protect the U.S. position in a new Asian balance featuring emerging world powers in China, Japan, and India" (2007, 80).

Ironically, the Japanese government has grasped this moment as a unique opportunity to forward its own political and military agendas. The administration of Prime Minister Shinzo Abe has chosen to produce a dangerous variety of geopolitical theater in its dispute with China over the Diaoyu or Senkaku Islands, and in its ostentatious tribute to the Yasukuni Shrine, where the remains of all the World War II Japanese war criminals were preserved to be worshiped by the Japanese public. Clinton's strategies and Japan's response explain China's otherwise inexplicable policy of reaffirming the necessity to defend the historical consensus among the allied forces during World War II. The fact that South Korea shares China's sentiments regarding "comfort women" and other Japanese war crimes reveals fissures in the alliances among the United States, Japan, and South Korea.

Clinton concluded her remarkable essay by reaffirming us exceptionalism as universalism: "Our capacity to come back stronger is unmatched in modern history. It flows from our model of free democracy and free enterprise, a model that remains the most powerful source of prosperity and progress known to human history" (2011, 63). With the us triumph over the Soviet Union in the Cold War as her tacit warrant, Clinton clearly believes the us pivot to the Asia Pacific is central to the revitalization of us power around the globe.

Without describing it as a response to Clinton's *Foreign Policy* essay, the *New York Times* published an article on November 20, 2011, bearing the sensational title "How China Can Defeat America." The piece was authored by Yan Xuetong, a Chinese political scientist trained at the University of California, Berkeley, in the early 1990s. Yan characterized the competition between the United States and China as a zero-sum game, but he argued that China was unlike the United States because China understood "the importance of morality in international relations." Rather than discussing China's grand strategy for global dominance, Yan criticized China's rampant domestic problems: "This means China must shift its priorities away from economic development to establishing a harmonious society free of today's huge gaps between rich and poor. It needs to replace money worship with traditional morality and weed out political corruption in favor of social justice and fairness."

In this piece, Yan was addressing the Chinese ruling elites—both the party functionaries and their think tanks—rather than the general US public. He called attention to the incompatibility between China's authoritarian political structure and the country's more liberal economic operations to underscore the urgency of reforming China's legal and juridical institutions. Tellingly, Yan did not recommend the adoption of democratic structures endorsed and promoted by the United States and Europe. Rather than applauding the neoliberal ideology of the United States and "the international community," Yan embraced notions of human rights and democracy that he found compatible with Confucian humanism.

Yan described militarism as the primary challenge in China's competition with the United States and other global or regional powers: "This will mean competing with the United States politically, economically and technologically. Such competition may cause diplomatic tensions, but there is little danger of military clashes." Refusing to accept the US model of exercising Western hegemony or the Japanese model of shedding Asia and joining Europe, Yan recommended that China return to the traditional path of Confucian wisdom that favors harmony rather than confrontation and convergence rather than divergence. But as Aaron Friedberg has explained, US policymakers' fidelity to "state rationality" will render it impossible for them to change their attitudes toward China as long as Chinese human rights policies remain authoritarian (2005, 44).

The Transpacific and Transnational American Studies: Cross-indigenous Studies, Oceanic Studies, and Asian/Asian American Studies

Throughout this introduction we have argued that transpacific studies are significant to transnational American studies at this historical juncture.

Without claiming to provide exhaustive coverage of the terrain, we want to conclude these introductory remarks by situating transpacific studies within a wide array of transnational practices at work in transnational American studies.

As a transnational practice, transpacific studies facilitated a critical examination of the neoliberal logic overseeing the processes of globalization that shaped the contours of the region. Scholars in transpacific studies who draw on what Chen defines as "deimperialization" will play a major role in critiquing the cultures of US exceptionalism, colonialism, and imperialism that Amy Kaplan and Donald Pease's *Cultures of United States Imperialism* initiated. In her introductory essay, "Left Alone with America," Kaplan located a pattern of denial of empire across the disciplines. She pointed out three absences in three interrelated fields: "the absence of culture from the history of U.S. imperialism; the absence of empire from the study of American culture; and the absence of the United States from the postcolonial study of imperialism" (1994, 11).

In "Culture, US Imperialism, and Globalization," John Carlos Rowe provided two of these missing elements by demonstrating the importance of imperialism to the history of US popular culture and by explaining how military imperialism is mediated by "a culture of fear that helps market late-capitalist products and encourages, rather than diminishes, military conflicts in the place of international diplomacy" (2004, 582).

Rob Wilson covered the third of Kaplan's absences in "Imagining 'Asia-Pacific' Today," which argued that the Asia Pacific is important to the postcolonial study of US imperialism. Wilson specifically explained how multicultural representations of the Asia Pacific "as imagined by authors as diverse as Melville and Epeli Hau'ofa, Maxine Hong Kingston and Patricia Grace, Haunan-Kay Trask and Li Ang, John Dominis Holt and Vilsoni Hereniko, Kenzaburo Oe and Lois-Ann Yamanaka" supplanted colonial and orientalist images by depicting the region as "a riddle and a maze, a rim and a charm, a struggle and a curse, both dream and slime, an ocean with ancient contents and cyborgian futures all cast into one strange regional poetic" (2002, 246).

In reevaluating the relationship between the global war on terror and the forgetting of the Vietnam War, William Spanos and Timothy Brennan have both stressed importance of resisting the US-centered global order that Michael Hardt and Antonio Negri have euphemistically referred to as "Empire." China studies scholars like Johnson supplemented the transnational American studies scholars' critiques of US colonialism, imperialism, and exceptionalism by revealing how the empire of military bases became embedded in the everyday practices of US citizens: "Our military empire is a physical reality with a distinct way of life but it is also a network of economic and political interests tied in a thousand different ways to American corporations, universities, and communities but kept separate from what passes for everyday life back in what has only recently come to be known as 'the homeland.' And yet even that sense of separation is disappearing—for the changing nature of the empire is changing our society as well" (2004, 9).

Although this transnational scholarship is significant for its range and scope, there are still areas that merit critical attention and intervention. These include the Korean War and the US military bases in Japan, South Korea, and Okinawa and on other Pacific islands, where history and imperialism, indigenous cultures and imperialism, and environment and imperialism have collided and then become conflated. Houston Wood wrote "Cultural Studies for Oceania" to redefine the field of cultural studies from a viewpoint forged out of the incompatibilities between Euro-American and Native Pacific Islander epistemologies: "It is especially important that the emerging cultural studies for Oceania prominently emphasize Pacific Islander ways of knowing. After centuries of colonialist-inspired neglect, indigenous researchers have begun documenting the complexity, subtlety, and validity of indigenous epistemologies" (2003, 341).

Matt Matsuda extended the reach of Wood's Oceania to include "small islands, large seas, multiple transits" throughout the Pacific (2006, 759). In bringing together the multiple conjunctures—"ancient navigations, colonial labor markets and migrations, strategic policy, and culture networks"—that "define the histories of an Oceanic Pacific" (ibid., 780), Matsuda concluded that transpacific studies should also sponsor the interweaving of Pacific Islanders' experiences with otherwise occluded indigenous spaces circulating throughout transnational narratives. Scholars in postcolonial Taiwan have recently founded a school of cultural studies that links Taiwan native studies to Native American transnational frameworks of extranational and transindigenous belonging, on the one hand, and to oceanic frameworks, on the other hand, so as to unsettle territorial ties to both the Chinese and US mainlands.

But Oceanic studies and cross-indigeneities studies scholars have not restricted their interventions to critiques of US imperialism; they have also engaged what Mignolo calls "the darker side of Western modernity" (2011, 1). Mignolo invented this phrase to describe the forces responsible for universalizing Western capitalism as modernization and development. Although oceanic and indigenous peoples and scholars sometimes romanticize and reinvent their objects of study, they never fail to mount critical resistance against the universality of neoliberal capitalism.

The 1990s increase of economic and cultural exchanges between East

Asia and North America stimulated collaborations among scholars in American studies, Asian studies, Asian American studies, and transpacific studies. In his account of the roots of Asian American studies and Asian studies, Sucheta Mazumdar asserted that these interrelated fields not only help understand the Asian dimension of US history but also benefit each other in terms of developing global, historical, and comparative perspectives and paradigms on race, ethnicity, diaspora, and modernity. Sau-ling Wong elaborated on Mazumdar's interest in the convergence of these fields by depicting globalization and transnationalism in Asian American studies as effects of what she calls "denationalization." Echoing Wong's and Mazumdar's claims, Susan Koshy has contended that "Asian American Studies is uniquely positioned to intervene in current theoretical discussions on ethnicity, representation and writing not despite of, but because of, the contested and contestatory nature of its formation" (1996, 342).

Lowe's *Immigrant Acts* and David Palumbo-Liu's *Asian/American* have provided important theoretical frameworks for transnational Asian American studies. By situating Asian immigration in relation to the history of US military interventions in Asia, Lowe defined Asian immigration as an arena for the critical negation of the nation-state: "it is a site that shifts and marks alternatives to the national terrain by occupying other spaces, imagining different narratives and critical historiographies, and enacting practices that give rise to new forms of subjectivity and new ways of questioning the government of human life by the national state" (1995, 29).

In a comparable intervention, Palumbo-Liu interrogated the constructed nature of the border separating Asia and America as a racial frontier, which marks both a distinction between Asian and American and a dynamic, unsettled, and inclusive movement within the US nation-state: "Asia/America resides *in transit* as a point of reference on the horizon that is part of both a 'minority' identity and a 'majority' identity. This constant transitivity evinces precisely the malleability and resistance of 'America' with regard to racial reformation" (1999, 5).

Building on Lowe's and Palumbo-Liu's theorizations, in *Transnational America* Inderpal Grewal laid out a theory that explained how the movement of human populations, the circulation of consumer products, and the popularization of human rights discourses in South Asia created transnational subjects. Yunte Huang wrote *Transpacific Imaginations* to show how the American literary imagination that emanated from different sides of the Pacific reflected different moments of the US empire. And Shirley Geok-lin Lim coedited *Transnational Asian American Literature* to explain how Asian American literature engaged with various historical dynamics related to the formation of the US nation at the same time that it articulated the diasporic, mobile, and transmigratory dimensions of each ethnic group within that collectivity. In a related exploration of transnational Asian American history, Erika Lee and Naoko Shibusawa persuasively argued that Asian American historians have always been "transnational in outlook by integrating transnational, diasporic, and global perspectives into analyses of the Asian American past" (2005, ix).

Janet Hoskins and Viet Thanh Nguyen recently edited *Transpacific Studies: Critical Perspectives on an Emerging Field*, which is based on the premise that the idea of the transpacific is an ongoing intellectual and political project as well as a material aspect of life in the twenty-first century. The editors describe transpacific studies as an enterprise involving multilateral relationships in multiple countries that allows for a reconsideration of dominant US-based fields from the perspective of emerging Asian- and Pacific-based fields.

As transnational American studies travels to the Pacific, there are many additional issues that merit critical attention. If decolonization now involves inventing a non-Western ontology and epistemology, is it possible to articulate an Asian or Pacific American ontology or epistemology as an alternative to the Euro-American ones? How do we create transpacific imaginaries that would cultivate recognition of the heterogeneity and multiplicity of Asian Pacific and Oceanic communities? How do we understand the historical differences and ongoing disputes among Asian nation-states in relation to US exceptionalism and interventionism, particularly in wake of the Obama administration's recent pivot to Asia? These are some of the critical issues that transpacific studies is positioned to address.

Transnational Practices in the Time of the Pivot to Asia

We have solicited fourteen essays for this volume and divided them into four sections: "Transnational Practices: Outside/Inside American Studies," "Deep Maps, Postracial Imaginaries, Diasporized Networks, and Other Transnational Literary Assemblages," "Remapping the Transpacific Turn: From the Black Pacific and Oceanic Eco-Poetics to Antipodean Transnationalisms," and "Decolonizing the Geopolitics of Knowledge for the Pacific Century."

Transnational Practices: Outside/Inside American Studies

Each of the contributors to the first section of this volume engaged the challenges and opportunities that transnationalist initiatives pose for American studies scholars. The section opens with Donald Pease's "How Transnational Studies Reconfigured the Field of American Studies: The Transnational/

Diaspora Complex," in which he formulates an account of what he calls the transnational-diaspora complex to distinguish different transnational dispositions. According to Pease, "the transnational/diaspora manifests the mistranslations and unequal exchanges that accompany and frustrate Americanist scholars who desire cross-cultural solidarity; the transnational/ diaspora complex discloses the mutual imbrications and unacknowledged reciprocities in cultures that Americanist scholars aspire to set in a relation of insuperable opposition." In the final section of his essay, Pease explains how American studies scholars who exercise the agency inherent in the transnational-diaspora complex can change the sites of the imperial state's exceptions into spaces of transnational critical resistance. Throughout his essay, Pease scrutinizes the ineluctably conflicted disposition of transnational American studies. Depending on where, how, and why it is practiced, transnational American studies can sustain, and conserve, or conduct an immanent critique of the imperatives of the US imperial state. Transnational American studies scholars can also turn the US imperial state into an object of analysis and critique.

Eva Cherniavsky's "Post-Soviet American Studies" argues that practitioners of the New American studies like Pease and Rowe remain wedded to the nation as the thing that they are committed to unthink. To avoid this impasse, Cherniavsky directs her critical attention away from the nation and to the state. Her study of post-Soviet American studies leads Cherniavsky to the discovery that agents of the US state are also committed to unthinking the nation. Instead of finding an equivalence between New Americanists and US state agents in post-Soviet Central Asia, however, Cherniavsky recommends that American studies scholars give up on the critique of the nation form and become attuned to the state's efforts to produce a different kind of citizen for the twenty-first century. Cherniavsky describes the transnational practices at work in post-Soviet American studies as a statist pedagogy intent on producing what she calls neocitizens for the neoliberal marketplace. According to Cherniavsky, when transnational American studies traveled to post-Soviet Central Asia, it shed the un-American disposition she attributed to the New Americanists and became subsumed within the US transnational state's pedagogical apparatus intent on educating neocitizens in how to become savvy operators in the global economic order.

In "Transnationalism, Planetary Consciousness, and American Studies," Yuan Shu deploys Mignolo's notion of "decolonial thinking" (2011, 108) and Gayatri Spivak's conceptualization of planetarity to move beyond the globalization of neoliberal capitalism by uncovering multidirectional non-Western and noncapitalist knowledge systems embedded in indigenous ontologies and epistemologies that have survived the incursions of Anglo-American capitalism. After he describes Confucianism as an indigenous epistemology that was appropriated for different purposes in China and Southeast Asia, Shu recommends that scholars consider Confucianism a possible epistemological alternative to both global neoliberal capitalism and the Chinese state.

Deep Maps, Postracial Imaginaries, Diasporized Networks, and Other Transnational Literary Assemblages

Each of the contributors to the second section of this volume is preoccupied with assembling, archiving, periodizing, categorizing, interpreting, or constellating literary formations in the twenty-first century. Shelley Fisher Fishkin's "Transnational Mark Twain," the first essay in this section, converts the transnational turn in American studies into an opportunity to collect, inventory, and begin to interpret contributions to American literature written in languages other than English. Fishkin turns writings about and translations of essays on Mark Twain's *The Adventures of Huckleberry Finn* in languages other than English and published outside the United States as her representative case study. Throughout this essay, Fishkin delights in the rewarding discoveries she makes while collecting items of overseas scholarship that open up the possibility of creating a "transnational Mark Twain." Digitizing these translations and commentaries from the nineteenth century to the present on a "Deep Map" called "Global Huck" allows Fishkin to engage in transnational, comparative, and multilingual studies that would have been all but impossible in an earlier era.

For Fishkin, "transnational" refers to scholarship written about Twain by scholars outside the United States in a language other than English. In "Racial Memory and the Modern Borders of the Nation-State," however, Rafael Pérez-Torres conceptualizes the United States itself as a plurinational state that included transnational formations within its borders. He focuses on the nexus of race and modernity within a Chicana/o context to bring the contradictions of American modernity into a relationship with Chicana/os' haunting memories of racial discrimination. In Pérez-Torres's view, colonial modernity was symptomatic of a systemic crisis brought about by modernization's dissolution of Chicano/as' transnational social networks. He situates Chicano/a literature between the systemic crisis of modernity and the lived crisis of racial disempowerment, to bear witness to the ways in which colonial modernity still haunts the racialized imagination of contemporary Chicano/a American culture.

Pérez-Torres does not believe that the movement into postmodernity fully erased the remnants of colonial modernity that persist within Chicana/o consciousness. But in "The Other Side of History, the Other Side of Fiction: Form and Genre in Susshu Foster's *Atomik Aztex*," Ramón Saldívar uses *Atomik Aztez,* a 2005 novel, as evidence of what he calls the post-postmodern phase of American debates on racial justice. Saldívar describes Atomic Aztex, Junot Díaz's *The Brief Wondrous Life of Oscar Wao* (2007), Salvador Plascencia's *The People of Paper* (2005), and Percival Everett's *Erasure* (2001) as works that represent the changing relationships between race and social justice, race and identity, and race and history, and that require American writers of color to invent a new postracial imaginary for thinking about the role of race in the construction of a just society. Saldívar considers the postracial imaginary to be an intercultural and transnational construct based on the shared desire to transcend the constraints of ethnicity or any national particularity. He argues that the aesthetic projects of this generational cohort engage, in formal and thematic ways, the issues of the transnational racial imaginary in a post-postmodern, post–civil rights moment.

Remapping the Transpacific Turn: From the Black Pacific and Oceanic Eco-Poetics to Antipodean Transnationalisms

Paul Gilroy invented the term "the Black Atlantic" to recover lost or forgotten Afro-American diasporic histories. Working with the scholarly legacies of the Black Atlantic, transpacific scholars have recently dug into records of an Afro-Asian diaspora. Brent Hayes Edwards has written about the anticolonial alliances Ho Chi Minh established with Africans and Vietnamese in France before World War II; Martin Luther King and Stokely Carmichael drew inspiration from Gandhi as well as Mao for the US civil rights movement; participants in the 1955 Bandung Conference forged bonds of Afro-Asian revolutionary solidarity in their shared struggle against colonialism and imperialism. Etsuko Taketani's essay for this volume, "The Manchurian Philosopher: W. E. B. Du Bois in the Eurasian Pacific," is drawn from her *The Black Pacific Narrative: Geographic Imaginings of Race and Empire between the World Wars,* published in 2014 by Dartmouth College Press. According to Taketani, Du Bois saw the Russo-Japanese War of 1904–5 as a sign of the historical awakening of the darker races. Du Bois considered the rise of the Japanese empire a salutary challenge to Western imperialism, and, despite the evidence of its authoritarianism and militarism in the 1930s, he remained a staunch lifelong defender of Japan's rise to world power. Taketani devotes much of her scholarly attention to Du Bois's hitherto neglected responses to Manchukuo (1932–45)—a Japanese puppet empire that was founded in Manchuria, Northern China, and that disappeared at the end of World War II—to reflect on the anticapitalist empire that inspired Du Bois to imagine a black Eurasian Pacific.

According to Taketani, Du Bois considered Japanese imperialism a historically necessary Asian alternative to Western colonial imperialism. But

Rob Wilson's essay, "Toward an Ecopoetics of Oceania: Worlding the Asia-Pacific Region as Space-Time Ecumene," calls attention to the damaging effects of both Japanese and Euro-American imperialism on ecosystems throughout the region, and he advocates on behalf of nonimperial, postcolonial modes of "worlding" the Pacific. Refusing Carl Schmitt's assertion that "Man is a terrestrial [being]" whose *nomos* of modernity measures belonging in terrestrial and territorial terms tied to a nation-state system (1997, 1), Wilson figures the Pacific as a subaltern regional category and a global and local vision of an ocean commons known as Oceania, which Wilson wants understood as the site of alternative modes of belonging inside Asia and the Pacific. Wilson moves to pluralize Oceania in all its discrepant histories and power differentials so as to figure the ocean in a more transpacific, affiliative way that makes possible an ecopoetics of translocal solidarity, place, and bioregional worlding.

Paul Giles's essay, "Antipodean Transnationalism: The Empire Lies Athwart," draws inspiration from the drastic changes 9/11 brought about in the world's geopolitical order. In Giles's view, the trauma of 9/11 and the radical post-2008 shifts in the world economy "will position Australia in particular as a potential American intermediary and ally against China, much as Britain was positioned against the Soviet Union in the 1950s." Remarking that this antipodean transpacific circuit was always made up of imperial crosscurrents as well as aquatic flows and island domains, Giles states that US excursions across the Pacific were complicated not only by encounters with native peoples but also by sporadic conflicts with Great Britain, the rival imperial power that used its base in Australia to exert influence over large sections of Pacific island space. Unlike Wilson's vision of Oceania, however, Giles does not place the antipodean imaginary in the service of Pacific Islanders or transpacific resistance movements. In Giles's estimation, "the challenge for antipodean transnationalism is to navigate among competing psychological and political positions, in a situation where mutual engagements of colonizer and colonized operate across a ubiquitous but amorphous force field in a state of constant transposition, rather than being confined to any kind of singular position susceptible of resolution within a conventional postcolonial . . . framework."

At a key moment in his essay, Giles tellingly recasts the empire writing back, which was how Bill Ashcroft, Gareth Griffiths, and Helen Tiffin depicted of Great Britain's response to the decolonization movement, in antipodean terms as the empire lying athwart to explain how his version of antipodean transnationalism negotiates the multidirectional nature of colonial legacies and crosscurrents by holding the contrary impulses of dominant and subordinate movements in dialectical tension. In the final essay in this section, "Transpacific Studies and the Cultures of US Imperialism," John Carlos Rowe endorses Giles's description of the colonial and imperial infrastructures saturating the region. But Rowe does not ratify Giles's image of the empire lying athwart as the backdrop for transpacific studies. Rowe's characterization of the transpacific as the aquatic habitat of formerly colonized states that all aspire to achieve cultural, economic, and political sovereignty in their relations to the Pacific region leads him to align the academic field of transpacific studies with these anticolonial struggles, "even when it is critical of specific postcolonial state formations in which the imperial heritage is still operative." Rowe specifically argues that the legacies of imperialism, indigeneity, and migration or diaspora must be read together in their layered simultaneity, and he recommends that indigenous rights figure centrally in transpacific studies. In championing the inclusion of transpacific studies within transnational American studies, Rowe identifies the following common concerns: hemispheric scope, attention to the consequences of imperialist expansion, respect for cultural and linguistic diversity, and concern with transcultural and transnational relations. Rowe concludes his essay by expressing the hope that transpacific studies might revitalize New American studies.

Decolonizing the Geopolitics of Knowledge for the Pacific Century

Rowe recommends that transpacific studies scholars add their knowledge to the transnational campaign to resist the institutions and infrastructures that were left over from the era of colonial imperialism and that have been repurposed to serve neoliberal capitalist modernity. But Rowe does not scrutinize his own methodology of knowledge production for signs of the colonial imperialism he opposes. In the essay Walter Mignolo contributed to the final section of our volume, "Geopolitics of Knowing/Understanding and American Studies: A Decolonial Argument or View from the Global South," he regards US American studies as an object to be studied from a US American imaginary situated outside the domain of American studies. Unlike most US American studies scholars, Mignolo does not think that the coloniality of knowing can be decisively separated from an imperialist disposition. He describes imperialization as a process designed to incorporate colonial subjects into structures of imperial management, on the one hand, and to convince imperial citizens of the legitimacy of colonization for the good of both the colonial subject and the citizen subject of the imperial nation-state, on the other hand. For Mignolo, deimperialization and decoloniality are concurrent and complementary projects that work on the imperial and the colonial subjects simultaneously. In the course of this exposition, Mignolo asserts that transnational American studies needs to decolonize the coloniality of knowledge at the foundation of American studies.

Mignolo's geopolitics of knowing is prompted by the following basic questions: who is intending to study what, when, why, where, and for what purposes? Viet Thanh Nguyen wrote his essay, "Industries of Memory: The Việt Nam War in Art," to uncover the rules of colonial difference at work in the industrial apparatus through which the United States produced, distributed, and sustained its official memory of the Vietnam War. Nguyen finds the US memory industry similar to the US arms industry in that both are structured through relations of exploitation and inequality. Memory's impact depends on vertical integration and economies of scale, with those who control the most significant means of production seeing to it that their memories exported. This inequity manifestly shaped the public presentation of memories of the Vietnam War. To the extent that Americans want to remember Vietnam and reconcile with it, they are mostly interested in their former Vietnamese enemies in Vietnam. They neither mourn nor remember the South Vietnamese, their former allies, many of whom have settled in the United States.

Nguyen sets what Mignolo described as the decolonial project to the task of liberating transpacific studies scholarship from the knowledge production of the US military-industrial apparatus. Alfred Hornung's essay, "ChinAmerica: Global Affairs and Planetary Consciousness," explores the intercultural relations between the United States and China—the two major global powers that he calls ChinAmerica—since the mid-nineteenth century in the countries' quest for enduring cooperation. Hornung hopes this transcultural constellation will serve as the basis for a new transnational consciousness in the twenty-first century, which includes a concern for the preservation of the planet. Unlike Mignolo and Nguyen, Hornung does not aspire to separate either of these global powers from their imperial proclivities. Rather than opposing either empire's exceptionalist convictions, Hornung tries to reconcile them: American exceptionalism acts on the evangelical desire to spread American values to every part of the world, while—in the words of Henry Kissinger—China "does not proselytize," but it does claim a "kind of cultural universality" (2011, xvi). Hornung finds that his effort to create a balance between the two exceptionalisms has been given symbolic expression in the pop cultural name Obamao (or Maobama). Hornung movingly interprets this amalgamation of the two names as the sign of collective hope for "transcultural convergence" in a way that would replace global competitiveness with the consensus of a transnational community as a vision for the twenty-first century.

We have made Yuan Shu's essay, "Negotiating the Technological Empire: Cosmopolitics, Colonial Modernity, and Early Chinese American Autobiographical Writing," the final chapter in the volume. In this essay Shu takes

China's reissuing of Yung Wing's *My Life in China and America* (1909) in a 1985 Chinese translation as the occasion for tracking the different framings and changing receptions of this Chinese American autobiographical text in its US and Chinese contexts. Refusing both Chinese and US national frameworks, Shu interprets Yung's autobiography in the transnational context of "colonial modernity." Conceptualizing colonial modernity as at once a historical condition and a critical concept, Shu connects Yung's experiences in the United States to his experience of the changing realities in China. Confronting what Mignolo theorizes as the rule of "colonial difference," Yung understood how that rule presupposed the knowledge regimes of the "coloniality of power" that translated nineteenth-century Western racial classification into hierarchical cultural values (Mignolo 2002, 58 and 60). In relating Yung's decolonial thinking to China's modernization process, Shu shows how it represented the Chinese tradition as a proleptic response to Western military, economic, and cultural dominance in the twentieth century. Shu also shows how Yung's decolonial thinking anticipates a different future for China and the United States in the twenty-first century.

Notes

1. See Alterman 2009.
2. See Feldman 2013.
3. See US Department of Defense 2012.
4. See Blaut 1993; Quijano and Wallerstein 1992.
5. See Perry n.d.
6. See Lowe 1995.
7. If Japan, according to Robert Rydell was highly honored as "the Great Britain of Asia" by a US newspaper, the *Daily Inter Ocean*, in a September 20, 1893, supplement (Rydell 1984) during the Chicago World's Columbian Exposition of 1893 because of the workmanship of the Japanese products on exhibition, then today the term is used mostly to highlight Japan's close political and military ties with the United States. On June 11, 2005, the blogger Sensuikan San posted on the topic. Clinton's emphasis on Japan's role in America's Pacific century certainly invokes the trope that has increasingly been articulated in political and military terms.

Bibliography

Alterman, Jon. 2009. "China's Soft Power in the United States." In *Chinese Soft Power and Its Implications for the United States*, edited by Carola McGiffert, 63–76. Washington: Center for Strategic and International Studies.

Baym, Nina. 2006. "Old West, New West, Post West, Real West." *American Literary History* 18 (4): 814–28.

Blank, Paul W. 1999. "The Pacific: A Mediterranean in the Making?" *Geographical Review* 89 (2): 265–77.

Blaut, James M. 1993. *The Colonizer's Model of the World: Geographical Diffusionism and Eurocentric History.* New York: Guilford.

Bové, Paul. 2002. "Can American Studies Be Area Studies?" In *Learning Places: The Afterlives of Area Studies,* edited by Masao Miyoshi and Harvey Harootunian, 206–30. Durham, NC: Duke University Press.

Brennan, Timothy. 2003. "The Empire's New Clothes." *Critical Inquiry* 29 (winter): 337–67.

Chen, Kuan-Hsing. 2010. *Asia as Method: Toward Deimperialization.* Durham, NC: Duke University Press.

Clinton, Hillary. 2011. "America's Pacific Century." *Foreign Policy* (November): 56–63.

Connery, Christopher L. 2001. "Ideologies of Land and Sea: Alfred Thayer Mahan, Carl Schmitt, and the Shaping of Global Myth Elements." *boundary 2* 28 (2): 173–201.

Cumings, Bruce. 1998. "Rimspeak; or, The Discourse of the 'Pacific Rim.'" In *What Is in a Rim? Critical Perspectives on the Pacific Region Idea,* edited by Arif Dirlik, 53–72. 2nd ed. Lanham, MD: Rowman and Littlefield.

———. 2009. *Dominion from Sea to Sea: Pacific Ascendancy and American Power.* New Haven, CT: Yale University Press.

———. 2010. *The Korean War: A History.* New York: Modern Library.

Daniels, Roger. 1988. *Asian America: Chinese and Japanese in the United States since 1850.* Seattle: University of Washington Press.

Dirlik, Arif. 1998a. "The Asia-Pacific in Asian-American Perspective." In *What Is in a Rim? Critical Perspectives on the Pacific Region Idea,* edited by Arif Dirlik, 283–308. 2nd ed. Lanham, MD: Rowman and Littlefield.

———. 1998b. "Introduction: Pacific Contradictions." In *What Is in a Rim? Critical Perspectives on the Pacific Region Idea,* edited by Arif Dirlik, 3–13. 2nd ed. Lanham, MD: Rowman and Littlefield.

Elliott, Emory. 2007. "Diversity in the United States and Abroad: What Does It Mean When American Studies Is Transnational?" *American Quarterly* 59 (1): 1–22.

Farrell, Theo. 2005. "Strategic Culture and American Empire." *SAIS Review* 25 (2): 3–18.

Feldman, Noah. 2013. *Cool War: The Future of Global Competition.* New York: Random House.

Fichter, James. 2010. *So Great a Proffit: How the East Indies Trade Transformed Anglo-American Capitalism.* Cambridge, MA: Harvard University Press.

Fishkin, Shelley Fisher. 2005. "Crossroads of Culture: The Transnational Turn in American Studies—Presidential Address to the American Studies Association, November 12, 2004." *American Quarterly* 57 (1): 17–57.

Fluck, Winfried. 2007. "Inside and Outside: What Kind of Knowledge Do We Need? A Response to the Presidential Address." *American Quarterly* 59 (1): 23–32.

Fraser, Nancy. 2014. "Transnationalizing the Public Sphere: On the Legitimacy and Efficacy of Public Opinion in a Post-Westphalian World." In *Transnationalizing the Public Sphere*, edited by Kate Nash, 8–42. Malden, MA: Polity.

Friedberg, Aaron L. 2005. "The Future of U.S.-China Relations: Is Conflict Inevitable?" *International Security* 30 (2): 7–45.

Grewal, Inderpal. 2005. *Transnational America: Feminisms, Diasporas, Neoliberalisms.* Durham, NC: Duke University Press.

Gulliver, Katrina. 2011. "Finding the Pacific World." *Journal of World History* 22 (1): 83–100.

Hardt, Michael. 2007. "Jefferson and Democracy." *American Quarterly* 59 (1): 41–78.

——— and Antonio Negri. 2001. *Empire.* Cambridge, MA: Harvard University Press.

Hoskins, Janet, and Viet Thanh Nguyen, eds. 2014. *Transpacific Studies: Critical Perspectives on an Emerging Field.* Honolulu: University of Hawaii Press.

Huang, Yunte. 2008. *Transpacific Imaginations: History, Literature, and Counterpoetics.* Cambridge, MA: Harvard University Press.

Jay, Paul. 2010. *Global Matters: The Transnational Turn in Literary Studies.* Ithaca, NY: Cornell University Press.

Johnson, Chalmers. 2004. *The Sorrows of Empire: Militarism, Secrecy, and the End of the Republic.* New York: Henry Holt.

Kaplan, Amy. 1994. "Left Alone with America." In *Cultures of United States Imperialism*, edited by Amy Kaplan and Donald Pease, 3–21. Durham, NC: Duke University Press.

——— and Donald Pease. 1994. *Cultures of United States Imperialism.* Durham, NC: Duke University Press.

Kaplan, Robert D. 2007. "America's Elegant Decline." *Atlantic*, November, 104–16.

Kissinger, Henry. 2011. *On China.* New York: Penguin.

Korhonen, Pekka. 1996. "The Pacific Age in World History." *Journal of World History* 7 (1): 41–70.

Koshy, Susan. 1996. "The Fiction of Asian American Literature." *Yale Journal of Criticism* 9 (2): 315–46.

Kuo, Ping Chia. 1930. "Canton and Salem." *New England Quarterly* 3 (3): 420–42.

Kwon, Heonik. 2010. *The Other Cold War.* New York: Columbia University Press.

Lee, Erika, and Naoko Shibusawa. 2005. "Guest Editor's Introduction: What Is Transnational Asian American History? Recent Trends and Challenges." *Journal of Asian American Studies* 8 (3): vii–xvii.

Leon W., M. Consuelo. 1994. "Foundations of the American Image of the Pacific." *boundary* 2 21 (1): 17–29.

Lewis, Martin W., and Karen Wigen. 1997. *The Myth of Continents: A Critique of Metageography*. Berkeley: University of California Press.

Lim, Shirley Geok-lin, John Blair Gamber, Stephen Hong Sohn, and Gina Valentino, eds. 2006. *Transnational Asian American Literature: Sites and Transits*. Philadelphia: Temple University Press.

Limerick, Patricia Nelson. 1992. "Disorientation and Reorientation: The American Landscape Discovered from the West." *Journal of American History* 79 (3): 1021–49.

Lowe, Lisa. 1995. *Immigrant Acts: On Asian American Cultural Politics*. Durham, NC: Duke University Press.

Matsuda, Matt K. 2006. "The Pacific." *American History Review* 111 (3): 758–80.

Mazumdar, Sucheta. 1991. "Asian American Studies and Asian Studies: Rethinking Roots." In *Asian Americans: Comparative and Global Perspectives*, edited by Shirley Hune, Stephen S. Fugita, and Amy Ling, 29–44. Pullman: Washington State University Press.

Mignolo, Walter D. 1995. *The Darker Side of the Renaissance: Literacy, Territoriality, and Colonization*. Ann Arbor: University of Michigan Press.

———. 2000. *Local Histories/Global Designs: Coloniality, Subaltern Knowledges, and Border Thinking*. Princeton, NJ: Princeton University Press.

———. 2002. "The Geopolitics of Knowledge and the Colonial Difference." *South Atlantic Quarterly* 101 (1): 57–96.

———. 2007. "From Central Asia to the Caucasus and Anatolia: Transcultural Subjectivity and De-Colonial Thinking." *Postcolonial Studies* 10 (1): 111–20.

———. 2011. *The Darker Side of Western Modernity: Global Futures, Decolonial Options*. Durham, NC: Duke University Press.

Palumbo-Liu, David. 1999. *Asian/American: Historical Crossings of a Racial Frontier*. Stanford, CA: Stanford University Press.

Patrick, Stewart M. 2011. "Obama's Message: An 'Atlantic Charter' for a Pacific Century." *Internationalist*, November 21. http://blogs.cfr.org/patrick/2011/11/21/obama%E2%80%99s-message-an-%E2%80%9Catlantic-charter%E2%80%9D-for-a-pacific-century/. Accessed May 15, 2015.

Pease, Donald E. 1993. "New Perspectives on U.S. Culture and Imperialism." In *Cultures of United States Imperialism*, edited by. Amy Kaplan and Donald E. Pease, 22–37. Durham, NC: Duke University Press.

———. 2006. "9/11: When Was 'American Studies after the New Americanists'?" *boundary 2* 33 (3): 73–101.

———. 2009. "Rethinking 'American Studies' after US Exceptionalism." *American Literary History* 21 (1): 19–27.

———. 2011. "Introduction: Re-Mapping the Transnational Turn." In *Re-Framing the Transnational Turn in American Studies*, edited by Winfried Fluck, Donald Pease, and John Carlos Rowe, 1–46. Hanover, NH: Dartmouth College Press.

Perry, Douglas. n.d. "Teaching with Documents: The Lewis and Clark Expedition." Washington: National Archives. http://www.archives.gov/education/lessons/lewis -clark/. Accessed February 19, 2014.

Quijano, Anibal, and Immanuel Wallerstein. 1992. "Americanity as a Concept, or the Americas in the Imaginary of the Modern World-System." *International Social Science Journal* 44 (4): 549–57.

Radway, Janice A., Kevin K. Gaines, Barry Shank, and Penny Von Eschen, eds. 2009. *American Studies: An Anthology.* Malden, MA: Wiley-Blackwell.

Reischauer, Edwin O. 1942. "Memorandum on Policy towards Japan." September 14. RG 407, Entry 360, Box 147, National Archives, College Park, Maryland.

Rowe, John Carlos. 2000. *Literary Culture and U.S. Imperialism: From the Revolution to World War II.* Oxford: Oxford University Press.

———. 2002a. *The New American Studies.* Minneapolis: University of Minnesota Press.

———. 2002b. "Postnationalism, Globalism, and the New American Studies." In *Futures of American Studies,* edited by Donald E. Pease and Robyn Wiegman, 167–82. Durham, NC: Duke University Press.

———. 2004. "Culture, US Imperialism, and Globalization." *American Literary History* 16 (4): 575–95.

———, and Rick Berg, eds. 1991. *The Vietnam War and American Culture.* New York: Columbia University Press.

Rydell, Robert W. 1984. *All the World's a Fair: Visions of Empire at American International Expositions, 1876-1916.* Chicago: University of Chicago Press.

Sakai, Naoki. 2010. "Transpacific Complicity and Comparatist Strategy: Failure in Decolonization and the Rise of Japanese Nationalism." In *Globalizing American Studies,* edited by Brian T. Edwards and Dilip Parameshwar Gaonkar, 240–65. Chicago: University of Chicago Press.

Saussy, Haun. 2006. "Exquisite Cadavers Stitched from Fresh Nightmare: Of Memes, Hives, and Selfish Genes." In *Comparative Literature in an Age of Globalization,* edited by Haun Saussy, 3–42. Baltimore: Johns Hopkins University Press.

Schmitt, Carl. 1997. *Land and Sea.* Translated by Simona Draghici. Washington, DC: Plutarch.

Sensuikan San. 2005. "Japan—the Britain of Asia"? Japan Forum, June 11. http://www .jref.com/forum/threads/japan-the-britain-of-asia.17745/. Accessed May 16, 2015.

Shambaugh, David L. 2005. "The New Strategic Triangle: U.S. and European Reactions to China's Rise." *Washington Quarterly* 28 (3): 7–25.

Spanos, William V. 2003. "A Rumor of War: 9/11 and the Forgetting of the Vietnam War." *boundary 2* 30 (3): 29–66.

Takeuchi, Yoshimi. 2005. *What Is Modernity? Writings of Takeuchi Yoshimi.* Edited, translated, and with an introduction by Richard F. Calichman. New York: Columbia University Press.

Twining, Daniel. 2007. "America's Grand Design in Asia." *Washington Quarterly* 30 (3): 79–94.

US Department of Defense. 2012. *Sustaining U.S. Global Leadership: Priorities for 21st Century Defense*. Washington: Department of Defense. http://www.defense.gov/news/Defense_Strategic_Guidance.pdf. Accessed May 15, 2015.

US Trade Representative. n.d. "Trans-Pacific Partnership (TPP)." https://ustr.gov/tpp. Accessed May 15, 2015.

Wang, Hui. 2011. *The Politics of Imagining Asia*. Edited by Theodore Huters. Cambridge, MA: Harvard University Press.

Wiegman, Robyn. 2011. "The Ends of New Americanism." *New Literary History* 42 (3): 385–407.

Wilson, Rob. 2000. *Reimagining the American Pacific: From South Pacific to Bamboo Ridge and Beyond*. Durham, NC: Duke University Press.

———. 2002. "Imagining 'Asia-Pacific' Today: Forgetting Colonialism in the Magic Free Markets of the American Pacific." In *Learning Places: The Afterlives of Area Studies*, edited by Masao Miyoshi and Harry Harootunian, 231–60. Durham, NC: Duke University Press.

Wong, Sau-ling C. 1995. "Denationalization Reconsidered: Asian American Cultural Criticism at a Theoretical Crossroads." *Amerasia Journal* 21 (1–2): 1–27.

Wood, Houston. 2003. "Cultural Studies for Oceania." *Contemporary Pacific* 15 (2): 340–74.

Yan, Xuetong. 2011. "How China Can Defeat America." *New York Times*, November 20.

Yui, David Z. T. 1930. "China and the Pacific World." *Pacific Affairs* 3 (1): 34–45.

Yung, Wing. 1909. *My Life in China and America*. New York: Henry Holt.

[I]

TRANSNATIONAL PRACTICES:
OUTSIDE/INSIDE AMERICAN STUDIES

1

DONALD E. PEASE

HOW TRANSNATIONALISM RECONFIGURED THE
FIELD OF AMERICAN STUDIES: THE TRANSNATIONAL/
DIASPORA COMPLEX

The Emergence of the Transnational/Diaspora Complex

The transnational turn in American studies has effected the most significant reimagining of the field of American studies since its inception. Transnational perspectives have changed the way Americanist scholars imagine
their relationship not just to the field in which they conduct their research,
but also to their work, their objects of study, and the disciplinary protocols through which those objects get interpreted, periodized, and distributed. In having this effect, the transnational has exercised a monopoly of
assimilative power that enabled it to subsume and replace competing spatial
and temporal orientations to the object of study—including multicultural
American studies, borderlands critique, postcolonial American studies, and
the more general turn to American cultural studies—within an encompassing geopolitics of knowledge. The transnational turn also brought about
changes in the disposition of American studies scholars.

The term "transnational" possesses a century-long pedigree in American
studies. Randolph Bourne coined the term "transnational America" in 1916
to celebrate the coexistence within the territorial United States of citizens
and immigrants who hailed from national cultures scattered across the
globe ([1916] 1964). But the term did not achieve popularity within American studies until the cessation of the Cold War in Europe led US American
studies scholars to consider a transnational framework to be a salutary alternative to American exceptionalism.

Throughout the Cold War, US ideological dominance was sustained in
part through the representation of the United States as an exception to the
rules through which it regulated the rest of the global order. American exceptionalism had legitimated US global sovereignty by founding it on representations of a dichotomized world order over which the United States

exercised the "legal" power to rule. But with the dismantling of the Soviet Union and the formation of the European Union, the United States lost its threatening socialist totalitarian Russian other as well as its destabilized and dependent European other. After the conditions that loaned the exceptionalist frame its plausibility passed away, the United States became answerable to the transcultural world historical processes to which it had described itself as an exception. With the disappearance of relations that were grounded in the Cold War's macropolitical dichotomies, multiple, interconnected, and heterogeneous developments came into view that were irreducible to such stabilized oppositions (Pease 2007; Rodgers 1998 and 2004).

Scholarship in the field of transnational American studies differs from scholarship produced during the Cold War in that transnational studies scholars presuppose globalization rather than exceptionalism as the horizon of intelligibility for their scholarship. The transnational interpretive frame facilitates the analysis of the disparate practices of spatialization at work in migrations, unincorporated territories, and borderland transactions that pose insuperable challenges to nationalist paradigms.

Shifts in the meaning of the term "transnational" depend on the disparate purposes for which it gets used. Transnational American studies can valorize deterritorializations that serve the interests of the world marketplace and transnational corporations. It can also endorse movements that advance the concerns of antiglobalization activists, nongovernmental organizations (NGOs), environmentalists, social movements, migrant laborers, refugees, and stateless peoples. And transnational American studies can ratify the presuppositions of the empires that were its original backers and beneficiaries. It can also ratify the initiatives of global formations that have emerged to resist the resurgence of empire. The transnational banner can be taken up by those who represent themselves as an integral part of state rule; it can also be embraced by those who feel beleaguered and oppressed by the state. Transnational initiatives can refer to efforts to expand or to impede the exercise of US power. Transnational scholarship can revalue social formations within national imaginaries or within the nonnational formations that would unsettle them. However, there is a world of difference between the transnational as an extension of the national framework and the transnational as a geopolitical formation that emerged in the wake of the Westphalian order (Briggs, McCormick, and Way 2008; Wald 1998).

As these observations suggest, the transnational is a highly contradictory concept, invested with multiple and incompatible significations. Since its significance gets particularized differently each time the transnational appears in a particular context, it is necessary to distinguish and clarify these different uses and meanings. There is no isomorphic relation between the transnational as a signifier and what it is made to signify. Over the last twenty years, scholars have offered multiple and contradictory accounts of transnational American studies. Carolyn Porter supplied a persuasive rationale for the shift to a transnational disposition in 2002 when she recommended that Americanists "reconceptualize a field that is clearly no longer mappable by any of the traditional coordinates . . . but that also resists the reconfiguration called for by its own historical and geographical expansion" (1994, 476). Samuel Huntington (1996) correlated the transnational aspect of the United States with the triumphalism of Western civilization. According to Shelley Fisher Fishkin, the transnational has effected a mutation of the nationalist orientation field: "Over the last ten years a web of contact zones has increasingly superseded 'the nation' as the basic unit of, and frame for, analysis" (2005, 42). Emory Elliott (2007) aligned the transnational imperatives of the field of American studies with cross-cultural exchanges that affirmed cosmopolitan liberal norms. Akira Iriye (1989) argued for a transnational cultural history to complement purely national developments. Brent Hayes Edwards (2007) correlated transnational American studies to a demotic cosmopolitanism and the struggle for minority rights. Johannes Voelz (2011) characterized transnationalism as the form of Americanization the US state assumed at the present juncture. José David Saldívar (2011) argued for a transnational, antinational, and outernational paradigm for American studies based on the "transnationality" of the Americas. Jeffrey Hole (2015) described transnational iterations of American studies as a pedagogy designed to refashion social relations and cultural practices according to the US neoliberal state's model.

It is evident from this list that advocates of transnational scholarship harbor different assumptions concerning its import and provenance. Although individual scholars would assign it a different value, each of these examples turns on an explicitly stated or implied distinction between the cultural, economic, social, and political activities of agents of core nation-states and the operations of agents inhabiting geographies, movements, and processes that are either autonomous of or excluded from the core states. The line of demarcation separating the projects and purposes of these disparate expressions of transnational American studies is itself a function of a juridical and political line dividing these transnational formations into contrary but coconstituting groups: transnational citizen-subjects who benefit from the transnational rules regulating the movement of goods, finances, and people in the newly globalized economic order; and the diasporic populations of refugees, nomads, indigenous peoples, migrant laborers, stateless peoples, and subalterns who lack such prerogatives (Cheah 1999; Trouillot 2003).

The fundamental category named by the transnational seems to be self-evident, but its conditions of representation vary greatly. The broad array of representations of the transactions between peoples of the diaspora and transnational citizen-subjects would include juxtaposition, subordination, mutual exclusion, reciprocal appropriation, subversion, exploitation, improvisation, evasion, hostility, and coexistence. I have devised the notion of a transnational/diaspora complex to take into account the US state's unequal distribution of economic, juridical, political, and economic rights as well as its asymmetrical inscription of mobility privileges on the bodies and goods of its citizens and subjects within as well outside US territorial boundaries. I also intend my use of the term to underscore the significance of the transnational in the transnational turn in American studies as an object of struggle rather than a fully achieved reality.

Transnational American studies originated in efforts to comprehend the incompatible scenarios in which the United States—as simultaneously a territorially bound nation-state and a deterritorialized imperial state of exception—negotiated and attempted to regulate the global economic system. The transnational/diaspora complex describes the agent and outcome of the operations through which transnational citizen-subjects and diasporic subjects undertake transactions with the state of exception and with the unruly processes of the global economic order. The line between transnational citizen-subjects and diasporic subjects is as arbitrary as the rules controlling the passage of people and goods at state borders. The transnational/diaspora manifests the mistranslations and unequal exchanges that accompany and frustrate Americanist scholars who desire cross-cultural solidarity; the transnational/diaspora complex discloses the mutual imbrications and unacknowledged reciprocities in cultures that Americanist scholars aspire to set in a relation of insuperable opposition.

While it does not exclude them, the term "diaspora" at work in the transnational/diaspora complex does not refer just to stateless peoples whose identity can be secured only in relation to a native land. The cultural differences organizing the denizens of the diaspora pose intractable challenges to the idea of a bounded, unitary nation to which they can return. The diasporic aspect of the transnational/diaspora complex refers both to the lived experience of migrants, nomads, and dispossessed peoples and to the processes that radically disrupt the lifeworlds of transnational citizen-subjects; it also uncovers the discontinuity in their identity formation. If the transnational citizen-subject continues to believe in a fixed universal and transcendental subject lying outside history and culture, the diasporic aspect of the transnational/diaspora complex locates the limit of the transnational subject that reverses its hegemony. In contrast, the transnational subject constitutes the identity within the US political and juridical order that an agent of the diaspora can provisionally assume to express the instances of economic, cultural, and social injustice that order perpetuates.

Transnational studies scholars are unlike agents involved in international exchanges in that the transnational/diaspora complex forecloses the possibility that either of the parties in the transaction will remain self-enclosed and unitary. In the nation, territory and people are fused; in transnational formations, they are disarticulated. The transnational is not the other of the nation. The transnational/diaspora complex does what the border does for the nation: it activates an undecidable economic, political, or social formation that is neither in nor out of the nation-state, yet confronts the latter with its own internal differences (Ickstadt 2002; Lenz 2002; Mignolo 2000).

It was in their production of sites—interzones, borderlands, intersections, and junctions—where the inside and the outside of America and other cultural domains were intertwined, and where more than one location, tradition, or practice came into play. The transnational/diaspora complex perforce changed the ways in which American studies scholars imagined their disciplinary objectives and the practical context for the articulation of their scholarly projects. Inherently relational, the transnational/diaspora complex involves a double move: to the inside, to core constituents of a given nation; and to an outside, where diasporic processes introduce different configurations.

Drawing on Americanist scholars' ambivalent investments in the transnational and diasporic aspects of their areas of study, the transnational/diaspora complex describes the reversibility of the regulatory and subversive processes that arise at the anxiogenic line separating transnational citizen-subjects from the diasporic figures who are constitutively excluded from transnational citizens' conditions of belonging. Rather than a unitary subject, transnational studies presupposes an inherently split subject position. This splitting makes it impossible to become wholly identified with the position of the transnational subject without simultaneously becoming affiliated with the figurations of diaspora that the transnational excludes.

By fostering the interaction of such contradictory strategies and irreconcilable interests, the transnational/diaspora complex has also brought about changes in the orientation of transnational American studies scholars. In what follows I will try to explain the significance of this reorientation through a consideration of the geopolitical situation in which transnational studies emerged; an account of the relationship of transnational American studies to the multicultural and postcolonial practices it supplanted; and a reflection on the changes the transnational/diaspora complex brought about in the field imaginary of transnational American studies scholars. To provide a conceptual context for these remarks, I will discuss the differences that transnational American studies effected in the encompassing discourse of American exceptionalism that previously supplied the field with intelligibility.

The Geopolitical Context

The emergence of transnational American studies was a symptom of a massive transformation in the world political economy. The geopolitical terrain that rendered the transnational a crucial cognitive framework was informed by a shift in the international norms governing states' relationships to bounded territories, migrant populations, and the sovereign will of national peoples (Barkin and Cronin 1994).

States undergo reimagining in significant ways during major systemic crises that precipitate changes in the rules governing the world system, such as the Great Depression, World Wars I and II, the termination of the Cold War, the decolonization of the Soviet empire, 9/11, and the financial meltdown of 2008. These crises result in differences in the international norms related to the legitimate agency of sovereignty. National sovereignty designates the people as the embodiment of a general will authorized to produce citizens, subjects, and laws. State sovereignty represents the state as the institutionalized government agency responsible for securing, regulating, and sustaining the nation (Barkin and Cronin 1994; Medovoi 2005; Miyoshi 1993; Sassen 2006). During periods when the norms of the international state system favor national over state sovereignty, the international community is more sympathetic to pleas for national self-determination at the expense of established states. In contrast, when international norms legitimize state rather than national sovereignty, the international community and its institutions defend the rights of established states against the nationalist claims of domestic ethnic groups (Barkin and Cronin 1994).

The globalization of markets and labor that implicated core states in the massively collateralizing networks of labor and finance capital precipitated a broad revaluation of states' relationship to their national societies. These global events created fissures in the connections between space, people, identity, and territorially bounded states. States around the planet influenced how their national populations understood these disruptions by forging rules that legitimized state rather than national sovereignty.

These newly minted rules were installed through the states' suspension of already existing contractual relationships with their national constituencies. The agency responsible for the installation and enforcement of these new rules and norms was the state of exception. The state of exception operates in a sphere that is separable from the logics of the nation and that cannot be reduced to its terms (Agamben 2005; Dawson and Schueller 2007). A state assumes this aspect when it suspends the laws and rules of an already constituted order so as to institute alternatives (Stoler 2006a). Transnational iterations of the field of American studies took center stage after the administration of President George W. Bush installed a state of exception (the homeland security state) to regulate the US national community's relationship to the social, economic, ideological, and cultural structures of exchange taking place across the planet (Pease 2009).

At the beginning of the twentieth century the diffusions of nationalism, colonialism, and large-scale wars constituted interrelated ways of regulating and controlling global processes. But the economic assumptions in play at the onset of the twenty-first century characterized nation-states and imperial warfare as inefficient technologies of management. The economic demands of the global marketplace redefined the state's mission, requiring that it downplay its obligations to the constituencies within a bounded national territory so as to meet the extranational needs and demands of global capital (Sassen 2006; Strikwerda 2000). The unruly capitalism that globalization sponsors reinstated an earlier alliance between capital and the state that restricted the states' role to that of protecting the newly emerging regional markets and local outposts of the global economy (Dirlik 2007).

At the beginning of the twenty-first century, market priorities reshaped sociopolitical agendas by characterizing the nation-state's social and political commitments as impediments to the efficient functioning of the global marketplace. Globalization necessitated the recentering of core nation-states into transnational regions like the European Union and the Association of Southeast Asian Nations. It also decentered peripheral nation-states in Central Europe; the Middle East; and recently decolonized spaces in Africa, South Asia, and the Caribbean.

Core states aspired to exempt themselves from contractual obligations to their national communities and to sever ties with every constituency except the entrepreneurial capitalists responsible for managing the global economy. Rather than representing the interests of the entire nation, managerial elites bifurcated nation-states into capitalist sectors fully integrated into the global capitalist order and regions whose premodern economic practices were subjected to the exploitative forces of the capitalist sector (Antonio and Bonanno 2000; Dirlik 2007; Gray 1998).

In the twentieth century, Westphalian norms defined state sovereignty in terms of the practices of vertical encompassment through which the state contained its economy, society, culture, and population within a bounded national territory. However, at the beginning of the twenty-first century, the globalization of capital, labor, and trade; NGOs; and the movement of migrants, refugees, and stateless peoples combined to pose insuperable challenges to the containment powers of sovereign states (Dimock 2006; Hardt and Negri 2000; Sassen 1996; Sharma and Gupta 2006). State sovereignty was undermined from below by the demands of subnational populations for decentralization and autonomy. It was pressured from above by the demands of supranational organizations like the World Bank, the World Trade Organization, and the G-7 for the coordination of military, environmental, and monetary policies. The verticality of the state's economic, political, and technological power was offset by horizontal networks of NGOs, political movements, migrant laborers, civil-society networks, missionary groups, care workers, and semiprivate organizations of all kinds with which the state was required to negotiate (Appadurai 1996; Sharma and Gupta 2006).

The importance of interconnected networks of finance, goods, labor, and peoples changed the definition of sovereignty to mean the monopoly of control over networks of interconnectivity (Friedman 1999; Pease 2010). One outcome of the diminution of the state's centralizing powers was the emergence of multiethnic and multicultural social formations. Another outcome was the impoverishment of state welfare apparatuses. The neoliberal global market's influence on the nation-state resulted in the unbundling of entitlements to civil, social, and political rights from national belonging; the marketization of public goods; the downsizing of welfare structures; the commodification of social insecurity; and the privatization and corporatization of public power into commercial or administrative competencies (Gilroy 2005; Gray 1998; Sassen 1996; Sharma and Gupta 2006).

The drastic reorganization of space on a global scale blurred familiar distinctions between here and there, center and periphery, and colony and metropole (Rowe 2002). But even as bounded places were unsettled and familiar lines of territorial demarcation became blurred, the social production of space continued to influence how people conceptualized themselves and the world (Dimock 2006). The generalized disorientation within the geopolitical realm incited the invention of a newly imagined geographical and juridical line. This juridical and political delineation at once founded and regulated the distinctions separating the transnational operations of agents of core states from the activities of agents of movements excluded from core states. If the fault line of the transnational that was specific to nation-states entailed the disjunction of national societies from the enactments of states of exception, that line of demarcation got reproduced on a global scale.

This juridical line became especially visible at territorial borders, airports, transfer sites, and other contact zones where asymmetrical rights and empowerments separated the members of transnational formations, who were entitled to move freely across boundaries, from members of diasporic populations, who were not. These constraints were enforced by the real enactments of states of exception (Cheah 1999; Trouillot 2003). The legally enforceable constraints extending rights and entitlements to transnational citizen-subjects traveling from core nation-states were not applicable to itinerant laborers and political refugees migrating from decentralized peripheral regions. In setting the unmarked transnational areas populated by core states apart from these marked geographies of diaspora, the juridicized geographical order rendered visible the rules and constraints that changed the ways in which stateless peoples were represented.

"Transnational" and "diaspora" refer to political and juridical as well as geographic designations. In juridical and geopolitical discourses, the unmarked transnational acted in opposition to the peripheralized geographies and diasporic populations that it marked. Cartographically, the transnational separated the stateless peoples of the diaspora from the members of the imperium organized out of globalism's core states. Geopolitically, transnational and diasporic populations referred to competing juridical and political configurations of identities formulated within and against the cultural legislation of the Western nation-state. Juridically, transnationals were separated from peoples of the diaspora by legislation that reproduced the distinction between core states and the periphery in laws pertaining to guest workers, indigenes, immigrants, illegal aliens, and migrants (Trouillot 2003).

Both transnational and diasporic formations challenge conventional understandings of the state as the core governance apparatus responsible for the regulation of social life and for the protection of territorial sovereignty. At the same time that they have drastically attenuated the state's authority, however, transnational political movements and organizations require the state to be the sovereign source of authority to which they can address their demands for recognition, rights, and entitlements: "Geographers of transnational space must clearly recognize the continuing power of nation-states in defining the framework and setting the terms within which transnational social relations take place" (Jackson, Crang, and Dwyer 2004, 5).

Juridical, political, and economic institutions constitute the structural frameworks that regulate the distinctions between the everyday experiences of transnational citizens and diasporic populations. Transnational studies scholars have represented transnational forms of citizenship as attributes that enable persons from core states with visas to pass freely across the boundaries of nation-states that would impede the movement of refugees, migrant laborers, stateless peoples, and other denizens of the global diaspora (Archibugi and Held 1995; Beck and Sznaider 2006; Guibernau and Held 2001). However, the challenges transnational migration and social movements have posed to state governments have reshaped citizenship into a multilayered process due to transnational migration and social movements that challenge state governments (Laguerre 2006; Werbner and Yuval-Davis 1999). The US state of exception became most clearly evident with the termination of the Cold War in Europe, when the United States intervened within the geopolitical realm to inaugurate a different set of rules concerning its relationship to transnational markets and regulatory commissions (Hardt and Negri 2000; Johnson 2000 and 2004). The transnational state of exception turned the diaspora into an unacknowledged yet pervasive precondition for transnational social relations. The state of exception exercises global sovereignty through its monopoly of the legitimate power to decide whether transnationals can maintain their civic identities. Since these decisions take place at and as the geographical and juridical line separating transnational citizens from diasporic subjects, that line of demarcation also discloses the reversibility of these subject positions.

This existential line is also the scene of origin of the transnational/ diaspora complex. Transnational citizen-subjects' generalized experience of anxious dislocation at this site reveals the condition they share with stateless migrants. By confronting transnational citizen-subjects with the geopolities they cohabit with diasporic populations, the transnational/diaspora complex undermines the self-other dichotomy that sustains transnationals' belief in their utterly secured, unitary identities and exposes them to diaspora as the shared condition of precariousness. Without the state as their guarantor, transnationals' rights would prove as inconsequential as those of the peoples of the diaspora to which they are set in opposition (Adas 2006; Sharma and Gupta 2006; Sharpe 2000b).

Carl Dahlman is surely correct in observing that "transnationalism is not a sufficient condition for diasporas, which additionally imply a common sense of territorial identity among its members" (2004, 486). But in the epoch of the transnational state of exception, the line demarcating transnational citizens from stateless subjects of the diaspora mutates into a process of interconnection when transnational citizen-subjects experience the foundational contingency of their civic identities. Although diaspora and transnational refer to different relationships to global economic processes, efforts to set the diasporic and transnational aspects of the transnational/diaspora complex in a relationship of mutual exclusion impedes recognition of their mutual imbrication.

Geographic spaces do not necessarily implicate single and stable identities. As Doreen Massey has observed, geographies of diaspora involve "social relations that connect people from different places," thereby disclosing "the internal differences and conflicts" in places that claim to be uniform in identity (1994, 5). Massey's insights inspired Stuart Hall to theorize cultural identity as itself an effect of the social and cultural differences implicit in the diaspora. Hall describes the diaspora as setting to work "this play of 'difference' within identity" that undermine the powers of the stabilizing self and produces complex and floating differential processes. The diasporic experience is "not defined by essence or purity, but by the recognition of a necessary heterogeneity and diversity; by a conception of 'identity' which lives with and through, not despite, difference" (Hall 1994, 396).

Following Hall's observations, we might think of the transnational/ diaspora complex as comprised of twinned yet contrary axes that operate simultaneously: the transnational vector of similarity and continuity and the diasporic vector of difference and rupture interconnected through diagonal forces (1994, 395). The transnational vector grounds the subject in continuity with the national past and correlates the subject with the intentionality of the state; the diasporic vector projects the experience of a profound discontinuity from the state's designs and promotes nomadic identifications.

Transnational citizen-subjects are always already mixed, heterogeneous, and even paradoxical entities that are themselves the effects of a tension inherent in the transnational/diaspora complex. Rather than buttressing the essentializing binary relation between self and other, the transnational/ diaspora complex introduces the experience of self-othering within transnational subjects that refuses to be displaced onto an external opposition between a coherent unified transnational self and an anarchic diasporic other. By "diasporizing" the privileged positioning of the transnational citizen-subject, the transnational/diaspora complex undermines the dichotomy between transnational self and diasporic other that would otherwise sustain a unitary subject position. Instead of a coherent identity, the diasporic subject releases "a cluster of flowing currents" dispersed in time and space, yet lacking a synthetic theme or a general equivalent to reconcile or harmonize them (Said 1999, 295).

The subjectivity of the transnational citizen-subject would appear to be constituted out of the radical exclusion of the diasporic other. Transnational subjects cannot identify with stateless refugees or nomads without forfeiting their identity. Yet the diasporic processes of self-differing precede and in some sense include the transnational agents whose subjectivity requires their exclusion. Although there is a tendency to split off this ongoing nomadism that cannot be stabilized into a unitary self, there nevertheless would appear to be an archaic unity between the transnational and diasporic processes. Indeed, the belief that the transnational and diasporic aspects are mutually exclusive rather than intertwined aspects of the transnational/diaspora complex is the effect of splitting this pervasive condition of nomadism into two separate aspects.

If we designate the diaspora as what takes place when forces of globalization break down the unitary sense of the national subject, we can say that the diaspora constitutes the limit that is internal to the transnational subject. A transnational citizen-subject might wish to impose the decisive distinction between transnational subject and diasporic subaltern, but if that person founded his or her identity on this dichotomy, she or he would be indistinguishable from a self-contained national subject. Transnational citizen-subjects cannot sustain the opposition between a transcendental self and its diasporic other because, unlike the national subject, the transnational subject is nonunitary: it lacks a unifying essence.

In its office as a transnational state of exception, the United States exercised the power to decide whether nation-states across the planet had been properly integrated within the global economic order or become so-called failed states. In extending its jurisdiction across national boundaries, the US state dissociated national communities from their presumption of territorial sovereignty. The contradictory provenance of the United States as a global state regulatory apparatus responsible for securing and maintaining the rule of law across the planet and as a territorially bound nation aroused anxieties among the citizen-subjects who were urged to reimagine themselves as internal exiles within the global homeland state (Johnson 2000 and 2004; Pease 2009).

In the twenty-first century the US state took up a transnational position in its negotiations with US citizen-subjects and extrastate institutions. The world market required the transnational state of exception to secure its transactions. Disparate transnational movements have invoked the norms of an imagined transnational civil society to check the power of the transnational state. These changes in the relationship between the state and national and international populations reflected changes in the global economic order. The mediator that separated the transnational state from the national society was the state of exception. It also regulated the relationship between transnational social formations, the global market, and the transnational state (Agamben 2005; Dawson and Schueller 2007; Miyoshi 1993).

Transnational American studies emerged in tandem with and in analytic relationship to the transnational state's and the global market's unruly transactions with transnational and diasporic formations. The transnational/diaspora complex describes the agency and outcome of the operations through which transnational and diasporic formations undertook unruly transactions with the national state, the transnational state of exception, and the global market. The work of the transnational/diaspora complex is discernible in the differences it effected in configurations of American studies.

The Emergence of Transnational American Studies
out of its Multicultural and Postcolonial Phases

The transnationalization of the field of American studies took place in three phases. The shift from anti-imperial to multicultural and then to transnational iterations of American studies was regulated by the field's construction of different imagined relations with the real state of exception. From 1968 to 1979, countercultural American studies scholars associated themselves with transnational social movements to oppose the Cold War state of exception. Multicultural American studies overlapped with the post–Cold War downsizing of the welfare state in the administrations of Presidents Ronald Reagan, George Bush, and William Clinton to adapt to the necessities of the transnational market. The emergence of transnational American studies coincided with global state of exception that President George W. Bush instituted in the wake of 9/11 (Rubin and Verheul 2009).

During the Cold War, American exceptionalism produced an image of US national unity in which gender, class, racial, and ethnic differences were massively downgraded. The discourse of American exceptionalism erected the image of a hardworking unified national monoculture to ward off the dangers posed by the globalizing of economic exchanges. It also represented internal differences between classes, genders, and ethnic groups as threatening national unity (Tyrrell 1991).

After the breakup of the Soviet empire, the United States inaugurated a new world order whose rules and norms would be enforced by a transnational state of exception. When the exception became the rule, the portions of the nation's history that had been hidden under the cover of exceptionalist history emerged into stark visibility. Racial, ethnic, and gender minorities who felt oppressed by exceptionalist norms called for a fundamental recasting of the American studies paradigm. American studies scholars who had organized their field identities out of exceptionalist norms had deployed the myths of the frontier and the melting pot to legitimate an assimilationist paradigm that overrode questions of diaspora and the state of multiculturalism. American studies scholars who embraced multiculturalist imperatives replaced the frontier and the melting pot with the borderland and the contact zone as the mythological sites grounding their negotiation with the multicultural domestic society. These scholars shifted the dominant US self-representation from a homogeneous national culture to a culture characterized by multiple ethnic and racialized cultures of very different, changing, and often conflicting kinds. In fostering the sociocultural empowerment of women, gay men, and lesbians as well as ethnic and racial minorities, these multiculturalist scholars adopted interpretive practices that brought exceptionalist norms into crisis (Lauter 2009; Lenz 1999; Sharpe 2000a; Werbner and Yuval Davis 1999; Žižek 1997).

But American studies scholars who construed the social and economic inequities within the multicultural society as the legacy of US imperial history insisted that colonial and postcolonial interpretive frameworks be brought to bear on these problems. When they described US immigration policies as postcolonial, these American studies scholars argued that multicultural problems could not be considered apart from the colonial institutions on which the United States was founded. In focusing their attention on the socioeconomic problems of groups within the multicultural society left unaddressed by US assimilationist policies, multicultural activists worked in tandem with postcolonial theorists to uncover US colonialism and imperialism as the unacknowledged legislators regulating the relationship between ethnic, racial, and gendered minorities and the dominant national identity (Mackenthun 2000; Sharpe 2000a; Sweeney 2006). The refugee, the alien from another country, the colonial subject, and the slave have always been the uncanny doubles of US citizens (Sharpe 2000a).

For the bulk of its history, the United States has been not only a nation-state but also an imperial power with colonial possessions (Stephanson 1995). According to Ann Laura Stoler, the US state's imperial and colonial forms of governance were founded on hierarchized variations of sovereignty and disenfranchisement and authorized by multiple and heterogeneous criteria for inclusion and exclusion. These contradictory criteria required constant juridical and political reassessments. US imperial governance implemented the construction of highly contradictory domains of jurisdiction wherein ad hoc exemptions from the law on the basis of racial and cultural difference resulted in the construction of exceptional spaces for exceptional peoples (Stoler 2006a, 57). The designers of the US imperial state created numerous exceptional spaces—Indian reservations, the frontier, unincorporated territories, internal colonies, protectorates, transfer stations, detainee centers, unincorporated territories, trusteeships, and possessions that belonged to the state but were not part of the US polity—to accommodate the disparate populations identified by the state's categorizations. The juridical and political decisions responsible for the production and justification of these anomalous sites of exception determined who was and who was not included within the US territorial state.

The legacy of colonialism was recognizably at work in US immigration policies' unequal treatment of ethnic and racial minorities, Third World immigrants, and members of diasporic communities. The categorizations the state invented to facilitate these policies—resident alien, guest worker, naturalized citizen, and citizen without voting rights—reflected disparate forms of assimilation and differentiation (Lauter 2009; Sharpe 2000a). After disclosing the persistence of institutionalized racism and sexism in US political arrangements, advocates of multiculturalism expanded the meaning of cultural differences beyond race and ethnicity to include gender, class, sexuality, and disability status.

However, transnational studies scholars raised doubts about the state's ability to incorporate differences and represent cultural diversity without radically changing governmental policies concerned with education and the remediation of social and economic inequalities. They specifically argued that the socioeconomic problems confronting US minority cultures and subcultures could not be understood apart from an analysis of the relationships of these subnational formations to migrant and diasporic communities around the globe. Transnational American studies scholars undermined the notion that national, cultural, and social formations were territorially bound. They installed an interpretive framework that supplanted multicultural and postcolonial narratives with cross-cultural and extranational accounts of domestic social problems (Elliott 2007; Sharpe 2000a). Through the construction of alternative terrains of collective aspiration responsible for the production and reproduction of the everyday social life of subjects and citizens, transnational American studies scholars argued that the extranational affiliations of domestic ethnic communities constituted indispensable linkages connecting the US socioeconomic polity with Asia, Africa, and Latin America as well as Europe. They did so to elucidate the interdependence of the inequities and oppressions within the United States and the problems that had arisen throughout the global economic order (Edwards 2007; Hall 2000; Hong 2007; Lionnet and Shih 2005; Lowe 1998; Montgomery 2003; Sharpe 2000b).

When they called attention to these intricate interdependencies, advocates of transnational American studies exposed the contradictory relationship between an increasingly interconnected world and a multicultural United States that remained tethered to exceptionalist assumptions. Knowledge produced in this emerging field reformulated multicultural conflicts that took place within the multicultural United States in terms of the cross-cultural processes carried out between national and transnational imaginaries. Rather than representing the multicultural United States as enclosed, transnational American studies scholars constructed models of knowledge production that conceptualized social movements and modes of cultural transmission as passing back and forth between disparate cultural systems. These scholars described cultural production and cultural change as complex, multidirectional processes that could no longer be mapped as the diffusion from a dominant center to a receptive periphery.

The transnational/diaspora complex mediated between American studies scholars' transnational and diasporic modes of knowledge production. Transnational scholars who identified with the transnational state's monopoly over the categories of cultural translation tethered diasporic others to the imperial state's taxonomy. But knowledges circulating throughout the diaspora included aspirations and freedom practices that were not answerable to the state's social logics. The diaspora's multitudinous processes of identification and disidentification disrupted and refracted the state's system of classifications and fostered identity formations within transnational scholars that were irreducible to the state's rubrics. In their assessment of the ways in which global economic processes exceeded the nation-state's regulatory practices, transnational American studies scholars elucidated disparate scales and practices of spatialization as evidenced in the geographies and movements of the diaspora.

However, the structural injustice at work in these spaces required creating postnational regulatory agencies and international courts of justice that have not yet materialized (Cheah 1999). Whereas the diasporic aspect of the transnational/diaspora complex communicated the aspiration of dispersed populations for such transnational tribunals of justice, the transnational aspect supplied a juridically recognized subject position that an agent of the diaspora could provisionally assume within a constituted order to express demands for a guest worker's rights or the undoing of a migrant laborer's debt peonage, and to contest the economic inequities and social and political injustice across the state's domain. As embodiments of the antagonism —enforced by enactments of local and global states of exception—between the nation-state's claims of sovereign self-determination and the constraints that sever migrant laborers from the right to a fair wage, housing, and health care, agents of the diaspora reinstated the questions of the multicultural and the postcolonial that transnational American studies scholars had displaced (Hall 2000; R. Saldívar 2006).

The Transnational/Diaspora Complex and the Emergence of a Transnational Field Imaginary

Thus far the discussion of the transnational/diaspora complex has focused attention on the disavowed diasporic figures within the transnational subject and ignored the geographies of diasporas on which transnational American studies scholarship were founded. The recent transnational turn in American studies inspired scholars to construct a plethora of cognitive and affective mappings that have replaced the naturalized geopolitics of nation-states and regions (Smith 2003).

Transnational scholars have located the transhemispheric, the transpacific, and the transatlantic as zones of cultural production informed by ineluctably transnational interactions. Transnational scholars have invented or restored transregional territories—Aztlan, the Black Atlantic, La Frontera, the Afro-Caribbean, the Pacific Rim, and the borderlands—that brought events from the disavowed history of US exceptionalism into stark visibility (Baucom 2005; Gilroy 2005; Go 2006; Richard 2001; J. Saldívar 1997). Insofar as all of these transnational geographies are inhabited by excepted peoples and spaces formerly under the dominion of US or European imperial states of exception, these sites are the locations of fieldwork for scholars in transnational American studies. Construed as localizations of the US imperial state of exception, these geographies of diaspora have brought about a reconfiguration of the imaginary of American studies: they have changed Americanists' field identities and their imagined communities, as well as their imagined relationships to both.

As the placeholder for the horrific events that took place at the obscene underbelly of American exceptionalism, each of these excepted territorializations pinpoints a site on which the US exceptional state had normalized its exceptions (Williams 1980; Zeitlin and Herrigel 2000). The state owned these territories by disowning the imperial predation and colonial violence that took place on them. When transnational Americanist scholars recovered the memories of the peoples who were the victims of Euro-American colonialism on these sites, they retrieved the imperial legacy that American exceptionalism had disowned. US American studies scholars who undertook the work of recovering this abjected past abandoned the self-representations that had formerly rendered them recognizable to themselves. They severed their ties to the exceptional national geography and forged bonds with a field that had become inseparable from these calamitous landscapes. After recovering this ignominious past, US American studies scholars who had inculcated American exceptionalist norms underwent a kind of self-abjection (Brown 2000; Traister 2010).

From its founding, American studies rendered the discourse of American exceptionalism as the mediator between the state of exception and its excepted spaces, peoples, and institutions (Castronovo and Gillman 2009). As a strategy of disavowal, American exceptionalism sustained Americanists' romance with America. Cold War Americanists' study of American literature and the objects structured out of American myths and symbols turned research in American studies into a secular version of a quest romance. Through their analysis of their objects of study, Americanist scholars aspired to achieve psychic wholeness through their integration with a transcendent Americanness. During the Cold War, the quest romance invested the subjects and objects of American studies with the affective relations sustained by the structures of misrecognition inherent in US exceptionalism (Fluck 2009). The romance broke down after Americanists uncovered the exceptions that the fantasy of exceptionalism had disavowed. Transnational Americanists' newly imagined territorializations of these excepted regions brought into stark visibility the disavowed exceptions—slavery, white settler violence, the forcible depopulation and genocidal extermination of native populations, internment camps, and transfer stations—that US exceptionalism had disavowed. By situating themselves within psychological topographies organized out of the shame-filled affects that exceptionalist historians had refused representation to, transnational American studies scholars produced new knowledge out of these foreclosed histories. Their collective acknowledgment of responsibility for these historical precedents also supplied affective resources for the transnationalization of the field.

The transnational reconfiguration of American studies specifically took place as a scenario within what I have elsewhere called the field imaginary (Pease 1989, 9–15). The field imaginary serves as a background of generally inarticulate yet efficacious metaphors and affects that provide the preconceptual orientation and unconsciously held collective beliefs and representations through which normative understandings get produced within the field. The paradigm-changing drama that the transnational/diaspora complex installed in the American studies field imaginary made a specific topic of analysis the role that the state of exception played in attaching US citizens (and Americanist scholars) to preexisting images and identities (Pease and Wiegman 2002). The state of exception was present at the joining of individuals and their mandated social identities. It was the state in its figuration as the exception that effected the individual's identification with a preexisting mandated image. The exception established a barrier between the subject that the individual became and his or her prior condition by recoding the individual as an alien, perverse, disorganized body whose threat to the integrity of the mandated subject justified its forcible exclusion by the state. Within the political arena the state correlated the individual's abject status with the figure of the refugee, the migrant, and other stateless subalterns from the global diaspora who the state excepted from the condition of belonging.

As the agency responsible for the internal act of hailing that transmuted the individual into a national identity, the state was other than the nation yet internal to the citizen-subjects its hailing produced (Bérubé 2003). In the transition from the Cold War nation-state to the transnational state of exception, the nation's subjects remained tethered to the state yet became severed from the coherent national identities to which the state had called them. In revealing the previously unimaginable space between the force through which the state tethered individuals to their mandated national identities and the as-yet-unidentified possible alternatives for these individuals, what could be called the transnational field imaginary disclosed the always already foreclosed difference between the mandated subject and the disorganized, unruly forces inherent in us national identity.

In bringing the national subject face to face with the diasporic figure who constitutes the limit of the national image repertoire, the transnational/diaspora complex detached the subject from its state-mandated subject position and facilitated its identification with processes of figuration that the transnational state had excepted. The transnational field imaginary thereafter fostered affiliations between transnational American studies scholars and excepted peoples within the global order. The figures that the transnational imaginary had rejected from the national imaginary supplied transnational Americanists with the identities through whom they took up these affiliations.

The transnational is an inherently split subject position embroiled in the transnational/diaspora complex. This splitting took place at the internal contact zone where the individual who had been removed from a preexisting subject position assumes a dual identification—with other core state transnationals as well as with the diasporic figures excluded by the state of exception. The splitting, which was inherent in the transnational subject, made it impossible to become identified with the transnational position without simultaneously becoming affiliated with the diasporic figures excepted by the transnational state, and vice versa. But since the figure through whom a transnational Americanist identified with peoples of the diaspora—the diasporized alien within—was itself subject to foreclosure by the psychic figuration of the state of exception, this dual identification required critical contestation with the juridical and political line installed by the transnational state of exception.

Internal to the national order but external to its regulatory norms, the state's exceptions embodied structures of psychic disavowal as well as the limits of its juridical rule. The change in the status of transnational Americanists' field identities to that of the transnational/diasporic split subject was accomplished through the dissolution of these psychic structures of disavowal. Given the state's intertwining of its juridical exceptions with psychosocial structures of disavowal, these psychic structures required that American studies scholars turn the state's exceptions into juridically actionable wrongs. But they could not accomplish this complex transaction without confronting the repressed histories of the imperial predations that these melancholic geographies remembered. The sights that severed us Americanists from their field identities unraveled the affective structures through which this knowledge had remained disavowed.

The geographies they dislocated from the state's excepted imperial history opened up nonstate spaces where alternative Americas became imaginable (Montgomery 2002). By situating themselves within psychological topographies that exceptionalist historians had disallowed representation, transnational American studies scholars produced new knowledge out of these foreclosed histories. More prescriptive than descriptive, these imaginary territories made up transnational alternatives to imperial and colonial histories that contributed to the transnational/diaspora complex's reconfiguration of the field imaginary. Individually and collectively, these transregional geographies from the underside of American exceptionalism enabled Americanist scholars to turn the state's exceptions to the rule into recognizable wrongs that demanded redress in a transformed geographical and juridical order (Pérez-Torres 2005).

In confronting transnational citizen-subjects with the transnational state of exception they shared with diasporic populations, the transnational/diaspora complex continues to call for projects within the field of transnational American studies capable of installing alternative understandings of the economic and political stakes of the global capitalist order.

Works Cited

Adas, Michael. 2006. *Dominance by Design: Technological Imperatives and America's Civilizing Mission*. Cambridge, MA: Harvard University Press.

Agamben, Giorgio. 1998. *Homo Sacer: Sovereign Power and Bare Life*. Stanford, CA: Stanford University Press.

———. 2005. *The State of Exception*. Chicago: University of Chicago Press.

Antonio, Robert J., and Alessandro Bonanno. 2000. "Conceptualizing the Global—a New Global Capitalism? From 'Americanism and Fordism' to 'Americanization-Globalization.'" *American Studies* 41 (2–3): 33–77.

Appadurai, Arjun. 1996. *Modernity at Large: Cultural Dimensions of Globalization*. Minneapolis: University of Minnesota Press.

Archibugi, Daniele, and David Held. 1995. *Cosmopolitan Democracy: An Agenda for a New World Order*. New York: Polity.

Barkin, J. Samuel, and Bruce Cronin. 1994. "The State and the Nation: Changing Norms and the Rules of Sovereignty in International Relations." *International Organization* 48:107–30.

Baucom, Ian. 2005. *Specters of the Atlantic: Finance Capital, Slavery, and the Philosophy of History*. Durham, NC: Duke University Press.

Beck, Ulrich, and Natan Sznaider. 2006. "Unpacking Cosmopolitanism for the Social Sciences: A Research Agenda." *British Journal of Sociology* 57 (March 20): 1–233.

Bérubé, Michael. 2003. "American Studies without Exceptions." *PMLA* 118 (1): 103–13.

Bogues, Anthony. 2010. *Empire of Liberty: Power, Desire, and Freedom*. Hanover, NH: Dartmouth College Press.

Bourne, Randolph. "Trans-National America." [1916] 1964. In *War and the Intellectuals: Selected Essays, 1915–1919*, edited by Carl Resek, 107–23. New York: Harper and Row.

Briggs, Laura, Gladys McCormick, and J. T. Way. 2008. "Transnationalism: A Category of Analysis." *American Quarterly* 60 (3): 625–48.

Brown, Wendy. 2000. "Resisting Left Melancholia." In *Without Guarantees: In Honour of Stuart Hall*, edited by Paul Gilroy, Lawrence Grossberg, and Angela McRobbie, 21–29. London: Verso.

Castronovo, Russ, and Susan Gillman, eds. 2009. *States of Emergency: The Object of American Studies*. Chapel Hill: University of North Carolina Press.

Cheah, Pheng. 1999. "Spectral Nationality: The Living On [*sur-vie*] of the Postcolonial Nation in Neocolonial Globalization." *boundary* 2 26 (3): 225–52.

Dahlman, Carl. 2004. "Knowledge and Development: A Cross-Section Approach." Washington: World Bank. Policy Research Working Paper No. 3366.

Dawson, Ashley, and Malini Johar Schueller, eds. 2007. *Exceptional State: Contemporary U.S. Culture and the New Imperialism*. Durham, NC: Duke University Press.

Dimock, Wai Chee. 2006. "Scales of Aggregation: Prenational, Subnational, Transnational." *American Literary History* 18 (2): 219–28.

Dirlik, Arif. 2007. *Global Modernity: Modernity in the Age of Global Capitalism*. Boulder, CO: Paradigm.

Doyle, Laura. 2009. "Liberty's Empire." In *American Studies: An Anthology*, edited by Kevin Gaines, Janice Radway, Barry Shank, and Penny Von Eschen, 59–68. Malden, MA: Blackwell.

Edwards, Brent Hayes. 2007. "Diaspora." In *Key Words for American Cultural Studies*, edited by Bruce Burgett and Glenn Hendler, 81–84. New York: New York University Press.

Elliott, Emory. 2007. "Diversity in the United States and Abroad: What Does It Mean When American Studies Is Transnational?" *American Quarterly* 59 (1): 1–22.

Fishkin, Shelley Fisher. 2005. "Crossroads of Culture: The Transnational Turn in American Studies—Presidential Address to the American Studies Association, November 12, 2004." *American Quarterly* 57 (1): 17–57.

Flatley, Jonathan. 2008. *Affective Mapping: Melancholia and the Politics of Modernism*. Cambridge, MA: Harvard University Press.

Fluck, Winfried. 2009. *Romance with America? Essays on Culture, Literature, and American Studies*, edited by Laura Bieger and Johannes Voelz. Heidelberg, Germany: Universitätsverlag.

Friedman, Thomas. 1999. *The Lexus and the Olive Tree: Understanding Globalization*. New York: Random House.

Gilroy, Paul. 2005. *Postcolonial Melancholia*. New York: Columbia University Press.

Go, Julian. 2006. "Imperial Power and Its Limits: America's Colonial Empire in the Early Twentieth Century." In *Lessons of Empire: Imperial Histories and American Power*, edited by Craig Calhoun, Frederick Cooper, and Kevin W. Moore, 201–14. New York: New Press.

Gray, John. 1998. *False Dawn: The Delusions of Global Capitalism*. London: New Press.

Guibernau, Montserrat, and David Held. 2001. "Globalization, Cosmopolitanism, and Democracy: An Interview with David Held." *Constellations* 8 (4): 427–41.

Hall, Stuart. 1994. "Cultural Identity and Diaspora." In *Colonial Discourse and Post-Colonial Theory: A Reader*, edited by Patrick Williams and Laura Chrisman, 392–403. New York: Columbia University Press.

———. 2000. "Conclusion: The Multicultural Question." In *Un/Settled Multiculturalisms: Diasporas, Entanglement, Transruptions*, edited by Barnor Hesse, 209–41. London: Zed.

Hardt, Michael, and Antonio Negri. 2000. *Empire*. Cambridge, MA: Harvard University Press.

Hole, Jeffrey. 2015. "Edward W. Said, the Sphere of Humanism, and the Neoliberal University." In *The Geocritical Legacies of Edward W. Said: Spatiality, Critical Humanism, and Comparative Literature*, edited by Robert T. Tally Jr., 1–25. New York: Palgrave Macmillan.

Hong, Grace Kyungwon. 2007. "The Ghosts of Transnational American Studies: A Response to the Presidential Address." *American Quarterly* 59 (1): 33–39.

Huntington, Samuel P. 1996. *The Clash of Civilizations and the Remaking of World Order*. New York: Simon and Schuster.

Ickstadt, Heinz. 2002. "American Studies in an Age of Globalization." *American Quarterly* 54 (4): 543–62.

Iriye, Akira. 1989. "The Internationalization of History." *American Historical Review*, 94 (1): 1–10.

Jackson, Peter, Philip Crang, and Claire Dwyer. 2004. *Transnational Spaces*. New York: Routledge.

Johnson, Chalmers. 2000. *Blowback: The Costs and Consequences of American Empire*. New York: Henry Holt.

———. 2004. *The Sorrows of Empire: Militarism, Secrecy, and the End of the Republic*. New York: Henry Holt.

Laguerre, Michelle S. 2006. *Diaspora, Politics, and Globalization*. New York: Palgrave Macmillan.

Lauter, Paul. 2009. "Multiculturalism and Immigration." In *American Multiculturalism after 9/11: Transatlantic Perspectives*, edited by Derek Rubin and Jaap Verheul, 23–34. Amsterdam: Amsterdam University Press.

Lenz, Guenter. 1999. "Internationalizing American Studies: Predecessors, Paradigms, and Dialogical Cultural Critique—a View from Germany." In *Predecessors: Intellectual Lineages in American Studies*, edited by Rob Kroes, 236–55. Amsterdam: VU University Press.

———. 2002. "Toward a Dialogics of International American Culture Studies: Transnationality, Border Discourses, and Public Culture(s)." In *The Futures of American Studies*, edited by Donald E. Pease and Robyn Wiegman, 461–85. Durham, NC: Duke University Press.

Lionnet, Françoise, and Shu-mei Shih. 2005. "Introduction: Thinking through the Minor, Transnationally." In *Minor Transnationalism*, edited by Françoise Lionnet and Shu-mei Shih, 1–27. Durham, NC: Duke University Press.

Lowe, Lisa. 1998. "The International within the National." *Cultural Critique* 40 (autumn): 29–47.

Mackenthun, Gesa. 2000. "America's Troubled Postcoloniality: Some Reflections from Abroad." *Discourse* 22 (3): 34–45.

Massey, Doreen. 1994. *Space, Place, and Gender*. Minneapolis: University of Minnesota Press.

Medovoi, Leerom. 2005. "Nation, Globe, Hegemony: Post-Fordist Preconditions of the Transnational Turn in American Studies." *Interventions* 7 (2): 162–79.

Mignolo, Walter. 2000. *Local Histories/Global Designs: Coloniality, Subaltern Knowledges, and Border Thinking*. Princeton, NJ: Princeton University Press.

Miyoshi, Masao. 1993. "A Borderless World? From Colonialism to Transnationalism and the Decline of the Nation-State." *Critical Inquiry* 19 (4): 726–51.

Montgomery, Maureen E. 2002. "Transculturations: American Studies in a Globalizing World—the Globalizing World in American Studies." *Amerikastudien/American Studies* 47 (1): 115–19.

Pease, Donald E. 1989. "New Americanists: Revisionist Interventions into the Canon." In. In *New Americanists: Revisionist Interventions into the Canon*, edited by Donald E. Pease, 1–37. Durham, NC: Duke University Press.

———. "Imperial Discourse." 1998. *Diplomatic History* 22 (4): 605–15.

———. 2007. "Exceptionalism." In *Key Words for American Cultural Studies*, edited by Bruce Burgett and Glenn Hendler, 108–12. New York: New York University Press.

———. 2009a. "Rethinking 'American Studies' after US Exceptionalism." *American Literary History* 21 (1): 19–27.

———. 2009b. *The New American Exceptionalism*. Minneapolis: University of Minnesota Press.

———. 2010. "American Studies after American Exceptionalism? Toward a Comparative Analysis of Imperial State Exceptionalisms." In *Globalizing American Studies*, edited by Brian T. Edwards and Dilip Parameshwar Gaonkar, 47–83. Chicago: University of Chicago Press.

——— and Robyn Wiegman. 2002. "Futures." In *The Futures of American Studies*, edited by Donald E. Pease and Robyn Wiegman, 1–44. Durham, NC: Duke University Press.

Pérez-Torres, Rafael. 2005. "Alternative Geographies and the Melancholy of Mestizaje." In *Minor Transnationalism*, edited by Françoise Lionnet and Shu-mei Shih, 317–38. Durham, NC: Duke University Press.

Porter, Carolyn. 1994. "What We Know That We Don't Know: Remapping American Studies." *American Literary History* 6 (3): 467–526.

Richard, Serge. 2001. "From Settler Colony to Global Hegemony: Integrating the Exceptionalist Narrative of the American Experience into World History." *American Historical Review* 106 (5): 1692–720.

Ritzer, George, and Elizabeth L. Malone. 2000. "Globalization Theory: Lessons from the Exportation of McDonaldization and the New Means of Consumption." *American Studies* 41 (2–3): 97–118.

Rodgers, Daniel. "Exceptionalism." 1998. In *Imagined Histories: American Historians Interpret the Past*, edited by Anthony Molho and Gordon S. Wood, 21–40. Princeton, NJ: Princeton University Press.

———. 2004. "American Exceptionalism Revisited." *Raritan* 24 (2): 21–47.

Rowe, John Carlos. 2002. "Postnationalism, Globalism, and the New American Studies." In *The Futures of American Studies*, edited by Donald E. Pease and Robyn Wiegman, 167–82. Durham, NC: Duke University Press.

Rubin, Derek, and Jaap Verheul. 2009. Introduction to *American Multiculturalism after 9/11: Transatlantic Perspectives*, edited by Derek Rubin and Jaap Verheul, 7–22. Amsterdam: Amsterdam University Press.

Said, Edward. 1999. *Out of Place: A Memoir*. New York: Vintage.

Saldívar, José David. 1997. *Border Matters: Remapping American Cultural Studies*. Berkeley: University of California Press.

———. 2011. *Trans-Americanity: Subaltern Modernities, Global Coloniality, and the Cultures of Greater Mexico*. Durham, NC: Duke University Press.

Saldívar, Ramón. 2006. *The Borderlands of Culture: Américo Paredes and the Transnational Imaginary*. Durham, NC: Duke University Press.

Sassen, Saskia. 1996. *Losing Control: Sovereignty in an Age of Globalization*. New York: Columbia University Press.

———. 2006. *Territory, Authority, Rights: From Medieval to Global Assemblages*. Princeton, NJ: Princeton University Press.

Shapiro, Michael J. 1997. *Violent Cartographies: Mapping Cultures of War*. Minneapolis: University of Minnesota Press.

Sharma, Aradhana, and Akhil Gupta. 2006. "Introduction: Rethinking Theories of the State in an Age of Globalization." In *The Anthropology of the State: A Reader*, edited by Aradhana Sharma and Akhil G. Gupta, 1–42. Oxford: Blackwell.

Sharpe, Jenny. 2000a. "Is the United States Post-Colonial? Transnationalism, Immigration, and Race." In *Postcolonial America*, edited by C. Richard King, 103–21. Urbana: University of Illinois Press.

———. 2000b. "Postcolonialism in the House of US Multiculturalism." In *A Companion to Postcolonial Studies*, edited by Sangeeta Ray and Henry Schwarz, 112–25. Oxford: Blackwell.

Smith, Neil. 2003. *American Empire: Roosevelt's Geographer and the Prelude to Globalization*. Berkeley: University of California Press.

Stephanson, Anders. 1995. *Manifest Destiny: American Expansion and the Empire of Right*. New York: Hill and Wang.

Stoler, Ann Laura. 2001. "Tense and Tender Ties: The Politics of Comparison in North American History and (Post)Colonial Studies." *Journal of American History* 88 (3): 829–65.

———. 2006a. "Imperial Formations and the Opacities of Rule." In *Lessons of Empire: Imperial Histories and American Power*, edited by Craig Calhoun, Frederick Cooper, and Kevin W. Moore, 53–72. New York: New Press.

———. 2006b. "On Degrees of Imperial Sovereignty." *Public Culture* 18 (1): 125–46.

Strikwerda, Carl. 2000. "From World-Systems to Globalization: Theories of Transnational Change and the Place of the United States." *American Studies* 41 (2–3): 333–48.

Sweeney, Fionnghuala. 2006. "The Black Atlantic, American Studies, and the Politics of Postcolonial Studies." *Comparative American Studies* 4 (2): 115–33.

Traister, Bryce. 2010. "The Object of Study; or, Are We Being Transnational Yet?" *Journal of Transnational American Studies* 2 (1): 1–23. http://www.escholarship.org/uc/item/864843hs?display=all#. Accessed February 7, 2015.

Trouillot, Michel-Rolph. 2003. *Global Transformations: Anthropology and the Modern World*. New York: Palgrave.

Tyrrell, Ian. 1991. "American Exceptionalism in an Age of International History." *American Historical Review* 96 (4): 1031–55.

Voelz, Johannes. 2011. "Utopias of Transnationalism and the Neoliberal State." In *Re-Framing the Transnational Turn in American Studies*, edited by Winfried Fluck, Donald E. Pease, and John Carlos Rowe, 356–73. Hanover, NH: Dartmouth College Press.

Wald, Priscilla. 1998. "Minefields and Meeting Grounds: Transnational Analysis and American Studies." *American Literary History* 10 (1): 199–218.

Werbner, Prima, and Nira Yuval Davis. 1999. *Women, Citizenship and Difference*. New York: Zed.

Williams, William Appleman. 1980. *Empire as a Way of Life*. New York: Dell.

Zeitlin, Jonathan, and Gary Herrigel, eds. 2000. *Americanization and Its Limits: Reworking US Technology and Management in Post-War Europe and Japan*. Oxford: Oxford University Press.

Žižek, Slavoj. 1997. "Multiculturalism, or, The Cultural Logic of Multinational Capitalism." *New Left Review* 1, no. 225: 28–51.

2

EVA CHERNIAVSKY

POST-SOVIET AMERICAN STUDIES

MY FOCUS IN THIS essay is on the proliferation of both American studies and, not incidentally, of American-style universities in the regions of the former Soviet bloc. This proliferation in both the revamped state acade- mies and the new private universities of Eastern Europe and Central Asia is funded in significant measure by the US Agency for International Devel- opment (USAID), which reflects, in turns, the foreign policy priorities of the Department of State. USAID generally operates in partnership with private foundations (for example, the Soros Foundation and; the Eurasia Founda- tion) and sometimes, though not always, the governments of host coun- tries. USAID's sponsorship of American studies evokes, of course, the history of Cold War–era public diplomacy, in which the promotion of American studies in client states was aligned with a wider effort to disseminate the American way. In this historical moment, the ambition of the United States to achieve global dominance was fused with an exclusive nationalist hail, which produced the dazzlingly contradictory mandate of the American cen- tury: because America is like no other nation, other nations should aspire to be more like America.

But despite the startling recurrence of the old paradigm in the infusion of Eastern European and Central Asian American studies with US government funding, the creation, institutional elaboration, and political imaginaries of what I am calling post-Soviet American studies speaks, instead, to the contemporary dissolution or divorce of the modern nation-state couple. In other words, American studies in the former Soviet bloc is not a vehicle for the interpellation of a local, comprador elite into the organizing ideologies of American political culture. Indeed, as I will suggest, post-Soviet American studies is not an ideological project at all, in the sense that we usually under- stand the term—though it is, without doubt, an imperial enterprise. More broadly, as I hope to show, post-Soviet American studies marks the extent to which the nation—the idioms and the affect of national belonging—is no longer the privileged pedagogical ground for the state's cultivation of its citizen-subjects.

To some extent, scholarship in transnational American studies has been alert to the shifting relations of nation and state in the contemporary moment. Certainly, work in the field has argued in important and compelling ways against narratives of national autogenesis and self-containment. It has detailed the porousness of national culture; the necessary failures of its constitutive exclusions; and the transnational migrations of peoples, discourses, and commodities that we addressed, not so long ago, as strictly national phenomena. It has documented the violence that alone sustains the production of sovereign territory, as well as the epistemic violence that produces the fictive ethnicity of the nation. But in its persistent, field-changing critique of nationalism, transnational American studies remains wedded to the nation as the thing that it is committed to unthink. The career of American studies in the regions of the former Soviet bloc—by which I mean both the conditions of its institutionalization, and the work it performs, on the ground, for Eastern European and Central Asian Americanists—is interesting, among other reasons, for the ways it invites us to revisit, or reframe, the meaning of our investment in the critique of the nation form.

In sketching the contours of post-Soviet American studies, I mean to make two claims. First, the stakes in our collective unthinking of the nation are quite specifically tied to the crisis of the left in the post-Reagan-era US Sometimes implicitly, but more often explicitly, the aspiration of transnational American studies has been to imagine new conditions for the left political mobilizations that seem so palpably foreclosed within the institutions and venues of US national politics. Leerom Medovoi encapsulates this sense of the field nicely when he suggests that the mission of transnational American studies is, or should be, to "deploy emergent post-national imaginaries on behalf of a counter-hegemonic globalization, oppositional narratives of cosmopolitan interests from below that confront the interests of post-Fordist capital with those of the life that it exploits (human and natural alike)" (177). To be sure, Medovoi's program orients transnational American studies toward the cultivation of a *global* left, yet increasingly I am moved to wonder whether the very preoccupation with global leftist solidarities is specific to American studies (and allied fields) in the US academy. At any rate, it does not take many hours of conversation with colleagues in Hungary, Georgia, Kyrgyzstan, or Azerbaijan to realize that the political imaginary of transnational American studies does not travel to the regions of the erstwhile Second World, even if much of the curricular content we associate with the transnational turn transfers easily enough. This is not to suggest that we have somehow failed to produce an authentic transnationalism, nor indeed to impose as the legitimating measure of transnational American studies that, to be what it claims, it must travel transnationally. But it is to suggest that the political imaginary of transnational American studies emerges more than we have cared to know from the parochial context of the United States: from the eclipse of representational politics within the simulacral scenes of American political life and the profound leftist melancholia it has engendered. Second, post-Soviet American studies reveals that the agents and agencies of the US state are also committed to unthinking the nation, so that the critique of nationalism within American studies offers relatively little insight into the workings of the contemporary US state. Alongside our own necessary reckoning with the legacies and afterlives of the modern nation-state form, we should remain attuned to the shifting relations of state to nation—and to the state's own elaboration of a postnational body politic.

American Studies in the Post-Soviet Academy

The study of US literature and history in the former Soviet Union and its satellite states considerably antedates the watershed years of 1989–90, but teaching and research related to American studies behind the Iron Curtain was most often an area of specialization within history departments or departments of literature and philology. The formation of American studies centers, programs, and departments both within the established (Soviet-era) academies and within a proliferating array of private, American-style academies dates with only a few exceptions (for example, the American Studies Center at the University of Warsaw, founded in 1976) to the early and mid-1990s. While not ascending to parity with the established disciplines— national academies and other institutions of accreditation have been typically slow to acknowledge new imports such as American and gender studies— American studies has nevertheless flourished in the post-Soviet context, in the form of research centers, degree-granting programs and departments, usually (though not always) with support from private foundations (such as the Soros Foundation and the Eurasia Foundation) and the US Department of State (for example, through embassy information centers and USAID).[1]

Although disparate local and regional histories make a significant difference in the issues and methods of American studies in these venues—not to mention, for instance, the disparities between Eastern European countries now entering the European Union (EU) and the newly independent republics of Central Asia—it is nonetheless productive to consider American studies in the broader post-Soviet context that the title of my essay proposes. Indeed, in a complaint (one of many) about what is known as the Bologna Process for standardizing higher education in the EU nations, Marek Kwiek explains the asymmetrical conditions of public higher education in Western Europe and in the "transition countries" of Central and Eastern Europe, in ways that illuminate the common conditions of the post-Soviet academy. "In a number of the transition countries escaping the model of command-driven economies," Kwiek writes, "the ideological position regarding the role of the state in the public sector differs considerably from the position taken, with few national exceptions, on a European level: the ideal of the state about to emerge once the chaos of the transition period is over is the American model of cost-effectiveness and self-restraint, rather than the 'European social model' of the EU 15" (769). The conditions of higher education that Kwiek identifies as characteristic of the transition countries in Central and Eastern Europe is broadly germane to the former Soviet regions of Central Asia, as well, where we see a shift from centralized state planning to a specifically American model of the reduced state, with the attendant crisis of the public sector and the underfunding of public higher education that this shift entails.

Of course, the American model of the postwelfare, neoliberal state is perhaps less about the reduction than about the redistribution of governance functions, what Liam Kennedy and Scott Lucas, writing on the topic of public diplomacy, aptly describe as a reterritorialization of what were once, in the not too-distant past, narrowly state-centered activities. Their central claim is that public diplomacy is not defunct in the post-9/11 era (not simply preempted, we might say, by the spectacle of force, or the strategy of shock and awe), but rather that its current failures are a consequence of this reterritorialization of state power:

> The failure of current attempts at U.S. public diplomacy can be attributed in part to their *dependence on an old paradigm of ideological warfare.* The conditions for the production and enactment of public diplomacy have changed significantly because of the way that global "interdependence" has radically altered the space of diplomacy. The founding premise of traditional diplomacy, that it was activity between states and their formal representatives, began to break down as the bipolar, state-centered context of the cold war gave way to multilevel relations conducted not only by national governments but by multinational corporations, nongovernment organizations (NGOS), private groups, and social movements using new technologies of communication to interact with and petition foreign publics. Moreover, this *dispersal and reterritorialization of public diplomacy* occurs amid the post-cold war (re)emergence of regional conflicts in international relations. American foreign policy is not only

rendered more global but more local by interventions in selected conflicts in
which issues of "cultural difference" magnify the problems of communication
encountered by American public diplomacy. *The difficulty of conducting a
"war of ideas" is compounded in a global information sphere that can swiftly
expose and interrogate contradictions of declared values and apparent policies
and actions.* (Kennedy and Lucas, 322; my emphasis)

The authors' enumeration of the changed conditions for public diplomacy usefully shorthands the context in which post-Soviet American studies emerged, the "multilevel relations" among governments, corporations,
and NGOs that produce, among other things, the funding streams for the
private, American-style universities that sprang up across the dismantled
Soviet empire, seemingly overnight, in the 1990s, and for the burgeoning
American studies programs throughout the region. In the prevailing analytic
discourse of the policymakers—the government and corporate administrators who conceive and elaborate them—these "multilevel relations" are routinely figured as a partnership among discrete sectors—states, markets, and
civil society—with civil society, in particular, framed as a "third way," an
alternative to market fundamentalisms that does not entail a return to state
regulation of the marketplace or a resurrection of the state as a primary
public service provider.[2] Post-Soviet American studies is, in many respects,
the brainchild of this partnership, but it is one that provides a telling perspective on the discourses and the institutional configurations of the reter-
ritorialized state, and especially on the way these operate (outside or apart
from the frame of national culture) to reproduce social subjects accommodated to present practices of governmental power. In the American studies
that emerges from this public diplomatic matrix, I will argue, the pedagogy
of citizenship is no longer lodged (or lodged primarily) in the discourse of
an assimilative nationalism.

In any case, we might note that the arrival of American studies in the
former Soviet bloc after 1990 coincides, roughly speaking, with the transnational turn in US-based American studies, alongside a new interest in the
possibilities of a critical internationalism that would cede US ownership of
the field. But where the inter- and transnationalism of American studies
appear complementary in the United States, that alignment seems tenuous,
at best, if we consider the post-Soviet academy as one arena of the field's
internationalization. In an essay describing the institutional and intellectual
history of American studies in Hungary, for example, Éva Federmayer compares the discontinuous investments that organize research and teaching
in the United States and in post-Soviet Hungary. Her portrayal of roughly
consonant thematics, on the one hand, and widely incommensurate critical

aspirations, on the other hand, is notable for its explicit and thoughtful consideration of a chasm that I have never failed to encounter in conversations with Americanists from the former Soviet bloc, but that goes usually unacknowledged—even, indeed especially, when I have sought to raise the question. Federmayer writes:

> The beginning of American Studies as an academic discipline at Hungarian colleges and universities is basically coterminous with the watershed years of 1989–1990 when the country made a radical shift from state socialism toward parliamentary democracy and a free economy. This political and economic about-face, which came hand-in-hand with the undermining of foundationalist certainties and the generation of new anxieties coincided, more or less, with the radical transformation that American Studies was undergoing between the 1990s and the early 2000s. Shaped by crucial scholarly debates in the U.S. American Studies community since the 1970s, "paradigm dramas" (as diagnosed by Gene Wise in 1979) fomented New American Studies with powerful agendas of pluralization and de-centering—a most challenging project that shows striking resonances with changes in Hungarian society and culture since 1990.
>
> However, the apparently easy parallel . . . is misleading. Whereas dominant discourses of New American Studies demonstrate a markedly "leftist" commitment to effect social change by remapping the relationship between culture, power, and social identities, current discourses in the highly charged political arena in Hungary demonstrate a shift toward conservative and/or populist agendas. To be sure, a country's political climate (nowadays saturated with nationalist concerns and economic anxieties, real or generated) should not be confused with the politics of another's scholarly community. What I seek to point out is the surprising discontinuities that a Hungarian Americanist is inevitably confronted with today when situating herself vis-à-vis subversive "post-Americanist" narratives about the transnational turn and critical internationalism typically dominating U.S. scholarly dialogue today. (Federmayer)

Here Federmayer lays out how certain elements of American studies—specifically, its embrace of identity politics and critical multiculturalism—dovetail with the contexts and preoccupations of Hungarian Americanists, while other elements, such as the "posting" of national contexts in preference to transnational and internationalist analytic frameworks, do not. Federmayer alludes, if only parenthetically, to the political crises of postsocialist Hungary that have followed from an upsurge of racialized ethnic nationalisms, fomented as one kind of familiar response to the incursions of transnational capital in both their cultural and economic manifestations (for example, the saturation of Hungarian mass media and public space with global popular culture, the impoverishment of the Soviet-era bourgeoisie, and the exponential increase in the gap between rich and poor). In this regard, no doubt, Hungarian politics are typical of conditions in many nations of the former Soviet bloc, as Federmayer's use of the undifferentiated "a country" (any country) implies. From the vantage of us-based American studies, one might surmise that the "post-Americanist" turn offers a useful analytic tool for Hungarian (and other post-Soviet) Americanists, who stand themselves (by and large) well to the left of racial populisms. But it is identity politics that meets the critical mandate to counter protofascist social mobilizations with a progressive representational politics, realized both in state protections for minority rights and in academic institutional sanctions of the knowledge projects that array nationalities, religions, and sexualities disqualified from the full rights and benefits of citizen as subjects of their own histories.

In contrast, both the transnational turn and, for that matter, the particular version of internationalism that is called critical internationalism invite attention to questions of political economy—to the historical relationship, for example, between nationalism and expansionist capital as it informs processes of immigration, migration, and diaspora. They call attention, as well, to the political economy of the modern university as an institutional guardian of national culture, which is, from this revisionist perspective, bound up in the relays of national identity, gendered and racial citizenship, entrepreneurialism (and other forms of professional-managerial competency), and imperial world making. Meanwhile, the intellectual identities of humanities-based scholars in the former Soviet bloc are routinely forged in opposition to the economic determinisms that have largely stood in for political economy as such within Soviet-era secondary and postsecondary education. In the intellectual's imaginary that attends the demise of the socialist state and the academy's projected retrieval from bureaucratic state control, moreover, the university is seen as a platform for public social engagement, rather than (as it does in the United States) an ivory tower marginal to the arenas where social change is wrought. From this perspective, a war of position—securing legitimacy and intellectual autonomy within the academy—seems more urgent than, say, unraveling the place of the contemporary university within neoliberal political economy. As Federmayer observed in response to a discussion of neoliberalism instigated by the us-based participants at a Central European University conference, to Hungarian academics—Americanists, feminists, and others committed to post-Soviet knowledge projects—neoliberalism simply does not seem like much of a problem, certainly nothing on the scale of the burgeoning ethnonationalist political parties and the perennial insecurity of identitarian knowledge projects (including American studies) in the academy. Although she did not dispute my suggestion that neoliberalism and ethnonationalism were linked phenomena, two sides of a coin, the linkage was evidently not compelling to her in the way it is to me, nor did it follow to her that critical analysis of the one could not and should not stand apart from critical analysis of the other.

To ask how American studies travels is not just to trace the uneven transmission of content across disparate institutional cultures and terrains but also, more fundamentally, to consider the subjects it arrays—the practices and fantasies (the two can never be separated) of political agency it sustains —which can never be simply inferred from interdisciplinary content. The contingent articulation of knowledge project to expert subject is especially marked in Enikö Bollabás's program for an internationalized American studies, even as she seems to offer a normative account that would reconcile regional incongruities:

> Therefore, in East-Central Europe the intellectual had to "do the sixties" in the 1990s, when finally there emerged a demand, say, for both feminist activism and feminist criticism, for gay and lesbian consciousness-raising as well as queer theory, for social activism in general as well as the desire for a finer understanding and critique. Together with all these new activities and ideas often packaged in the United States, there came an unprecedented influx of U.S. products. U.S. business and cultural presence has proved equally difficult to figure out; *this is where American studies is beginning to have a social role: to help identify what is desirable and what is not desirable to import—whether politically, socially, culturally, or conceptually.* In order to be able to do this, American studies must substantiate both the appreciation and the critique of U.S. culture; it must, in other words, balance the "respect mode" [of Cold War American studies] with the "attack mode" [of contemporary New Americanist work]. This balancing act is, I believe, the true meaning of the internationalization of American studies, so memorably and powerfully called for by Jane Desmond and Virginia Dominguez. (565; my emphasis)

The conceptual linchpin of this passage, it seems to me, is not the call to balance with which it concludes (as though one could simply split the difference between apology and critique), but rather the way it situates American studies in Eastern and Central Europe as an expert knowledge that can mediate between cultural nationalism and cosmopolitanism within the public sphere. Certainly, this way of imagining the "social role" of American studies and the cultural authority of the scholar has no analog in the US context (we can scarcely imagine American studies in the United States today operating on a national ethical imperative to distinguish desirable from undesirable cultural forms). But it is also not possible to position this set of investments as backward with respect to US American studies, or as less sophisticated—

or even, I would argue, to locate Central and Eastern European American studies to the right of its leftist US counterpart. After all, Bollobás's version of Central and Eastern European American studies is also seeking to disseminate a (limited) critique of capital flows within a public sphere in which expressly reactionary discourses have tended to predominate. So unless we in the United States care to legislate that nationalist discourses (for example, about what is desirable or not for the nation) are always and everywhere toxic (in other words, unless we choose to impose our own postnationalism as a universal critical norm), then we must concede that left and right travel no better than transnational American studies. It does not require extensive contact with intellectuals from countries in the former Soviet bloc to recognize that Marxism, as the principle of Soviet-era bureaucratic state control and as the critique of capital, is at least as likely to signify right reaction as left opposition (and that, too, all forms of Marxist-derived political economy, including those we might tend to define as much by their distance from classical Marxism as by their indebtedness to it, code as part of a relatively undifferentiated Marxist analytic).

From this vantage point, the task of defining something like the ideological cast of American studies sponsored by the US state and US donors in the former Soviet bloc—as we aspired to do, not so long ago, in our critical retrospectives of the field as a Cold War export—is not only difficult, but also, as I take it, a blind alley. As Federmayer, Bollobás, and others attest, American studies in the former Soviet bloc has served as a point of entry for a range of critical practices, including feminism, multiculturalism, and poststructuralism, if only because fluency in English (as well as familiarity with researching US archives and publications) permits access to these critical orientations.[3] So the originators and initial faculty members of American studies centers and departments after 1990, especially within the state academies, were often literary scholars and historians whose work on things American (within foreign literatures or modern history departments, for example) had brought them into contact with the critical conversations that were reshaping those disciplines in the 1980s United States. No doubt, for those of us trained entirely in the US academy, it is hard to imagine American studies as the way into, say, deconstruction or radical lesbian feminism. But the history of American studies' emergence in the former Soviet bloc and the contemporary investments of Central and Eastern European and Central Asian Americanists both suggest that American studies functions as a conduit and staging ground for a heterogeneous array of critical projects—and that if the transnational turn is not well marked in these regional iterations of American studies, neither are they aligned with an unreconstructed or celebratory Americanism.

Despite the "surprising discontinuities" that confront the Hungarian Americanist, then, and that confront others in the region, American studies in Central and Eastern Europe and Central Asia feels approximately in time with US-based American studies. Perusing course offerings, for instance, I read titles that are not much different from what I would expect to find in core or cross-listed US American studies curricula. A few representative course titles include "Ethnicity, Nation, National Minority: A Comparative Approach" and "Black Modernism, or the New Negro Renaissance" (Eötvös Loránd University); "Interrogating Whiteness: From Identity to Imperialism" and "Gender and Sexuality" (American University of Central Asia; and "Delving into the Heart of the Matrix" and "Political Violence and Terrorism" (Baku State University).[4] Titles are only gestural, to be sure, but they nevertheless index a traffic in organizing motifs and critical preoccupations. My point is that post-Soviet American studies is not simply the old exceptionalism dressed up in more current fashions (for example, referring to diversity in lieu of the melting pot)—at least not to any greater extent than we find contemporary idioms grafted onto abiding exceptionalist frameworks within the American studies curricula of US academic institutions. Rather, post-Soviet American studies curricula appear to sample the issues and methods of their US equivalents and thus to reproduce something of the scattered quality of US American studies, as it ranges across liberal and critical multiculturalisms and their different orientations to such key topoi as identity, freedom, justice, nation, and markets.

The State as Educator

What are the aspirations of the US state and its funding partners for American studies abroad, if it is not (or no longer) bound to the dissemination of an exceptional—at once inimitable and assimilative—Americanism? If indeed the issues and methods of American studies abroad are variably oriented to a range of analytic and political priorities? Ideology is always a restless traveler, to be sure, inasmuch as the same content produces disparate effects in different times and locations. But my point is that the shape of American studies in the region does not resolve into a content from which we might derive its sponsors' agenda for the post-Soviet knowledge consumer (however unevenly that agenda might be realized on the ground). If delivery of an ideological content is not the agenda, then what are the aspirations, to cite Antonio Gramsci's still resonant formulation, of the state as educator?[5]

The role of the state as educator is plain enough in the historical context of the modern nation-state, where the institutions and offices of the state govern in the name of a national people and in conformity to the law that embodies the people's sovereign will. Where the legitimacy of the state is based on the premise of popular sovereignty, the state as educator cultivates a particular kind of modern subject: a "free" subject whose emancipation (as citizen or as individual) requires his voluntary accession to the distribution of power and privilege that the law secures. The "individual is interpellated as a (free) subject," Louis Althusser tells us, "in order that he shall (freely) accept his subjection" (136). Or, in Michael Warner's memorable formulation, the citizen who is both sovereign and subject must enact "consent to his own coercion" (111). Emancipation entails domination cathected as choice—and it is precisely the business of the state to sustain that cathexis through the mediation of a normative nationalism that sutures atomized (self-owning) individuals to the abstract body of the American people.

But does the legitimacy of state power depend any longer on the exercise of popular sovereignty—on the claim to represent a national people? Or, to put the question in a slightly different way, does the viability of the state depend any longer on the appearance of legitimacy? What if freedom is no longer the name of the game, despite the ways in which the idioms of freedom continue to circulate residually, as the fragments of what Medovoi calls "a ruined ideology" (171)? In the remaining sections of this essay, I suggest how post-Soviet American studies, as a joint project of the US state and the nongovernmental actors of civil society, sets us on the trail of precisely such a transformation, in which the state no longer frees the individual but operationalizes her: assesses and selectively cultivates her capacities. At the site of the emergence of new postnational relays between the state and civil society, relays that are keyed in turn to the contemporary organizations of global capital and flexible accumulation, we encounter a different model of citizen—let's call her the neocitizen—who is interpellated as functional, rather than as free, where functionality entails ease of interface with administrative networks on different scales (local, regional, and global); an analytic orientation to social relations as data and a facility in the evaluation of data based on such measures as risk, compliance, outcomes, and capacity; a cosmopolitan orientation to diversity; and (preferably) fluency in the lingua franca of global governance, English. Unlike freedom, functionality is not a putatively generalized condition but indexes a differentially distributed condition of social and political agency. And unlike the free citizen, the neocitizen is interpellated into a set of administrative protocols that are framed as the instrument for the pursuit of broadly heterogeneous political aspirations. In fact, the real heterogeneity of the neocitizens' identifications and convictions are entirely functional for this structure of governance, since they index exactly the social dispositions and formations to be accounted, risk-assessed, and managed by the institutions of the extended state. Neocitizenship is thus enacted not in the form of sovereign consent, but in the acquisition of a professionalized civic competence that entails belief only in the instrumental value of the organizations, institutions, and media to which this competency opens access. The relationship of the neocitizen to the structure of governance in which she participates is expressly and openly opportunistic, in other words, rather than consensual—and by extension there is no option for the performative withdrawal of consent, only for the tactical rejection of functionality as means. If the withdrawal of consent represents the ultimate realization of the sovereign citizen's prerogatives, to reject functionality is simply to resign one's neocitizenship.

So it follows that the pedagogies of neocitizenship would differ in kind from the pedagogies of the modern citizen-subject. Writing in a theoretical rather than a historical frame, Althusser famously suggests that ideology subjects us under the sign of freedom. The voice that hails me affirms the reality of my existence, but it also demands that I inhabit this reality—the one in which I find myself already represented, and which therefore appears to be naturally and rightfully my own. Although Althusser presents ideology (on the model of the unconscious) as eternal, I suggest that this concept of ideology is forged instead in the specific historical contexts of popular sovereignty, disciplinary society, and the modern nation-state. Increasingly, it strikes me that the present moment, marked by more or less radical transformations in each of these historical formations, demands at the very least that we reopen the question of how ideology works on the subject—as well as the question of how its subjects work. Yet it is no easy matter to think outside of or apart from this understanding of ideology as freeing—subjection cathected as self-realization—when it is precisely on this model that our critical practices have been developed.

In reflections on "the end of liberal democracy" Wendy Brown takes up the question of ideology today in terms of its vexed and uncertain relation to neoliberalism (37). Insisting on the increasing vacuity of the liberal democratic tropes that circulate, oddly enough, in tandem with the elaboration of a specifically "neoliberal rationality," Brown suggests that neoliberalism sustains a parasitical relationship to the ideological discourses that its rationality supplants. "The post-9/11 period," she notes, "has brought the ramifications of neoliberal rationality into sharp focus, largely through practices and policies that progressives assail as hypocrisies, lies, or contradictions but that may be better understood as *neoliberal policies and actions taking shape under the legitimating cloth of a liberal democratic discourse increasingly void of substance*" (47; my emphasis). So it appears that "neoliberalism can become dominant as governmentality without being dominant as ideology" (49). Brown's provocative formulation helps explain the limited efficacy of the "ruthless denaturalization" Medovoi recommends (175), insofar as neoliberalism has already denatured (or voided of substance) the ideological idioms it appropriates. And by imagining a power that prevails politically and organizationally but not ideologically, Brown also marks the limits of interpellation in Althusser's terms and the inauguration of quite a different subject of power. In what sense can we speak of a neoliberal subject if neoliberalism is not mediated (or mediated primarily) through its proper ideological figures? How do we apprehend at the level of the subject a practice of power that does not act to reproduce the apparent substance—the "free" assent—of the individual?

In the present iterations of post-Soviet American studies, I find the outlines of a neocitizen who is operationalized or mobilized, but not emancipated and so not required to believe in the institutions, discourses, and practices that subject her. Brown suggests that neoliberalism seeks "legitimation" through the citation of liberal democratic discourse, but at the same time the vacuous nature of these citations transforms the ideological hail into so much ideological noise. From this perspective, the cynical response of the contemporary us electorate on which Brown also remarks indexes not so much the failure of these neoliberal legitimation strategies as the increasing irrelevance of conviction and consent. "Interpellation" (if we choose to retain the term at all) is no longer about cultivating attachment to what is right and natural, but simply about inserting the subject into the relays of power that she or he may choose to revere or revile. To do the work of the extended state, the neocitizen need only be networked, poised to navigate and proliferate the relationships that link foundations (state and corporate donors), civil society (organizations and associations), regulatory agencies (state-based and international ones), and the public sphere (corporate and alternative media).

Consider, for instance, the "civil society" mandate of the Eurasia Foundation, a privately managed nonprofit organization supported by USAID, which is also a major donor to the American University of Central Asia and its American Studies Department:

> Goal: *Increased citizen participation in political and economic decision-making.*
> Central to the Eurasia Foundation's mission is the belief that local communities are best able to determine their own needs and priorities. The Foundation promotes the development of effective mechanisms for citizen participation in political and economic decision-making by engaging and strengthening civil society. In particular, the Foundation has encouraged independent media to act as a voice for their communities and community-based civic organizations to advocate for public policies that further democratic and market reforms.

The Foundation's civil society program has emphasized projects that advance the financial sustainability and create a more nurturing legal and regulatory environment for the civil society sector as a whole (Eurasia Foundation).

One of a trio of mandates (the other two are "private enterprise development" and "public administration and policy"), the "civil society" mandate cites elements or keywords of a familiar discourse of participatory democracy, while reimagining the relations between state and civil society in which the norms and practices of civic "participation" are historically anchored. Here we find ourselves squarely on the terrain of "multilevel relations" among governments, corporations, and NGOs that Kennedy and Lucas describe. Thus a USAID-funded, privately managed nonprofit cultivates civic organizations and independent media that advocate for reforms (political and market freedoms), especially those that enhance the prospects for development and expansion of the "civil society sector." By a curiously circular logic, then, the political activities of organizations in civil society address the state primarily, if not exclusively, for the purpose of securing its own continuing viability ("creat[ing] a more nurturing legal and regulatory environment"). Indeed, in this networked arena of "multilevel" governance, one is hard put to decide what the citizen participates in, since the primary aspiration of the "civil society sector" appears to be to establish and secure its own position as a nodal point (or "level") through which governmental power flows. So, too, the citizen-participants are characterized not by a set of normative political commitments, but by their administrative capacity: "Like their counterparts in the private sector, leaders of civic and media organizations need to develop new skills to operate their organizations effectively. The Eurasia Foundation has supported the development of training programs that provide civil society leaders with the financial management skills they need to operate financially viable and effective institutions" (Eurasia Foundation).

The task of civic leadership, then, is to secure and manage revenue streams, especially by developing "local models of philanthropy and volunteerism" (Eurasia Foundation). For this reason, the Eurasia Foundation sets a "high priority on projects aimed at mobilizing community resources, both financial and human, around community development issues" (Eurasia Foundation). If the language of community-funded community activism evokes the romance of grass-roots politics, however, what drops from view in this iteration of "citizen participation" is a critical orientation to the state. Instead, we find citizens' group "advocating for public policies" in some unspecified domain where public policy is forged (in corporate boardrooms, at international aid agencies, in government at the every level, and in the proliferating private organizations to which governmental functions are outsourced). On the terrain of "multilevel" governance, moreover, the neocitizen is no longer sovereign: her posture is one of "advocacy" vis-à-vis a range of organizations that are under no a priori obligation to recognize her (as their practice of power does not depend on the claim to represent). Within the discursive world of the Eurasia Foundation's mandates, community politics is about creating sustainable organizations of citizen-advocates, situated in the networks through which flow funds, personnel, and the social data that are the stuff of policy debate.

To a certain extent, it would appear that the Soros Foundation's Open Society Institute (OSI)—which also supports a range of educational and civil-society-oriented initiatives in Eastern Europe and Central Asia, including the American University of Central Asia—holds instead to the modern conception of citizenship as the relation of sovereign subjects to the state. "The Open Society Foundations work to build vibrant and tolerant societies whose governments are accountable and open to the participation of all people," we are told, although in what follows, as in George Soros's own writing, "accountability" has less to do with the lawful exercise of state power than with good accounting practices (Open Society Foundations). An accountable government, according to these terms, is one that functions efficiently and cooperatively within the networked terrain of multilevel governance. Such efficiency and cooperation includes complying with laws and treaties and upholding basic citizenship rights (OSI is especially concerned with rights of minority populations).[6] Yet despite the reappearance of these familiar touchstones of liberal democracy, the emphasis at OSI is not on cultivating the practice of popular sovereignty within formerly socialist state bureaucracies, but rather on cultivating civil society as the provider of professionalized advocacy within the wider field of networked governance. To this end, corrupt, autocratic governments must be either pressured or motivated to participate "accountably" in the network of international agencies, NGOs, and foundations through which governmental power operates. Implicit in the OSI mission statement, this understanding of governance and of civil society becomes explicit in Soros's own writings on globalization, "open society," and "social entrepreneurship" (Soros, 69).

Taken as a whole, Soros's prolific writing on these topics might be characterized as a critique of capital from the standpoint of capital. His overarching concern is with strategies for redressing and mitigating the scope and scale of economic and social inequities that destabilize regimes, provoke opposition, and imperil social and economic infrastructures—in other words, his concern is with inequity conceptualized as systemic risk. In this regard, he shares much with Joseph Stiglitz, the former World Bank chief economist who has called for reforming and restructuring the institutions of global governance and development assistance in an attempt to reduce immiseration and the threat of mass insurgencies it brings (Stiglitz 21–22; see also 119). Soros's assessment of root causes, however, differs from Stiglitz's in several ways, including an insistence on "bad government" as the central factor in the production of poverty. "Making the promotion of open society the goal differs from the internationally endorsed goal of poverty reduction in emphasizing the importance of the political arrangements prevailing in individual countries," Soros writes, "but the fact is that poverty and misery are usually associated with bad governments" (59). This analysis underlies his two-part agenda: providing "public goods on a global scale" and "fostering economic, social, and political progress in individual countries" (58). Responsibility for the former is assigned to wealthy nations, acting through international agencies and NGOs. "There is an urgent need for the provision of public goods," Soros observes, "and the rich countries ought to pay for them. Wealth redistribution used to take place on a national scale until globalization rendered progressive taxation counterproductive; now it ought to be practiced on a global scale" (106). "Public goods" in this view include resources for health, education, and environmental protection, as well as some provision for a "social safety net" (64). "Governments" (of the nonwealthy nations) serve as possible although not necessary relays in the delivery of public goods; thus, in cases of persistent corruption, Soros proposes that aid should flow directly to NGOs. Because "governments are not the most efficient economic agents" under the best of circumstances, he contends, "there is something wrong with international assistance if it serves to increase the role that governments play in the economy" (68–69). The transfer of responsibility for the provision of public goods away from "governments" reduces the role of the receiver states, in any case, to providing a kind of legal and administrative infrastructure.

Ultimately, then, we return to the conceptual framework of the Eurasia Foundation's mandates. The "promotion of better governments," Soros sums up, "includes not only an efficient and honest central and local administration and an independent and reliable judiciary but also the rule of law and an appropriate relation between the public and private spheres: a society that is not dominated by the state, a private sector that is not in cahoots with government, and a civil society whose voice is heard" (58). But heard where and by whom, exactly? In this network of governments (rich and poor), international agencies, foundations, and NGOs, there is no longer a privileged constitutive relationship between the state and its citizens. Good government is a service provider that secures, among other things, the conditions for civil society; the quantity and quality of "public goods" are reckoned on a cost-benefit analysis (their costs and benefits to state and private-sector providers); and responsibility for their delivery is dispersed. Included among these "public goods" are the educational institutions that secure the production of the professionalized neocitizen.

"Neoliberal Zombies" and the New Imperialism?

I have been arguing that the foundations of and partnerships between state and private donors sponsoring American studies departments and centers in the new American universities, as well as in the refurbished state academies of countries in the former Soviet bloc and newly independent Soviet republics, have prioritized the social production of the professionalized neocitizen, and that the pedagogies of neocitizenship are relatively content-neutral. American studies in this iteration is hospitable to any number of knowledge projects, which are left to the discretion, so to speak, of local faculty members, academic administrators, and students in particular national and regional contexts. Indeed, American studies in the former Soviet bloc, like the wider regional apparatus of higher education as a "public good" sponsored by a "rich" country (in Soros's terms), could hardly be more sensitive or more receptive to local initiative and variations. The language of the donor foundation mandates is not the exceptionalist discourse of the city on a hill. It does not promote American values even if, from time to time, donors or the academies themselves opportunistically recycle some of that language. They can do so precisely because there is no proper neoliberal ideology that might be vitiated by such borrowings, as Brown suggests. Rather, American studies in the former Soviet bloc is bound up in an apparatus of higher education that cultivates a specific form of civic participation as professionalized advocacy. From the perspective of the interests that operate this apparatus, it matters relatively little what one wishes to advocate for, as long as the advocacy takes place within the relays of multilevel governance that Kennedy and Lucas describe. Students in the region pursuing American studies training or degrees are not asked to produce an identification with America, nor in general do they do so. What the programs offer is a capacity for neocitizenship that functions (or promises to function) tactically in the service of any number of political, social, or entrepreneurial agendas. Thus American studies at the American University of Central Asia specifically cites the placement record of its graduates, who "work at organizations like the U.S. Embassy in the Kyrgyz Republic, UNICEF, Counterpart International, and in other NGOs or private firms in their respective countries" (American University of Central Asia), while the Department of American Studies at Eötvös Loránd University asserts in similarly sweeping terms that "graduates have entered into academia, the civil and diplomatic service, as well as the political and economic spheres" (Eötvös Loránd University).

If American studies and American academies in the former Soviet bloc represent the contemporary neoliberal culture of US imperialism, it is not a cultural politics we can think by analogy to the old, however much the present forms of world making feel like the changing same. In many ways, I would agree with Madina Tlostanova's scathing account of Westernized higher education in the Central Asian republics of the former Soviet Union that situates it in the context of an all too familiar imperial history. "These locales can be attractive only as symbolic signs of geo-strategic dominance (which does not require any capital investment) or a place for the erection of new military bases for the future 'righteous' wars for oil," she writes, "while the local population either is added to the dispensable lives or is indoctrinated by neo-liberal ideologies by means of opening the American universities, distributing of grants, and if need be, organizing the fruit and flower revolutions to replace the ex-Soviet bosses with the neo-liberal zombies" (3). But the ruptures are no less decisive than the continuities. If modern empire and colonization entailed cultural imposition (the civilizing mission) without political incorporation (citizenship rights did not extend to the colonized), the neoliberal variant, it seems to me, entails very nearly the reverse: effective incorporation in networks of transnational, multilevel governance, where the watchwords are efficiency, output, excellence, accountability, compliance, flexibility, capacity—in short, an arsenal of administrative benchmarks that set the conditions of participation but do nothing to compel belief. Neoliberal culture, such as it is, does not operate normatively to produce identifications, but rather takes account and operationalizes identifications (national, regional, ethnic, gendered, sexual, and so forth) that are produced in other arenas and idioms of social and political life. Reading somewhat against Tlostanova's grain, I take the zombie as a possible figuration of the neocitizen, since the zombie, after all, is an animated corpse that acts with relentless purpose and an utter lack of faith or conviction. What other forms—more or less hopeful—the neocitizen may yet assume remains, of course, to be seen.

Notes

1. In the absence of external foundation support, these programs are vulnerable to cost-cutting measures and the kind of curricular streamlining that tends to accompany the implementation of the Bologna process (Éva Federmayer, personal communication).

2. For this "third way" discourse on civil society, see, for example, Edwards, *Civil Society*; Salamon et al., *Global Civil Society*.

3. For this understanding of the history of the field in the former Soviet bloc regions, I am crucially indebted to Olga Bogacheva and Sabina Manfova (personal communications).

4. My information on the American studies curriculum at Eötvös Loránd University is taken from the department's graduate program handbook, edited by Tibor Frank. For details of course offerings of the American Studies Center at Baku State, I thank Sabina Manfova for forwarding the center's newsletter (personal communication, June 9, 2004). The course titles in American studies at the American University of Central Asia were posted online (American University of Central Asia).

5. Gramsci develops this concept in *Selections from the Prison Notebooks* (257–64).

6. The continuation of the quoted statement emphasizes this latter point: "To achieve its mission, OSI seeks to shape public policies that assure greater fairness in political, legal, and economic systems and safeguard fundamental rights. On a local level, OSI implements a range of initiatives to advance justice, education, public health, and independent media. At the same time, OSI builds alliances across borders and continents on issues such as corruption and freedom of information. OSI places a high priority on protecting and improving the lives of people in marginalized communities" (Soros Foundation).

Works Cited

Althusser, Louis. "Ideology and Ideological State Apparatuses (Notes towards an Investigation)." In *Mapping Ideology*, edited by Slavoj Žižek, 100–140. New York: Verso, 1994.

American University of Central Asia. "Department of American Studies." http://www
.auca.ky/en/academics/Degree_Program/american-studies. Accessed November 20, 2008.

Bollobás, Enikö. "Dangerous Liaisons: Politics and Epistemology in Post-Cold War American Studies." *American Quarterly* 54, no. 4 (2002): 563–79.

Brown, Wendy. *Edgework: Critical Essays on Knowledge and Politics*. Princeton, NJ: Princeton University Press, 2005.

Edwards, Michael. *Civil Society*. Cambridge: Polity, 2004.

Eötvös Loránd University, Department of American Studies. http://das.elte.hu/. Accessed February 8, 2015.

Eurasia Foundation. "Programs." http://www.eurasia.org/programns/grantmaking.aspx. Accessed February 21, 2009.

Federmayer, Éva. "American Studies in Hungary." *European Journal of American Studies* 1, no. 1 (2006). http://ejas.revues.org/document451.html. Accessed February 7, 2015.

Frank, Tibor, ed. *PhD Program in American Studies*. Budapest: Eötvös Loránd University, 2002.

Gramsci, Antonio. *Selections from the Prison Notebooks.* Edited and translated by Quinton Hoare and Geoffrey Nowell Smith. New York: International, 1971.

Kennedy, Liam, and Scott Lucas. "Enduring Freedom: Public Diplomacy and U.S. Foreign Policy." *American Quarterly* 57, no. 2 (2005): 309–33.

Kwiek, Marek. "The Emergent European Educational Policies under Scrutiny: The Bologna Process from a Central European Perspective." *European Educational Research Journal* 3, no. 4 (2004): 759–76.

Medovoi, Leerom. "Nation, Globe, Hegemony: Post-Fordist Preconditions of the Transnational Turn in American Studies." *Interventions* 7, no. 2 (2005): 162–79.

Open Society Foundations. "About Us." http://www.opensocietyfoundations.org/about/mission-values. Accessed May 22, 2015.

Salamon, Lester M., et al. *Global Civil Society: Dimensions of the Nonprofit Sector.* Baltimore, MD: Johns Hopkins Center for Civil Society Studies, 1999.

Soros, George. *George Soros on Globalization.* New York: Public Affairs, 2002.

Soros Foundation. "Mission Statement and Values." http://www.soros.org/about/overview. Accessed February 21, 2009.

Stiglitz, Joseph. *Globalization and Its Discontents.* New York: W. W. Norton, 2002.

Tlostanova, Madina. "Why Cut the Feet in Order to Fit the Western Shoes? Non-European Soviet Ex-Colonies and the Modern Colonial Gender System." Unpublished paper.

Warner, Michael. *The Letters of the Republic: Publication and the Eighteenth-Century Public Sphere.* Cambridge, MA: Harvard University Press, 1990.

TRANSNATIONALISM, PLANETARY CONSCIOUSNESS, AND AMERICAN STUDIES

THE 1990S NOT ONLY witnessed dramatic political changes on the global map, culminating in the collapse of the Soviet and East European Communist bloc, but the decade also experienced the emergence and flourishing of critical discourses, from those about globalization to postcolonial theories. American studies has equally been affected by these changes and thoughts. In 1994, with the publication of Carolyn Porter's seminal essay, "What We Know That We Don't Know," the hemispheric dimension of American literature was first brought to the attention of Americanists and the notion of the transnational entered the language of American literary studies. A decade later, at the American Studies Association's annual convention in Atlanta, Shelley Fisher Fishkin delivered her presidential address, "Crossroads of Cultures," which explored the possibility of centering the transnational as the new field imaginary of American studies. As she instantiated the transnational in tropes and concepts such as the borderlands, crossroads, and contact zones, she redefined the notion as historically informed and shaped "multidirectional flows of people, ideas, and goods and the social, political, linguistic, cultural, and economic crossroads generated in the process" (2005, 21–22). Fishkin envisioned transnational American studies as an inclusive and expanding field that investigates issues from diverse perspectives, ranging from critique of US exceptionalism to Chicano border studies, from imagining a Black Atlantic to Chinese exclusion historiography, from representation of the Japanese American internment experience to Native American activism for social and environmental justice, from public memory of the Holocaust to German scholarship in American studies. This remapping of the field not only integrated the Pacific into its object of study but also pointed to a future that promised equal attention to all transnational crossroads of cultures. Fishkin concluded by reaffirming the

United States as "a transnational crossroads of cultures" that would continue to facilitate the transmission of ideas and imagination across national and cultural boundaries.

As the transnational turn took off as a catchphrase for conference themes, writing topics, and teaching interests, its political and cultural implications have come under critical scrutiny. Based on her case study of Robert Greenhow's transnational American historiography, Anna Brickhouse interrogates "the transnational turn" with skepticism and self-reflexivity: "Might the transnational turn in American studies be simply the most recent incarnation of Western academic imperialism? Is the hidden hand of NAFTA behind all our scholarly efforts, nudging us toward every formulation?" (2008, 716). She not only raises questions about the impact of neoliberal capitalism on academic scholarship in the United States but also calls attention to the lack of theoretical underpinnings for the transnational turn in American studies so far. In the same vein, in his introduction to the volume *Re-Framing the Transnational Turn in American Studies*, Donald Pease recapitulates the challenges that transnational American studies has raised in theory and practice and foregrounds a common concern among New Americanists that "transnational American studies scholars dismantled the foundational tenets and premises informing the methodology, periodization, and geographical locations of U.S. American studies" but have not yet "added a coherent order of intelligibility to the field" (2011, 3). To Pease, the transnational turn exposes a field whose discourse, object of analysis, and practitioners have remained "in transit and transaction" (ibid., 6).

Indeed, on what theoretical terrain should we investigate the multidirectional flows of people, ideas, and goods and understand the implications of the crossroads of cultures that such flows have generated? More specifically, in what critical ways should we trace the non-Western and noncapitalist roots underlying the multidirectional flows, which have started and evolved with, and complicated, Anglo-American capitalism? It is in this sense that we should move beyond the globalization of neoliberal capitalism and read the transnational turn in terms of planetarity, which would relate to what the decolonial theorist Walter Mignolo articulates in terms of indigenous epistemology (2000, 23–33) and would serve as an alternative to neoliberal capitalism, which has asserted itself as the teleological end of history. This new sense of planetary consciousness, embedded in indigenous ontologies and epistemologies, will reinscribe non-Western and noncapitalist knowledge systems such as "Pachamama" in the indigenous people of the Andes and Confucianism in East Asia and proliferate new forms of knowledge production and circulation from Third World perspectives and positions.

Planetary Consciousness, Neoliberal Capitalism,
and Indigenous Epistemology

When Mary Louise Pratt first employed the term "planetary consciousness" in her critique of European colonialism and imperialism in the Americas, it had entirely different denotations and connotations (2008, 29). Reading the two important historical events that took place in Europe in 1735, the publication of *The System of Nature* by the Swedish naturalist Carl Linnaeus and the launching of Europe's first major scientific expedition around the globe, Pratt argues that they marked "important dimensions of change in European elites' understanding of themselves and their relations to the rest of the globe" (ibid., 15). On the one hand, as a descriptive apparatus that had sought to classify all the plants and species on the planet, natural history constructed meanings for Europeans on a planetary scale, extracting "specimens not only from their organic or ecological relations with each other, but also from their places in other peoples' economies, histories, social and symbolic systems" (ibid., 31). On the other hand, Europe's technology and experience in navigation and cartography had made circumnavigation of the globe a possibility. Precisely in this sense, taxonomy and global circumnavigation produced Europe's "planetary consciousness," which would embolden the European elites—particularly merchants and industrial capitalists—to appropriate land for colonization, natural resources for exploitation, and non-European markets for expansion. As Pratt further observes, this intellectual awareness and knowledge production coincided with the height of the slave trade, the plantation system, and colonial genocide in North America and South Africa and transformed plantation agriculture into a crucial setting for the Industrial Revolution and mechanization of production in Europe. In conclusion, Pratt observes that Europe's planetary consciousness evolved into the basic element in the construction of modern Eurocentrism and the legitimation of European colonialism and imperialism around the globe.

If Europe's planetary consciousness in the eighteenth century defined the beginning of Western capitalist exploitation, expansion, and colonization, which reached their heyday in the nineteenth century, then neoliberalism in the late twentieth century pointed to the culmination of capitalism, which had dominated the planet in both spatial and temporal terms. In *A Brief History of Neoliberalism*, David Harvey presents the years 1978–80 as "a revolutionary turning-point in the world's social and economic history" (2005, 1), in which deregulation, privatization, and the withdrawal of the state from sectors of social provision became the standard theory and practice of the nation-state, and freedom was articulated in terms of individual entrepreneurial choices and skills within an institutional framework characterized by free markets and free trade. Harvey features three defining moments across the globe during this historical period. First, in 1979, British Prime Minister Margaret Thatcher authorized the use of tactics to constrain trade union power and reverse the inflationary stagnation that Britain had suffered during the preceding decade. Second, in 1980, Ronald Reagan, the newly elected president of the United States, not only endorsed and extended Paul Volcker's drastic monetary measures to control inflation at the Federal Reserve but also developed and implemented harsh policies to control labor power and deregulate industry, agriculture, and resources extraction, as well as to liberate the financial market both domestically and globally. And third, in an entirely different sociopolitical and cultural context on the other side of the Pacific, Chinese Vice Premier Deng Xiaoping, who reemerged at the center of Chinese political power after Mao's purge during the Chinese Cultural Revolution of1966–76, began an unprecedented liberalization of a communist-ruled economy in 1978. After his brutal crackdown on the student demonstration in Tiananmen Square in 1989, he stepped up his efforts to produce a hybrid economy in 1992 and totally ignored students' demands that he address the problems of unfair distribution of wealth and the rampant corruption generated through the dual-track price system in China's reform and open-door policy during the previous decade. According to Harvey, "there has everywhere been an emphatic turn towards neoliberalism in political-economic practices and thinking since the 1970s" (ibid., 2).

Harvey's narrative of neoliberalism is conspicuous in two senses. First, he not only incorporates the recent economic development and performance in China into neoliberal history as its critical constituting part, but he also equates Chinese neo-authoritarianism with Anglo-American neoliberalism, which certainly serves a good purpose. Indeed, following Deng's belief that the state should let a small group of people get rich first and then have them lead the masses onto the path of common wealth, the Chinese elites have indeed accumulated enough wealth for themselves by dismantling the social welfare network and job security system for the masses—but they never committed themselves to sharing the increasing wealth with the masses, which contradicted the promise of the so-called master designer of China's economic reform. Second, Harvey never accounts for the impact of the collapse of the Soviet Union and the East European Communist bloc as the last barrier to the expansion and domination of neoliberal capitalism around the globe, which would finally triumph as the only hegemonic discourse and practice on the planet in the early 1990s. Indeed, with the flowering of academic and popular publications on the collapse of Soviet communism as the victory of neoliberal capitalism in a cause-and-effect relationship—publications including Francis Fukuyama's *The End of History and the Last Man* and Thomas Friedman's *The Lexus and the Olive Tree*—the US-centered global order has been described as the final stage of human history and celebrated in the trope of a "golden straitjacket" that would fit all human conditions and enhance economic prosperity throughout the globe (Friedman 1999, 101). In *Empire*, an academic blockbuster, Michael Hardt and Antonio Negri joined the chorus from the left and read neoliberal capitalism in terms of "Empire"—which, as a new global order, a new logic, and a new structure of rule has reconfigured the globe in spatial totality and temporal linearity: "Empire is the political subject that effectively regulates these global exchanges, the sovereignty power that governs the world" (2000, xi). To Hardt and Negri, our political task as we face the totalizing effect of neoliberal capitalism is "not simply to resist these processes but to reorganize them and redirect them toward new ends" (ibid., xv).

Even though the use of the term "Empire" has been challenged by scholars from different critical traditions, as exemplified by the work of Timothy Brennan and Gopal Balakrishnan,[1] questions have arisen about new means of resistance to globalization and neoliberal capitalism.[2] It is precisely at this critical moment that Gayatri Spivak's reappropriation of the term "planetarity" may supplement Harvey's critique of neoliberalism and suggest a different way of resistance to the globalization of neoliberal capitalism. In *Death of a Discipline*, Spivak revamps comparative literature by moving beyond both the prototypical European paradigm and the postcolonial South Asian model, with the latter revolving around India and the Sartrean Frantz Fanon, and articulates planetarity as a new method of constituting human experiences as well as a political strategy of resistance to neoliberal capitalism. She proposes that the presumed collectivities should "attempt to figure themselves—imagine themselves—as planetary rather than continental, global, or worldly" when they cross borders under the auspices of comparative literature (2003, 72). This sense of planetary consciousness, according to Spivak, operates at three different levels. First, geopolitically speaking, Spivak invokes planetary consciousness as an alternative system to neoliberal capitalism in terms of alterity and transcendental figurations and cultivates the notion as resistance to globalization, which she reduces to the working of electronic capital on the global grid and "the imposition of the same system of exchange everywhere" (ibid.). She thus describes planetarity as a "particular mindset" as well as a "structure of feeling" (in the sense of Raymond Williams): "If we imagine ourselves as planetary subjects rather than global agents, planetary creatures rather than global entities, alterity remains underived from us; it is not our dialectical negation, it contains us as much as it flings us away" (ibid., 73). It is at this point that we may reach beyond neoliberal capitalism and reimagine ourselves in the precapitalist cultures of the planet. Second, at the institutional level, by redefining humanity in terms of a disposition to move toward the other and by instantiating the origin of the other in the figurations of "mother, nation, god, and nature" (ibid.), Spivak not only dismantles the Eurocentric legacy of comparative literature as a discipline but also implements a new planetary legacy, which will be supplemented by area studies and substantiated by the concept of alterity. In this light, she envisions a new robust comparative literature, which would embrace the three old minorities of Africans, Asians, and Hispanics in demographic terms and expand the geopolitical understanding of the Asia Pacific beyond East Asia to incorporate Southeast Asia, Micronesia, Polynesia, New Zealand, Australia, Hawaii, and California—"each with different histories of the movements of power" (ibid., 84–85). Third, by returning to the textual as a cultural critic, Spivak reinscribes the notion of "the uncanny" in the Freudian sense of psychoanalysis, which signifies a certain unpredictability and disruptiveness, and through which she moves the tropes and figurations created for women and related to women's bodies away from the phallocentric signification of the term so that it can sustain a new version of humanity taken from precapitalist and planetary cultures. She further contests the notion of "the uncanny" in the writings of José Martí and W. E. B. Du Bois and investigates the possibility of displacing and reconfiguring their works in planetary terms. She notes that "in our historical moment, we must try persistently to reverse and displace globalization into planetarity—an impossible figure and therefore calling on teleopoiesis rather than istoria" (ibid., 97). Unable to tease out the exact meaning of planetary consciousness, for which she admits she "cannot offer a formulaic access" (ibid., 78) and with which she claims she is writing for "a future reader" (ibid., 93), Spivak finally defines the planet as "a catachresis for inscribing collective responsibility as right" and resorts to "the right of the textual to be so responsible, responsive, answerable" (ibid., 102).

If Spivak's response to what Harvey calls the fundamental contradictions of neoliberal capitalism is to invoke the Freudian uncanny at both the political and textual levels, then Mignolo's strategy is to question the formation of the uncanny in terms of geopolitics of knowledge and to unravel its underlying power structure, which had rendered it as "subjugated knowledge" and "subaltern knowledge" (2000, 337–38). Mignolo begins by interrogating how classification of the planet, particularly the varieties of blood and skin in its human population, in the modern and colonial imaginary could metamorphose differences into values and hierarchies, which he theorizes first as "colonial differences" in the peak period of colonialism of the nineteenth century and then as "imperial differences" at the pinnacle of neoliberalism in the late twentieth century (ibid., 13). What underlies this cultural metamorphosis is the "coloniality of power," (ibid., 17) a critical notion that Mignolo borrows from the Peruvian sociologist and humanist Anibal Quijano and that he locates in European capitalism from the fifteenth to the eighteenth centuries. Mignolo develops Quijano's theory and foregrounds four different ways in which the coloniality of power constitutes itself and exercises its influences. First, while Linnaeus was credited with naming 8,000 plants, as best illustrated in *The System of Nature*, there simultaneously existed another system of classification and reclassification of the human population on the planet, through which the concept of culture had emerged and assumed a crucial role. Second, such classifications were articulated and maintained through an institutional structure that consisted of the state apparatus, the university, and the church, among others. Third, spaces were redefined in accordance with the classifications and as a way to substantiate their goals. Fourth, such classifications generated an epistemological perspective from which the meaning and implication of the new matrix of power were articulated and through which the new production of knowledge was channeled. It was precisely at this critical juncture that Europe's local knowledge and histories were projected onto the global stage and accorded a universal status, which Mignolo theorizes as "global designs" (ibid., 17). He designates this evolving process as encompassing both the tangible and intangible and often using a mechanism of reflexivity and self-reflexivity: "The expansion of Western capitalism implied the expansion of Western epistemology in all its ramifications, from the instrumental reason that went along with capitalism and the industrial revolution, to the theories of the state, to the criticism of both capitalism and the state" (2002a, 59).

When capitalism shifted its center from the Mediterranean to the North Atlantic in the seventeenth and eighteenth centuries, "global designs" marked the organization and restructuring of knowledge in a universal scope, which would privilege the geopolitical space of Western Europe while eliminating the possibility of incorporating into its corpus other knowledge from local histories of China, India, and the Islamic world. Such elimination was rationalized and practiced through what Mignolo calls "a double bind" (ibid., 70), in which non-Western philosophy either was too similar to Western philosophy to make any contribution to knowledge production or was too different from Western philosophy to qualify as philosophy in the Western sense of the word. In differentiating between modernity and the modern world system by linking the former to literature, philosophy, and the history of ideas and by associating the latter with the social sciences,

Mignolo not only foregrounds coloniality and the colonial difference as "loci of enunciation" but also suggests the importance of innovating "the double movement of appropriation and radical criticism from the perspective of the indigenous to the point of revealing the colonial differences in the social sciences" (ibid., 74).

In "Coloniality and Social Classification," Mignolo further compares the complexity of the ancient Greek term *nomos* with that of *chakra* in ancient Quechua. While *nomos* (often translated as "the law of the land") designates a type of experience that would connect human communities with what we call the environment today, *chakra* (a term still used today) refers to a land where people work to live and have a nurturing relationship with other living organisms (2008, 324–31). To the Greeks, Gaia was the goddess of the earth and the mother of time; to the Andeans, Pachamama not only instantiates mother earth and space-time in the same way but also points to the Greek concept of cosmos. The point Mignolo makes is that all human communities had shared this basic common ground and, in that sense, there had been a polycentric planet before 1500. It was in the sixteenth century when "the first nomos of the earth" was destroyed, and later the notion was deployed in three fundamental classificatory maneuvers, as an example of what Carl Schmitt calls "the global linear thinking" (quoted in ibid., 327). These maneuvers reduced all human-land socio-spiritual configurations to the Greek master concept of *nomos* in time and space and consequently reestablished *nomos* as the only rule of the game, which Mignolo critiques as the nature of "the global linear thinking" and reinterprets as "the global racial thinking" (ibid., 329).

Mignolo feels it imperative to return to the indigenous epistemology and ontology that would diversify knowledge production and reconfigure the system of knowledge for all humanity. Deploying the Ecuadorian and Bolivian model of university as his prime examples, he explores Amawtay Wasi,[3] which means interculturality, earning wisdom, and the good way of life among the indigenous population as a noncapitalist alternative to the competitive and technologically oriented model that defines the Western university. In this sense, Mignolo envisions a new sense of planetary consciousness that emphasizes "diversality" rather than universality: "I'm talking about diversality, a project that is an alternative to universality and offers the possibilities of a network of planetary confrontations with globalization in the name of justice, equity, human rights, and epistemic diversality. The geopolitics of knowledge shows us the limits of any abstract universal, even from the left, be it the planetarization of the social sciences or a new planetarization of a European fundamental legacy in the name of democracy and repoliticization" (2002a, 90). Though romantic and idealistic in its reimagining of indigenous epistemology and ontology, Mignolo's theory does offer us a new way to rethink knowledge production, particularly with regard to the multidirectional flows investigated by transnational American studies.

Confucian Humanism as Alternative Epistemology and Knowledge Production System

Mignolo challenges the Western dominance of knowledge production as well as the neoliberal teleology of history by reimagining a noncapitalist, indigenous epistemology and ontology in Latin America. It is important to extend his critical insights to non-Western traditions and knowledge production in East and Southeast Asia, which are supposed to have benefited from the rule of neoliberal capitalism. Proliferation of Confucianism in East and Southeast Asia from the late twentieth century to the present would offer us a case study in the difficulty and complexity of developing an indigenous epistemology in relation to neoliberal capitalism. Not only has Confucianism been represented in different lights and for different purposes in East and Southeast Asia, but it has also been articulated with the "Beijing Consensus" in contrast to the "Washington Consensus" and neoliberal capitalism (Dirlik 2007, 140). If the Chinese state has evolved to practice what Harvey calls "neoliberalism with Chinese characteristics" (2005, 120), why and how has the Chinese state promoted Confucianism? What are the major differences between Chinese and Anglo-American neoliberal capitalisms? These questions are not only crucial to our understanding of changing meanings of cultural traditions in East and Southeast Asia under neoliberal capitalism but also central to our investigation of what underlies the multidirectional flows in transnational American studies.

Confucianism was first promoted by political leaders in Southeast Asia in the 1980s, two to three decades after their independence from European colonial powers. The most conspicuous spokesperson was Lee Kuan Yew, the founding prime minister of Singapore, who had employed Confucianism as an explanation in cultural terms for the successes of what were called the Four Asian Tiger Economies. Even though in the 1960s Lee had blamed Confucianism for economic stagnation and technological backwardness in Asia, in the 1980s—after the four tiger economies had taken off—he embraced Confucianism and urged the elites in the region to reinvent themselves as "modern Asians," "Confucian capitalists," and "successful Asian entrepreneurs" (Shu 2005, 90). Lee's initial purpose may have been to create a cultural identity for the elites in East and Southeast Asia in relation to the middle and upper middle classes in the more advanced capitalist societies in Western Europe, North America, and Japan, but the meaning of Confucianism changed slightly in the process of its circulation in the global media, evolving to serve as a neoconservative response to Western "decadence" (Ong 1999, 74) in terms of personal lifestyle and the social welfare state as well as a gesture to claim the high moral ground for East and Southeast Asian nation-states in the global political structure.[4]

The discourse of Confucianism took a different turn during the first decade of the twenty-first century, when China became a global economic powerhouse. Advocated by two presidents of the Chinese state, Jiang Zemin and Hu Jintao, Confucianism has played different roles inside and outside mainland China. As neoliberal capitalism penetrated China through the combined practice of market extremism, neoconservatism, and neo-authoritarianism, polarization between wealth and poverty, social inequality, environmental degradation, unemployment, and government corruption have become rampant in Chinese society and culture. As Wang Hui points it out in *China's New Order*, "this finally reached the point that neoliberalism was obliged to employ the theory of 'transition' to maintain its myths of free markets and globalization" (2003, 120). By using the euphemistic term "transition," the Chinese ruling elites have not only transformed themselves from party functionaries and state bureaucrats to bureaucratic capitalists and entrepreneurs, but they have also legitimized systemized corruption and social inequality, which the old socialist regime had promised to eliminate—a goal it never accomplished. It was precisely during this prolonged "transition," when social unrest and massive protest became widespread in China, that the country's political leaders decided to resort to the Confucian ideal of harmony. Jiang first emphasized the necessity for the elites to rule by virtue, which he elaborated as restraining oneself from participating in corruption; Hu later discussed the urgency of building a harmonious society, which would practice a form of control over dissidents and manage discontent.

In the global context, the Chinese state has deployed Confucianism as a way to ease the concerns and anxieties of neighboring countries and the Western powers about China's growing economic influence. Two Chinese authors thus rationalize China's rise and determine that it is peaceful: "The nonaggressive nature of China is nurtured by a long tradition of Confucianism, which sees human relations as essentially interconnected and advocates harmony in such relations: harmony between man and nature, harmony among members of society, and harmony among states."[5] Though they never elaborate on how Confucianism can regulate the trajectory of Chinese neoliberal capitalism rather than vice versa, the authors' argument nevertheless demonstrates how the Chinese state attempts to reassure the rest of the world, particularly Southeast Asian nation-states, that its rise would bring more opportunities rather than pose any challenge to the political and economic status quo. The Chinese political strategist Yan Xuetong, dean of the Institute of Modern International Relations at Tsinghua University and editor in chief of the *Chinese Journal of International Politics*, argues in an article in the *New York Times* that the race between China and the United States has become a zero-sum game, and that China can win the race by using morally informed leadership as its new political capital in the global arena. Yan offers two prescriptions for the Chinese neo-authoritarian/neoliberal state to address its mounting problems. Domestically, the Chinese ruling elite should replace its obsession with gross domestic product and economic development with a new commitment to building a harmonious society that would bridge the widening gap between the rich and the poor. Globally, the Chinese state should stop buying political influence from Third World nation-states and instead offer an alternative to the US model in terms of moral leadership. By cultivating what he calls more "high-quality diplomatic and military relationships" than Washington, Yan believes that China can win the race with the United States politically, economically, and technologically without risking any military showdown.[6]

Unable to define moral leadership or relate it to the urgent issues of human rights, environmental justice, and sustainable economic development in the global context, Yan's argument remains a discourse of self-cultivation in the Chinese tradition and fails to capture the imagination of the global audiences as a validation of the Chinese model. Tracing the different trajectories and histories of Western and Eastern capitalisms, Giovanni Arrighi recognizes the subversive power that China's continuing economic expansion has accumulated but highlights three problems that may disrupt its current course, with emphasis on the unsustainability of the Chinese model and the possibility of US intervention. He notes: "But the more unsustainable the Chinese economic expansion will have become socially and ecologically, the easier it will be for the United States to mobilize locally and globally forces capable of slowing it down or bringing it to an end."[7] With growing social inequality and ecological degradation in China, Arrighi concludes that China may not succeed in competing with the United States in terms of global moral leadership.

Precisely because Confucianism has been represented in different ways and used for different purposes in China and Southeast Asia, we have to reinvent it in order to consider a possible alternative epistemology in the transnational context, both in response to global neoliberal capitalism and in relation to the Chinese state. At this point, it is important to introduce what James Clifford calls "articulation theory," (2001, 477) based on Stuart Hall's model. Hall defines an articulation as "the form of connection that can make a unity of two different elements under certain conditions." He notes that "the theory of articulation asks how an ideology discovers its subject rather than how the subject thinks the necessary and inevitable thoughts which belong to it; it enables us to think how an ideology empowers people, enabling them to begin to make some sense or intelligibility of their historical situation, without reducing those forms of intelligibility to their social-economic or class location or social position" (1986a, 53). In extending the theory, Clifford emphasizes that articulation "offers a non-reductive way to think about cultural transformation and the apparent coming and going of 'traditional' forms" (2001, 478). Moreover, he also understands the question of authenticity as secondary in that "the process of social and cultural persistence is political all the way back" (ibid., 479). In this light, advocating Confucianism does not mean a return to an original point but highlights its humanist dimension and discards its tendency to create a social hierarchy and cultural patriarchy.

Indeed, in his description of Confucianism in relation to the Chinese cosmos, Tu Weiming evokes the "uncanny" notion of qi, which is not intelligible in modern Western philosophy, but which has functioned as "a way of conceptualizing the basic structure and function of the cosmos" as well as "a mode of thought that synthesizes spirit and matter as an undifferentiated whole" for the Chinese for centuries (1998b, 107). He argues that qi provides "a metaphorical mode of knowing, an epistemological attempt to address the multidimensional nature of reality by comparison, allusion, and suggestion" (ibid., 108). As a spontaneously self-generating life process, which permits all modalities of existence, in Tu's theorization qi possesses the three basic principles of continuity, wholeness, and dynamism, through which competitiveness, domination, and aggression in the Western sense can be transformed and humanity can be articulated as one body in connection to the universe. Tu thus summarizes his argument: "The great transformation of which nature is the concrete manifestation is the result of concord rather than discord and convergence rather than divergence" (ibid., 110).

Tu's articulation of Confucianism as a new planetary consciousness is significant in many ways. To begin with, Tu does not simply represent Confucianism as a supplement to Western philosophy in terms of community versus individuality, nor does he measure it by using Western philosophy as his frame of reference. Rather, he defines Confucianism in relation to other spiritual resources that include Christianity, Hinduism, Buddhism, Islam, and tribal traditions around the planet. In that sense, his description of Confucianism has not only "deprivileged" and "provincialized" Western discourses as the center of knowledge production around the globe for centuries,[8] but it also exemplifies what Mignolo calls "diversality" in the true sense of the word. Accentuating the "concentric circles" of "self, family, community, society, nation, world, and cosmos," Tu reinvents and recaptures Confucianism as a new planetary consciousness among many others, an approach that would be anthropocosmic rather than anthropocentric (1998a, 17).

Moreover, in Tu's depiction of Confucianism, he emphasizes that Chinese culture does not have a creation myth and employs the "uncanny" notion of *qi* to describe the combination of spirit and matter as "an undifferentiated whole." He further considers *qi* in relation to the system of yin and yang and in light of the five elements of water, fire, wood, metal, and earth, which the Chinese believe are constituents of the universe. In this process, Tu re-imagines Confucian humanism but exorcizes its patriarchal and hierarchical dimensions, which have dominated Chinese culture and society for over two thousand years and which have continued to serve the interests of the current Chinese regime and its ruling elites for the purposes of social stability and political control.

Finally, Tu's description of Confucianism also defines a new politics of representation, which may have implications for Chinese or Asian American everyday practices and cultural representation. In moving beyond global neoliberal capitalism and articulating humanity in unity with the universe, he envisions a new grand harmony that encompasses all modalities of life and all dimensions of existence. It is in this sense that Tu's definition of Confucianism moves beyond the simple *telos* of serving as the Chinese and Chinese American epistemologies and points to the possibility of the emergence of a new planetary consciousness.

Confucianism, Articulation, and Chinese American Epistemology

Though it was not until the late 1960s that Asian American literature emerged as part of what David Palumbo-Liu describes as "the ethnic canon," (1995) the relevance of Confucianism to the Chinese American experience has been crucial throughout Chinese American history and culture. The first effort to articulate Confucianism as an epistemology was in the late nineteenth century, when Chinese American autobiographical writing started to appear in the mainstream media in the United States. In his polemic essay, "Why Am I a Heathen?," published in 1887, against the hostile background of the Chinese Exclusion Act of 1882, Wong Chin Foo explored the possibilities of inventing Confucianism as a Chinese American epistemology and of employing it as a critical lens in his examination of Protestant ethics and the capitalist mode of production. Expressing confusion about the contradictory doctrines and practices of different denominations of Christianity in the United States, Wong challenged the business orientation of the country's institutions, the everyday practices of a technologically centered capitalist culture and society, and the imperialist impulses underlying the Western civilizing missions in China. His argument coincided with the fact that there had been common ground for all human societies before 1500 in what Mignolo calls "the first nomos of the earth."[9] Wong went on to present Chinese culture as based on Confucianism:

> In the course of our national existence, our race has passed, like others, through mythology, superstition, witchcraft, established religion, to philosophical religion. We have been "blest" with at least half a dozen religions more than any other nation. None of them were rational enough to become the abiding faith of an intelligent people; but when we began to reason we succeeded in making society better and its government more protective, and our great Reasoner, Confucius, reduced our various social and religious ideas into book form, and so perpetuated them. (1887, 174)

In response to rampant prejudice, discrimination, and institutional racism in US culture and society in the late nineteenth century, Wong adopted a chauvinistic tone to describe the diverse religious theories and practices in China and identify Confucianism as the secular teaching of rationality and morality. Wong made a serious appeal to the Christian populace of the United States to come to the secular Confucius. Through his critique of social and racial problems in the United States and his challenge to the US civilizing mission and the British imperialist war in China, Wong expressed his concerns about the consequences of unrestricted capitalism coupled with Protestant ethics and sought to establish Confucianism as an epistemology for Chinese Americans living and working in the United States. In addition to advocating Confucianism, Wong started the first Chinese American newspaper in 1883 and helped organize the first Chinese civil rights organization in the United States in 1892.[10] Wong also allegedly challenged Denis Kearney, a leader of the Workingmen's Party of California and a notorious agitator against Chinese immigration, to a debate and a duel.[11]

Against the background of Chinese exclusion, Wong's promotion of Confucianism was significant in many important ways and even started a debate on religion among Chinese in North America.[12] To begin with, despite the semicolonial and semifeudal conditions in China in the late nineteenth century, Wong did not simply buy into what Mignolo theorizes as "the colonial difference" and "the imperial difference" but vigorously reinvented Confucianism as a Chinese American epistemology to fight racism in the United States and Western imperialism in China. Moreover, following the Confucian vision of a grand harmony of humanity, Wong also critiqued the ruthlessness of the capitalist mode of production and offered Confucian humanism as an alternative to Western colonial and imperial expansions around the globe.

The issue of Chinese American epistemology resurfaced at an Asian American literature and creative writing conference held in Hawaii in 1978, at which authors debated the meaning of Chinese America.[13] This debate, I argue, not only called attention to the relevance of the Chinese/Asian tradition to the Chinese/Asian American cultural production but also raised questions about how the Confucian tradition should be represented to and adapted for the general public in the United States. If Frank Chin called Maxine Hong Kingston's work "fake" at the conference[14] and identified with the Euro-American model of masculinity in the anthology *Aiiieeeee*, then he endeavored to reinvent Confucianism as a new epistemology for Chinese or Asian Americans in the sequel to that anthology, *The Big Aiiieeeee*: "In Confucianism, all of us—men and women—are born soldiers. The soldier is the universal individual. No matter what you do for a living—doctor, lawyer, fisherman, thief—you are a fighter. Life is war. The war is to maintain personal integrity in a world that demands betrayal and corruption. All behavior is strategy and tactics" (1991a, 6). Similarly, in his novel, *Donald Duk*, Chin presents Sun Tzu's *The Art of War* in terms of the broader rubric of Confucianism and reclaims some of the neglected history of early Chinese Americans—building the transcontinental railroad in North America in the late nineteenth century—and to ground that history in what he has reinvented as a new Chinese American epistemology.

If Chin's fictional work reinvents a masculine Confucianism for Chinese or Asian America, then Kingston's new work points to a different approach to Confucianism for Chinese and Chinese or Asian Americans. In *The Fifth Book of Peace*, Kingston structures her narrative around the basic Chinese elements of fire, wood, water, and earth and narrates her own journey in search for peace. Beginning with a fire that destroyed her house, her book manuscript on peace, and her family heirlooms, Kingston displays empathy for the victims of war in Iraq and reflects on the possibility of excavating the ancient Chinese books of peace, the destruction of which has been connected to fires throughout Chinese history—from book burning during the reign of the first emperor to the destruction of cultural artifacts in the Cultural Revolution.

During Kingston's journey to search for "Three Lost Books of Peace" in China, she meets many writers and scholars, one of whom is Wang Meng, a prolific writer and former minister of culture. Wang not only understands the nature of Kingston's efforts but also supports her use of poetic license: "You yourself imagined Books of Peace. And since you made them up, you are free to write whatever you like. You write them yourself" (2003, 52). In this light and recognizing the connection between Chinese culture and her artistic work, Kingston redefines her work as an extension and reinvention of a new Chinese American epistemology: "I learned: it is my responsibility to pull the Book of Peace out of nothing. I'd been hoping to get a jump start, but not a quote, line, or word of it did the Chinese have" (ibid., 53). Most importantly, Kingston extends the meaning of peace beyond Chinese America and articulates its importance on a global scale: "it had to be fiction, because Peace has to be supposed, imagined, divined, dreamed. Peace's language, its sounds and rhythms, when read aloud, when read silently, should pacify breath and tongue, make ears and brain be tranquil" (ibid., 61).

Indeed, Kingston defines peace both in relation to community and humanity and in opposition to war and nationalism. She substantiates the notion of peace in everyday life throughout the chapters on water and earth. Kingston has held numerous workshops on writing as a healing process for veterans of the Vietnam War, which bring together US and North Vietnamese veterans and peace activists. She later extended the workshops to veterans of all US wars around the globe. At this point, Kingston does not openly challenge US military interventionism and imperialism explicitly but embraces the Confucian and humanistic view of harmony by helping veterans and bringing together pro- and antiwar activists. Furthermore, she does not confine herself to broadly defined Confucianism but also draws inspiration from Buddhist traditions, particularly the theory and practice of the Vietnamese pacifist and meditation master, Thich Nhat Hanh. To Kingston, the notion of peace has to be reinvented over and over again for different audiences and occasions: "The images of peace are ephemeral. The language of peace is subtle. The reasons for peace, the definition of peace, the very idea of peace have to be invented, and invented again" (2003, 402). She concludes her work with an appeal to people across the planet: "Children, everybody, here's what to do during war: In a time of destruction, create something. A poem. A parade. A friendship. A community. A place that is the commons. A school. A vow. A moral principle. One peaceful moment" (ibid.). From the three allegedly lost Chinese books of peace to her own work of ontology and epistemology, Kingston expresses her own sense of planetary consciousness that is nurtured by US antiwar movements and embedded in Confucian and Buddhist traditions, and that should be accessible to people throughout the planet.

Toward a Planetary American Studies?

In her critical reflection on modernist studies, Susan Stanford Friedman envisions and articulates planetarity as a new methodology that moves beyond the Western expansionist model but is centered on "the far-reaching implications of the linkage of modernism with modernity" (2010, 474).

Developing four strategies of revisioning, recovering, recirculating, and collaging, Friedman not only addresses the problem of Eurocentrism at the theoretical level but also defines the specific ways in which we can implement and practice what Mignolo describes as "diversality." It is precisely in terms of diversality that we should consider a possible paradigm shift in transnational American studies from the traditional transatlantic to the emerging transpacific studies, and from globalization to planetary studies. In East Asia and the Asian Pacific, where the old Cold War has never ended, a new Cold War has already started. While Asian Pacific countries have attracted global attention by their superb economic performance and expansion in recent decades, the Asia Pacific has also become a new site of tensions and conflicts, where forces of neocolonialism and decolonization, neoimperialism and deimperialization, and old and new global powers will continue to compete in the decades to come. This is precisely the point that transnational American studies should engage and intervene.

So what would American studies look like if the transnational rather than the national were at the center of its field imaginary? In reiterating Fishkin's question and returning to our starting point, I suggest that centering the transnational should not only foreground different indigenous and alternative epistemologies that underlie the multidirectional flows but should also initiate a movement toward a planetary American studies beyond the globalization of neoliberal capitalism and transnational studies that privileges what Mignolo calls "the Atlantic commercial circuit" (2002a, 81). A planetary American studies would not only guarantee the continuation of multidirectional flows of people, ideas, and goods between North America and Latin America, between North America and West Europe, and between North America and East Asia but would also underscore the historical roots of those flows in other social, cultural, and economic systems, which would finally raise critical questions about whether the capitalist mode of production and its global expansion are the only way to manage our planet. This offers precisely what Pease calls "a coherent order to intelligibility" (2011, 3) of the field.

Notes

1. See Brennan 2003; Balakrishnan 2003. For other responses to Hardt and Negri, see Passavant and Dean 2004.

2. See Cooppan 2003.

3. Walter Mignolo wrote in an e-mail message to me in 2015: "Amawtay-Amauta was the name of a wise man that Franciscans translated—in their own narrow minds and limitations—as a philosopher. Y qualifies as the wisdom of the anawta and wasi means

house. That is, House where the wisdom of the amauta dwells. Short translation in Spanish is 'Casa de la Sabiduria' and in English 'House of Wisdom.'"

4. See Shu 2005.

5. Wang and Zhao 2006, 121.

6. Yan 2011. His argument here is more domestically than globally oriented. I suspect that the title was edited by the editors at the *New York Times* to achieve a sensational effect.

7. Arrighi 2007, 280.

8. I am borrowing the expressions "deprivileging" from Chen 2010 and "provincializing," from Chakrabarty 2000.

9. Mignolo 2008.

10. See Zhang 1998.

11. Moyers 2003.

12. Yan Phou Lee, a Chinese American who had just been converted to Christianity and graduated from Yale College, wrote an essay in response to Wong titled "Why I Am Not a Heathen" in the *North American Review* in September 1887. In his counterargument, Lee documented his own journey from being a "heathen" to becoming a Christian and downplayed Wong's advocacy of Confucianism as a symptom of what historians today call "sinocentrism" (K. Wong 1998, 20). Basing his subscription to "cosmopolitanism" on the premise that "other nations are superior to her [China] in science and the arts," Lee called for a "real" Christianity as opposed to a "false" one and envisioned Christian humanism as the solution to social injustice and racial inequality in the United States: "I fervently believe that if we could infuse more Christianity into politics and the judiciary, into the municipal government, the legislature and the executive, corruption and abuses would grow beautifully less" (1887, 311).

13. See Newman 1979.

14. In the essay "Come All Ye Asian American Writers of the Real and the Fake" featured in *The Big Aiiieeeee* (a sequel to the 1974 anthology *Aiiieeeee*), Chin not only challenges Kingston's sense of Chinese American identity and community, but he also presents her use of the autobiographical form as a symptom of subjection to Western desire. He argues that autobiography, with its basis in the Western metaphysical tradition and Christian confession, could never capture the sensibility or imagination of Chinese America, which has its sources in Chinese folklore and tradition, and that Kingston misinforms her readers about gender and identity configuration in Chinese American culture: "She takes Fa Mulan, turns her into a champion of Chinese feminism and an inspiration to Chinese American girls to dump the Chinese race and make for white universality" (1991a, 3).

Bibliography

Arrighi, Giovanni. 2007. "States, Markets, and Capitalism, East and West." *Positions* 15 (2): 251–84.

Balakrishnan, Gopal, ed. 2003. *Debating Empire*. New York: Verso.

Brennan, Timothy. 2003. "The Empire's New Clothes." *Critical Inquiry* 29 (2): 337–67.

Brickhouse, Anna. 2008. "Scholarship and the State: Robert Greenhow and Transnational American Studies 1848/2008." *American Literary History* 20 (4): 695–722.

Briggs, Laura, Gladys McCormick, and J. T. Way. 2008. "Transnationalism: A Category of Analysis." *American Quarterly* 60 (3): 625–48.

Chakrabarty, Dipesh. 2000. *Provincializing Europe: Postcolonial Thought and Historical Difference*. Princeton, NJ: Princeton University Press.

Chen, Kuan-Hsing. 2010. *Asia as Method: Toward Deimperialization*. Durham, NC: Duke University Press.

Chin, Frank. 1991a. "Come All Ye Asian American Writers of the Real and the Fake." In *The Big Aiiieeeee! An Anthology of Chinese American and Japanese American Literature*, edited by Jeffery Paul Chan, Frank Chin, Lawson Fusao Inada, and Shawn Wong, 1–92. New York: Penguin.

———. 1991b. *Donald Duk: A Novel*. Minneapolis, MN: Coffee House Press.

Chow, Rey. 2001. "How (the) Inscrutable Chinese Led to Globalized Theory." *PMLA* 116 (1): 69–74.

Chowdhury, Kanishka. 2006. "Interrogating 'Newness': Globalization and Postcolonial Theory in the Age of Endless War." *Cultural Critique* 62:126–61.

Clifford, James. 1986. "On Ethnographic Allegory." In *Writing Culture: The Poetics and Politics of Ethnography*, edited by James Clifford and George E. Marcus, 98–121. Berkeley: University of California Press.

———. 2001. "Indigenous Articulations." *Contemporary Pacific* 13 (2): 468–90.

Cooppan, Vilashini. 2005. "The Ruins of Empire: The National and Global Politics of America's Return to Rome." In *Postcolonial Studies and Beyond*, edited by Ania Loomba et al., 80–100. Durham, NC: Duke University Press.

Desai, Gaurav. 2006. "Capitalism, Sovereignty, and the Dilemmas of Postcoloniality." *boundary 2* 33 (2): 177–201.

Dirlik, Arif. 1998. "The Asia-Pacific Idea: Reality and Representation in the Invention of a Regional Structure." In *What Is in a Rim? Critical Perspectives on the Pacific Region Idea*, edited by Arif Dirlik. 15–36. 2nd ed. Lanham, MD: Rowman and Littlefield.

———. 2007. *Global Modernity: Modernity in the Age of Global Capitalism*. Boulder, CO: Paradigm.

Fishkin, Shelley Fisher. 2005. "Crossroads of Culture: The Transnational Turn in American Studies—Presidential Address to the American Studies Association, November 12, 2004." *American Quarterly* 57 (1): 17–57.

Friedman, Susan Stanford. 2010. "Planetarity: Musing Modernist Studies." *Modernism/Modernity* 17 (3): 471–99.

Friedman, Thomas L. 1999. *The Lexus and the Olive Tree*. New York: Farrar, Straus and Giroux.

Fukuyama, Francis. 1992. *The End of History and the Last Man.* New York: Free Press.

Hall, Stuart. 1986a. "On Postmodernism and Articulation: An Interview with Stuart Hall." *Journal of Communication Inquiry* 10 (2): 45–60.

———. 1986b. "Gramsci's Relevance for the Study of Race and Ethnicity." *Journal of Communication Inquiry* 10 (2): 5–27.

———, Doreen Massey, and Michael Rustin. 2013. "After Neoliberalism: Analysing the Present." *Sounding* 53: 8–22.

Hardt, Michael, and Antonio Negri. 2000. *Empire.* Cambridge, MA: Harvard University Press.

Harvey, David. 2003. *The New Imperialism.* New York: Oxford University Press.

———. 2005. *A Brief History of Neoliberalism.* New York: Oxford University Press.

———. 2006. *Spaces of Global Capitalism.* New York: Verso.

———. 2014. *Seventeen Contradictions and the End of Capitalism.* New York: Oxford University Press.

Johnson, Chalmers. 2004. *The Sorrows of Empire: Militarism, Secrecy, and the End of the Republic.* New York: Henry Holt.

Kingston, Maxine Hong. 2003. *The Fifth Book of Peace.* New York: Vintage.

Krishnaswamy, Revathi. 2008. "Postcolonial and Globalization Studies: Connections, Conflicts, Complicities." *The Postcolonial and the Global,* edited by Revathi Krishnaswamy and John C. Hawley, 2–21. Minneapolis: University of Minnesota Press.

Lee, Yan Phou. "Why I Am Not a Heathen." *North American Review* 145 (September 1887): 306–12.

Lim, Shirley Geok-lin, John Blair Gamber, Stephen Hong Sohn, and Gina Valentino, eds. 2006. *Transnational Asian American Literature: Sites and Transits.* Philadelphia: Temple University Press.

Mignolo, Walter D. 2000. *Local Histories/Global Designs: Coloniality, Subaltern Knowledges, and Border Thinking.* Princeton, NJ: Princeton University Press.

———. 2002a. "The Geopolitics of Knowledge and the Colonial Difference." *South Atlantic Quarterly* 101 (1): 57–96.

———. 2002b. "The Many Facets of Cosmopolis: Border Thinking and Critical Cosmopolitanism." In *Cosmopolitanism,* edited by Carol Brockenridge, Sheldon Pollock, Homi K. Bhabha, and Dipesh Chakrabarty, 157–87. Durham, NC: Duke University Press.

———. 2006. "Citizenship, Knowledge, and the Limits of Humanity." *American Literary History* 18 (2): 312–31.

———. 2008. "Coloniality and Social Classification." *La Dialectique du Dialogue.* http://www.alati.com.br/pdf/2008/LaDialectiqueduDialogue/pdf254.pdf. Accessed May 16, 2015.

———. 2011. *The Darker Side of Western Modernity: Global Futures, Decolonial Options.* Durham, NC: Duke University Press.

Mitchell, W. J. T., and Wang Ning. 2005. "The Ends of Theory: The Beijing Symposium on Critical Inquiry." *Critical Inquiry* 31 (2): 265–70.

Miyoshi, Masao. 1993. "A Borderless World? From Colonialism to Transnationalism and the Decline of the Nation-State." *Critical Inquiry* 19 (4): 726–51.

Moyers, Bill. 2003. *Becoming American: The Chinese Experience*. PBS. March.

Newman, Katherine. 1979. "Hawaiian-American Literature Today: The Cultivation of Mangoes." *MELUS* 26 (2): 46–77.

Ong, Aihwa. 1999. *Flexible Citizenship: The Cultural Logic of Transnationality*. Durham, N.C.: Duke University Press.

——— and Donald M. Nonini, eds. 1997. *Ungrounded Empires: the Cultural Politics of Modern Chinese Transnationalism*. New York: Routledge.

Palumbo-Liu, David. 1995. Introduction to *Ethnic Canon: Histories, Institutions, and Intervention*, edited by David Palumbo-Liu, 1–27. Minneapolis: University of Minnesota Press.

Passavant, Paul A., and Jodi Dean, eds. 2004. *Empire's New Clothes: Reading Hardt and Negri*. New York: Routledge.

Pease, Donald E. 2006. "9/11: When Was 'American Studies after the New Americanists.'" *boundary 2* 33 (3):73–101.

———. 2008. "Immigrant Nation/Nativist State: Remembering against an Archive of Forgetfulness." *boundary 2* 35 (1): 177–95.

———. 2009. "Re-Thinking 'American Studies after U.S. Exceptionalism.'" *American Literary History* 21 (1): 19–27.

———. 2011. "Introduction: Re-Mapping the Transnational Turn." *Re-Framing the Transnational Turn in American Studies*, edited by Winfried Fluck, Donald E. Pease, and John Carlos Rowe, 1–46. Hanover, NH: Dartmouth College Press.

Porter, Carolyn. 1994. "What We Know That We Don't Know: Remapping American Literary Studies." *American Literary History* 6 (3): 467–526.

Pratt, Mary Louise. 2008. *Imperial Eyes: Travel Writing and Transculturation*. 2nd ed. New York, Routledge, 1992.

Shu, Yuan. 2005. "Globalization and 'Asian Values': Teaching and Theorizing Asian American Literature." *College Literature* 32 (1): 86–102.

Spivak, Gayatri Chakravorty. 2003. *Death of a Discipline*. New York: Columbia University Press.

Tucker, Mary Evelyn, and John Berthrong, eds.1998. *Confucianism and Ecology: The Interrelation of Heaven, Earth, and Humans*. Cambridge, MA: Harvard University Center for the Study of World Religions.

Tu Weiming. 1998a. "Beyond the Enlightenment Mentality." In *Confucianism and Ecology: The Interrelation of Heaven, Earth, and Humans*, edited by Mary Evelyn Tucker and John Berthrong, 3–21. Cambridge, MA: Harvard University Center for the Study of World Religions.

———. 1998b. "The Continuity of Being: Chinese Visions of Nature." In *Confucian-*

ism and Ecology: The Interrelation of Heaven, Earth, and Humans, edited by Mary Evelyn Tucker and John Berthrong, 105–21. Cambridge, MA: Harvard University Center for the Study of World Religions.

Venturino, Steven J. 2005. "Inquiring after Theory in China." *boundary 2* 33 (2): 91–113.

Viviano, Frank. 2005. "China's Great Armada." *National Geographic*, July, 28–53.

Wang Hui. 2003. *China's New Order: Society, Politics, and Economy in Transition.* Edited by Theodore Huters. Cambridge, MA: Harvard University Press.

Wang, Shouren and Zhao Wenshu. 2006. "China's Peaceful Rise: A Cultural Analysis." *boundary 2* 33 (2): 117–27.

Wong, Chin Foo. 1887. "Why I Am a Heathen?" *North American Review* 145 (August): 169–79.

Wong, K. Scott. 1998. "Cultural Defenders and Brokers: Chinese Responses to the Anti-Chinese Movement." In *Claiming America: Constructing Chinese American Identities during the Exclusion Era*, edited by K Scott Wong and Sucheng Chan, 3–40. Philadelphia: Temple University Press.

Yan, Xuetong. 2011. "How China Can Defeat America." *New York Times*, November 20.

Yu, Bingyi, and Lu Zhaolu. 2000. "Confucianism and Modernity—Insights from an Interview with Tu Wei-ming." *China Review International* 7 (2): 377–87.

Zhang, Qingsong. 1998. "The Origins of the Chinese Americanization Movement: Wong Chin Foo and the Chinese Equal Rights League." In *Claiming America: Constructing Chinese American Identities during the Exclusion Era*, edited by K. Scott Wong and Sucheng Chan, 41–63. Philadelphia: Temple University Press.

DEEP MAPS, POSTRACIAL IMAGINARIES, DIASPORIZED NETWORKS, AND OTHER TRANSNATIONAL LITERARY ASSEMBLAGES

TRANSNATIONAL MARK TWAIN

"TRAVEL," MARK TWAIN WROTE, "is fatal to prejudice, bigotry, and narrow-mindedness, and many of our people need it sorely on these accounts."[1] Twain, who spent a third of his life living outside the United States, was one of America's first truly cosmopolitan writers, as at home in the world as he was in his own country. His works traveled widely as well: they have been translated into virtually every language in which books are printed. Twain critics, however, have largely confined their gaze to a relatively parochial, easy-to-access body of material: writing on Twain published in English and the original English-language versions of his texts.

When it comes to this focus, the critics are not out of step with their colleagues, even those at the forefront of efforts to make American literary studies more transnational. However, during the past fifteen years, in both monographs and anthologies of primary and secondary materials, scholars have increasingly focused on American literature in languages other than English. Works by Merle Bachman, Nicholas Kanellos, Mark Shell, Werner Sollors, Hana Wirth-Nesher, Xiao-huang Yin, and others have helped make it possible for what I call the transnational turn in American studies to embrace American literature originally written in Spanish, French, Chinese, Yiddish and other languages and have drawn our attention to the ways in which other languages have inflected the timbres and tones of American literature in English.[2] This work has succeeded in making US-based scholars more attentive to voices that were previously beyond their hearing and has helped reduce the damage that an English-only myopia has inflicted on our field since its start.

But this ferment of multilingual recovery and recognition has been limited by self-imposed restrictions rooted in genre and geography, privileging fiction and poetry written within the boundaries of what is now the United States. This essay explores what we can learn by focusing on a different geography and different genres. Its geographical focus is on work published in languages other than English outside of the United States. The genres it considers are translations of American literary texts on the one hand, and critical writing on American literature on the other hand. These geographical and generic choices open up to our scrutiny vast continents of writing that critics of American literature have previously ignored. What kinds of questions does this body of writing challenge us to ask? I will take as my case study writing about and translations of work by Mark Twain.

Writers and critics around the world have been writing about Twain for at least 140 years in languages other than English, but US-based critics have been largely oblivious to this body of work. And although Twain's works began to be translated soon after they first appeared, the topic of translation has received relatively little critical attention from Twain scholars. This essay will probe the ways in which recently translated writing about Twain that was originally published in Chinese, Danish, French, German, Italian, Japanese, Spanish, Russian, or Yiddish can help us understand both Twain's achievement as a writer and his impact on world literature.[3] The essay will also explore what we can learn about how American literature travels when it leaves home by examining some of the decisions, elisions, and misprisions involved in translating Twain into French, German, Japanese, and Spanish. I will then suggest how digital technologies may facilitate new insights into the cultural work that Twain's writings have done around the world. Finally, in addition to looking at how Twain's texts have traveled, I will explore some aspects of the impact that Twain's own travels had on those texts to begin with. My goal is, by example, to open American literary studies to a range of new and fruitful transnational approaches and perspectives, taking Mark Twain as my case study.

If we set out to look for an American author most likely to achieve a world readership, we would be hard-pressed to find a less promising candidate, at the start of his career, than Mark Twain. Twain's first national fame came with a sketch about a storyteller in a Western mining camp and the uptight Easterner whom this storyteller regaled with a tale about an inveterate gambler and all the animals he bet on. That story was the lead piece of Twain's first book, *The Celebrated Jumping Frog of Calaveras County and Other Sketches*.[4] An early French reader, Thérèse Bentzon, wrote that "it was quite difficult for us to understand, in reading the ["Jumping Frog"] story the '*roars of laughter*' that it has brought in 'Australia and India, New York and London,' the title of 'inimitable' that it has been granted by admiring critics in the English press."[5] "What is most impossible to translate," she wrote, "is the original and mordant style, the idiomatic language, a strange and often picturesque mixture of neologism, dialect and what the Americans call *slang*."[6]

If European readers found the idiomatic language and slang of Twain's first book hard to penetrate, the insults he hurled at them in his second book were downright insufferable. The idea that the author of *The Innocents Abroad* would one day be the toast of Europe probably seemed even more preposterous than the idea that the author of "The Jumping Frog" would one day get an honorary degree from Oxford. *The Innocents Abroad*, the record of a trip Twain took to Europe in the company of a group of middle-class, middle-brow fellow Americans, was, in the opinion of the German writer Eduard Engel, "a thoroughly irritating book."[7] It wasn't written for readers like him. It was written for readers back home, designed to help armchair travelers see Europe and the Holy Land as they might have seen it with their own eyes. It was designed to let Twain's fellow Americans see Europe at his side, learning something along the way, but not in a manner that constantly reminded them of how new their own country was and how lacking in all the conventional trappings of civilization. Recall Henry James's lament about all that was absent from American life—no sovereign, no court, no palaces, no castles, no manors, etc. Of course Americans had an inferiority complex about Europe. *The Innocents Abroad* was designed to let Americans feel unself-conscious before the great icons of European culture—to let them learn something about the Old World while keeping their self-respect. Engel was not amused. Writing in 1880, he found the book crude and "unforgiveable," and he opined that "if the muses are in favor of Mark Twain, they will not allow him to cross the Atlantic again."[8]

Twain expected readers in Europe to hate *Innocents Abroad*. The book was garnering largely positive reviews from newspapers across the United States when, in October 1870, Twain read in the *Boston Advertiser* that a solemn, serious critique of the English edition of his book had just appeared in the London *Saturday Review*. Before he even set eyes on that review, Twain could not resist writing a parody of what a humorless, literal-minded review of his book might look like, nor could he resist publishing it in the December issue of *Galaxy* in the "Memoranda" section that he edited—supposedly reprinted from the London journal. Twain's review of his own book began like this: "Lord Macaulay died too soon. We never felt this so deeply as when we finished the last chapter of the above-named extravagant work. Macaulay died too soon—for none but he could mete out complete and comprehensive justice to the insolence, the impertinence, the presumption, the mendacity, and, above all, the majestic ignorance of this author."[9]

Later in the "review" Twain added: "That we have shown this to be a remarkable book, we think no one will deny. That it is a pernicious book to place in the hands of the confiding and uninformed, we think we have also shown. That the book is a deliberate and wicked creation of a diseased mind, is apparent upon every page."[10]

Twain confessed to the hoax in the next issue of *Galaxy*, writing that "the idea of such a literary breakfast by a stolid, ponderous British ogre of the quill was too much for a naturally weak virtue, and I went home and burlesqued it—revelled in it, I may say. I never saw a copy of the real 'Saturday Review' criticism until after my burlesque was written and mailed to the printer."[11]

The real review must have been a bit of a letdown. It contained no exasperated fulminations about "the insolence, the impertinence, the presumption, the mendacity, and . . . the majestic ignorance of this author." Although the English critic did acknowledge that the reader of the review might be persuaded that "Mr. Twain is a very offensive specimen of the vulgarest kind of Yankee," he added: "And yet, to say the truth, we have a kind of liking for him. There is a frankness and originality about his remarks which is pleasanter than the mere repetition of stale raptures."[12]

"The mere repetition of stale raptures," as the English reviewer put it, was de rigueur in travel books of the day, but Twain's book was different. In *The Innocents Abroad* and later works, Twain broke out of the mold with such originality that many Europeans who justly could have been offended were intrigued instead. Bentzon, who found his slang so impossible to translate, found that she couldn't deny the "unquenchable verve" of his prose.[13] A little over a decade later, one of her countrymen, Henry Gauthier-Villars, would be so taken with Twain's refreshing style and the humor that infused it that he would claim Twain as a new model for the kind of writing his fellow Frenchmen should strive to produce.[14] Gauthier-Villars had lost patience with the "precious" and "tangled-up" sentences carefully crafted by the "refined stylists" then in vogue in his country.[15] He strongly preferred the "lively . . . incisive . . . bold irony" so abundant in Twain's work.[16] The first book on Mark Twain published anywhere turns out to be the one Gauthier-Villars published in French in 1884. In *Mark Twain*, Gauthier-Villars wrote: "Hello then, charming writer with no model or imitator! I bid you welcome among us, newcomer with endless verve; the sound of the hurrahs you have raised has already crossed the ocean. We have been waiting for you, for we are tired of the grubby woes that have taken over too many of our countrymen. We have not forgotten that 'Laughter is the best medicine' and we want to learn American humor from you, the cheerful Yankee with the ringing laugh, the inimitable Mark Twain!"[17]

Even Engel, who found Twain's first European travel book "thoroughly irritating," had to admit that Twain's comments on German in his second

European travel book were remarkably sound. Engel wrote that "the best
Mark Twain has ever accomplished is his appendix to [*A Tramp Abroad*]
titled 'The Awful German Language.' Here, ignorance, good humor, and
wit form such a strange mixture that when reading it one really does not
know if one should get angry or laugh. I preferred the latter and advise any
reader of this appendix to do the same. . . . [O]ut of his mouth—as out of
the mouth of children and sucklings—come some truths quite worth taking
to heart."[18]

Engel, the great turn-of-the-century authority on German, credits Twain
with having somehow aptly hit on many "a sad truth" about the language,
such as when he deplores the "parenthesis disease" that allows a "sort of lu-
minous intellectual fog" to substitute for "clearness," or when he considers
the frequently convoluted, interminable quality of German sentences.[19] (In
a later work, Twain will convey his critique of the length German sentences
with admirable economy when he calls German a language in which a man
can "travel all day in one sentence without changing cars."[20]) Engel claimed
in 1880, concerning one point Twain raised, that it was "well-known" that
"a reform . . . is on its way," one that he wagered Mark Twain could witness
if he "visits Germany again in another ten years."[21] But Valerie Bopp, who
translated Engel's comments on Twain for *The Mark Twain Anthology*, notes
that over a century later, that reform has still not come to pass.[22] While in
1880 Engel had called Twain's first travel book "crude and unforgiveable,"
by the time he published his *Geschichte der englischen Literatur von den
Anfängen bis zur Gegenwart. Mit einem Anhang: Die nordamerikanische
Literatur* (History of English Literature from the beginning to the present.
With an Appendix: North American Literature) in 1897, he had changed his
mind: he called Twain's "eye for the ridiculous" in *The Innocents Abroad*
"wonderful."[23]

Other Europeans initially appalled by what Twain had to say about them
also came around eventually. "To think how he mistreated Italians in his
early travel writings!" exclaimed Italian writer Livia Bruni in 1905.[24] She
quotes Twain's description of the Civita Vecchia in *The Innocents Abroad*:

The people here live in alleys two yards wide, which have a smell about them
which is peculiar but not entertaining. . . . These alleys are paved with stone,
and carpeted with deceased cats, and decayed rags, and decomposed vegetable-
tops, and remnants of old boots, all soaked with dish-water, and the people
sit around on stools and enjoy it. . . . They work two or three hours at a time,
but not hard, and then they knock off and catch flies. This does not require
any talent, because they only have to grab—if they do not get the one they
are after, they get another. It is all the same to them. They have no partialities.

Whichever one they get is the one they want. They have other kinds of insects, but it does not make them arrogant. . . . They have more of these kind[s] of things than other communities, but they do not boast.[25]

Writing more than three decades after Twain wrote this, Bruni adds: "Maybe he wasn't all that wrong, given the miserable situation in our country!"[26]

When I accepted an invitation to keynote a symposium on Twain in Lisbon in the fall of 2010, I rather timidly asked Teresa Alves, the colleague who invited me, whether I should avoid mentioning *The Innocents Abroad*, given Twain's offensive comments about the Portuguese Azores in that book. She wrote back: "My Dear, he is completely forgiven, to the point that we are launching a translation of the book with the Symposium!"[27] (This translation by Margarida Vale de Gato, *A Viagem dos Inocentes*, marked the first time that *The Innocents Abroad* was translated into Portuguese.[28] When she read aloud some of the offending passages from her translation at the Lisbon symposium on October 8, 2010, the Portuguese audience's unrestrained, raucous laughter was ample testimony to the accuracy of Alves's view that Twain was, indeed, "completely forgiven.")

Although it sometimes seemed as if Twain managed to find new ways of offending European readers every time he published a book, each book ultimately ended up earning him more admirers than detractors. When *A Connecticut Yankee in King Arthur's Court* came out, for example, the British writer William Stead daringly selected it as the Novel of the Month in the English publication *Review of Reviews*. He wrote that he realized that many would rebuke him for doing so, charging that the book "profaned" English institutions, that it was "not a novel" but rather "a ponderous political pamphlet, and so forth and so forth." Nevertheless, he went on, "to those who endeavour to understand what the mass of men who speak English are thinking . . . this book of Mark Twain's is one of the most significant of our time." Praising the "irreverent audacity of its original conception," Stead noted that "Mark Twain gets 'directlier at the heart' of the masses" than any of the "superfine literary men of culture who pooh-pooh the rough rude vigour of the American humorist."[29]

Charles Darwin kept *The Innocents Abroad* on his bedside table, within easy reach when he wanted to clear his mind and relax at bedtime.[30] Chancellor Otto von Bismarck committed favorite parts of that book to memory to share with his grandchildren. Friedrich Nietzsche offered to send *Tom Sawyer* to some good friends as a gift.[31] Joseph Conrad often thought of *Life on the Mississippi* when he "was in command of a steamer in the Congo and stood straining in the night looking for snags."[32] The Nobel Laureate Kenzaburō Ōe cites *Huckleberry Finn* as the book that spoke so deeply to his condition in war-torn Japan that it inspired him to write his first novel, as discussed below.

Fellow writers have long strained to convey their wonder at how Twain managed to transform the rough, raw material of American life into transcendent art. "Literature is now an occupation for gilders. It urgently needs to be an occupation for miners. The hands hurt more, but you extract, with strong hands, pure metal," José Martí wrote after hearing Twain read from a book about to be published that turned out to be *Huckleberry Finn*.[33] Unlike those effete gilders of the genteel tradition, Martí wrote, Twain had "been in the burning workshops where the country was forged."[34] Maxim Gorky wrote that Twain "has always impressed me as a blacksmith who stands at his anvil with the fire burning and strikes hard and hits the mark every time."[35]

Writers the world over marveled at the art Twain wrought from the speech of ordinary people—speech whose previous appearance in literature had most often been treated with ridicule. Jorge Luis Borges observed that in *Huckleberry Finn* "for the first time an American writer used the language of America without affectation"; the book, Borges believed, "taught the whole American novel to talk."[36] Mark Twain's dazzling experiments with the vernacular helped inspire writers around the world to create art out of the language spoken by their countrymen—writes like Johannes Jensen, the first great modern Danish author. In 1910 Jensen wrote in an editorial in *Politiken*, a newspaper in Denmark, that "*vitality* is the word that almost fully covers Mark Twain's nature. There is something singularly rested and awake about him, he rears, challenges, he is new, and there is a new world around him. His essence is a new beginning."[37] Jensen was proud of having imparted something akin to that vitality to his own country's literature: in his Nobel Prize acceptance speech in 1944, he wrote, "I inspired a change in the Danish literature and press by introducing English and American vigour, which was to replace the then dominant trend of decadent Gallicism."[38] The Nobel Prize committee had applauded the "bold, freshly creative style" that Jensen had developed when it gave him the award; the "American vigour" and vitality Jensen attributed to Twain's prose probably helped shape the ways in which Jensen transformed Danish writing in the twentieth century.[39]

Multifaceted and complex, Twain appealed to diverse readers for a multitude of different reasons. As she shows in a poem she wrote in 1905, the Russian poet Marina Tsvetaeva recalled the ways in which Twain's books about children—*Huck Finn*, *Tom Sawyer*, and *The Prince and the Pauper*—enticed her into intoxicating realms of the imagination (during a childhood in which her family discouraged her own aspirations as a writer, this experience proved especially important).[40] G. K. Chesterton wrote in 1910 that he was attracted to Twain's "splendid explosive little stories," in which "the excitement mounts up perpetually" as "they grow more and more comic"; Chesterton was drawn to the "mad logic" of Twain's "wild wit" and to the "truly mountainous and almost apocalyptic" humor that he found in Twain's work.[41] Jesús Castellanos, a leading Cuban public intellectual a generation younger than Martí, delighted in Twain's "delicious" "way of saying things precisely as they are not," while Theodor Herzl, who met Twain when he was working as a journalist in Paris, found Twain's humor "immense, overpowering, and shattering."[42]

Writers around the world endeavored to place Twain in their own national literary traditions, alongside the titans of world literature who were more familiar to them and their readers. The Yiddish critic Maks Eric, for example, writing in a Yiddish paper in Vilna in 1924, wrote an extended comparison of Twain with Sholem Aleichem;[43] the Spanish novelist Angel Guerra and Martí both compared Twain with Cervantes.[44]

William Dean Howells found it hard to account for Twain's worldwide popularity. Referring to Twain's humor, Howells wrote, "When I think how purely and wholly American it is, I am a little puzzled at its universal acceptance."[45] It is all the more remarkable that Twain won such a fervent international following when we realize that many readers around the world were often encountering his work in translations of very mixed quality. As Gauthier-Villars, the Frenchman who wrote the first book on Twain reminds us, we need to "be aware that the old Italian saying *traduttore, traditore* is especially true when applied to Mark Twain—to translate him is to betray him."[46] Gauthier-Villars cautions that translations may not "capture the joyous temerity of the American prose, or the joyous eccentricity of the expressions Twain creates from whole cloth, nor the sharp edges of the humor to which the original use of slang adds irresistible comedy."[47] This observation resonates with that of the Japanese writer Okakura Kakuzo, who wrote that "translation is always a treason and can at its best be only the reverse side of a brocade—all the threads are there, but not the subtlety of color or design."[48]

Some translations of Twain's work were remarkably apt, as we learn from the great Chinese writer Lu Xun, widely viewed as the father of modern Chinese literature, the first author to write short stories and prose poems in the language everyday Chinese people actually speak, rather than in the traditional literary language. In 1931 Lu's two-year-old son found an old copy of *Eve's Diary* by Mark Twain in a pile of trash left by a Westerner who had just moved out of the house next door in Shanghai. Lu was entranced by both the text and Lester Ralph's striking illustrations. He asked a friend, Li Lan, to translate the book into Chinese, and she did. Lu wrote the preface to the Chinese edition of *Eve's Diary*, which was first published in a small edition later that year, the first book-length publication of Twain's work in Chinese. Lu said that the "translator's faithful, simple and natural rendering" of Twain's language would lead people to almost think that "it wouldn't have been any better if Eve had kept her diary in Chinese."[49]

But the felicitous result of Li's translation of *Eve's Diary* could not have been more different than the experience of one of Twain's early Japanese translators, Hara Hoitsuan. Indeed, as Indra Levy tells us, Hara's efforts to translate Twain constitute an episode of early twentieth-century literary history that has long lived in infamy as a cautionary tale among scholars of translation studies in Japan. Levy's 2011 article, titled "Comedy Can Be Deadly: Or, How Mark Twain Killed Hara Hoitsuan," tells us that in April 1903 *Asahi Shimbun* published a translation of a burlesque by Twain called "The Killing of Julius Caesar 'Localized,'" by Hara, a best-selling translator. Levy writes: "This minor translation of a minor text by a world-famous American author quickly sparked a knock-down, drag-out fight between Hara and another translator, Yamagata Iso'o."[50] Yamagata attacked Hara for having failed to understand both Twain's sense of humor and the moral purpose behind it. Levy observes: "In response to Hara's dismissals of both the humor and the sense of justice he has imputed to Twain, Yamagata makes the following claim: 'by looking at his humorous writings [kokkei bunshō, glossed with the transliteration yūmorasu raichingusu], the person who is truly capable of understanding humor should be able to see that in his jokes he satirizes the dark side of life and lambastes the hypocrisy of people, that there are hot tears within the laughter, and moral indignation within the quips.'"[51] In Yamagata's formulation, Levy notes, "there is nothing particularly admirable in the literary provocation of laughter for its own sake, and he thus dismisses the Japanese tradition of comic fiction as nothing more than pandering to the vulgar tastes of an unenlightened public. What distinguishes the humorous writings of an author like Twain is a deeper critical purpose, one informed by 'hot tears' and 'moral indignation.' He thus brands Hara's understandable failure to 'get' a rather elaborate foreign joke as a mark of his intellectual, cultural, and even spiritual inferiority."[52]

As Levy tells us, Yamagata was incensed by Hara's failure to grasp Twain's subtle sense of humor and decided to deliver a final, devastating slam: an annotated retranslation of the same text, published in book form along with the original text itself and a blow-by-blow account of his altercation with Hara, replete with verbatim citations from both sides. Within a year of the publication of Yamagata's book, Hara was committed to a psychiatric hospital, reportedly as a result of a suicide attempt. He died eight months later.[53] This sensational tale of one translator's demise "has become the stuff of legend in the annals of Meiji literary history."[54] Levy's startling paper limns a complicated answer to the question of how a translator's "descent into madness and death" could be connected to "his failure to convey an essentially foreign sense of what is funny."[55]

Although later Japanese translators of Twain avoided Hara's tragic fate, they nonetheless sometimes produced seriously flawed translations. Tsuyoshi Ishihara describes some of the changes that Kuni Sasaki made when he translated *Tom Sawyer* as a book for Japanese children.

For instance, Sasaki deleted the well-known scene in which Tom and Becky say "I love you" and exchange kisses, after which Tom reveals to Becky's dismay that she is not the first girl to whom he has been engaged. In Sasaki's version there is no engagement, no "I love you," and no kisses. Instead, Tom tries to win Becky's affection by promising that he will invite her to his circus every day when he becomes a clown. "Sasaki's alteration," Ishihara continues, "seems reasonable in light of the conservative tradition in Japanese children's literature and the differences in the custom of courtship between America and Japan. To say 'I love you' is still embarrassing for most Japanese."[56] Despite these changes, Ishihara notes, Sasaki's introduction of "bad boy" figures like Tom and Huck to "contemporary Japanese children's literature," where no equivalent tradition of bad-boy stories existed, "was truly revolutionary." "Most of the boys in Japanese stories," Ishihara tells us, "were loyal, well-tamed children without much vitality." Sasaki's translation of *Tom Sawyer* "opened up Japanese children's literature to fresh perspectives." Sasaki's translation of *Huckleberry Finn*, in contrast, so sentimentalized Huck and made him so respectable that the Huck first encountered by readers of Japanese would be hard for a reader of English to even recognize.

Sasaki's version of Jim is even more removed from Twain's. Sasaki simply omits two of Jim's most important scenes in the novel—the scene where he rebukes Huck for fooling with him after they're separated in the fog, after which Huck forces himself to apologize, and the scene where Jim recalls, with deep shame, the time he beat his little daughter 'Lizbeth for not doing as she was told before he realized that she was deaf. In addition, Sasaki simply omits exchanges that are central to the book's satirical look at racism —such as the famous exchange between Huck and Aunt Sally about the steamboat explosion. (Lest we judge Sasaki too harshly, it is worth pointing out that many readers in the United States in this period also misunderstood the book's satire on racism.)

It is fortunate that a much more accurate Japanese translation of *Huckleberry Finn* by Tameji Nakamura appeared in 1941. It was this inexpensive paperback edition from a prestigious Japanese publisher that Kenzaburō

Ōe read as a young boy in the remote mountain village of Shikoku. His mother managed to barter some rice for a copy of this book, telling her son that his father, who had passed away the year before, had said that it was "the best novel for a child or for an adult." Since Japan was then at war with the United States, his mother warned Ōe that "if your teacher ask you who is the author, you must answer that Mark Twain is the pseudonym of a German writer."[57] After the war, when Ōe read the book again—this time in English—he called it "a work that 'opened the door to the world of literature' for him."[58] Ōe's translator, John Nathan, notes that "it was Huck's moral courage, literally Hell-bent, that ignited his imagination. For Ōe the single most important moment in the book was always Huck's agonized decision not to send Miss Watson a note informing her of Jim's whereabouts and to go instead to Hell. With that fearsome resolution to turn his back on his times, his society, and even his god, Huckleberry Finn became the model for Ōe's existential hero."[59] When I met Ōe in Austin, Texas, in 1996, and asked him whether his first book, *The Prize* (or *The Catch*), was a direct response to Twain's most famous novel, Ōe wrote in my copy of a book by him that I had brought for him to sign, "Yes, I agree with your opinion about Huck, the narrative of my first novel is under the shadow of Huck." The Japanese scholar Shoji Goto "has suggested that since Ōe's works have had a tremendous impact on postmodern Japanese literature," *Huckleberry Finn*, through Ōe, has played an important role in the development of that literature as well.[60]

By far the vast majority of translators of *Huckleberry Finn* fail to meet the challenge of translating the multiple dialects Twain crafted with such painstaking care, noting: "In this book a number of dialects are used, to wit: the Missouri negro dialect; the extremest form of the backwoods Southwestern dialect; the ordinary 'Pike County' dialect; and four modified varieties of this last. The shadings have not been done in a haphazard fashion, or by guesswork; but painstakingly, and with the trustworthy guidance and support of personal familiarity with these several forms of speech."[61] Sometimes, as is the case with a 1944 Spanish translation of the book by G. López Hipkiss, the translator states a reason for this: "Creamos en la mente del lector una impression falsa. El carácter de los personajes sera español y no extranjero" (We create a false impression in the mind of the reader. The characters would become Spanish and not foreign.)[62] More commonly, translators simply omit the dialect without explanation, as Sasaki did when he translated the book into standard Japanese, or as is the case in twelve of the thirteen Spanish-language editions of the novel that Jessica Harris examined.

Occasionally, however, a translator came up with a creative alternative to at least a part of the dialect issue. Although Andrés Mateo's 1967 Spanish translation of *Huckleberry Finn* published in Mexico has Huck speak standard Spanish, Harris demonstrates that he has Jim and several of the other African American characters in the book speak a variant of Spanish that is markedly different from the Spanish that Huck speaks. Harris argues persuasively that "Mateo's translation of Jim's speech is based in reality, on an actual, observable Mexican dialect of Spanish as it is described in an anthropological report by Gonzalo Aguirre Beltrán," who in 1958 studied a community in Oaxaca of "descendants of African slaves brought by the Spanish conquistadores to supplement the slave labor provided by the indigenous peoples of what is now Mexico."[63] In Harris's view, "Jim's dialectal Spanish as written by Andrés Mateo exhibits too many of the features of Spanish dialect described in *Cuijla* for the similarity to be coincidental." Harris believes that Mateo consciously chose "a dialect spoken by africano-mexicanos" for Jim. She writes: "By attempting a dialectal form of Spanish for Jim's speech, Andrés Mateo retains some of Twain's original vernacular energy. By basing Jim's dialect on an actual, spoken dialect, Mateo follows even the spirit of Twain's explanation of his dialects as written according to observation and experience. And by choosing a dialect most likely spoken by the descendants of former African slaves, Mateo's Jim would be recognizable as belonging to a formerly subjugated and persecuted class of people."[64] For Harris, Mateo's translation succeeded where the twelve other Spanish translations she examined failed.

Francisco José Tenreiro made a similarly creative choice when crafting the speech of black characters in his Portuguese translation of *Huckleberry Finn*. Tenreiro, who was born in São Tomé, was a respected African poet (as well as a geographer) who was inspired by the Francophone poet Aimé Césaire as well as by Langston Hughes. Tenreiro is credited with having introduced the concept of negritude to Afro-Portuguese poetry. In his translation of *Huckleberry Finn*, Jim and other black characters speak in a Cape Verde dialect.[65]

Scholars working in French and German are increasingly looking at the ways in which the asymmetrical or symmetrical forms of address that Jim and Huck use for each other in translations of the book have changed over time, reflecting, in part, changes in racial attitudes in the French-speaking, Spanish-speaking, and German-speaking countries in which translations have been published. While early French translations of *Huckleberry Finn* undercut the novel's subversive critiques in various ways, including having Jim use the formal *vous* to address Huck while Huck used the informal *tu* in addressing Jim, Ronald Jenn notes that Susanne Nétillard's 1948 translation for the Communist publishing house, Les Éditions Hier et Aujourd'hui departed from this pattern, having both Jim and Huck use *tu*. Jenn writes that Nétillard made "every effort to render the linguistic subtleties of the novel" and "painstakingly worked at rendering the polyphony of the original."[66] Judith Lavoie has similarly high praise for the superiority of Nétillard's translation to those that preceded it.[67] Raphaele Berthele has conducted analogous research on changes in the representation of Jim's speech in the history of German translations of the novel.[68]

According to statistics only through 1976, Twain's books have been published in fifty-five countries and translated into seventy-two foreign languages. According to Robert Rodney, who gathered these numbers, Twain was enormously popular from early in his career in Germany (with Swiss and Austrian audiences reading German editions of his work). Indeed, by 1976 over six hundred German-language editions of Twain's works had been issued, along with over 500 Spanish-language editions and "well over two hundred editions each in French and Italian, and almost two hundred in Swedish, over one hundred in Dutch for the Netherlands and Belgium, and more than one hundred editions each in Danish and Portuguese, with a large output of the latter in Brazil."[69] In addition to enjoying tremendous audiences in English-speaking countries—Great Britain, Canada, Australia, New Zealand, and South Africa—Twain was particularly popular in Spain, Italy, Russia, Yugoslavia, Japan, France, Hungary, Norway, Sweden, Brazil, and India. He also had sustained popularity during various periods in Mexico, Czechoslovakia, the Netherlands, Belgium, Denmark, Turkey, Romania and Israel. Rodney notes that Twain also reached substantial audiences in at least twenty-three other countries—including Norway, Iceland, Chile, Columbia, Uruguay, and China.[70] After World War II, multiple editions of Twain's work were published in Cuba, Albania, Greece, Iran, Egypt, Pakistan, Indonesia, Malaysia, Taiwan, and Korea; there were more than a hundred Serbo-Croation editions of his work; and by the 1960s at least one edition of his work had been published in Peru, Morocco, Ceylon, Burma, Singapore, the Philippines, and Thailand, with translations appearing in Burmese, Tagalog, Indonesian, Malay and Thai. Rodney notes that in the twentieth century, Twain's major works were translated into Polish, Finnish, Yiddish, Bohemian, Magyar, Bulgarian, Croation, Serbian, Slovak, Slovene, Albanian, Macedonian, Greek, Estonian, Latvian, Lithuanian, and Ukranian, among others. Between 1950 and 1976 there were at least thirty-nine editions of Twain's works published in Turkish and at least twenty-four Hebrew editions, and there were translations into Arabic and Farsi as well. *Tom Sawyer*, *Huckleberry Finn*, and *The Prince and the Pauper* were the most frequently translated works. Rodney notes that "after Indian independence in 1947," *Tom Sawyer* and *Huck Finn* were translated into Assamese, Bengali, Hindi, Malayalam, Marathi, Oriya, and Tamil, as well as other languages.[71] Sixty-three Chinese-language editions of Twain's works were published between 1931 and 1969, and there have been well over seventy-five editions of various works translated into Japanese. Taken collectively, Rodney reports, Twain's novels "were published in more than thirty-four hundred international editions, his stories and sketches in more than nine hundred editions, and his travel works in approximately five hundred editions. It is safe to say that by the mid-twentieth century readers of almost all nationalities and cultures had been exposed to something from Mark Twain."[72] Twain's "literary legacy" "continued to grow," Rodney writes, "and eventually included every nationality with a publishing enterprise large enough to support the translation and publication of his writings."[73] It would be hard to find a writer with the geographic coverage and duration of Mark Twain.

Although Rodney does not mention this point, recent scholarship has demonstrated that foreign translations of Twain's works are occasionally doubly translated, surely a recipe for miscommunication if ever there was one. For example, Jessica Harris notes the translator Carlos Pereyra's 1939 complaint about the propensity of Spanish translators (with a better command of French than English) to translate Twain's works from the French translations available to them, and Margarida Vale de Gato has noted that Portuguese translators similarly translated Twain from French translations rather than from the original English.[74] Similarly, Xilao Li notes that a 1904 Chinese translation of "Cannibalism in the Cars" by the well-known writer and translator Chen Jinghan (under his pen name Leng Xue) turned out to be a retranslation from an unacknowledged Japanese source—in fact, from a translation by none other than the ill-fated Hara Hoitsuan![75] And in a 2010 article written in Japanese and published in the Japanese *Journal of Mark Twain Studies*, Liang Yan, a Chinese student getting her PhD from Kyushu University in Japan, notes that other works by Twain, such as "The Californian's Tale," were also translated not from the original English but from Japanese translations.[76]

Certain works by Twain spoke especially to particular countries at specific moments in time. For example, as Ishihara tells us, "the undemocratic atmosphere of imperial Japan at the turn of the century significantly shaped the Japanese reception of Twain. Japan was not yet ready for Twain's anti-authoritarian stories, such as *Tom Sawyer* and *Huckleberry Finn*. The Prince and the Pauper, on the other hand, seemed acceptable."[77] In a way, Ishihara writes, *The Prince and the Pauper* is "a story about the loyalty of subjects to a sovereign, which was a common theme in Japanese juvenile stories. Moreover, while the story denounces the undemocratic elements of feudalistic society, reform is made from the top to the bottom. As a result, the strict social hierarchy of royal rule remains unchanged, which was quite acceptable to imperial Japan."[78]

The work that spoke to the Cuban revolutionary and national hero José Martí was *A Connecticut Yankee*. A few weeks after the book was published in the United States, Martí, who was living in that country at the time, wrote in *La Nación*, an Argentinian newspaper, that the book was "fueled by indignation" and that reading it made him want to congratulate its author in person.[79] He recognized that Twain was committed as a writer and as a citizen of a democracy to values that Martí shared: both men rejected the claims of aristocracy to deference and legitimacy, both abhorred injustice, both sympathized with the downtrodden and disempowered, and both disdained writing that was pretentious and affected. Martí clearly saw in Twain a kindred spirit. Viewing *A Connecticut Yankee* as much more than a satire of medieval chivalry, Martí recognized it as compelling criticism of contemporary injustice. He wrote that Twain "makes evident—with an anger that sometimes borders on the sublime—the vileness of those who would climb atop their fellow man, feed upon his misery, and drink from his misfortune."[80] Twain "handles his subject with such skill," Martí writes, that we get much more than scenes that are faithful to "that age [of] kings and bishops, villagers and serfs. [Instead] a picture emerges of that which is starting to be seen in the United States today: virtuous men who are scourged by whips, armed by nature, with only solitude and hunger, men who go forth with a pen for a lance and a book for a shield to topple the money castles of the new aristocracy. There are paragraphs in Twain's book that make me want to set off for Hartford to shake his hand."[81]

Martí clearly saw Twain as a writer whose critique of the exploitative aspects of modern society paralleled Martí's own critique in important ways. Martí also admired (and emulated) Twain's rejection of the belabored, ornamental "gilded" literary conventions with Old World pedigrees in favor of a more rough-hewn, natural prose style better suited to the exigencies of the New World.[82] Indeed Martí, who would title his most widely reprinted essay "*Nuestra América*" ("Our America"), referred to the author of *A Connecticut Yankee* with affection as "nuestro Mark Twain" (our Mark Twain).[83] (Castellanos similarly claimed Twain as a kinsman from a continental standpoint, writing in 1910 that there is only "one in all the continent who can call himself truly American. . . . No one else has presented such astonishing discoveries of expression, feeling, ideas, language."[84])

The Twain whom Martí celebrated as an impassioned critic of the lack of social justice in American society was also the Twain praised by writers in China and the Soviet Union for much of the twentieth century. But until the 1990s, this Twain was largely unknown to readers in the United States. Writing in *Scanlan's Monthly* in 1970, the unjustly neglected critic Maxwell Geismar penned the following indictment of the dangerously limited ways in which his fellow Americans had engaged Twain: "During the Cold War era of our culture, mainly in the 1950s although extending back into the '40s and forward far into the '60s, Mark Twain was both revived and castrated. The entire arena of Twain's radical social criticism of the United States— its racism, imperialism, and finance capitalism—has been repressed or conveniently avoided by the so-called Twain scholars precisely because it is so bold, so brilliant, so satirical. And so prophetic."[85] Probably at least in part because Chinese and Soviet writers and critics lauded the Twain who was a radical social critic, American writers and critics felt free to largely ignore that Twain as a construct of Chinese and Soviet propagandists. America's Twain, in the Americans' view, was a writer worth celebrating not for his satire and social criticism, but for his marvelous humor. Clearly the Chinese and Soviets did find Twain's social criticism well-suited to the propagandistic purposes for which they used it. But it is unfortunate that the rivalries of the Cold War encouraged Americans to neglect the valid aspects of Twain's critiques.

Lao She was one the leading Chinese authors of the twentieth century. In 1960, as president of the National Association of Writers, he delivered a speech in Beijing to commemorate the fiftieth anniversary of Twain's death.[86] Twain was one of the few foreign writers whose works were allowed to be translated and published in China after the founding of the People's Republic, as Xilao Li has noted. The anti-imperialist, antiwar aspects of his work were emphasized, and Lao's speech fits this mold.[87] But alongside some of the expected Cold War jargon, one finds some insightful readings of pieces by Twain that were largely unknown in the United States at the time.[88] These pieces—and the ideas they put forward—would not become central to scholarship on Twain in the United States until the 1990s.

In his speech in 1960, Lao wrote that he considered Twain's "reprimand of the imperialist aggressive powers and sympathy for the anti-colonialist Asian and African people" to be "*the part of his literary heritage we should value most.*"[89] But American critics paid little attention to this aspect of Twain until the 1992 publication of Jim Zwick's *Mark Twain's Weapons of Satire*.[90] Zwick's book helped set in motion a process of reevaluation that continues today.[91]

One of the comments Lao made in his 1960 speech noted that the anti-imperialism for which Twain became well known in 1900 dates back at least to 1868: Twain, he notes, "gave strong support to the Chinese people's fierce struggle against imperialist aggression. As early as 1868, in his essay entitled 'Treaty with China,' he berated the shameless invaders for their forceful setting up of concessions."[92] But even to this day relatively few Americans have even heard of "Treaty with China," an article Twain published in the New York *Tribune* in 1868. It is so obscure that its first reprinting since the year of its initial publication was in the spring of 2010, in the second issue of the *Journal of Transnational American Studies*, which also features an analysis of it by Martin Zehr.[93]

Lao was not the only writer to fault American critics at midcentury for their neglect of Twain's anti-imperialism. Writing in *Literaturnaya Gazeta* in 1959, the Soviet critic Yan Bereznitsky charged that Charles Neider, in his 1959 edition of *Mark Twain's Autobiography*, had allowed previously unpublished "inoffensive trifles" such as "Twain's meditations on baldness, on the value of hair-washing," and so on to displace Twain's "indignant notes about the predatory wars which the United States carried on half a century ago" or his critiques of the "knights and henchmen of American expansionism."[94]

Lao had similarly complained that American critics were reducing a bracing, satirical social and political critic to a figure who told trivial humorous anecdotes. "Twain by no means was a mere humorist," he said in 1960. "He was a profound and excellent satirist."[95] Indeed, in the United States the idea that what matters most about Twain is his humor dominated writing on Twain throughout the twentieth century and continues to do so in the twenty-first century.[96] But as Twain himself once said, "humor must not professedly teach and it must not professedly preach, but it must do both if it would live forever."[97] If the extended appraisals of Twain's long arc of anti-imperialist writing by Lao and Bereznitsky had been more familiar to Americans, critics of the late twentieth and early twenty-first centuries might have been less prone to periodize Twain's anti-imperialism as incorrectly as they have. For example, if Americans had been more aware of Twain's 1868 anti-imperialist "Treaty with China" (which Lao lauded in 1960), perhaps Amy Kaplan would have recognized the error of her assertion that Twain was aligned with pro-imperialist forces until the last decade or so of his life, an attitude that, she argued, was central to making him the writer he became.[98]

John Carlos Rowe warns us that "Twain's public statements about his 'change of mind'" about imperialism belie "the continuity of his thinking about imperialism from *Connecticut Yankee* to his overtly anti-imperialist satires of the period 1898–1905."[99] But "Treaty with China" suggests that he began expressing anti-imperialist views twenty years before he published *A Connecticut Yankee*. "The great achievement" of Twain's "critique of European and emerging U.S. imperialisms," should not be trivialized, Rowe warns, adding that few of Twain's peers "were able to understand and even fewer were willing to challenge the emerging imperium of the United States."[100] The Chinese and Soviet critics Lao and Bereznitzky focused on precisely these issues decades before US critics began pay them serious attention.

The proliferation of digitization around the world offers some potentially exciting opportunities for exploring in fresh ways the kinds of issues this essay has raised. Technology that allows us to digitize both translations of and commentaries on Twain from the nineteenth century to the present, combined with technology that allows us to locate these publications at the geographical sites where they were written or published, can make it possible for us to engage in transnational, comparative, and multilingual studies that would have been much more difficult in an earlier era. I coined the acronym DPMPS (or "Deep Maps") to refer to what I call Digital Palimpsest Mapping Projects, a concept I describe in an article in the *Journal of Transnational American Studies*.[101] In nodes on an interactive map, Deep Maps would embed links to archival texts, images, and interpretive materials in different locations and different languages. To construct such maps, scholars would mine digital archives around the world for material to include as links, using the durable URL of the text or image in the digital archive in which it resides, as well as additional relevant source information. Scholars would also scan previously undigitized materials and put them online. Ideally, the materials would be accessible at no cost to as broad an international audience as possible and would be available as pedagogical tools to any teacher or student with access to the Internet. Deep Maps would be palimpsests in that they would allow multiple versions of events, texts, and phenomena to be written over each other—with each version still visible under the layers of the other versions. The gateway into any topic would be a geographical map. Deep Maps would be projects rather than products because they would be open-ended, collaborative works in progress.

I have begun to collaborate with colleagues around the world on a Deep Map called Global Huck that would make it easier to explore in comparative ways many of the kinds of materials discussed in this essay. While existing digitized translations of *Huckleberry Finn* would be the most convenient texts to link to, it might also be possible (under fair use) to digitize portions of previously undigitized translations for inclusion on the Deep Map. If the same key sections of the novel were digitized across an array of different languages and translations from different periods, scholars would be able to pursue comparative studies of them in ways that were previously prohibitively difficult. And links to selective commentaries on these translations would provide scholars with road maps to help them understand the cultural work the translations have done in the countries in which they were published. Colleagues with whom I am collaborating on Global Huck include Selina Lai (Hong Kong University), who is an expert on Chinese translations; Tsuyoshi Ishihara (Waseda University), who is an expert on Japanese translations; Seema Sharma (Mumbai University) and Aparajita Nanda (University of California, Berkeley), who are exploring Hindi and Bengali translations; Paula Harrington (Colby College), who is pursuing a systematic study of French translations; Eleftheria Arapoglu (University of California, Davis), who is exploring Greek translations; Chris Suh (Stanford University), who is examining Korean translations; and Aruni Kashyap (a writer from Guwahati), who is examining an Assamese translation. Global Huck might be one website or a portal to linked websites. The idea would be to bring together in one place as many digitized translations of the book as possible—either housed on the site or available through links to the institutions that digitized the text, using maps as a gateway—as well as links to both critical commentary on the book in a range of languages and covers and illustrations with metadata about them. Ideally, it would be possible to take a specific passage in the book—such as Pap's "Call this a guvment" speech—and make it easy for users to look at multiple translations within one language and across many languages, as well as critical discussions of those translations. The Omeka platform, developed at the Roy Rosenzweig Center for History and New Media at George Mason University, is one promising platform for Global Huck. It was developed for archivists and has a template for inputting all of the relevant metadata; it is also fairly simple to use. It has the advantage of allowing multiple scholars in different locations to upload texts in different languages, which can then be organized into exhibits based on a particular time period or geographical region. In addition, Omeka has developed an interface with the Neatline platform built by the University of Virginia, which may make it increasingly easy to show the geographical location of archival materials on maps. Omeka may well become the technology of choice for Deep Maps. But other platforms may be useful, as well.

There is a growing interest in translation studies, suggesting that now is the right time to launch a project like Global Huck. Princeton University has recently instituted a major in translation and intercultural communication; the University of Michigan, Kent State University, and the University of California, Santa Barbara, offer PhDs in translation studies; and Stanford recently established a translation studies minor.

While, for a range of reasons, Global Huck might be the best place to start when it comes to Deep Maps involving Mark Twain, it is certainly not the place to stop. There would be clear advantages to having scholars collaborate on a Global Twain project that would bring together a range of translations and critical studies. As I noted above, many Spanish and Portuguese translations were made from earlier French translations rather than English originals, and a number of Chinese translations were made from Japanese translations. Making the different generations of translations available in one place might yield interesting insights into what happens when translators play the multilingual equivalent of the game of telephone. The growth over the past few years in a range of crowd-sourced translation ventures suggests that engaging scores of people around the globe in analyzing the choices that translators made in various editions of *Huck Finn* might not be the chimera it may appear to be, as Dana Oshiro's overview in 2009 makes clear.[102] Enterprises like the ones Oshiro discusses could serve as models for Twain scholars around the globe when it comes to identifying and translating the most important criticism on *Huck Finn* that has been published in languages other than English. It could also suggest some ways of crowd-sourcing the annotation of the potentially hundreds or even thousands of translations that could eventually be digitized and made available to a global audience. Throughout his career, Twain was intrigued—as well as horrified—by the fate of his texts in translation, as is clear from his piece in *Sketches New and Old* titled "The 'Jumping Frog.' In English. Then in French. Then Clawed Back into a Civilized Language Once More By Patient, Unremunerated Toil."[103] And Twain, a celebrated early adopter, was famously captivated by technology. Global Huck and Global Twain Deep Maps would honor Twain's fascination with languages and technology as they would encourage scholars around the world to pioneer in melding technology, translation, and comparative cultural studies in fresh and engaging ways.[104]

Mark Twain traveled throughout the world more than any other American writer of his era. His travels helped give him global perspectives on such issues such as racism, imperialism, and anti-Semitism.[105] It was often when he was abroad that he gained the clearest understanding of his own country. For example, when he was in Bombay in 1896, the sight of a German abusing a native servant triggered memories of similar scenes involving the abuse of slaves that he had witnessed during his childhood in the South.[106] He had not described those scenes from his childhood in print before. It was only when he was about as far away from Hannibal, Missouri, as he could be that he was able to write about the brutality he had witnessed there half a century before.[107]

The time Twain spent outside the United States was key to the enlargement of his moral awareness. The anti-Semitism he observed in the Reichsrath of the Austro-Hungarian empire and the Dreyfus affair resonated with the racism that fueled lynchings in the United States, and with the racist assumptions that underlay Western powers' imperialism in Asia and Africa.[108] Prejudice, racism, the exercise of unjust authority—these qualities crossed borders, and as Twain had the chance to see them in a range of contexts, his insights into the dynamics of these phenomena were sharpened profoundly.

Twain viewed travel as the best antidote to "prejudice, bigotry and narrow-mindedness," believing that "broad, wholesome, charitable views of men and things can not be acquired by vegetating in one little corner of the earth all one's lifetime."[109] As Richard Bridgman has noted, travel "had powerful attractions for a skeptical intelligence like Twain's. Its formal displacements generated the very situations that produce humor: values clashed, perspectives underwent abrupt shifts, and around the next corner, surprise."[110] Twain's traveling had a profound impact on the development of his understanding of world affairs, on his sensibilities as a writer, and on his compassion toward his fellow human beings. One of his most important stories, "The War-Prayer," which was not published until after his death, is rooted, as the critic Hua Hsu tells us, "in the lessons one learns looking beyond borders, studying the dynamics of international power and politics and noting the hypocrisy of spreading ideas like freedom, liberty and salvation by force."[111] Hsu goes on to suggest that "it isn't merely the creation of a great humorist or social critic; it is the creation of one of American culture's great travelers. Roughing it on the road, Twain achieved insights into the human condition and the tenuousness of national affiliations that were unavailable to his more provincial peers." Hsu believes that "the success of 'The War-Prayer' as a cogent and prescient piece of criticism calls for a reappraisal of Twain as a trans-Pacific traveler, an American with a consciously *global* viewpoint."[112]

Twain's travels allowed him to make connections and recognize patterns that others did not. They allowed him to witness myriad forms of prejudice, hatred, and injustice promulgated by so-called civilized nations. ("There are many humorous things in the world," he wrote in *Following the Equator*. "Among them is the white man's notion that he is less savage than the other savages."[113]) And they allowed him to question the idea of American exceptionalism with the characteristic confidence and wit he deployed to challenge so many other pieties: "I think that there is but a single specialty with us, only one thing that can be called by the wide name 'American.' That is the national devotion to ice-water."[114]

Mark Twain's works have traveled more widely than those of any other American author, and travel was central to the development of his thinking and of his art, a key factor in shaping his rejection of American exceptionalism and his embrace of a border-crossing compassion and openness to cultures beyond his own. For these reasons and others, it is appropriate to allow Twain's writings to inspire some of our boldest efforts to forge new border-crossing, transnational habits of scholarship.

Notes

Portions of this essay reprise some of the points I made in "American Literature in Transnational Perspective: The Case of Mark Twain," in *Companion to American Literary Studies*, edited by Robert Levine and Caroline Levander (Oxford: Wiley-Blackwell, 2011), 279–93; and in *Writing America: Literary Landmarks from Walden Pond to Wounded Knee—A Reader's Companion* (New Brunswick, NJ: Rutgers University Press, 2015), introduction.

1. Mark Twain, *The Innocents Abroad* (1869; paperback repr. ed., ed. Shelley Fisher Fishkin, New York: Oxford University Press, 2009), 650.

2. See Merle Bachman, *Recovering "Yiddishland": Threshold Moments in American Literature* (Syracuse, NY: Syracuse University Press, 2007); Nicolas Kanellos, *Herencia: The Anthology of Hispanic Literature of the United States* (New York: Oxford University Press, 2003); Marc Shell and Werner Sollors, eds., *The Multilingual Anthology of American Literature: A Reader of Original Texts with English Translations* (New York: New York University Press, 2000); Werner Sollors, ed., *Multilingual America: Transnationalism, Ethnicity, and the Languages of American Literature* (New York: New York University Press, 1998); Hana Wirth-Nesher, *Call It English: The Languages of Jewish American Literature* (Princeton, NJ: Princeton University Press, 2008); Xiao-huang Yin, *Chinese American Literature since the 1850s* (Carbondale: University of Illinois Press, 2000).

3. The recently translated pieces cited in this essay are all translations that I commissioned as editor of *The Mark Twain Anthology: Great Writers on His Life and Works* (New York: Library of America, 2010).

4. Mark Twain, *The Celebrated Jumping Frog of Calaveras County and Other Sketches* (1867; paperback repr. ed., ed. Shelley Fisher Fishkin, New York: Oxford University Press, 2009).

5. Thérèse Bentzon, excerpt from "Les Humoristes Américains: Mark Twain," *Revue des Deux Mondes*, July 15, 1872, 313–15; translated by Greg Robinson as "From 'The American Humorists: Mark Twain,'" in *The Mark Twain Anthology*, ed. Fishkin, 25. "Roars of laughter" appears in English in the original.

6. Ibid., 28. "Slang" appears in English in the original.

7. Eduard Engel, "Mark Twain: Ein Amerikanischer 'Humorist,'" *Magazin für die Literatur des Auslandes*, 98 (1880): 575–79; translated by Valerie Bopp as "From 'Mark Twain: An American Humorist,'" in *The Mark Twain Anthology*, ed. Fishkin, 33.

8. Ibid., 31.

9. Mark Twain, "Memoranda: An Entertaining Article," *Galaxy* 10 (December 1870): 876–85 in *The Mark Twain Anthology*, ed. Fishkin, 19.

10. Ibid., 22.

11. Mark Twain, "Memoranda: A Sad, Sad Business," *Galaxy* 11 (January 187) 158–59; in *The Mark Twain Anthology*, ed. Fishkin, 17.

12. "*The Innocents Abroad* by Mark Twain," *Saturday Review* (London), October 8, 1870, 467–68, in *Mark Twain: The Contemporary Reviews*, ed. Louis J. Budd (Cambridge: Cambridge University Press, 1999), 83, 86.

13. Bentzon, "The American Humorists," 26.

14. Henry Gauthier-Villars, *Mark Twain* (Paris: Gauthier-Villars, 1884).

15. Henry Gauthier-Villars quotation from his *Mark Twain*, translated by Shelley Fisher Fishkin in *The Mark Twain Anthology*, ed. Fishkin, 56.

16. Henry Gauthier-Villlars, *Mark Twain*, translated by Greg Robinson, in *The Mark Twain Anthology*, ed. Fishkin, 58.

17. Ibid.

18. Eduard Engel, excerpt from "Mark Twain: Ein Amerikanischer 'Humorist'" in *Magazin für die Literatur des Auslandes 98* (1880): 575–79; translated by Valerie Bopp as "Mark Twain: An American 'Humorist,'" in *The Mark Twain Anthology*, ed. Fishkin, 37.

19. Ibid, 38. Engel is quoting from Mark Twain, "The Awful German Language," Appendix D, *A Tramp Abroad* (Hartford, CT: American, 1880).

20. Mark Twain, *Christian Science* (1907), the Oxford Mark Twain, ed. Shelley Fisher Fishkin (New York: Oxford University Press, 1996), 4.

21. Engel, 38.

22. Valerie Bopp, personal communication, March 6, 2009.

23. Engel, "Mark Twain," excerpt from *Geschichte der englischen Litteratur von den Anfangen bis zur Gegenwart. Mit einem Anhang: Die nordamerikanische Litterattur* (History of English Literature from the beginning to the present. With an Appendix: North American Literature); translated by Valerie Bopp, in *The Mark Twain Anthology*, ed. Fishkin, 40.

24. Livia Bruni, "L'Umorismo Americano: Mark Twain," *Nuova Antologia di Lettere, Scienze ed Arti*, 4th series, January–February 1905, 696–709; translated by Patricia Thompson Rizzo as "American Humor: Mark Twain," in *The Mark Twain Anthology*, ed. Fishkin, 112.

25. Quoted in ibid., 110.

26. Ibid., 112.

27. Teresa Alves, personal communication, March 7, 2010.

28. Mark Twain, *A Viagem dos Inocentes. Ou a Nova Rota Dos Peregrinos*, translation of *The Innocents Abroad* by Margarida Vale de Gato (Lisbon: Ediçōtildees tinta-da-china, 2010).

29. William T. Stead, "Mark Twain's New Book: A Satirical Attack on English Institutions," *Review of Reviews* (London), 1 (February 1890): 144–56; in *Mark Twain: The Contemporary Reviews*, ed. Budd, 307–8.

30. Sir Harry Britain relates Darwin's comments on this subject (comments relayed

to him and William Dean Howells by a friend of theirs and Darwin in "My Friend Mark Twain," *Mark Twain Journal* 11, no. 3 (1961): 2.

31. Friedrich Nietzsche, letter to Franz Overbeck, November 14, 1879, in *Penguin Portable Nietzsche*, ed. and trans. by Walter Kaufmann (New York: Penguin, 1954), 73.

32. Quoted in "Conrad Pays Tribute to Mark Twain," *Mentor* 12 (May 1924): 45.

33. José Martí, "Escenas Norteamericanas," *La Nación* (Buenos Aires), January 11, 1885; translated by Edward M. Test as "From 'North American Scenes,'" in *The Mark Twain Anthology*, ed. Fishkin, 49–50.

34. Ibid., 50.

35. Quoted in "Gorky and Twain Plead for Revolution Committee Formed to Raise Funds for Russian Freedom to Arm Revolutionists," *New York Times*, April 12, 1906.

36. Jorge Luis Borges, in collaboration with Esther Zemborain de Torres, *An Introduction to American Literature*, trans. and ed. L. Clark Keating and Robert O. Evans (Lexington: University Press of Kentucky, 1967), 37. Borges is agreeing with the statement by John Mason Brown: "*Huckleberry Finn* taught the whole American novel to talk."

37. Johannes V. Jensen, "Mark Twain," *Politiken* (Copenhagen), April 23, 1910); translated by Jan Nordby Gretlund, in *The Mark Twain Anthology*, ed. Fishkin, 119.

38. Nobelprize.org, "The Nobel Prize in Literature 1944: Johannes V. Jensen," http:// nobelprize.org/nobel_prizes/literature/laureates/1944/jensen-autobio.html, accessed February 9, 2015.

39. Nobelprize.org, "Johannes V. Jensen—Facts," http://www.nobelprize.org/nobel _prizes/literature/laureates/1944/jensen-facts.html, accessed March 14, 2015.

40. Marina Tsvetaeva, *Knigi v krasnom pereplëte* (Books bound in red), in *Vechernii al'bom* (Evening Album) (Moscow: Stixi, 1910); translated by Yuri Tretyakov as "Books Bound in Red," in *The Mark Twain Anthology*, ed. Fishkin, 115–16.

41. G. K. Chesterton, "Mark Twain," *T. P.'s Weekly* (London), April 19, 1910, 535– 36; in *The Mark Twain Anthology*, ed. Fishkin, 129.

42. Jesús Castellanos, "Mark Twain," in *Los Optimistas* (Madrid: Editorial América, 1910), 115–20; translated by Edward M. Test, in *The Mark Twain Anthology*, ed. Fishkin, 133–36; Theodor Herzl, excerpt from *Feuilletons* [1903], translated by Alexander Behr as "Mark Twain in Paris" and reprinted in *Mark Twain Quarterly* (winter 1951), 16–20, in *The Mark Twain Anthology*, ed. Fishkin, 83.

43. Maks Erik, excerpt from *Tog* (Vilna), May 23 and 30, 1924; translated by Zachary M. Baker as "From 'Sholem Aleichem and Mark Twain: Notes on the Eighth Anniversary of Sholem Aleichem's Death,'" in *The Mark Twain Anthology*, ed. Fishkin, 151–57.

44. Angel Guerra, excerpt from *Prólogo: Mark Twain, Cuentos Escogidos* (Madrid: Libreria Moderna, 1903); translated by Edward M. Test as "From 'Prologue to Mark Twain: Selected Tales,'" in *The Mark Twain Anthology*, ed. Fishkin, 105; José Martí, "Escenas Norteamericanas," *La Nación* (Buenos Aires), February 20, 1890, reprinted in *Obras Completas de Martí* (Havana: Editorial Trópico, 1941), 38:186; translated by

Rubén Builes and Cintia Santana as "From *North American Scenes*," in *The Mark Twain Anthology*, ed. Fishkin, 53.

45. William Dean Howells, *My Mark Twain: Reminiscences and Criticisms* (New York: Harper and Brothers, 1910), 140.

46. Gauthier-Villars, "Mark Twain," 59.

47. Ibid.

48. Quoted in Ulrich Steindorff, "Mark Twain's Broad German Grin—New Translations Have Helped to Restore a Lost Sense of Humor," *New York Times*, July 13, 1924.

49. Lu Xun, excerpt from *Xiawariji "Xiaoyin"* (A short introduction to "Eve's Diary") (Shanghai, 1931); translated by Gongzhao Li as "Preface to Mark Twain, 'Eve's Diary,'" in *The Mark Twain Anthology*, ed. Fishkin, 174.

50. Announcement of a paper by Indra Levy presented on April 14, 2010, at the Stanford University (Center for East Asian Studies, http://ceas.stanford.edu/events/event _detail.php?id=1351, accessed March 14, 2015). The paper was revised and published as "Comedy Can Be Deadly: Or, How Mark Twain Killed Hara Hoitsuan," *Journal of Japanese Studies* 37, no. 2 (2011): 328–40.

51. Levy, "Comedy Can Be Deadly," 340. The bracketed material is from Levy.

52. Ibid., 341.

53. Ibid., 329.

54. Announcement, http://ceas.stanford.edu/events/event_detail.php?id=1351.

55. Levy, "Comedy Can Be Deadly," 328.

56. Tsuyoshi Ishihara, *Mark Twain in Japan: The Cultural Reception of an American Icon* (Columbia: University of Missouri Press, 2005), 16.

57. Quoted in ibid., 59.

58. Ibid.

59. John Nathan, introduction to *Teach Us to Outgrow Our Madness: Four Short Novels by Kenzaburō Ōe*, trans. John Nathan (New York: Grove, 1977), xii.

60. Ishihara, *Mark Twain in Japan*, 59.

61. Mark Twain, *Adventures of Huckleberry Finn* (1885), the Oxford Mark Twain, ed. Shelley Fisher Fishkin (New York: Oxford University Press, 1996), 7.

62. Quoted in Jessica M. Harris, "When the Right Word Is Not Enough: Spanish-Language Translations of Huck Finn," honors thesis, University of Texas at Austin, 2001, 9. The English translation is Harris's.

63. Ibid., 47–48. See Gonzalo Aguirre Beltrán, *Cuijla, Esbozo etnográfico de un pueblo negro* (Mexico City: Fondo de Cultura Económica, 1958), 9–11. Harris goes on to describe in detail the linguistic characteristics that Beltrán observed among the Cuijleños, and their relationship to the ways in which Mateo translates Jim's speech in the novel.

64. Harris, "When the Right Word Is Not Enough," 51.

65. Mark Twain, *As Aventuras de Huckleberry Finn*, trans. Francisco José Tenreiro, 2nd ed. (Lisbon: Inquérito, 973). I am grateful to Isabel Caldeira for bringing this translation to my attention, and to Isabel Oliveira Martins for having shown it to me in the

exhibit she produced with Maria De Deus Duarte at the Biblioteca Nacional de Portugal on October 9, 2010. See the exhibit catalogue, Isabel Oliveira Martins and Maria de Deus Alves Duarte, *Mark Twain em Portugal* (Lisbon: Biblioteca Nacional de Portugal, 2010).

66. Ronald Jenn, "From American Frontier to European Borders: Publishing French Translations of Mark Twain's Novels *Tom Sawyer* and *Huckleberry Finn* (1884–1963)," *Book History* 9 (2006): 235–60.

67. Judith Lavoie, "La Parole Noire en Traduction Française: Le Cas de *Huckleberry Finn*," Ph.D. diss., McGill University, 1998. See also the book into which the dissertation was revised, Judith Lavoie, *Mark Twain et La Parole Noir* (Montreal: Les Presses de l'Université de Montreal, 2002).

68. Raphaele Berthele, "Translating African-American Vernacular English into German: The Problem of 'Jim' in Mark Twain's *Huckleberry Finn*," *Journal of Sociolinguistics* 4, no. 4 (2000): 588–613.

69. Robert M. Rodney, ed. and comp., *Mark Twain International: A Bibliography and Interpretation of his Worldwide Popularity* (Westport, CT: Greenwood, 1982), xxiv.

70. Ibid.

71. Ibid., xxvi.

72. Ibid., xliii.

73. Ibid., xxiii.

74. Harris, "When the Right Word Is Not Enough," 11; Margarida Vale de Gato, personal communication, October 8, 2010.

75. Xilao Li, "The Adventures of Mark Twain in China: Translation and Appreciation of More Than a Century," *Mark Twain Annual* 6, no. 1 (2008): 65–76.

76. Liang Yan, "'The Californian's Tale' no chugokugo-yaku 'Yamaga-kigu' ni kansuru kenkyu" (A study of "The Californian's Tale" in Chinese translation), *Mark Twain: kenkyu to hihyo* (Journal of Mark Twain Studies) (Japan) 9 (April 2010): 86–93. I first heard about Liang's work from Tsuyoshi Ishihara, a professor at Waseda University, who is mentoring her work on Twain. I met Liang when I lectured in Fukuoka, Japan, in September, 2010, and she gave me a copy of her article.

77. Ishihara, *Mark Twain in Japan*, 14.

78. Ibid.

79. Martí, "North American Scenes," 54.

80. Ibid.

81. Ibid., 53–54.

82. Ibid. 48–53.

83. José Martí, "Escenas Norteamericanas," *La Nación* (Buenos Aires), February 20, 1890. Reprinted in *Obras Completas de Martí* (Havana: Editorial Trópico, 1941), 38:186. Translated by Rubén Builes.

84. Castellanos, "Mark Twain," 134.

85. Maxwell Geismar, "Mark Twain and the Robber Barons," *Scanlan's Monthly*, March 1970, 33.

86. Lao She, "Mark Twain: Exposer of the 'Dollar Empire.' A Speech by Lao She Commemorating the Fiftieth Anniversary of the Death of Mark Twain," trans. Zhao Yuming, Sui Gang, and J. R. LeMaster, *US-China Review* 19 (Summer 1995): 11–15; in *The Mark Twain Anthology*, ed. Fishkin, 283–88. Although it is undisputed that Lao She delivered this speech, and although the text is now widely credited to him in print in China, the well-known Chinese poet and scholar Yuan Kejia claimed in a Chinese journal in 1985 that he was paid to write this speech for Lao She to deliver, and that he is its actual author. "In Feb. 1985, *Foreign Literature Review*, run by the Institute of Foreign Literature, China Academy of Social Sciences, published a note by Yuan Kejia, in which he pointed out the mistake in publishing, in the 4th issue of *Foreign Literature Review* in 1984 (p. 132), the essay under the name of Lao She. He also described the circumstance under which Lao She read the essay. It was read at a national conference in memory of Mark Twain in 1960. They made the agreement that Yuan was to write the essay, and Lao She was to read the essay under his name, but the payment for the writing was to go to Yuan. Yuan said in the note that it was not uncommon for one to write an essay and for another to read it under his name. But for publication, it was another matter. The essay should be given its right author's name to avoid confusions in the future" (Gongzhao Li, personal communication, July 8, 2010).

87. Xilao Li, "The Adventures of Mark Twain in China: Translation and Appreciation of More than a Century," *Mark Twain Annual* 6, no. 1 (2008): 65–76.

88. The two leading exceptions to this situation in the United States were the critics Philip Foner and Maxwell Geismar. See Philip S. Foner, *Mark Twain, Social Critic* (New York: International, 1958); Maxwell Geismar, "Mark Twain and the Robber Barons" and *Mark Twain: An American Prophet* (New York: Houghton Mifflin, 1970). While these works by Foner and Geismar were not totally neglected, they did not generally set the agenda for scholarship when they were published. Their real impact would not be felt until the 1990s, when their approach resonated with new publications—by Jim Zwick, in particular—that underlined the importance of the texts to which they had drawn Americans' attention two decades earlier. The fact that International Publishers, the publishing firm of the US Communist Party, published Foner's *Mark Twain, Social Critic* may have prevented the book from setting scholars' agendas as much as it might have. Meanwhile, Geismar was marginalized as a critic at least in part because of his progressive politics.

89. Lao, "Mark Twain," 283–84 (emphasis added).

90. Jim Zwick, *Mark Twain's Weapons of Satire: Anti-Imperialist Writings on the Philippine-American War* (Syracuse, NY: Syracuse University Press, 1992).

91. See, for example, Shelley Fisher Fishkin and Takayuki Tatsumi, eds., "New Perspectives on 'The War-Prayer,'" special forum, *Mark Twain Studies* 2, republished in the "Reprise" section of *Journal of Transnational American Studies* 1, no. 1 (2009), http://www.escholarship.org/uc/acgcc_jtas?volume=1;issue=1, accessed February 10, 2015.

92. Lao, "Mark Twain," 284.

93. Martin Zehr, "Mark Twain, 'The Treaty with China,' and the Chinese Connec-

tion," *Journal of Transnational American Studies* 2, no. 1 (2010), http://escholarship.org/uc/item/5t02n321, accessed February 10, 2015.

94. Yan Bereznitsky, "Mark Twain on the Bed of Procrustes," *Literaturnaya Gazeta* (Moscow), August 18, 1959; translated by Robert Belknap, in *Mark Twain and the Russians: An Exchange of Views*, ed. Charles Neider (New York: Hill and Wang, 1960), 13–15. See also Yan Bereznitsky, "The Question Is Significantly More Profound: A Letter to Charles Neider," *Literaturnaya Gazeta* (Moscow), December 12, 1959, translated by Robert Belknap, in *Mark Twain and the Russians*, ed. Neider, 19–24. Both items are in *The Mark Twain Anthology*, ed. Fishkin, 278–79.

95. Lao, "Mark Twain," 287.

96. For an example of the continuation of this view in the twenty-first century, see the 2001 edition of Louis J. Budd's 1962 book, *Mark Twain: Social Philosopher*, in which the author concludes his preface to the new edition with this comment: "Though I consider sociopolitical ideas—or the art of how we do and must live together—supremely important, we care about [Twain's] particular questions and answers primarily because of his gift for humor" (Bloomington: Indiana University Press, 2001, xvii).

97. Mark Twain, *Autobiography of Mark Twain*, ed. Charles Neider ([1959]; Harper-Perennial Edition, New York: Harper and Row, 1990, 358).

98. Amy Kaplan, *The Anarchy of Empire in the Making of U.S. Culture* (Cambridge, MA: Harvard University Press, 2002), 52.

99. John Carlos Rowe, *Literary Culture and U.S. Imperialism: From the Revolution to World War II* (New York: Oxford University Press, 2000), 125.

100. Ibid., 139.

101. Shelley Fisher Fishkin, "DEEP MAPS: A Brief for Digital Palimpsest Mapping Projects (Dpmps or 'Deep Maps')," *Journal of Transnational American Studies* 3, no. 2 (2012), http://escholarship.org/uc/item/92v10ot0, accessed February 10, 2015.

102. Dana Oshiro, "Changing the World with Open Translation," ReadWriteWeb, July 16, 2009, http://www.readwriteweb.com/archives/changing_the_world_with_open_translation.php, accessed February 10, 2015.

103. Mark Twain. "The 'Jumping Frog.' In English. Then in French. Then Clawed Back into a Civilized Language Once More By Patient, Unremunerated Toil," in *Sketches, New and Old* (1875), the Oxford Mark Twain, ed. Shelley Fisher Fishkin (New York: Oxford University Press, 1996), 28–45.

104. This discussion of Global Huck draws on three papers I delivered and the discussions that followed: "Recent Developments in Transnational American Studies," at the Transnational Ethnic and American Studies Working Group, University of California, Berkeley, Humanities Center (October 13, 2011); "A Digital Palimpsest Mapping Project (DPMP)—'Deep Map'—on 'Global Huck,'" at the annual meeting of the American Literature Association (May 26, 2012, San Francisco); and "Transnational American Studies: Next Steps," at the Hong Kong University Conference on Oceanic Archives and Trans-

national American Studies (June 6, 2012) and at the Tsinghua University Conference on Transnational American Studies as Theory and Praxis (June 7, 2012, Beijing).

105. For more on this topic, see Shelley Fisher Fishkin, "Mark Twain and the Jews," *Arizona Quarterly* 61, no. 1 (2005): 135–66.

106. Mark Twain, *Following the Equator* (1897), the Oxford Mark Twain, ed. Shelley Fisher Fishkin (New York: Oxford University Press, 1996), 650.

107. See Shelley Fisher Fishkin, "Mark Twain's Historical View at the Turn of the Twentieth Century," in *Proceedings of the 1999 Kyoto American Studies Summer Seminar*, ed. Hiroshi Yoneyama (Kyoto: Center for American Studies, Ritsumeikan University, 2000), 123–39.

108. See Fishkin, "Mark Twain and the Jews."

109. Twain, *The Innocents Abroad*, 650.

110. Richard Bridgman, *Traveling in Mark Twain* (Berkeley: University of California Press, 1987), 3.

111. Hua Hsu, "The Trans-Pacific Lesson of Mark Twain's 'War-Prayer,'" *Mark Twain Studies* 2, republished in the "Reprise" section of *Journal of Transnational American Studies* 1, no. 1 (2009), http://escholarship.org/uc/item/666369jq#page-1, accessed February 10, 2015.

112. Ibid.

113. Twain, *Following the Equator*, 213.

114. Mark Twain, "What Paul Bourget Thinks of Us," in *How to Tell a Story and Other Essays* (1897), the Oxford Mark Twain, ed. Shelley Fisher Fishkin (New York: Oxford University Press, 1996), 196–97.

RACIAL MEMORY AND THE MODERN BORDERS
OF THE NATION-STATE

DISCUSSIONS ABOUT THE NEXUS between race and modernity need to consider how notions of time and historical narratives form often unrecognized borders bounding how we think of ethnicity. Though much new scholarship is undertaken to counteract the trend, there has been a tendency in ethnic studies to view the period prior to the civil rights movements of the 1950s and 1960s as a kind of prehistory to our current notions of the multirelational ethnic subjectivities living in the borderlands of postmodern America.[1] Here I refer to America understood most broadly as a transnational circuit of physical, economic, and cultural exchange. Thus my current project focuses on how the nexus of race and modernity within a Chicana/o or Mexican-American context generates the consciousness of the contemporary and helps forge constituencies in the modern nation-state.

The study of this nexus between race and the modern is of course not new. From the transatlantic work of Paul Gilroy in *The Black Atlantic* (1993) to the hemispheric studies of José Saldívar in *The Dialectics of Our America* (1991) and the examination of Greater Mexico in José Limón's *American Encounters* (1998), the powerful transformations wrought by modernity have formed a sharp critical lens for those critics interested in Latina/Latino and postcolonial constituencies whose lives are lived on the margins in North American society.[2]

The present discussion is but a preliminary attempt to consider the relationship between the promises and contradictions of modernity and the memory of racial distinction that marks Chicana/o experiences in the United States. Modernity stands as a response to modernization characterized by increasing technologization and the rise of monopoly capitalism on an economic level as well as claims to equality and increased rights in the political realm. This response is at once ambiguous and alienating. Modernity corresponds to the dissolution of well-worn social networks due to the processes of modernization. Yet modernity also considers the manner in which new constituencies seek to engage issues of justice and liberty.

Race—at least in the context of the United States—represents one formulation by which the demand for social justice may be enacted. Indeed, race is one instantiation of the colonial encounters that have formulated life in this hemisphere. Here I am thinking of Gilroy's words in *The Black Atlantic*: "Where lived crisis and systemic crisis come together, Marxism allocates priority to the latter while the memory of slavery insists on the priority of the former" (1993, 40). The racial memory of colonial encounters marks the lived crisis that individuals and communities have endured. Modernity marks one such moment of crisis, a shift in the manner of producing and living. The memory of racial injustice and connection manifests that crisis in the flesh of the living. My discussion, then, emerges from between these double crises, the systemic and the lived, the modern and the racial, the haunted and the remembered, to trace how modernity haunts the racialized imagination of contemporary Chicana/o culture.[3]

In considering the relationship between modernity and racial memory, I must acknowledge the important scholarly work already undertaken that interrogates the relationship between modernization and lived Chicana/o experiences. The historians David Montejano (1987), David Gutiérrez (1995), Emma Pérez (1999), and George Sánchez (1993) provide a clear understanding of how modernization helped foster the conditions for Chicana/o subjectivity. The cultural critics Ramón Saldívar (2006), José Limón (1992), and María Saldaña-Portillo (2004) offer us exceptional work on the intricacies of Chicana and Chicano cultural expression in its troubled relationship to the conditions of modernity.

What I seek to add to these discussions of modernity in the context of Mexican-American life is the element of racial memory, one that provides a lived memory of colonial encounters. To better illustrate the relationship between race and modernity, it is useful to turn to a few passages from two texts that have in their own ways become canonical within the corpus of Chicana/o literary production: *George Washington Gómez* (1990), by Américo Paredes, and *The Rain God*, by Arturo Islas (1991).[4]

There are a number of reasons why these works are significant. Both novels locate the formation of an ethnic identity in South Texas, both involve the dissolution of patriarchal power, and both reveal the impact of modernity on the characters. As Limón says of Paredes's novel, it is "an account of the dilemmas inherent in the search for identity in the face of modernity, as seen through the life of a young man in the context of Greater Mexico" (1998, 24). In both novels, this search is characterized by a systemic crisis, one that—at least in the case of Paredes's work—is marked, as Limón has

noted, by "the coming of a rapidly advancing Anglo-American capitalist political economy and culture to the area" of south Texas between 1870 and
1930 (1994, 85). I take up this issue of systemic crisis below in this essay.
What I turn to here is the central parallel that can be drawn between the
disruption of male warrior heroes in Paredes's and Islas's books.

A large part of Paredes's narrative focuses on the manner in which the
eponymous protagonist seeks to carve out an identity for himself, not just
in the face of modernity but in the face of the family patriarch, his Uncle
Feliciano, who—against his better judgment—seeks to find a way to steer
the youth to become (as his family had hoped) "a great man who will help
his people" (1990, 16). In Islas's novel, the narrative is driven by the way
the family patriarch—Miguel Angel, called Miguel Grande—seeks to control the other members of the family, particularly his slightly fey young son,
Miguel Chico. Miguel Grande struggles both to retain a sense of order in the
family and to maintain his position of patriarchal privilege. This privilege is
undone when the two women who form the core of his emotional life—his
wife and his mistress—manage his life rather than him managing them.

Both novels—written in very different historical eras but published within
a few years of each other—are haunted by the manner in which clearly demarcated modalities of behavior associated with a regulated and patriarchal
society are ruptured by the incursion of the modern. To put it another way, as
Paredes writes in *With His Pistol in His Hand*, in the Mexico-Texan world
before modernity, "social conduct was regulated and formal, and men lived
under a patriarchal system . . . [in which] decisions were made, arguments
were settled, and sanctions were decided by the old men of the group, with the
leader usually being a patriarch" (1971, 11–12). In the worlds of the novels,
this patriarchal system is broken down by the incursion of modernity—the
dissolution of traditional social networks and the assertion of new forms of
equality that cut cross lines of gender, race, and even sexual identification.
The break the modern brings disrupts a patriarchal order that contains both
a measure of moral surety and a reliance on inherent social inequalities.[5]

From one perspective, articulated by Renato Rosaldo among others, this
disruption leads to a quest for greater equality and justice—we might recall
Rosaldo's reading of Paredes's *With His Pistol in His Hand* and its valoriza-
tion of the male warrior hero against the mock-epic tone found in Ernesto
Galarza's *Barrio* Boy (1971). "In Galarza's autobiography," Rosaldo writes,
"both the warrior hero and the Edenic myth occupy central places, but they
are mocked rather than treated with poetic reverence" (1989, 156). While
Paredes's work traces the struggle between a patriarchal society in confrontation with an encroaching Anglo-American world, Galarza's text focuses
on the movement into that world—based on his own experiences as a "bar-

rio boy" struggling to formulate a new, empowered identity that does not (indeed, cannot) rely on the model of the warrior for survival. Yet, as Limón and both José Saldívar (1997) and Ramón Saldívar (2006) argue, the disruption of a patriarchal and heroic model—one in which a sense of moral stability ostensibly exists—leads inexorably to a sense of anxiety, alienation, and irony. These are conditions of the modern.

I must confess that my present interest in modernity arises from my longtime interest in postmodernity. I still believe that modernity exists within postmodernity, just as colonialist thought exists in postcolonialist critique. Here, those of you who may have skimmed my first book on poetry (1995) will recognize a central tenet of my argument: Chicana and Chicano culture emerges from a space of rupture. Chicana/o critical discourse forms part of a contemporary strategy for self-definition and self-determination even as it reveals the discontinuities, tensions, and disjunctures evident in the construction of a relevant cultural identity. These ruptures reveal the difficult position marked by the term "Chicano." This term, after all, emerges from an extraordinarily violent and exploitative history. One element of this history, and one central rupture, is the passage from the premodern to the modern. Therefore modernity is a key moment in the development of Chicano and Chicana consciousness. At the same time, I argue that though modernity represents a moment of rupture in Chicana/o culture, the movement into postmodernity does not fully erase modernity as a relevant condition for Chicana/o critical consciousness or study.

Part of my intellectual interest has to do with the definition of Latino and Latina studies in the United States: that is, the study of movements involving both culture and labor across sometimes capricious national borders. I have argued that Chicana/o culture moves both through the gaps and across the bridges of numerous cultural practices that are associated with particular geographies: the United States, Mexico, Texas, California, the rural, and the urban. The geographies are also associated with particular cultural practices: the folkloric, the postmodern, the popular, the elite, the traditional, the tendentious, and the avant-garde. Chicana/o culture moves against and with these diverse sites. It variously participates in the practices inherent in the sites while simultaneously positing a critique of their practices.

Chicana and Chicano cultural practices are, in short, adept at transformation and adaptation. They assume a self-identity that knows itself as simultaneously self and other. This consciousness allows for an ability to move through numerous realms without becoming a part of or fully submitting to them. On a theoretical plane, Chela Sandoval's notion of the methodology of the oppressed forms a key node of critical intervention: "people of color in the United States, familiar with historical, subjective, and political dislocation

since the founding of the colonies, have created a set of inner and outer technologies to enable survival within the developing state apparatus, technologies that will be of great value during the cultural and economic changes to
come" (2000, 79). These technologies enable a subtle shifting and differential
movement that matches the transformations of late capitalist consumption.

Marginal political practices parry the logic of all-consuming late capitalism.
The very movement of laboring bodies contests the notion that globalizing capitalism has contained all its subjects. Roger Rouse has famously provided an
exemplary moment of late capitalist consumption and community in his essay
"Mexican Migration and the Social Space of Postmodernism" (1991), which
addresses the practices of a migrant community from Aguililla, Michoacán,
taking up residence in Redwood City, California. Rouse describes a type
of transnational social organization and personal identification—based on
the simultaneous occupation of two distinct geocultural sites—that disrupts
received notions of nationalism and cultural identity.

Chicana/o culture has long developed through and against the various
economic and cultural transformations undergone by the United States. As
an integral part of the labor force that has driven North American production, Chicanas/os know all too intimately the reality of decentered subjectivity and the violence that results from the pursuit of master narratives—
progress, expansion, and modernization. Chicanas/os have lived through and
survived (which can be a form of triumph over some times) the disparities
wrought by modernity. Yet, as we will see at the close of this essay, survival
is not always triumphant and can, indeed, be based on denial and delusion.

One manner in which Chicana and Chicano critical discourse has sought
to thematize its struggle with social disparity has been, at least since the
political movements of the 1960s, the assertion of a new racial consciousness. The affirmation of a mestiza/o identity served a pointed political and
cultural end. It was a way to affirm difference and to stake that difference
on inclusion in the very body of the United States.

While the idea of *mestizaje* emerges from a history of essentialized and
biologized racial discussions, the term has come to be used in Chicana/o
discourse as a way to move beyond binary constructions of racial identity
and identity politics. Consequently, *mestizaje* has come to occupy a highly
valued—though not unproblematic—position in our critical discourse because it embodies the idea of multiple subjectivities. It opens our understanding of racial/ethnic identity to greater complexity and nuance. Critical
mestizaje helps indicate how people live their lives in and through their
bodies as well as in and through ideology. A disjuncture (or rupture) in ideology becomes apparent through the dislocations experienced by mestiza/o
bodies. This dislocation means that ideological constructs of subjectivity

cannot always hail Chicana or Chicano subjects successfully. *Mestizaje* in a Chicana/o context has sought to articulate the critical nature of this failure.

Chicana/o *mestizaje* represents the double nature of Chicano identity. It allows for the forging of new multivalent identities and it imbeds identity in already constraining social relations. To better understand this point, we might look back at one cultural response to how the racial nature of Mexican identity serves the contradictory purposes of national identification.

Let us direct our attention to the opening scene of Paredes's *George Washington Gómez*. The novel, written between 1936 and 1940, is a fascinating creative narrative by a restless young writer who, after drafting the novel, set it aside for nearly half a century.

The novel presents the story of a family forced from the llano of the Mexican-American border region into the town of Jonesville-on-the-Grande. The conflicts between the Sediciosos—seditionists stirring up a plot to secede from the United States—and the Texas Rangers make for violent and unstable conditions. These conditions lead to the death of a young father, Gumersindo Gómez, at the hands of the Texas Rangers. His dying wish is that his brother-in-law, Feliciano Garcia, never reveal to Gumersindo's newly born son the manner in which his father died. Gumersindo's dying words are: "'My son. Mustn't know. Ever. No hate, no hate'" (1990, 21). Feliciano takes the family to Jonesville, where—as a part of the political machine run by the Anglo Texan Judge Bob Norris—he grows in wealth and status. There he raises Gumersindo's family as his own, becoming the patriarch whose position and power forms at first a source of pride and later a target of scorn for the sole boy of the family, George Washington Gómez. Saldaña-Portillo (2004) and Ramón Saldívar (2006), among others, have written about the novel and focus, quite rightly, on the complex and contradictory interpellation of the main character. My interest here has less to do with the main characters and more to do with the interstices of the narrative, those moments when the narrative focuses on setting and context. It is these moments that are telling about the relationship between race and modernity.

As the book opens, Gumersindo is with Doc Berry, racing in the doctor's Model T Ford across the open plain to get to Gumersindo's wife, who is having a baby. Gumersindo is described as "a stocky, red-haired man of about thirty" (Paredes 1990, 11).

> Gumersindo and Doc are stopped by a quartet of Texas Rangers keeping an eye out for seditionists and smugglers. Two of the Rangers stare at Gumersindo, as if trying to place him. The man fidgeted in his seat and avoided their eyes. Finally one of the Rangers spoke, "What's your name, feller?"
> "He doesn't speak much English," Doc Berry said.

"Mexican, eh?" said MacDougal. "For a minute there I thought he was a white man." He looked steadily at the man, who began to show signs of nervousness.

"He's a good Mexican," Doc said. "I can vouch for him."

"He's okay if you say so, Doc," MacDougal answered. "But it's getting kinda hard these days to tell the good ones from the bad ones. Can't take any chances these days. But he's all right if you say so." (ibid.)

Of course this encounter is necessary for the exposition of the story, revealing the tension between the different populations living in the region around the border. What is interesting to me is the manner in which racially encoded identities in this passage are undone. Gumersindo does not look like a Mexican but is mistaken, even if only for a minute, for a white man. The mistake is immediately corrected, and with his racial category determined, the Ranger and Doc can go on to discuss whether Gumersindo is a good Mexican or a bad one—evidently, the only two categories by which a Mexican can be understood. Even that distinction, the Ranger laments, is getting harder and harder to ascertain.

From the beginning of the book, an anxiety over racial categorization becomes a central form of social ordering. Just before encountering Gumersindo and Doc, the Rangers had come across the smuggler Lupe García and his driver, El Negro. The Rangers remark on the man driving the carriage, a big man with "Negroid features" (ibid., 10): "'A nigger,' one of them said, 'a nigger-greaser. What do you think of that?'" (ibid., 11). The Rangers in these passages speak from a racial paradigm prevalent in the United States that assumes there is a clear distinction between racial identities. Yet here, in the Texan borderlands of Paredes's novel, this distinction seems undone at every point: a white man who turns out to be Mexican, a Mexican who appears black.

In part, the undoing of racial distinction may be the result of two different racial paradigms coming into contact as a result of the US colonization of territories that had once been Spanish or Mexican. In the United States, the one-drop rule and its ideology of racial binarism predominated in the period of Paredes's narrative (I would argue that this binarity remains at the heart of US racial ideology). In Mexico, a more fluid system of racial categorization emerged. In *Recovering History, Constructing Race*, Martha Menchaca traces the development of nineteenth-century racial formation in what is now the US Southwest. Her book takes note of the racial diversity and fluidity in Mexico under colonial Spanish rule. The famous *casta* (caste) system—though meant to discursively contain the myriad combinations of racial couplings—underscored the porousness of racial identity and identification. The categories were basically limited to Spanish, black, Indian, mestizo, *castizo*, mulatto, *morisco*, *lobo*, *coyote*, and occasionally *chino* (Katzew 2004, 44). This does not mean that race did not matter under Spanish colonialism. Rather, as Menchaca notes, by the time of Mexican independence in 1821, the caste system had been collapsed for the purposes of the census categorization into two groups: *gente de razón* (those people who accepted Spanish rule, language, and culture) and *indo* (those who maintained their own governing systems) (Menchaca 2002, 167). Members of both groups belonged to the empire culturally, legally, and legislatively, and race played a less important role in identity and identification.

However, Menchaca clearly points out that in the US context, racial stratification and identification were inexorably part of the civil social order. By the end of 1849, "Congress [had] racialized the Indians of the Southwest and determined they were distinct from Mexicans" (ibid., 218). Legally, Mexican Americans were considered white. The historian Ernesto Chávez explains that when the United States annexed Mexican lands and citizens after 1848, "the U.S. government, owing to the provisions of the 1790 naturalization act, made ethnic Mexicans legally white. However, socially, they were not given the privileges of whiteness and faced de facto segregation" (2002, 2). Despite the legal standing of Mexican Americans, the racial ideology of the frontier held more powerful sway than structures of legal protection. Indeed, the force of the law would soon be used to ensure the subaltern position of the Mexican-descended American. Tomás Almaguer reminds us that working-class people of Mexican origin in the United States were "often denied their legal rights by being categorized as Indians" (1994, 57). The racial categorizations of nineteenth-century America on an ideological level served to constrain the mestiza/o body on the social and economic levels.

The mestiza/o body came to occupy an ambiguous position in US society. In Paredes's novel, this ambiguity is produced as a result of modernization. We are told that, after its founding in 1846 as Jonesville, Texas, "for more than half a century Jonesville remained a Mexican town, though officially part of the United States" (1990, 36). Then "came the railroad early in the 20th century, and with it arrived the first real-estate men and the land-and-title companies, and a Chamber of Commerce, of course, which renamed the little town 'Jonesville-on-the-Grande' and advertised it to suckers from up north as a paradise on earth: California and Florida rolled up into one" (ibid.).

The incursion of the railroad leads to land speculation and housing development. The process of advertising—implying mass production and mass media—generates consumer capitalism along with those "suckers" who end up victims of capitalism's duplicity. But, of course, those suckers are not the only victims caught in the shell game of consumer capitalism: "Mexicans labored with axe and spade to clear away the brush where the cattle of their ancestors once had roamed. To make room for truck farming and citrus groves. And the settlers poured in from the U.S. heartland, while Mexicans were pushed out of cattle raising into hard manual labor. It was then also that Jonesville-on-the-Grande came to have a Mexican section of town" (ibid.).

The railroad not only brought land speculators, it also generated modern agribusiness—whose development was aided by the technology of the railroad as a means of mass transportation. By the mid-1920s, for example, Texas produced twenty to thirty percent of the world's cotton crop (Gutiérrez 1995, 42). And the railroad provided the means of getting that cotton to the world. More important here, the technology that brings corporate capitalism to south Texas pushes the Mexican away from independence and instead subjects him to a new regime as laborer and segregated citizen. Even more compelling in Paredes's narrative is the sense that there is a pathos, an inevitability, to the Mexican's subjugation: "It was the lot of the Mexicotexan that the Anglosaxon should use him as a tool for the Mexican's undoing. The chaparral had been the Mexicotexan's guarantee of freedom. While it existed, it served as a refuge to the *ranchero* fleeing from alien law. The chaparral and the flats had made cattle-raising possible; and even the small farmers—their little parcels of land tucked deep in the brush—had been comparatively independent" (Paredes 1990, 42).

The disruption wrought by modernization is underscored narratively by the sentence fragment that stands at the center of this passage: "To make room for truck farming and citrus groves." This formal fragmentation parallels the disruption experienced by the Mexicotexans. Their independence is lost, casting them in the ironic position of performing their own undoing. The undoing of independence is coupled, again ironically, within the narrative with a kind of revealing, an emergence from the chaparral into the clear light of history and the exploitative system of agribusiness. With the arrival of American settlers—with what Ramón Saldívar calls "the limitless power of Americanization and modernization" (2006, 155)—the Mexican moves from subject to subjugation. And in this process, the Mexican becomes just a tool:

> But the American had begun to "develop" the land. He had it cleared and made it into cotton fields, into citrus orchards and towns. And it was the Mexicotexan's brown muscular arms that felled the trees. He wielded the machete against the smaller brush and strained his back pulling tree stumps out of the ground. For this he got enough to eat for the day and the promise of more of the same tomorrow. As day laborer clearing chaparral, as cotton and fruit picker for as few cents a day as he could subsist on. Every stroke of the ax, every swing of the mattock clinched his own misfortune. (Paredes 1990, 42)

Again, on a formal level the fragmentation of social life is underscored, here with the sentence fragment, "As day laborer clearing chaparral, as cotton and fruit picker for as few cents a day as he could subsist on." Of more significance is the position of the Americans as agents in history, the planners and commanders of modernization. By contrast, the Mexicans act as the unwitting means of modernization. In the narrative, this role of the Mexican laborer is embodied and racialized—it is "brown muscular arms" that clear the land for development. Once again, the systemic rupture represented by modernity is incarnated via racial allusion. The tone of this passage strikes exactly the sense of pathos that imbues the novel, as Ramón Saldívar notes: "Paredes's subjects for the substance of his narrative are not warrior heroes but the nonheroic innocents who dwell darkly in the shadows of history and live its internal contradictions and hierarchical complexities in the mode of irony" (2006, 156). Although there is much to admire in Saldívar's work, his observation is not entirely correct. In large part, the novel traces precisely how George Gómez's life is haunted by the dream of the warrior hero. From his family's hope that he will be a leader of his people to his uncle's reluctant secret about Gumersindo's death and his own recurring dream of battling over Houston on the Mexican side of the US-Mexico War, the novel is infused with the dream of a heroic subjectivity. It is true, however, that by the end of the novel, the protagonist has become precisely the type of nonheroic character Saldívar describes.

George Washington Gómez is, finally, an individual bound by modernity to fail to attain an integral identity. Moreover, he is bound by the racial logic that his own somatic presence would seem to deny. He is forever a Mexican, and consequently always racialized. As his future father-in-law comments in the last section of the novel: "'They sure screwed you up, didn't they, boy? . . . . You look white but you're a goddam Meskin. And what does your mother do but give you a nigger name. George Washington Go-maize'" (Paredes 1990, 284). His identity is shot through with the racial discourses he cannot escape. Significantly, the fact of his Mexican character is underscored by the name he chooses for himself by narrative's end: George G. Gómez, "the middle G for García, his mother's maiden name" (ibid.). Intentionally or not, he incorporates a matrilineal genealogy that, of course, does nothing to liberate his own sense of identity or place him in a position that would empower an ethnic consciousness.

It is possible to go on at length with a discussion of the numerous racial memories imbedded in Paredes's novel—from the perception that George Washington Gómez's mispronounced name, Guálinto, is an Indian one to his ejection from the nightclub La Casa Mexicana because he is Mexican and his doting on the photos of his sister's children and remarking "more than once on their blue eyes and light-colored hair" (ibid., 290). Such a discussion can be set aside for the moment to refocus on the conjoining of race and modernity that is evident in the interstices of the book and that emerges, finally, at the close of the novel where, much to George's dismay, his former classmates have decided to organize for political rights.

While the critic Hector Pérez finds hope in this element of the narrative, he admits that the overall tone of the novel is one of despair: "The clash of cultures is powerful and pervasive. The task is an impossible one and therein lies the root of the oppressive frustration for Guálinto and his community" (1998, 42). More specifically, I would argue, the cultures in contestation that Pérez cites are themselves the embodied practices of modernity's contradictions. These contradictions are certainly evident in the manner in which Mexicans of all races were unequally incorporated into the expanded United States following the War with Mexico in 1848. "Enfranchisement," Saldaña-Portillo observes insightfully, "required disavowal of a rich, racial logic of inclusion. It required the abandonment of the very terms of sovereign Mexican character, its mestizo and Indian heritage" (2004, 158). By the close of the novel, the minor characters reject the contradictions of modernity embodied, as John Cutler observes, by "Guálinto's incomplete psychic repression of his Mexicanness" (2015, 44) in favor of social equality and incorporation that are also a part of modernity. George's classmates at the novel's close are claiming for themselves "the rights of our people" (Paredes 1990, 292). The enfranchisement that George's old friends envision for themselves is one that does not reject a racial logic of inclusion—on the contrary, this sense of enfranchisement demands that inclusion be premised on a racial logic of self-identification and self-assertion. They seek to become racialized agents in history, not merely "brown muscular arms" clearing the way for their own misfortune.

The twin elements of modernity—alienation and enfranchisement—manifest themselves quite clearly in George Washington Gómez. Given that Paredes wrote the novel at a time when modernization was still a process at work in south Texas, it makes sense that his narrative would incorporate the divisions and promises wrought by modernity. But my assertion is that the problems and promises of modernity haunt Chicana/o cultural and critical production past the moment of the modern.

The Rain God, a novel by another son of Texas, tells the story of three generations of the Angel family and their struggles with each other and with their border lives in the United States. The novel, written and rewritten over a number of years from the 1970s to early 1980s was the first published book by Stanford University Professor Arturo Islas. Originally published by the small Alexandrine Press of Palo Alto in 1984, it has become a standard—perhaps classic—text in Chicana/o literature. Though admired, it has also generated a good deal of criticism, primarily because it does not more overtly champion the queer sexuality of the central character, Miguel Chico, an accusation that is at once unfair and problematic.[6]

My focus here is on how the novel manifests the connection between race and modernity. It is valuable because it helps connect the world of Texas, where most of the action takes place, with the world of California, where the protagonist goes to study and write and, conveniently, escape the judgments of his family. *The Rain God* is a novel that, like Paredes's work, examines the manner in which patriarchy forms a significant but lost model of male behavior. Most important, the book insists that modernity generates the complex context that drives the action. The Angel family aspires to social and economic enfranchisement, pursuing the American Dream with varying success. The family also finds it is continually haunted by racial disavowal and, almost literally, the ghost of modernity. That is, the family lives the central contradictions of the modern.

Critics have noted the manner in which the novel relies on literary modernism to formulate its narrative. Marta Sánchez informs us that "Islas has appropriated specific modernistic techniques (especially self-conscious narration, but also non-linear spatial and temporal sequences) and those of psychoanalysis from the dominant culture and has 'grafted' them onto Mexican-Chicano culture" (1990, 295). Just as Limón has argued that Paredes's creative work joins other emerging literatures that "represent a strong continuation of a critical modernism" (1992, 165), Sánchez views Islas's use of modernist techniques as a critical reinvigoration. José Saldívar also traces the literary influences on Islas to Wallace Stevens and Willa Cather, as well as to Octavio Paz, Juan Rulfo, and Gabriel García Márquez (1991, 18). In the very form of Islas's novel, modernity continues to spawn a critical response.

In order to unpack this observation a bit more, I would like to focus our attention on the opening of Islas's novel. It begins by considering a photograph:

A photograph of Mama Chona and her grandson Miguel Angel—Miguel Chico or Mickey to his family—hovers above his head on the study wall beside the glass doors that open out into the garden. When Miguel Chico sits at his desk, he glances up at it occasionally without noticing it, looking through it rather than at it. It was taken in the early years of World War II by an old Mexican photographer who wandered up and down the border town's main street on the American side. . . . Because of the look on his face, the child seems as old as the woman. The camera has captured them in flight from this world to the next. (1991, 3–4)

This passage, recounted from the vantage point of Miguel Chico, demonstrates the manner in which the narrative uses this photograph to draw attention to the process of representation, or the question of presentation and self-reflexivity, a hallmark of postmodern literature as well as of modernist aesthetics. The photograph becomes a metonym for the novel itself. In particular, the peculiar line about the boy and the old woman captured "in flight from this world to the next" can be interpreted in a variety of ways—in flight from the world of mortals to the world of eternity, or from the world of the past to the world of the present. This evocation of time and its passage reflects a central concern in the novel: the movement through modernity into the present. Miguel Chico's meditation on the photograph takes place some thirty years after it was taken, at the cusp in US history between modernity and postmodernity. The evocation of time and the movement through time collapse into the narration itself. For the passage can also suggest a flight by the characters from "this world" of the fiction to "the next" of the real—cleverly evoking the vexed relationship between art and life, and between signifier and signified. While Rosemary King argues that the book is a "journey of self-discovery" (2004, 95), I consider it a meditation on self-construction and self-critique. After all, if this is about Miguel's process of self-discovery, that process is one in which the distracted observer glances up at the representation "without noticing it." The self-discovery would be almost accidental. Rather, the novel revolves around the effects that historical time has on the book's characters.

One more element in this passage is worth noting. Photography itself is a technology of the modern, as Walter Benjamin reminds us in "The Work of Art in the Age of Mechanical Reproduction." Benjamin observes: "photographic reproduction, with the aid of certain processes . . . can capture images which escape natural vision" (1988, 218). Though of course Benjamin is discussing photography as a means of removing the auratic from the work of art, his point about the role of photography in the modern age is salient. The moment of this border experience, fleeting in reality, here is forever captured via the technology of the photograph. It is a small but nevertheless significant point that the technology of the modern opens the narrative.

It is significant because, by the end of the narrative, we realize that Mama Chona—Miguel Chico's grandmother—has become the agent through which the lives of the characters are informed by the disavowal of racial memory and haunted by the rumblings of modernity in Mexico. Though Mama Chona is a powerful figure throughout the novel, it is not until the last chapter of the book that the reader learns about her tragic past. As the family matriarch, she has much to do with teaching the contradictory family values related to class and race that reflect a kind of colonial con-

sciousness. She associates ignorance and poverty with the Indian heritage of
Mexican identity, a heritage she continually disavows despite the presence
of the Indian in her somatic features: "As much as she protected herself from
it, the sun still darkened her complexion and no surgery could efface the Indian cheekbones, those small very dark eyes and aquiline nose" (Islas 1991,
27). As Antonio Márquez argues, "the novel brims with tragic irony when
Mama Chona denies her Indian heritage. . . . . Denying the Indian blood that
courses through her veins, Mama Chona personifies a not uncommon will-
fulness and a pathetic self-deception" (1994, 13). Her act is, of course, the
enacting of a colonizing ideology. Cutler illustrates how the novel "attends
to a longer racial legacy associated with the doubling of the coloniality of
power in the Southwest" under the rule of both the Spanish empire and the
US nation-state (2015, 98). Mama Chona's denial of her racial connection
to a people and a culture is not the "pathetic self-deception" that Márquez
sees. Rather, narratively, it is a means by which a rich and troubling history
of white supremacy becomes evoked. For the diegesis of the novel, her racial
denial is part of a complex survival strategy that, no matter how damaging,
proves to be more than self-delusion.

Toward the end of the narrative, we learn through Miguel Chico the tragic
history of Mama Chona's first son, Miguel Angel—in whose memory both
Miguel Chico and his father, Miguel Grande, had been named. The first
Miguel Angel was "Mama Chona's only child born of the love she had felt
for her husband" (ibid., 162). At the beginning of the Mexican Revolution—
the convulsive event that was Mexico's own manifestation of modernity—
Miguel Angel was gunned down while walking home from the university in
San Miguel de Allende. It is unclear whether government troops or revolutionary guerrillas fired the shot that cut down the only son born to Mama
Chona out of love. This ambiguity is significant in that the revolution as an
event, not the actions of individual men or political positions, bears responsibility for the death of the promising young student.

This death haunts Mama Chona her entire life, and it is what causes her
to deny the country and history from which she proceeds. She has, in a very
real sense, become a victim of modernity. Islas tells us: "She renounced all
joy on the day they buried Miguel. She was thirty-two" (ibid., 164). Her
children born subsequently become a trial to her, and she lives her life in denial of her race, her sexuality, and her past. The denial represents a deluded
but not a pathetic response to an accidental loss occasioned by Mexico's
own painful grappling with the modern.

In this sense, the Chicana and Chicano subjectivities in the novel are shot
through with the harsh contradictions and violent eruptions occasioned by
modernity. Those eruptions certainly disrupt the patriarchal order Miguel

Grande is so determined to maintain. But they also allow for queer sexual identities to name themselves and enable female characters to assert power. Moreover, the eruptions of modernity allow for a critical interrogation of the underpinnings of the ideology—racial, familial, religious, cultural—that Mama Chona has sought so diligently to instill in members of her family but that they eventually alter or abandon. Modernity makes it possible to acknowledge and engage differences within identity.

This is one compelling issue in tracing what remains of both the dreams and the disruptions wrought by modernity. The location of race in this equation offers a productive way to consider how the systemic crisis that modernity represents is experienced and lived. Race becomes a key, within Chicana and Chicano critical discourse, to the extremely contradictory and complex ways the remnants of modernity are lived today and to the manner in which it is possible to acknowledge difference within sameness.

This difference (in one register represented by the racial/ethnic others that are becoming the majority populations in many parts of the United States) within sameness represented by the imagined community of the nation-state is one challenge that, it could be argued, is represented by the ascension of Barack Obama to the presidency. More specific to my own work, the call for racial equality, the insistence on social justice for communities histori-cally aggrieved, the demand for sexual and gender equality across a variety of lines, and the hope for a community of like selves (which itself implies a kind of exclusivity) are all issues that are linked to modernity and that remain at the core of what Chicana/o activism seeks.

We all inherit a vexed legacy as a result of modernization that simulta-neously promises both enfranchisement and empowerment and actualizes alienation and exclusion. It is in the flesh that those contradictions are felt and through which the hope for new lived experiences can be sensed. For this reason, it rewards us to interrogate memories of race so we may better understand the qualities of modernity that still haunt our postmodern ex-istence and help formulate new and more empowered relationships to a still emerging nation-state.

Notes

1. For examples of current work that presents a countervailing perspective on the relationship between present and past configurations of race and ethnicity, see Alemán and Streeby 2007; Bost 2003; López 2011; Streeby 2002. In a related manner, the Recov-ering the U.S. Hispanic Literary Heritage Project at the University of Houston has been working to recover a literary heritage fully engaged with issues of class privilege, racial construction, and ethnic identification and disidentification.

2. We might keep in mind the proposal Gilroy makes regarding his notion of the Black Atlantic: "The specificity of the modern political and cultural formation I want to call the Black Atlantic can be defined, on one level, through desire[s] to transcend both the structures of the nation-state and the constraints of ethnicity and national particularity. These desires are relevant to understanding political organizing and cultural criticism. They have always sat uneasily alongside the strategic choices forced on black movements and individuals embedded in national and political cultures and nation-states in America, the Caribbean, and Europe" (1993, 19). The interconnectivity and, in many instances, mutual denial between the constructions of ethnicity and of national identities forms a primal dynamic in the formation of the modern nation-state.

3. The present discussion takes up several issues I explore in my book *Mestizaje: Critical Uses of Race in Chicano Culture* (2006). There I take up the vexed relationship between racial self-identification and disidentification that is involved in the affirmation of a mestizo/a racial consciousness.

4. The novels are united by more than their status in the field of Chicana/o letters. They also share a highly vexed publication history. In *Dancing with Ghosts* (2005), Frederick Aldama recounts the terrible time Islas had in finding a publisher for his book, revising his manuscript each time he received a rejection notice from one of the publishing houses that considered the novel. Alexandrian Press—a small publisher in Palo Alto, California—eventually published the first edition of the book in 1984. In 1991, it was republished by Avon, now an imprint of HarperCollins. In the case of Paredes, as a young man in the late 1930s, he put aside the manuscript for *George Washington Gómez*. It was not until 1989, after much convincing by friends, that he agreed to try to publish the book, which appeared in 1990. However, the publication was a printing of the original manuscript without any revision or rewriting.

5. The uniformity and completeness of the patriarchal world of the vaquero is itself illusory, of course, as the work of Jovita González suggests. See José Limón's introduction to her collection of stories *Dew on the Thorn* (1997) for a discussion of the antipatriarchal slant to her writing.

6. For intelligent and illuminating discussions of homosexuality in Isla's life and his work, see Ricardo Ortiz's argument that Isla's corporeal life in terms of both sexuality and disability inform the shape and function of his literary texts (2007, 399 and 420) and Cutler's observation that *The Rain God* foregrounds the experience of what Eve Sedgwick terms the "epistemology of the closet" (quoted in 2015, 100).

Works Cited

Aldama, Frederick Luis. 2005. *Dancing with Ghosts: A Critical Biography of Arturo Islas*. Berkeley: University of California Press.
Alemán, Jesse, and Shelley Streeby, eds. 2007. *Empire and the Literature of Sensation:*

An Anthology of Nineteenth-Century Popular Fiction. New Brunswick, NJ: Rutgers University Press.

Almaguer, Tomás. 1994. *Racial Faultlines: The Historical Origins of White Supremacy in California.* Berkeley: University of California Press.

Benjamin, Walter. 1988. *Illuminations: Essays and Reflections.* Edited by Hannah Arendt. Translated by Harry Zorn. New York: Schocken.

Bost, Suzanne. 2003. *Mulattas and Mestizas: Representing Mixed Identities in the Americas, 1850–2000.* Athens: University of Georgia Press.

Chávez, Ernesto. 2002. *"¡Mi Raza Primero!" ("My People First"): Nationalism, Identity and Insurgency in the Chicano Movement in Los Angeles, 1966–1978.* Berkeley: University of California Press.

Cutler, John Alba. 2015. *Ends of Assimilation: The Formation of Chicano Literature.* New York: Oxford University Press.

Galarza, Ernesto. 1971. *Barrio Boy.* Notre Dame, IN: University of Notre Dame Press.

Gilroy, Paul. 1993. *The Black Atlantic: Modernity and Double Consciousness.* Cambridge, MA: Harvard University Press.

González, Jovita. 1997. *Dew on the Thorn.* Introduction by José Limón. Houston: Arte Público.

Gutiérrez, David G. 1995. *Walls and Mirrors: Mexican Americans, Mexican Immigrants and the Politics of Ethnicity.* Berkeley: University of California Press.

Islas, Arturo. 1991. *The Rain God.* New York: Avon.

Katzew, Ilona. 2004. *Casta Painting: Images of Race in Eighteenth-Century Mexico.* New Haven, CT: Yale University Press.

King, Rosemary A. 2004. *Border Confluences: Borderland Narratives from the Mexican War to the Present.* Tucson: University of Arizona Press.

Limón, José E. 1992. *Mexican Ballads, Chicano Poems: History and Influence in Mexican-American Social Poetry.* Berkeley: University of California Press.

———. 1994. *Dancing with the Devil: Society and Cultural Poetics in Mexican-American South Texas.* Madison: University of Wisconsin Press.

———. 1998. *American Encounters: Greater Mexico, the United States, and the Erotics of Culture.* Boston: Beacon.

López, Marissa K. 2011. *Chicano Nations: Imagining the Americas, Inhabiting America.* New York: New York University Press.

Márquez, Antonio C. 1994. "The Historical Imagination in Arturo Islas's *The Rain God* and *Migrant Souls.*" *MELUS* 19 (2): 3–16.

Menchaca, Martha. 2002. *Recovering History, Constructing Race: The Indian, Black, and White Roots of Mexican Americans.* Austin: University of Texas Press.

Montejano, David. 1987. *Anglos and Mexicans in the Making of Texas, 1836–1986.* Austin: University of Texas Press.

Ortiz, Ricardo L. 2007. "Arturo Islas and the 'Phantom Rectum.'" *Contemporary Literature* 48 (3): 398–422.

Paredes, Américo. 1971. *With His Pistol in His Hand*. Austin: University of Texas Press.
———. 1990. *George Washington Gómez: A Mexicotexan Novel*. Houston: Arte Publico.
Pérez, Emma. 1999. *The Decolonial Imaginary: Writing Chicanas into History*. Bloomington: University of Indiana Press.
Pérez, Héctor. 1998. "Voicing Resistance on the Border: A Reading of Américo Paredes's *George Washington Gómez*." *MELUS* 23 (1): 27–48.
Pérez-Torres, Rafael. 1995. *Movements in Chicago Poetry: Against Myths, against Margins*. Cambridge: Cambridge University Press.
———. 2006. *Mestizaje: Critical Uses of Race in Chicano Culture*. Minneapolis: University of Minnesota Press.
Rosaldo, Renato. 1989. *Culture and Truth: The Remaking of Social Analysis*. Boston: Beacon.
Rouse, Roger. 1991. "Mexican Migration and the Social Space of Postmodernism." *Diaspora* 1 (Spring): 8–23.
Saldaña-Portillo, María Josefina. 2004. "'Wavering on the Horizon of Social Being': The Treaty of Guadalupe-Hidalgo and the Legacy of Its Racial Character in Américo Paredes's *George Washington Gómez*." *Radical History Review* 89 (Spring): 135–64.
Saldívar, José David. 1991. *The Dialectics of Our America: Genealogy, Cultural Critique, and Literary History*. Durham, NC: Duke University Press.
———. 1997. *Border Matters: Remapping American Cultural Studies*. Berkeley: University of California Press.
Saldívar, Ramón. 2006. *The Borderlands of Culture: Américo Paredes and the Transnational Imaginary*. Durham, NC: Duke University Press.
Sánchez, George J. 1993. *Becoming Mexican American: Ethnicity, Culture and Identity in Chicano Los Angeles, 1900–1945*. New York: Oxford University Press.
Sánchez, Marta. 1990. "Arturo Islas' *The Rain God*: An Alternative Tradition." *American Literature* 62 (2): 284–304.
Sandoval, Chela. 2000. *Methodology of the Oppressed*. Minneapolis: University of Minnesota Press.
Streeby, Shelley. 2002. *American Sensations: Class, Empire, and the Production of Popular Culture*. Berkeley: University of California Press.

6

THE OTHER SIDE OF HISTORY, THE OTHER
SIDE OF FICTION: FORM AND GENRE IN
SUSSHU FOSTER'S *ATOMIK AZTEX*

BARACK OBAMA WAS ELECTED president of the United States with only 39 percent of the white electorate voting for him. What are we to make of this astonishing fact? One possibility I would like to propose is that the United States has entered not so much a postrace era, but something perhaps even more startling: a postwhite era, by which I mean white politicians can no longer afford to underestimate the voting power of the people of color in the United States. How did that happen? When did it happen in the case of Obama's second election? What caused the change? Some of those questions were the hot topics of debates between pundits, commentators, and election experts of all sorts. Still, some answers are already intriguingly obvious. Right at the top of explanations are the ones that we have been debating in the United States for almost the entirety of the twentieth century and now well into the second decade of the twenty-first century: the ways in which race, ethnicity, gender, and labor, particularly the ethnicity of labor, could affect the outcome of a presidential election in the United States.

In the days immediately following the election, Dorian Warren, a professor of international and public affairs at Columbia University, proposed that "people of color delivered the election, and more accurately, people of color in combination of several constituencies." Warren asked: Since a smaller percentage of independent voters voted for Obama in 2012 than in 2008 (45 percent and 52 percent, respectively), where did the votes come from? Warren lists several key factors:

1. Nonwhite voters (a major factor in the victory, since only 39 percent white voters voted for Obama)
2. African American voters (98 percent voted for Obama; the Republican strategy of voter and voting suppression backfired)

3. Latinos (75 percent voted for Obama)
4. Women (55 percent voted for Obama, maintaining their 2008 level)
5. Labor and union voters (65 percent voted for Obama, including
   white men, but predominantly the new demographic of women in the
   labor unions)
6. Revenge of the nerds and Big Data (Nate Silver predicted this outcome completely correctly); triumph of empirical evidence over
   punditry.[1]

If there is anything to be learned about Obama's election to a second
term in 2012, certainly it is that the idea of what it means to be a racialized
person in the United States is in flux today. Numerous events and incidents
in the years immediately following the 2012 election have served to underscore the fact that being in a postrace period does not mean the end of racism.
Instead, it may well refer to a new stage in the continuing historical drama of
American debates on racial justice, racial politics, and what W. E. B. Du Bois
famously termed "the color line."

Fascination with the changing demography and topography of race is
not unknown in literature and literary studies, of course. But its expressions
in the twenty-first century have taken an unusual turn. As an instance of
this fascination with the shifts in American racialization, I wish to offer the
instance of Sesshu Foster's 2005 novel, *Atomik Aztex*.[2] In an introductory
note to an excerpt from *Atomik Aztex* published in the *Amerasia Journal*,
Sesshu Foster had this to say about the novel: "*Atomic Aztex* reconceives
Los Angeles as the Aztec underworld and Land of the Dead, where unquiet spirits victimized by History are presumed to speak. An Aztec warrior
speaks from the other side of life about some other side of History. From a
limbo of genocidal amnesia and official forgetting. Even the dead have their
complaints—especially the dead."[3]

Like many ethnic writers, Sesshu Foster is concerned with history, memory, and their relationship to a better future. This concern arises from the
conviction that in the struggle for social justice, the enemy is so implaca-
bly determined to deny you justice, freedom, and dignity that no one and
nothing is safe from the possibility of complete historical annihilation and
"genocidal amnesia." In "Theses on the Philosophy of History" Walter Benjamin had famously stated as much.[4] For this reason alone, *Atomik Aztex*
fits within the grand tradition of social protest fiction by us ethnic writers.
But at the same time it may also be the wildest example of that mode that
one could imagine, as it takes on, in formal and thematic ways, the issues of
the racial imaginary. Foster's novel, though it may be an odd example, is far
from the only example one could cite.

In addition to Foster, a host of other writers are exploring a post-postmodern, post–civil rights moment in American racial formations. I refer to writers such as the Latinos Yxta Maya Murray, Salvador Plascencia, Junot Díaz, Marta Acosta; the African Americans Percival Everett, Colson Whitehead, Dexter Palmer, and Darieck Scott; the Asian Americans Larissa Lai and Charles Yu; and the Native American Sherman Alexie. A case can also be made for including in this cohort Michael Chabon, Gary Shteyngart, and Jonathan Safran Foer's recalibrations of Jewish and Yiddish ethnicity.[5]

Foster's weird novel is part fantasy; part hallucinatory Global South realism; part muckraking novel; part historical novel; part chronicle in the tradition of the *crónicas de Indias*, the Spanish narratives of the discovery and conquest of the Americas; part history of the Aztec (Nahua, Mexica) pre-Columbian world; part Los Angeles cartoon noir; and wholly science fiction alternative and counterfactual history. For these reasons, *Atomik Aztex* elegantly illustrates the modes of speculative realism and historical fantasy that I have been considering in my current work on speculative realism and historical fantasy in contemporary ethnic fiction.

Features of a New Aesthetic

My hypothesis about these works is that they are not inconsequentially similar. On the contrary, they represent a distinctive turn in the history of contemporary ethnic and general fiction. These novels share at least these four distinctive features.

1. *Speculative realism is a mode in critical dialogue with the aesthetics of postmodernism.* The shared generational history among writers of the post–civil rights era leads to a dialogical relationship between postmodernism and US ethnic literature. Rather than seeing the rise of postmodernism and ethnic literature in the postwar era as two distinct and unrelated phenomena, viewing both within the domain of a shared aesthetic matrix allows us to see how postmodern and ethnic fiction were shaped by the same institutional histories and practices of creativity.[6]

Seeing postmodern and ethnic writers within a dialogic context allows us to raise questions such as: Why have minority writers, with few exceptions, found postmodernism such an inhospitable domain for their representations of contemporary social conditions? Díaz's *The Brief Wondrous Life of Oscar Wao*, Plascencia's *The People of Paper*, and Everett's *Erasure* are exemplary instances of this dialogic, critical relation between contemporary ethnic fiction and postmodern metafiction.

2. *Speculative realism draws on the history of genres and mixes generic*

forms. These authors share a second feature that, like the first one, reflects a historical dimension, but in a different context—namely, that of genre history and the mixing of generic forms. The turn within ethnic narrative that I am describing here parallels a development that occurred at the end of the eighteenth century and the beginning of the nineteenth. In the midst of the revival of romance from the mid-eighteenth century to the early nineteenth, writers like Walter Scott and James Fenimore Cooper invented a new narrative form as a reaction against neoclassical, antiromantic strains of fiction, in favor of the sublime, the imaginary, and gothic strains of magic, enchantment, and wonder.

The mixed generic modes that we see appearing in numerous contemporary narratives mirror this historical phenomenon, but with a curious twist. Now the mixing of genres includes not just the canonic paradigms of classical, neoclassical, romantic, realist, and modernist origin, but also the outcast, low-brow, vernacular, not to say kitschy varieties of what has come to be known as genre fiction, including the fantasy, science fiction, gothic, noir, and erotic speculative writings of the postwar era. And they do so to focus on one theme: the curious status of race at the beginning of the twenty-first century. There are numerous possible instances of this feature of contemporary ethnic fiction. For example, Scott's *Hex* and Chabon's *Yiddish Policemen's Union* mix historical fiction and science fiction alternative history; Alexie's *Flight* and Lai's *Salt Fish Girl* blend myth and fantasy with elements of the traditional bildungsroman; and Acosta hilariously blends feminist bildungsroman with Chicano vampire stories in novels such *as Happy Hour at Casa Dracula.* All of these raise as formal and thematic concerns the very nature of genre, especially as it relates to matters of racial identity. I will return to this issue momentarily, but for now note that this second feature concerns the oxymoronic blending of history and the speculative genres.

3. Speculative realism is invested in the real while working in the mode of historical fantasy. The third feature concerns the topos and form of realism and the real in literary production, literary studies, and philosophy, but in the revised form of what I am calling here speculative realism, a hybrid of the fictional modes of the speculative genres, naturalism, social realism, surrealism, magical realism, "dirty" realism, postpositive realism, and metaphysical realism. That is why I find myself fascinated by the weird realism emerging from the group of contemporary philosophers that includes Alain Badiou, Ray Brassier, Quentin Meillassoux, and Graham Harman.[7] Prominent in the writings of Junot Díaz, speculative realism is a form that is also pervasive in Murray's *The Conquest*, Whitehead's *John Henry Days* and *Zone One*, Yu's *How to Live*

Safely in a Science Fictional Universe, and Shteyngart's *Super Sad True Love Story*.

4. *Speculative realism explores the thematics of race, seeking a new racial imaginary in twenty-first-century America.* Here we enter the fraught territory of the fascination with and anxiety over the term "postrace." How? Why? For this generation of writers, born for the most part in the 1960s and 1970s, the heroic era of the struggle for civil rights is not a personal memory but a matter of social history. At the beginning of the twenty-first century, changing relationships between race and social justice, race and identity, and race and history now require American writers of color to invent a new imaginary for thinking about the nature of a just society and the role of race in its construction. While all of the authors I have referred to emphasize this specific aspect of the aesthetic I am describing, Foster's and Murray's novels, like Díaz's works, Everett's novels (including especially *Erasure*), and Whitehead's works do so with the particular aim of reconfiguring the thematics of race.

I wish to account for these four aspects common to the writings of contemporary ethnic writers and the defining aesthetic that results from a new racial imaginary that is being forged around us. As a generational cohort, these authors share these characteristics, I repeat, not as a merely contingent and random assemblage of features common to a vaguely defined spirit of the age, but as matters that go to the heart of their aesthetic projects and their concern with a new racial imaginary.

Form and Genre in Atomik Aztex

The two central concerns of *Atomik Aztex* are a reconceptualization of the way that race affects the formations of history and the reshaping of the form of the novel in order to represent that reconceptualization.

The formal characteristics of the novel give us the strongest clues as to how to read it. These characteristics include the muckraking tradition and form; *crónicas de Indias* and the history of conquest; the Mesoamerican calendrical narrative form, especially concerning fate and time in Mexican cosmology; the realist historical novel, in its depiction of the Battle of Leningrad and the conquest of Mexico; and science fiction, counterfactual worlds, and alternative and virtual history.

Foster begins by situating his narrative in an alternate universe where Aztecs have conquered the European invaders, launching into the world their own culture of totemic powers and blood sacrifices. In this separate reality the protagonist (Zenzontli, "Keeper of the House of Darkness") has hallucinations, nightmares, and doomsday visions of another horrific world, where things are run apocalyptically by Europeans, and where consumerism reigns supreme—that is, a world that looks and feels a lot like our own. Simultaneously, in a surreal alternative present, Aztecs armed with automatic weapons and ancient totemic powers conquer and colonize 1940s Europe, while ghosts of the twentieth century's world wars emerge from the Farmer John Meatpacking Plant (an actual abattoir in contemporary Los Angeles) to haunt the present.

The first and perhaps most obvious of the forms and traditions that shape *Atomik Aztex* is the muckraking novel. A muckraker investigates and reports on a host of social issues, broadly including crime and corruption and often involving elected officials, political leaders, and influential members of business and industry. The term is associated with a number of important writers who emerged in the 1890s through the 1930s, a period roughly concurrent with the Progressive Era in the United States. These writers focused on issues having to do with social justice broadly and early versions of environmental justice, in particular.

Atomik Aztex follows this pattern closely enough that it's impossible to ignore it as a precursor model in theme (protest fiction) and form (social realism). Moreover, the muckraking focus of the realist segments of Foster's novel draw on scenes from the actual Farmer John Meatpacking Plant located in the town of Vernon, California, a pig slaughterhouse and abattoir that has been in that location since 1931. Probably the most striking visual feature of the actual plant is the huge mural on the external walls of the compound.

The mural depicts idyllic cartoon landscapes of fields, trees, corn crops, barns and other farm buildings, and of course, lots of pigs, big and small, engaged in a variety of activities. Some of the pigs are happy and carefree, lying in the grass, playing in the mud or with each other, piloting airplanes, sleeping in hammocks, and interacting with everyone from a buxom hillbilly girl to a boy who is fishing. This is the "Farmer John pork packing plant . . . with a wraparound porky pig mural you can see when you drive by" that Zenzontli mentions early in the book (AA 44) and again later (AA 169 and 179).

According to Anthony Lovett and Matt Maranian, the abattoir, "located in the exquisitely dismal industrial area of Vernon, . . . is one of the last slaughterhouses in a region that once teemed with factories that turned mammals into meat."[8] *Atomik Aztex* focuses on a different kind of muck to rake. Here the topic is not socialism as a necessary response to unbridled capitalism. Instead, the issue is the way that, even in an alternative history, the grand, soggy compendium of untold stories, erasures, disappearances,

and genocides that constitutes the archive of current events and contemporary daily history constitutes a different kind of reality, requiring a different
realism to capture its bizarre perversity and absurdity.

Crónicas de Indias: History of Conquest of Tenochtitlán

In addition to the muckraking form, another narrative of history drives *Atomik Aztex*—the advent of modernity in the Americas with the conquest of
the Aztec and other pre-Columbian Mesoamerican empires. On a world
historical level, the history of the conquest of Mexico served as a model for
European-native relations for centuries after the fall of Tenochtitlán. The
lesson it taught was that Europeans would triumph over natives, however
formidable the apparent odds, because of cultural superiority that manifested itself visibly in equipment but resided much more powerfully in mental and moral qualities.[9]

As counterpoint to the Spanish version of the result of warfare between
Indians and Europeans in America in the early sixteenth century, *Atomik
Aztex* offers a different representation of the rules of war as experienced on
the Russian front in the winter of 1942.[10]

Calendrical Narrative: Fate, Time in Mexican Cosmology

More importantly, the Aztec scenes and the entire temporal structure of the
novel depict Mexican Indian notions of fate and time.[11] Other novels, most
notably, Leslie Marmon Silko's *Almanac of the Dead* and Karen Tei Yamashita's *Tropic of Orange*, have conceptualized preconquest Mesoamerican time
as multidimensional and eternally recurrent.[12] Here Foster uses indigenous
Mesoamerican calendrical systems of temporality to show how time, and
history, could work otherwise.

Think of a calendar that keeps track only of every Christmas or Thanks-
giving Day or some other holiday, clustering them together as a separate unit
of reckoning. Contrast this marking of time passing to one that keeps track
of the flow of time between these exceptional moments by emphasizing only
the sequential flow of days, weeks, and months. Now combine these two
circular and linear trajectories. Within this doubled calendric count, any
one day is thus essentially linked to at least two sign systems: the sequential
days of a year cycle and the recurring cycle of ritual days, both of which
contained within a repeating fifty-two year pattern.

The important part of this for my discussion of Foster's novel is that any
particular event can be understood as unfolding in a dynamic process modeled by some past situation.[13] The essential character of the controlling time
is manifested in subtle ways, largely masked from human eyes. In human
experience, outcomes remained contingent until manifested.[14]

This is the temporal pattern that Foster is alluding to in this novel when Zenzontli cautions his fellow warriors that "what's happening here should be news to no one. Probably you've all gone thru similar experiences in multiple past lives" (AA 101). The historical doubling in Zenzontli's narrative comes with the additional complication that the temporality of his life unfolds in at least two geospatial worlds: an alternate one in which Chicanos or Aztecs have colonized Europe, and the familiar one of contemporary late capitalism and "stupefying consumerism" (AA 89), which dulls time into a sequence of linear causality.

The Battle of Stalingrad and the Conquest of Mexico

As if this wasn't confusing enough, there is yet one more narrative model to contend with in *Atomik Aztex*. In addition to the muckracking novel and the multiply compounded narrative based on Mesoamerican chronology, there is also the narrative model of the battle memoir and realist historical novel. *Atomik Aztex* uses the form of the great Russian novels about the Battle of Stalingrad—in particular, Vasily Grossman's superb novel, the Russian masterpiece you have probably never heard of, *Life and Fate*.[15] Itself a retelling in twentieth-century form of Tolstoy's nineteenth-century masterpiece *War and Peace*, Grossman's novel, surprisingly little known in this country, is typical of this war novel genre. Both Grossman and Foster follow the stories of a large cast of characters at the time of the Battle of Stalingrad, between July 1942 and February 1943. *Atomik Aztex* is an exact parallel of Grossman's novel, in particular in its narration of the massive bloodletting on both sides in the attacks and counterattacks at the "Red Oktober Traktor Factory" (detailed in AA 90–103). The long desperate siege on the banks of the Volga River provides the backdrop against which Foster's allegorical Chicano, Latino, or Aztec characters try to discern meaning in their lives.

Science Fiction, Counterfactual Worlds, and Alternative and Virtual Histories

There is one last model of narrative form: science fiction itself, particularly in the mode of counterfactual worlds and alternative and virtual histories. While science fiction typically deals with a future waiting to happen just beyond this or that shift in history, after an imagined cataclysm or impending world-destroying apocalypse unleashes another universe waiting to be born, alternative histories—or "allohistory"[16]—take us in other directions.[17] *Atomik Aztex* works within this mode of allohistory: "Rather than a tightly bound cause-and-effect process linking a given present (all aspects of which supposedly constitute a single *total* world) with a single future world, history [now] becomes a variety of paths that disperse into disjunct alternatives."[18] With these alternative realities come alternative values.

Reading Atomik Aztex: *The Applied Aztek Sciences of the Human Heart*

So, given all this, what makes *Atomik Aztex* not simply postmodern meta-fiction?[19] If a case can be made for *Atomik Aztex* being distinctive, it must be related to the nature of the racial discourses of the novel and the ways that those discourses are represented: through an urban metro-Spanglish, negropolitan, Chicano *caló*, spoken by all of the characters—that is, in the modified form of what we might call multicultural science fiction specula-tive realism. This discursive feature suggests the disturbance of ethno- and racial centrism that is one feature of the fiction I am highlighting here. It rep-resents the attempted achievement of a perspective from which one's own racial or ethnic culture is only one of a number of possible positions, no one of which acquires unproblematic ascendancy or transcendence. In fact, *Atomik Aztek* represents this failed transcendence in how it mocks, paro-dies, criticizes, and denaturalizes the cultural norms of both mainstream postmodern metafiction and ethnic fiction having to do with the dystopian mid-twentieth century and the *fin de siécle*.

The double-edged effect of this feature of Foster's novel is to render the exotic—a contemporary world ruled by Aztec social, political, and aesthetic ideologies—as a means of undermining the self-assurance of the superiority of any possible subaltern utopias. In the end, the difference between the im-perium of European coloniality and conquest, the racism of national social-ism, the ruthless tyranny of Stalinism, the unchecked predation of modern mass consumer capitalism, and the pre-Columbian "applied Aztek Sciences of the Human Heart" (AA 5) remain undifferentiated.

Given this concern with allohistories and different futures, it is not sur-prising that in considering the relationships between history, memory, and the future, Benjamin can serve as a final touchstone. In "Theses on the Phi-losophy of History," he points to just the conjuncture of past, present, and future of which Foster writes by referring to a 1920 painting by Paul Klee:

A Klee painting named "Angelus Novus" shows an angel looking as though he is about to move away from something he is fixedly contemplating. His eyes are staring, his mouth is open, his wings are spread. This is how one pictures the angel of history. His face is turned toward the past. Where we perceive a chain of events, he sees one single catastrophe which keeps piling wreckage and hurls it in front of his feet. The angel would like to stay, awaken the dead, and make whole what has been smashed. But a storm is blowing in from Paradise; it has got caught in his wings with such a violence that the angel can no longer close them. The storm irresistibly propels him into the future to which his back is turned, while the pile of debris before him grows skyward. This storm is what we call progress.[20]

In *Atomik Aztex*, angels of history are figured by the "novus" and the "novum," the awakening of the dead by the catastrophes of history and "progress." These "unquiet spirits" speak from "the other side of life about the some other side of History." They utter their complaints from the depths of what Foster refers to as "a limbo of genocidal amnesia and official forgetting." From each of these perspectives, history is what still lies before us, to be salvaged from the catastrophe of progress.[21]

This attention to the narrative possibilities of realism as a concern of ethnic fiction in the late twentieth and early twenty-first centuries, in my opinion, amounts to a radical revaluation of the trajectory of the development of narrative form. In returning to the real in its heterogeneous forms, ethnic realism acquires a different quality than the one literary history has assigned it over the past forty years. Instead of a timeline that takes us from naïve realism to plodding social realism, triumphant modernism, and demystified parodic postmodernism, something else results: when placed within a horizon that includes naturalism, realism, social realism, surrealism, magical realism, post-positive realism, and perhaps speculative realism, realism emerges as the substratum of narrative that has never been entirely superseded in the history of narrative forms. The aesthetic and political implications of this revision of literary history are immense and yet to be fully explored.

Notes

1. Dorian Warren, "Boxing Out: Race, Walmart, and the Politics of Market Regulation from Below," talk at the Research Institute of the Center for Comparative Studies in Race and Ethnicity, Stanford University, November 8, 2012. See also "Changing Face of America Helps Assure Obama Victory," Pew Research Center, November 7, 2012, people-press.org/2012/11/07/changing-face-of-america-helps-assure-Obama-victory, accessed April 29, 2015.

2. Sesshu Foster, *Atomik Aztex* (San Francisco: City Lights, 2005). Quotes in the text from this work will be cited as "AA."

3. Sesshu Foster, "Prefatory Note to *Atomik Aztex*," *Amerasia Journal* 27, no. 2 (2001): 1.

4. Walter Benjamin, "Theses on the Philosophy of History," in *Illuminations: Essays and Reflections*, ed. Hannah Arendt, trans. Henry Zohn (New York: Schocken, 1968), 253–64.

5. See Yxta Maya Murray, *The Conquest: A Novel* (New York: Rayo, 2002); Salvador Plascencia, *The People of Paper* (San Francisco: McSweeney's, 2005); Junot Díaz, *The Brief Wondrous Life of Oscar Wao* (New York: Riverhead, 2007); Marta Acosta, *Happy Hour at Casa Dracula* (New York: Pocket Star, 2006); Percival L. Everett, *Erasure: A Novel* (Hanover, NH: University Press of New England, 2001); Colson Whitehead, *The*

Intuitionist (New York: Anchor, 1999), *John Henry Days: A Novel* (New York: Doubleday, 2001), and *Zone One* (New York: Doubleday, 2011); Dexter Palmer, *The Dream of Perpetual Motion: A Novel* (New York: St. Martin's, 2010); Darieck Scott, *Hex: A Novel of Love Spells* (New York: Carroll and Graf, 2007); Larissa Lai, *Salt Fish Girl* (Toronto: Thomas Allen, 2002); Charles Yu, *How to Live Safely in a Science Fictional Universe* (New York: Pantheon, 2010); Sherman Alexie, *Flight: A Novel* (New York: Black Cat, 2007); Michael Chabon, *Yiddish Policemen's Union* (New York: Harper, 2007; Gary Shteyngart, *Super Sad True Love Story* (New York: Random House, 2011); Jonathan Safran Foer, *Extremely Loud and Incredibly Close* (Boston: Houghton Mifflin, 2005).

6. In his characterization of the post-1945 era of fiction writing in the United States as one shaped in significant ways by the rise of creative writing programs, Mark McGurl argues for a necessary critical realignment of the relationship between postmodern fiction and the so-called ethnic, minority American fiction. See Mark McGurl, *The Program Era: Postwar Fiction and the Rise of Creative Writing* (Cambridge, MA: Harvard University Press, 2009).

7. See Ray Brassier, Iain Hamilton Grant, Graham Harman, Quentin Meillassoux, "Speculative Realism: A One-day Workshop," *Collapse* 3 (November 2007): 307–449.

8. Anthony Lovett and Matt Maranian, *L.A. Bizarro: The All-New Insider's Guide to the Obscure, the Absurd, and the Perverse in Los Angeles*, 2nd ed. (San Francisco: Chronicle, 2009, 282). "Appreciating the Art at Farmer John's Slaughterhouse" http://labizarro .com/2010/08/23/farmer-johns/.

9. Inga Clendinnen, "'Fierce and Unnatural Cruelty': Cortés and the Conquest of Mexico," *Representations* 3 (winter 1991): 65.

10. Ibid., 78.

11. Ibid., 84.

12. Leslie Marmon Silko, *The Almanac of the Dead* (New York: Simon and Schuster, 1991); Karen Tei Yamashita, *Tropic of Orange* (Minneapolis, MN: Coffee House, 1997).

13. Clendinnen, "'Fierce and Unnatural Cruelty,'" 85.

14. Ibid.

15. Vasily Grossman, *Life and Fate: A Novel*, trans. Robert Chandler. (New York: Harper and Row, 1985).

16. Istvan Csicsery-Ronay, *The Seven Beauties of Science Fiction* (Middletown, CT: Wesleyan University Press, 2008), 102.

17. Ibid., 77–78.

18. Ibid., 94.

19. *Atomik Aztex* falls within the tradition of novels that retell the history of the conquest of Mexico, but with a difference. See Orson Scott Card, *Pastwatch: The Redemption of Christopher Columbus* (New York: TOR, 1996); Murray, *The Conquest*; Christopher Evans, *Aztec Century* (London: Victor Gollancz, 1993).

20. Benjamin, "Theses on the Philosophy of History," 257–58.

21. Foster, "Prefatory Note to *Atomik Aztex*," 1.

[IIII]

REMAPPING THE TRANSPACIFIC TURN: FROM THE BLACK PACIFIC AND OCEANIC ECOPOETICS TO ANTIPODEAN TRANSNATIONALISMS

7

THE MANCHURIAN PHILOSOPHER:
W. E. B. DU BOIS IN THE EURASIAN PACIFIC

The vast struggle in the Pacific which broke out at Pearl Harbor on December 7, 1941, was merely the logical result of the events which began in Manchuria. The road to World War II is now clearly visible; it has run its terrible course from the railway tracks near Mukden to the operations of two bombers over Hiroshima and Nagasaki.
—Henry L. Stimson, *On Active Service in Peace and War*

THERE IS PERHAPS NO greater cinematic representation of the Cold War symbolism of Manchuria than *The Manchurian Candidate* (1962), a political science fiction film based on the 1959 best-selling novel of the same name by Richard Condon and starring Frank Sinatra. What this Cold War film represents, among other things, is the "terror" of Chinese communist brainwashing, for which Manchuria, a historical name given to a geographic region in Northeast Asia, stands as a potent metaphor. The film depicts how the Soviets and the Chinese Communists brainwashed American POWs during the Korean War (1950–1953), and in particular how they turned Staff Sergeant Raymond Shaw (Laurence Harvey) into a sleeper agent, or an amnesiac assassin. The brainwashing takes place in a research pavilion decorated with portraits of Joseph Stalin and Mao Tse-tung, in Manchuria, where the captured POWs are flown by helicopter. Following his conditioning in Manchuria, Shaw's chief mission in the United States is to assassinate the presidential nominee at the Republican National Convention, so that Senator John Iselin (Shaw's stepfather) is installed as US president. The red-baiting Senator Iselin, a stand-in for Senator Joseph McCarthy, is in fact a puppet—the Manchurian candidate—whose strings are pulled by his wife (Shaw's mother), who is a communist agent. In the final climactic sequence of the film, Captain Bennett Marco (Frank Sinatra), a brainwashed ex–Korean War POW himself, understands the whole story of the international communist conspiracy: that "the Soviet Union and the People's Republic of China conspired with purported American anti-Communists, who linked themselves with fascist tendencies in American life, in order to destroy the American republic."[1]

Manchuria served as the linchpin of modern regionalism in East Asia. In the 1950s, the region gained a new geopolitical valence associated with the neologisms "the Manchurian candidate" and "brainwashing" of the popular Cold War lexicon in the United States. At the end of World War II, the regional order of the Japanese Empire had collapsed. Manchukuo,[2] the Japanese puppet state of Manchuria, was invaded by the Soviet Union—which declared war on Japan on August 8, 1945, two days after the atomic bomb was dropped on Hiroshima. Manchuria subsequently became a site of the civil war fought between the Chinese Communist Party (CCP), led by Mao, and the Kuomintang (KMT), the governing party of the Republic of China under Chiang Kai-shek. As historian Victor Shiu Chiang Cheng observes, Mao imagined China's "Madrid" in Manchuria. "With its political, strategic, economic, and geographical importance," Manchuria, though covered by the Sino-Soviet Treaty of August 1945 and hence in the hands of the KMT, was what Mao coveted for the Communists' expansion. In April 1946, Mao's army seized Hsinking (Changchun), the old capital of Manchukuo. This military conquest "symbolized the Communists' control of Manchuria." "The civil war in Manchuria," Cheng remarks, "foreshadowed the open general war in China over the next three years," which would end with Mao's proclaiming the establishment of the People's Republic of China in mainland China in October 1949.[3]

We now know—thanks to Bernardo Bertolucci's epic film *The Last Emperor* (1987)—that somehow the symbolic apogee of the dissolution of Manchukuo was a successful effort by the Chinese Communists to reeducate Pu Yi, the last emperor of the Ch'ing (Manchu) Dynasty and puppet emperor of Manchukuo. The opening set of the film is a train station on the Chinese-Russian border in Manchuria. The scene depicts the repatriation of a trainload of "war criminals," including the middle-aged and worn Pu Yi (John Lone), from the Soviet Union. Pu Yi, who had been captured by the invading Soviet troops at the end of World War II, is now handed over to the recently proclaimed People's Republic of China in 1950. The train brings Pu Yi home to Manchuria, which he now has to learn to call the "Northeast" (Northeast China), and to the detention center of the Fushun Bureau of Public Security, otherwise a reeducation camp. After undergoing ten years of rehabilitation as "Prisoner 981," the ex-emperor is released as a reformed citizen of Mao's China. As the prison governor (Ying Ruocheng) declares, "As a result of remolding through labor and ideological education during his captivity, he has shown that he has genuinely reformed." The final scene of the movie shows China during the Cultural Revolution in 1967. In the penultimate episode that appears exterior to Pu Yi's autobiography *From Emperor to Citizen* (1964–1965), the main source of Bertolucci's screenplay, Pu Yi comes unexpectedly upon a parade of Red Guards brandishing pictures of Mao and waving little red books. They herd before them a group of "traitors," among whom is his former prison governor made to wear a dunce cap and a chest placard reading "counter-revolutionary." Pu Yi witnesses the humiliation of the governor, his former "teacher," at the hands of the fanatical Red Guards and his being forced to "kowtow to Chairman Mao"—a command that renders Mao Communist China's emperor. *The Last Emperor* ends with scenes of a horde of modern American tourists in China in the 1980s. The tour guide, with her Klaxon emitting the notes of Yankee Doodle, leads the tourists into the Hall of Supreme Harmony, the ancient imperial throne of the Ch'ing Dynasty, where Pu Yi was crowned at age three, and announces that he died in 1967. The film thus leaves the viewer with a question that historian John K. Fairbank astutely frames: wasn't Pu Yi, the mortal representative of the puppet state Manchukuo, in the end "the world's champion puppet—first under the Ch'ing court, then under the Japanese militarists, [and] finally under the Chinese Communists"?[4]

I begin with this brief discussion of post–World War II paradigmatic cinematic representations of Manchuria because they point in the direction of a series of interrelated issues that I want to discuss in relation to W. E. B. Du Bois, the preeminent African American scholar-intellectual who is generally thought to have become a dedicated Stalinist and Maoist in the 1950s. These include the hitherto ignored experiences and responses of Du Bois to Manchukuo, the unsubstantiated rumors in the US Congress that Du Bois was a (puppet) propagandist for the Japanese imperial government, and the ambivalence at the heart of Du Bois's symbiotic sympathies both for Soviet Russia and socialism and for the Japanese Empire in pre–World War II Asia.[5] While Du Bois is known to have become a devoted admirer of Communist China in the 1950s, in the 1930s, as Gerald Horne has observed, "Du Bois, a socialist of sorts and a friend of Soviet Russia, sought to reconcile [China] with Japan as this unlikely prospect steadily slipped away in reality."[6]

Du Bois's problem indicated by Horne is succinctly described by Bill Mullen in what he considers to be the problem of "Afro-Orientalism," which Mullen defines as both emerging from and revising "Marxian analytical contributions on colonialism and imperialism." Asia played a complex role in the grand arc of Du Bois's internationalism after Japan's defeat of Tsarist Russia in 1905, and Du Bois continued to champion the ascent of Japan to power and to colonialism and imperialism. In Mullen's view, Du Bois's seemingly radical failure to oppose the Japanese Empire was partly due to the influence of the complex of events of the 1930s and was partly "fostered by selective support for Japanese nationalists in the United States," among whom was Yasuichi Hikida, "an agent of Japanese expansionism." The evolution of the political and cultural thought of Du Bois and Afro-Orientalism, however, did not end there. Indeed, argues Mullen, "it was later reflection and rumination on his Japanese 'mistake' that moved Du Bois ultimately and decidedly in the firm direction of a materialist analysis of imperialism, race, and capitalism."[7] Du Bois's encounter with the Japanese Empire thus moved him in the counter-direction of support for Mao's China, the right political objective that Du Bois attained in the end.

Compelling though Mullen's teleological narrative of interpretation is, I would like to rethink this Asian arc of Du Bois's internationalism over time by teasing out, not so much a discontinuity (and counter-direction) that is obvious, as a continuity that is more subtle but also critically important. The difficulty of seeing the mutual implications of his support both for the Japanese Empire and for Mao's China and the Soviet Union perhaps means that many of us who work on Du Bois and Asia tend to remain caught in a prevalent (that is, post–World War II) geopolitical map of East Asia—a framework in which Manchukuo (1932–1945), once a regional linchpin and a source of international conflict, is conspicuously absent, erased as it is into the People's Republic of China (1949–). Based on Du Bois's actual travel narrative that tells a story of the now-defunct Empire of Manchukuo, this essay proposes to examine a black Eurasian Pacific geography that Du Bois charted.[8]

At the center of this essay is an analysis of Du Bois's largely neglected 1936 Eurasian continental rail tour that took him from Nazi Germany via Soviet Russia to China. Du Bois landed in Manchuria as the first African American reporter to cover Manchukuo—a new colored nation on the Pacific Rim that had appeared in atlases only four years prior, with demarcated territory bordering the Soviet Union, the Republic of China, and Korea under Japanese colonial rule. My primary texts in this essay are a chapter entitled "I Gird the Globe" from Du Bois's unpublished, book-length manuscript "Russia and America," and dispatches that he sent to the *Pittsburgh Courier* from Manchuria. As with *The Last Emperor*, Du Bois's point of entry into Manchuria is a train station on the Chinese-Russian border (then the Manchukuo-Soviet border). In 1934, writing in his signature editorial "As the Crow Flies" in *Crisis*, the official organ of the National Association for the Advancement of Colored People (NAACP), Du Bois had offered his congratulations to Pu Yi on his assuming the imperial title of the Emperor Kang Teh of Manchukuo. In Du Bois's view, the coronation marked an important step toward the union of the Empire of Japan and the Empire of Manchuria, heralding a regionally integrated Asia. Du Bois writes, "Watch, colored America, with beating heart, the first fateful step toward a new united Asia. When the Emperor, Kang Teh, mounts the imperial throne and joins Japan and Manchuria in one white world–defying state."[9] However, in Du Bois's 1936 travel narrative, neither Pu Yi nor the Japanese militarists are central characters of Manchukuo. Instead, Yosuke Matsuoka, Japanese diplomat and president of the South Manchuria Railway (SMR) Company, emerges as the architect of Manchukuo. Against the backdrop of the dominant understanding of Manchukuo as a state created by Japanese militarists with Pu Yi as their puppet, Du Bois offers an alternative Manchurian narrative. My intention in the present essay is to tap the critical potential of this Manchurian narrative that tells about the geopolitical awareness Du Bois gained when he thought he was witnessing the actualization of a new model of government for colored peoples.

Du Bois and Japanese Imperial Propaganda

Important recent theoretical work posits the centrality of Asia to Du Bois's internationalism.[10] However, a major problem surfaces when scholars consider the implications of the African American intellectual's apology for the Japanese imperium that expanded by military dominance in East Asia. As biographer David Levering Lewis has shown, Du Bois issued unnervingly pro-Japanese messages in his newspaper columns and lectures at black colleges in the 1930s.[11] As discussed below, in 1939 Du Bois's actions gave rise to rumors in the US Congress that he was a paid propagandist for the Japanese imperial government. Further, it led to his investigation by the Federal Bureau of Investigation (FBI), which opened a file on Du Bois in 1942. The FBI found no evidence that Du Bois engaged in subversive activities. Nonetheless, it placed Du Bois on a list of persons to be held in "Custodial Detention" in the event of a national emergency.[12] One document included in the file quoted Du Bois as having allegedly claimed that "in the Japanese he saw the liberation of the negroes in America, and that when the time came for them to take over the United States, they would find they would have help from the negroes in the United States"[13] when he made a speech during his stay in Japan in 1936.

There is a growing consensus among scholars of Du Bois that his defense of the Japanese Empire in the 1930s is not just an embarrassing anomaly but also a complex result of multiple factors of influence. One notorious example is Japanese propaganda operations that targeted the preeminent black intellectual. In his prize-winning biography of Du Bois, Lewis pointed out that Du Bois's circle of acquaintances included Yasuichi Hikida, an alleged Japanese agent. In Lewis's account, Hikida began his approach by making the acquaintance of Arthur Schomburg, a Harlem bibliophile, whose sponsorship enabled Hikida to infiltrate "the inner circles of the Talented Tenth" of black America. This group included, in addition to Du Bois, James Weldon Johnson, George S. Schuyler, Walter White, Claude McKay, Dorothy West, William Pickens, Rayford Logan, Claude Barnett, and Percival L. Prattis. Du Bois, according to Lewis, was "the outspoken representative of a group mind-set ideally made for Hikida's purposes" to sway black public opinion. Having established himself in this circle, Hikida drew sufficiently close to Du Bois to facilitate the Asian leg of Du Bois's tour in 1936, which included five months in Germany sponsored by the Oberlaender Trust and a journey across the Soviet Union to visit China and Japan. Hikida arranged Du Bois's stay in Japan as a quasi-state guest.[14]

Lewis's suggestion that Du Bois's trip to Japan was partly a product of Japanese "negro propaganda operations" would certainly explain why Du Bois's trip unfolded so differently from the journey that Langston Hughes undertook three years previously. The poet, arriving in Japan from Moscow in 1933, quickly fell under suspicion of being a communist "international courier" and was expelled from Japan by the Tokyo police.[15] In contrast, the Japanese authorities treated Du Bois as an honored guest. Upon entering Japan, he found that special arrangements had been made for his lecture tour around the country. However, I would like to question this suggested relationship between Du Bois and Japan's "negro propaganda operations."

A file in Japan's national archive reveals that a detailed plan for Du Bois's stay was well in order prior to his arrival. The plan includes both official and nongovernmentally sponsored activities.

December 11 (Friday)
Morning: Arrival at Tokyo station
A.M.: A ceremonial call at the grounds of the Imperial Palace and Meiji Shrine
Noon: Luncheon at the Pan-Pacific Club
P.M.: Visits to newspaper offices
Evening: A reception hosted by the Information Department, Ministry of Foreign Affairs
December 12 (Saturday)
A.M.: A visit to the Tokyo Imperial Household Museum
P.M.: A visit to the Kabuki Theater upon the invitation of the Kokusai Bunka Shinkokai (KBS)
December 13 (Sunday)
A sightseeing tour to Nikko (KBS)
December 14 (Monday)
A day trip to Kamakura and Yokosuka (KBS)
December 15 (Tuesday)
A.M.: A visit to Tokyo Imperial University

P.M.: A visit to Waseda University
A banquet hosted by the Nippon P.E.N. Club
December 16 (Wednesday)
A.M.: Visits to department stores
P.M.: Lecture at Senshu University
A banquet hosted by KBS
December 17 (Thursday)
Embark from Yokohama[16]

Among the government-sponsored activities in which Du Bois participated (not reflected on this itinerary) was a geisha party for the visiting
intellectual hosted by a foreign ministry official.[17] The Ministry of the Navy,
moreover, extended to Du Bois the privilege of conducting a tour of "inspection" of Japan's Combined Fleet at Yokosuka. The fleet at the time included
the *Nagato*, the first battleship in the world mounted with sixteen-inch guns
and the most powerful warship in the world at the time of its commissioning
in 1920, as well as her sister ship *Mutsu*.[18] Both the *Nagato* and the *Mutsu*
had undergone renovation and updating in the year of Du Bois's visit. In
1941, the *Nagato* began the Pacific War as the flagship of the Combined
Fleet. The order to attack Pearl Harbor was issued from its decks.[19]

Among the nongovernmental organizations—cultural and educational
institutions—that hosted Du Bois, the Kokusai Bunka Shinkokai (KBS; Society for International Cultural Relations) honored the black intellectual
with a party at the Kabuki Theater, as well as a banquet presided over by "a
Count who was educated at Amherst with [Calvin] Coolidge and [Dwight]
Morrow," as Du Bois reports in a dispatch to the *Pittsburgh Courier* from
Japan. KBS also arranged sightseeing tours for Du Bois to Nikko, Kamakura, and Yokosuka. The Pan-Pacific Club had invited Du Bois to attend
its monthly luncheon (as it did Hughes), and the Nippon P.E.N. Club invited
Du Bois along with two Chinese writers to its monthly dinner party. Du Bois
presented lectures at a number of universities, including Tokyo Imperial
University, "the largest and most noted in Japan," where he lunched with
the president and "inspected" the library, in the collections of which he
"found some of [his] own books."[20]

However, there is reason to doubt that he was indeed the target of Japanese "negro propaganda operations," as scholars suggest, despite the obvious privileges and courtesies accorded to Du Bois. Hikida was a clerk in
the Japanese consulate in New York from 1938 to 1941 and was an em-
ployee of Japan's Foreign Office in Tokyo after 1942, during which he drafted
a proposal entitled "Wartime Negro Propaganda Operations" in January 1943.
However, no official or unofficial program that could be termed "negro prop-

aganda" targeting black Americans in general or Du Bois in particular has been shown to exist at the time of Du Bois's peacetime visit to Japan in 1936. An attempt to account for Du Bois's seeming embrace of the expanding Japanese imperium in East Asia should therefore not begin with the unsupported premise of such an influence. Let us rather begin by asking how, even in the absence of "negro propaganda operations," Japan seems to have shaped Du Bois's perceptions to elicit a response from the thinker that so deeply supported its cause.

The answer to this question lies not in Japan's interest in the ostensibly central fact of Du Bois's identity as black but rather in his status as an influential visitor from the West. It is for this reason that Du Bois's primary host in Japan was KBS.[21] Founded in 1934 under the auspices of the Foreign Ministry to coordinate Japan's cultural diplomacy, KBS was charged with making systematic use of the "soft power" of culture and values to influence foreign public opinion. Under H.I.H. Prince Takamatsu (a brother of Emperor Hirohito) as its honorary president and Prince Fumimaro Konoye (and future prime minister of Japan) as its president, KBS counted among its advisers Japan's prime minister, minister of the imperial household, minister of foreign affairs, and minister of education, as well as "more than 130 representatives of the people" from the political, economic, social, and scholarly world who served on its body of councilors.[22] Thus, coordinated by both state and nonstate actors, KBS directed Japan's cultural diplomacy at influential statesmen, businessmen, scholars, thinkers, novelists, artists, and, in particular, journalists from the West. The efforts of KBS to "enlighten" foreigners on Japanese civilization, and courtesies that it extended to them, such as free train passes, were intended to influence these people of influence to spread favorable views of Japan via lectures, radio, or books in their home countries.[23] Du Bois received a complimentary first-class train pass in Japan and was taken to see expressions and demonstrations of both Japan's ancient traditions and its modern technological achievements. These included Kabuki performances; the Shinto shrines, temples, and Buddhas; and warships. These courtesies were a measure of his status as a press representative of the *Pittsburgh Courier* and a professor at Atlanta University. Notably, many of the institutions that hosted Du Bois's tour in Japan were headed by KBS councilors.[24]

Beyond the self-described objective of KBS to "introduce and encourage interest in, and study and knowledge of, Japanese culture based upon the ideal of furthering worldwide exchange of cultural relations in the cause of international peace and better understanding,"[25] Japan's exercise of soft power was imperative in the context of the diplomatic crisis that Japan faced in the early 1930s. The military occupation of Manchuria, known as the Manchurian Incident, marked a new phase of Japanese imperialism in its continental thrust. It led Japan into direct conflict with the US Open Door policy in China, affirmed as international law in the Washington Naval Conference of 1921–1922. Subsequently, Japan withdrew from the League of Nations (in which Japan had been a charter member and one of four permanent league council members) in 1933. Japan needed new channels to influence international public opinion. KBS, founded as such a channel in 1934, was thus linked ideologically to Japan's continental advance in Manchuria. The ultimate aim of the agency, to borrow the words of historian Tomoko Akami, was "to show that Japan was a civilized and sophisticated country, and was capable of 'guiding' its puppet state" of Manchukuo.[26]

In this regard, it is noteworthy that the successive presidents of the SMR Company served on the board of councilors for KBS, and that Yosuke Matsuoka, Japan's chief delegate to the League of Nations who pulled the nation out of the league, was installed in 1935 as president of SMR and as a KBS councilor. SMR was far more than Japan's railway company in Manchuria. Founded in 1906, the company was a giant conglomerate that propelled the development of southern Manchuria, crown jewel of the Japanese Empire. In addition to running freight and passenger services, SMR owned coal mines and wharves and controlled diverse subsidiary corporations in Manchuria. In the railway zone under its control, SMR acted as an alternative administration to the local Chinese government, providing health care, education, and employment to Chinese as well as Japanese. It also managed schools, hospitals, libraries, museums, and a large research institute. With a president—who was Matsuoka at the time of Du Bois's visit—appointed by the Japanese government, SMR was, moreover, a quasi-state organ whose activities in Manchuria were directed "in accordance with foreign policy and national security aims."[27] After the provocation of the Manchurian Incident and the subsequent Japanese establishment of the puppet regime of Manchukuo, SMR served as the brains trust for Manchukuoan development, while also assuming management of Manchukuo's state railways.

In this light, the active role of SMR—rather than of Hikida—in the Asian leg of Du Bois's world tour emerges to demand our careful attention. As disclosed in a letter from Du Bois to Chih Meng of the China Institute in the United States, the African American intellectual had originally planned to travel from Europe across the Soviet Union "by way of the Trans-Siberian Railroad" and to proceed directly to Peiping (Peking), China, via Mukden in Manchukuo.[28] Meng, associate director of the China Institute in New York, and spokesperson for the Republic of China, had denounced Japan's establishment of Manchukuo in his book *China Speaks*, asserting that "the Chinese people have been colonizing Manchuria peacefully for centuries" and that "the Manchus in Manchuria today are somewhat in the position of Indians in the United States, except that the Manchus have been entirely assimilated into Chinese culture."[29] At the suggestion of the Japanese personnel of the SMR Company,[30] however, Du Bois altered his itinerary, adding a weeklong tour to "inspect" the new state of Manchukuo. SMR employees arranged a package tour of sorts for Du Bois along SMR's Manchurian rail lines, with accommodation provided by the Yamato Hotel chain that the company operated. SMR thus functioned in the role of unofficial publicity agent promoting Manchukuo through tourism and exercised soft power to influence international public opinion. This tour, as I shall discuss further, was a defining experience for Du Bois. It shaped his perceptions and understanding of Manchuria, becoming what we might call a black Manchurian narrative.

A Week in Manchuria

In his unpublished "Russia and America," Du Bois included a chapter entitled "I Gird the Globe" in which he relates his experiences during his Eurasian continental trip in 1936. Du Bois traveled the international trunk lines, riding the rails to national borders and traversing these borders to follow the steel rails onward. The lines he followed traced the divergent paths of the major socioeconomic systems on the continent—those of Nazi Germany, the Soviet Union, and Manchukuo. International railway links provided a connection between these divergent paths for the traveler. Through his grand tour, Du Bois came to imagine Manchuria radically as a testing ground for "some form of socialism."[31]

The new colored state of Manchukuo on the Pacific Rim, with territory bordering the Soviet Union, first appeared in atlases in 1932. Its presence redrew diplomatic relations across the Eurasian continent—a development that would have interested Du Bois, the international tourist, in 1936. While in Berlin, Du Bois was able to obtain a visa to Manchukuo through a "Manchukuo trade mission office" that had been established there as a result of a "Germany-Manchukuo trade agreement" concluded in the spring of that year.[32] This agreement, a trilateral arrangement between Germany and the economic bloc of Japan and Manchukuo (the yen bloc), amounted to Germany's "de facto recognition of Manchukuo" and set the stage for the Anti-Comintern Pact that Germany and Japan would conclude on November 25, 1936,[33] only days following the end of Du Bois's tour of Manchukuo. The Soviet government, meanwhile, denied Du Bois a visa to make extended stops in Soviet Russia. Du Bois recalls in his travel manuscript "I Gird the Globe" that Moscow "was not welcoming visitors, especially from the United States and en route to Japan." However, he was granted permission for "passage through to Manchuria," which he undertook on a ten-day-long ride on the Trans-Siberian Railway from Moscow to Manchouli, the station on the frontier of Manchuria (RA, 102–3).

The principal effect of the establishment of Manchukuo on international relations was to alter the balance of power in the Far East, sharply straining Japanese-Soviet relations in particular. In response to the strategic threat of Japan bringing northern Manchuria—formerly a buffer zone—under its armed control, the Soviet Union had concentrated its energies on strengthening its military forces. These were deployed along both the Manchukuo-Soviet border and the border between Manchukuo and the Mongolian People's Republic, a satellite state that the Soviet Union had established in Outer Mongolia in 1924. In his travel manuscript, Du Bois recalls the prolific military activity—"soldiers, arms, factories, all for war preparation"—that he witnessed as his train passed through Siberia and approached Manchuria. He reports feeling "the earth beneath [his] feet smoldering and quaking with the flames of coming war." However, the thinker "could not believe it" and "would not," perhaps because, in 1936, "next to Russia, Japan intrigued [him] as holding the destiny of the darker [workers in] its hands." For Du Bois, Soviet Russia was "a state seeking to replace private profit with public welfare" and the Japanese were "leaders of the world fight against white imperialism" (RA, 126–27). Du Bois's sympathies thus were divided between two states whose spheres of influence were encroaching on one another, creating an explosive situation on the continent.

Du Bois's travel manuscript records a tension-ridden border between the Soviet Union and Manchukuo at Manchouli, which he reached on November 12. When his train stopped at the "fatal border," Du Bois and his fellow travelers from Europe had to change to a different train on the Manchukuoan side, passing through both Russian and Manchukuoan customs inspections en route (RA, 128). In 1936, Manchouli was no longer the quiet frontier station on the Chinese Eastern Railway connecting Russia with China that it had been. After the establishment of the puppet state, border clashes had taken place. Consequently, the Soviet government decided to sell its interests in the Chinese Eastern to Manchukuo.[34] The sale of these railway interests in March 1935 represented Stalin's de facto recognition of Manchukuo. On the Manchukuoan side at Manchouli, customs officers were posted to secure the border, and entry into the country was not always guaranteed.[35] Du Bois reports that as a guest of SMR he was courteously ushered into "the station-master's private parlor" but that he saw an English lady struggle with a rough Manchukuo inspector who rummaged through her luggage, fingering the negatives of some films. The woman turned to Du Bois with pleading eyes and said, "For heaven's sake don't leave me" (RA, 129).

Following his account of the border crossing in "I Gird the Globe," Du Bois offers a descriptive map of Manchukuo based on his travels along the rails that crisscrossed the country. He intended to probe not only the geography but also the meaning of Manchukuo, a colored *imperium in imperio*, on his tour—its arrangement with SMR, unofficial publicity agency for the (puppet) state, notwithstanding. In his journey along the rail lines as both traveler and passenger, Du Bois traced the paths of Manchuria's coloniality and its modernity, which created contingent national and transnational forms of community in that region. Manchukuoan Manchouli served as his point of departure; he described the settlement as "a straggling town on a dusty plain, with Russian and Chinese signs" (RA, 129), and a much smaller town in proportion to its railway station than most because the station was built first and the town developed around it. Du Bois reported Harbin, the next stop, to be a thriving city that had developed with the Russian construction of the Chinese Eastern and was "the only remaining center of Czarist Russia on earth" (RA, 130).

Du Bois then describes the urban cityscape of Hsinking, which burst into sight as the train rode out of the northern desert. "The whole scene changed as if by magic," Du Bois writes. Hsinking was a crossroads of international traffic where the Chinese Eastern and SMR converged. A small riverside town only a few years before, Hsinking was in the process of growing into the capital city of Manchukuo.[36] From his room in the SMR-operated Yamato Hotel in Hsinking,[37] Du Bois saw to the right the old Chinese town, "huddled and crouching, with its strange signs and ancient insignia," and to the left, "the beginning of the new Japanese city, or the city of the new Manchoukuo, planned by the Japanese." Highlighting the differences between the Chinese and Japanese districts of the city that represented pre- and post-1932, Du Bois, whose language is encoded with what might be termed a black Orientalist or colonial discourse, justifies Manchukuo—proxy imperialism—as a modernizer in Asia. "Clearly this colonial effort of a colored nation is something to watch," Du Bois concludes (RA, 130).

Indeed, with a new SMR station as its focal point and center, Hsinking was being built according to a geometrical plan, with state-of-the-art roads radiating out from the station, and with monumental state buildings, public offices, and the palace of the emperor Pu Yi lining them in various stages of completion: "some finished, some yet building, some only projected" (RA, 130). As one historian describes it, the architecture of public buildings in the capital of Manchukuo was, characteristically, "stark but imposing modernist bodies made of reinforced concrete, topped with Chinese or Japanese-inspired ornamental roofs"—a touch of Manchukuo's "Pan-Asianism."[38] Du Bois also may have observed that Hsinking was furnished with city parks, botanical gardens, and decorative lakes, as well as a modern public hygiene system with water closets installed in all residential, commercial, and industrial buildings—the first such system in Asia. Planned and constructed as a "futuristic cityscape," the capital of Manchukuo was intended to project "the power of the colonial state as the agent of modernity," in the words of historian Louise Young.[39]

Speeding southward in "Japanese cars better than Pullmans" on SMR's streamlined super-express train, the Asia Express, Du Bois traveled to Mukden, the ancient capital of the Manchu Dynasty. In Du Bois's accurate description, the Manchus "for 267 years ruled China" until the 1911 Revolution (RA, 130). The Chinese revolution culminated in the establishment of the Republic of China and the abdication of the last Manchu emperor, Pu Yi—the same being installed twenty years later as the emperor of Manchukuo. Thus, two modern states in East Asia, the Republic of China and Manchukuo, branched off separately from the trunk line of the Chinese Empire. Du Bois found Mukden "a singular city," divided into "an ancient walled town, three hundred years old"—with a dignified palace and two royal mausoleums—and "a new Japanese city, broad and square, busy and beautiful" in the SMR zone. A war memorial had been erected in the Japanese district to commemorate the battle of Mukden in the Russo-Japanese War—a war that enabled Japan to take "her place among the Powers." Recently added to this memorial were the names of soldiers who had fallen in the Manchurian Incident,[40] in which the Japanese Kwantung Army burst from the SMR zone to occupy Manchuria, enabling the creation of Manchukuo under the (nominal) rule of Pu Yi. In reflecting on Mukden during his stay, Du Bois decided, "This is surely the place to pause and ask what is this Manchurian venture of Japan, and what does it mean?" (RA, 130–31).

His grappling with this question eventually led Du Bois to write two bold, provocative dispatches for the *Pittsburgh Courier* in which he justified Japan's Manchurian venture. He sent these dispatches, which were published in 1937, from Dairen, which was not only the final stop on his tour of inspection and the terminus of the SMR trunk line but also the location of the headquarters of SMR. In Dairen, the *Manshu Nichi-Nichi*, Manchuria's biggest SMR-affiliated newspaper, reported on Du Bois's arrival and published a photograph of the visiting dignitary.[41] Du Bois delivered a lecture on "the Problem of Race Segregation in the United States" to the SMR Club (the conference room of which was packed to overflowing with an audience of a hundred and several tens). At a dinner in the club following the lecture, Du Bois led a round-table talk on the "Future of the Black Race" and other racial matters.[42] Du Bois noticed that "graduates of several American universities were present" at this event.[43] These were most likely Japanese Americans. As historian John J. Stephan observes, Japanese Americans sometimes fled the racial tensions that afflicted them in America, the land of opportunity for whites, and sought "a multi-ethnic land of opportunity" in Manchukuo.[44] In Manchukuo, "equal treatment" among the so-called quinque racial makeup of the populace (Han Chinese, Japanese, Manchus, Mongols, and Koreans), in addition to "people of other nationalities who wish to reside permanently" within the territory, was established as a principle—though not a practice—in the declaration of the founding of the state issued in 1932.[45] Ethnic diversity was thus a defining feature of Manchukuo; there were also communities of Germans, Jews, Ukrainians, Poles, and Crimean Tartars, as well as British, American, French, and Italian expatriates, let alone White Russians. The SMR Company employed dozens of such Japanese Americans seeking a multiethnic land of opportunity in Manchukuo during its existence from 1906 to 1945.[46]

The first of the dispatches that Du Bois sent to the *Pittsburgh Courier* during this visit, captioned "Yosuke Matsuoka," describes an interview Du Bois conducted in Dairen with Matsuoka, president of SMR. Matsuoka was also a graduate of the University of Oregon in the United States. While his dispatch leaves out many details of his conversation with Matsuoka—at the time one of the best-known Japanese personages in the world, having recently pulled Japan out of the League of Nations—Du Bois's text clearly represents Matsuoka as the architect of Manchukuo. Du Bois reports that Matsuoka "ranks as a viceroy and premier," holding "the destinies of thirty millions [the inhabitants of Manchukuo] in his hands," and shouldering "the responsibility of proving to the world that colonial enterprise by a colored nation need not imply the caste, exploitation and subjection which it has always implied in the case of white Europe."[47] In the declaration of the founding of Manchukuo on March 1, 1932, the "will of thirty million people" had been offered as grounds for the establishment of the state and its secession from the Republic of China.[48]

Du Bois's symbolic coupling of Matsuoka and Manchukuo is significant, implying that Du Bois understood Japan's Manchurian venture to be a project of the SMR Company, not of Japanese militarists. Indeed Du Bois's account contains no mention either of the Chinese resistance or of the sometimes tense collaboration of Chinese local elites with the Japanese authorities.[49] Partly, this may reflect how the Japanese—rather than the Chinese—controlled the means of representation of Manchukuo that affected Du Bois while in Manchuria. In Du Bois's view, which was clearly influenced by his dialogue with Matsuoka, the prime force for "the development and independence of the colored peoples" in Manchukuo was SMR—Japan's half state-owned and half privately owned corporation that had long acted since

1906 in Manchuria as an alternative administration to the local Chinese government.[50] Because SMR worked to break down the boundaries between metropole and colony, between industry and culture, and between private capital and public welfare, the state of Manchukuo that it had helped build, albeit an *imperium in imperio*, seemed to him to disrupt the exploitative racial and social order forged between Western maritime empires and their colonies beyond oceans.

Thus, in the second of his dispatches to the *Pittsburgh Courier*, captioned "Japanese colonialism," Du Bois compares the "colonial situation" in Manchuria with "colonies in Africa and the West Indies, under white European control" in this light. He enumerates five constituent elements that make the former different from the latter: (1) "Absence of racial or color caste"; (2) "Impartial law and order"; (3) "Public control of private capital for the general welfare"; (4) "Services for health, education, city-planning, housing, consumers' co-operation and other social ends"; and (5) "The incorporation of the natives into the administration of government and social readjustment." Du Bois thus made a strong case for empire—that is, liberal empire—in East Asia. With these advantages in view, Du Bois brushes aside as "immaterial" the question of whether Manchukuo is an independent state or a colony. He then broaches what he deems "the main question," that is, "What is Japan doing for the people of Manchuria and how is she doing it? . . . Is she reducing the mass of the people to slavery and poverty? Is she stealing the land and monopolizing the natural resources?"[51]

The answer that Du Bois offers in this second *Courier* dispatch from Dairen is based on his understanding that "Japanese colonialism" in Manchuria is an integrated industrial and cultural system in which capitalism is carefully controlled for the public good. Du Bois observes:

The people appear happy, and there is no unemployment. There is public peace and order. A lynching in Manchoukuo would be unthinkable. There are public services to improve crops, market them and increase their prices. Manchoukuans are in the police force and the schools and public services. . . . The Japanese hold no absolute monopoly of the offices of the state. The new housing and new cities take account of the Chinese as well as the Japanese. There has been private investment of capital on a considerable scale; but the railroads are partially owned by the state; electricity, water, gas, telegraph and telephone are public services. The largest open cut coal mine in the world is in Manchuria. . . . [T]hey have schools, library, hospital, water, sewage and parks. Electricity for a large part of Manchuria is made here—a total of 130,000 kilowatts. Yet all this is not only half owned by the government, but the private employer is under strict government control and regulation.

In concluding his *Courier* dispatch, Du Bois argues that although the Manchukuo government was not "controlling capital for the benefit of the workers" as he thought it should, "neither, so far as that is concerned, is Japan. There is, however, no apparent discrimination between motherland and colony in this respect. Nowhere else in the world, to my knowledge, is this true." Du Bois suggests that the Manchurian venture aims not at unilateral dominion but at a contiguous regional community that transcends nationalism. He ends his dispatch with an affirmation of the venture, declaring that "no nation should rule a colony whose people they cannot conceive as Equals."[52]

In accordance with Du Bois's view, an anti-laissez-faire ideology was indeed at work in the state-planned and state-controlled economy in Manchukuo.[53] As Young describes, the SMR Company was staffed with Japanese leftists and Marxists who were politically marginalized at home in Japan. In Manchuria, they "tried to turn the new empire into a kind of social laboratory, a controlled environment in which to test out theories of social transformation."[54] The *Economic Construction Program of Manchukuo*, drafted by the SMR Company and issued by the Manchukuo government in 1933, stipulates that, in view of "the baneful effects which capitalism when unbridled may exert," the government of Manchukuo will "apply a certain amount of national control" and "prevent any exclusive class of people from monopolizing the natural resources and the development of industries, thus enabling all to enjoy such benefits."[55] Following the example of Soviet economic planning, SMR issued a draft proposal for the first Five-Year Industrial Development Plan for Manchukuo in October 1936, a month before Du Bois's visit, to be implemented in 1937.[56]

What lies at the heart of Du Bois's sympathy with the Manchurian venture is his affirmation of Manchukuo's socioeconomic experiment of departing from a capitalist development. In "I Gird the Globe," Du Bois demarcates four power nuclei in the world of 1936: Great Britain and Western Europe, Italy and Eastern Europe, the Union of Soviet Socialist Republics, and the Japanese Empire (RA, 132). Precisely because he looked upon Japan as "the hope of the colored world" (RA, 101), Du Bois was "curious to know just how far" Japanese imperium in Asia would "follow the western model," or alternatively would "follow some form of socialism." For Du Bois, the future course of Asia had grave implications for the future of the darker "workers." As he toured Manchukuo, Du Bois speculated that "for historic and other reasons," the Japanese Empire in Asia would not pursue the model of the Soviet Union on the Eurasian continent but that at the same time, "there was at least equal reason for refusing the lead of Great Britain or France or the United States," that is, Western maritime empires (RA, 132).

His interview with Matsuoka enabled Du Bois to envision an alternative to both the Soviet Russian and Western models—a "third way" toward which the Manchurian venture pointed.

In the most crucial passage of his travel manuscript (portions of which were published in the aforementioned dispatch captioned "Yosuke Matsuoka"), Du Bois recalls that he and Matsuoka "talked of industry, capitalism and communism." This conversation led them to share a stunning theory that, in Du Bois's account, framed Matsuoka's understanding of the Japanese Empire: "In some ways Japan [is] the most communistic of modern states." What Matsuoka had in mind, of course, was not communism as a social or political system but rather communism as a deeply rooted aspect of Japanese culture. As Du Bois reports Matsuoka to have explained it, "In Japan there had never been that strong sense of individual ownership of property that characterizes so many people[s]. There was, on the contrary, through the family and clan a strong sense of common ownership of all wealth, of willingness to give to others and sacrifice for the common good" (RA, 133). In Matsuoka's view, the Japanese—whose society was grounded in the sense of communal ownership and the common good—were morally communistic.

Embracing this idea, Du Bois "ventured boldly to add" that perhaps the Japanese could evolve, without revolution, into a state capable of replacing private profit with public welfare: "You Japanese, by your marvelous national discipline, were able without revolution to transform Japan from Feudalism to Industrialism. May it not be possible, again without revolution, and with that same discipline and sacrifice, for Japan to make that further inevitable change from private profit to public welfare?" (RA, 133).[57]

Perhaps to protect Matsuoka (the advocacy of communism—which was tantamount to endorsing the overthrow of the emperor system—was a criminal offense under Japanese law), Du Bois chose not to mention in the Courier dispatch that "Matsuoka expressed agreement with [him]." However, Du Bois asserts in his travel manuscript that Matsuoka did agree with him, and Du Bois concludes, "I think he was sincere" (RA, 133).

In any case, Matsuoka quite clearly restated what he said to Du Bois five years later, to Joseph Stalin. As Japan's foreign minister in 1941, Matsuoka described the common ground that Japan shared with Soviet Russia to Stalin with the resonant phrase "moral communism" in the course of concluding the Japanese-Soviet Neutrality Pact. The pact was intended to establish the partnership and ensure the mutual territorial integrity of the two states and their respective territories of Manchukuo and the Mongolian People's Republic. Stalin's de jure recognition of Manchukuo and a formation called the Eurasian Continental Bloc (discussed in the last section of this essay) were a result. As if anticipating and endorsing this continental bloc, Du Bois describes gazing from a hill at Port Arthur out across the Yellow Sea and concluding that "Manchuria is the natural mainland of the isles of Japan" (RA, 131).[58]

In his travel manuscript, Du Bois thus comes to regard Manchukuo as a state developing through the agency of SMR toward "some form of socialism" rather than as an autarchic regional empire under Japanese militarists, functioning as a cornerstone for new regionalism in East Asia. His journey onward to the Republic of China, and in particular a luncheon meeting with a group of Chinese at the Chinese Bankers' Club in Shanghai (arranged through Chih Meng and "the American-supported University of Shanghai" [RA, 138]),[59] only strengthened Du Bois's conviction that the Manchurian venture offered hope for darker workers in Asia. Du Bois's encounters with the elite in the Republic of China—represented at the luncheon meeting by the editor of the China Press, the secretary general of the Bank of China, the general manager of the China Publishing Company, the director of the Chinese Schools for Shanghai, and the executive secretary of the China Institute of International Relations—convinced him that they were trying to extricate themselves from the snares of European capital "by the method of establishing [their] own capitalistic control."[60] The Chinese elite, Du Bois gathered, "proposed to out-capital capital" rather than to displace capitalism (RA, 140).

The luncheon meeting also gave Du Bois a sense of the indignation that the Chinese felt toward the Japanese (they "hate Japan more than Europe when [they] have suffered more from England, France, and Germany than from Japan"), which he believed to derive partly from a Chinese sense of cultural superiority. In Du Bois's view, the Chinese felt that Japan, which they regarded as "the culture child of China," was arrogantly trying to "show China the way of life" (RA, 139–40). However, such sentiments, presupposing Japan's cultural inferiority to China, did not sway Du Bois, perhaps due to the subsequent influence of the cultural diplomacy of KBS, which fostered his appreciation of both ancient and modern Japanese civilization from the time he landed in Japan after leaving Shanghai, as we have seen. Upon returning to the United States and lecturing in Harlem "to an eager audience, which overflowed the Y.W.C.A. auditorium," Du Bois concluded that "the Japanese were creating an incredibly fine state out of the conquered territory" in Manchuria—thus assuming the role of unofficial publicity agent promoting Manchukuo in his home country as KBS may have hoped he would.[61]

The Battle of Shanghai

A major ramification of the Manchurian venture, in historical actuality, was a full-fledged war that broke out between the Republic of China and the Empire of Japan in July 1937, six months after Du Bois's return from Asia.

Initially a small military clash at the Marco Polo Bridge in the suburbs of Peking, the conflict became a full-scale (though undeclared) armed conflict between the National Revolutionary Army of the Republic of China and the Imperial Japanese Army and Navy, spreading rapidly to Shanghai. The war acted as a catalyst for the formation of an anti-Japanese alliance between the KMT and the CCP, in which the Red Army became the Eighth Route Army of the National Revolutionary Army in a united Chinese front. Nonetheless, the Japanese gained control of Shanghai after a fierce three-month battle. The rapid development of hostilities in Shanghai complicated Du Bois's black Manchurian narrative significantly.

More broadly, in the African American community, the Battle of Shanghai was represented in multiple and conflicting ways. The *New York Amsterdam News*, Harlem's leading black weekly, reported that the Sino-Japanese conflict divided public opinion. In Harlem, "a soap-boxer" on a street corner damned Japan for being "just as Fascist-minded as can be," while elsewhere "a trio of curbstone debaters" applauded Japan for showing the white world that "if they can gobble up China and everywhere else, Japan can do some gobbling, too."[62] According to another black weekly, the *Pittsburgh Courier*, the situation was "seriously argued in Aframerican gatherings." On one side, pro-Japanese blacks believed that Japan was "fighting the battle of the colored peoples of the world against a China backed by white imperialists." On the other, pro-Chinese blacks "fiercely resent[ed] Japanese aggression and the effort to destroy Chinese independence so laboriously created after twenty-six years of revolution and counter-revolution."[63]

The disparate conceptions of the Battle of Shanghai are directly reflected in the African American representations of China and Japan. On the left of the spectrum of black political thought, Langston Hughes, Richard Wright, and Paul Robeson regarded the CCP-led China as fighting an anti-imperialist war. Hughes published his poem "Roar China!" in September 1937, shortly after the outbreak of the Battle of Shanghai. Opening with a direct address, the imperative to "Roar, China! / Roar, old lion of the East!," the poem calls for resistance to Japanese and Western imperialists, for which the foreign concessions of Shanghai were the historical symbol.[64] Wright was Harlem Bureau editor of the *Daily Worker*, the newspaper of the Communist Party of the United States of America (CPUSA)—a capacity in which he served for over a year from 1937 to 1938. He reported in September 1937 on a massive Harlem rally "to protest Japan's undeclared war against China." Staged by Harlem workers—"Negro, Chinese, and white"—under the auspices of the American Friends of the Chinese People and the American League against War and Fascism, the rally included as speakers black American leaders James W. Ford, organizer of the Harlem Division of the CPUSA, and

Ashley L. Totten of the Brotherhood of Sleeping Car Porters.[65] Similarly, the singer-activist Robeson "openly declared his support for China in her heroic struggle against Japanese imperialism."[66] Steadfast in his support of Chinese aspirations for self-determination throughout the Sino-Japanese War, Robeson and Liu Liang-mo, secretary of the Shanghai YMCA, would eventually release an album in the United States in 1941, entitled *Chee Lai! (Arise!)*, to aid the Chinese war of resistance. Robeson performed the title song—the future national anthem of the People's Republic of China—in English and Chinese, calling upon the Chinese masses "who refuse to be bond slaves" to "stand up and fight for liberty and true democracy." Proceeds from the sale of the album were donated to "the China Aid Council of United China Relief."[67]

During the Battle of Shanghai, the mainstream US media discourse adopted the theme of humanitarianism. The October 4, 1937, issue of *Life* magazine, founded by Henry Luce, printed images of the Japanese bombing the civilian population from the air. In one heartrending photo, which *Life* estimated was seen by 136,000,000 people around the world, a Chinese baby, wounded by a bomb, bawls pitifully amid the ruins of Shanghai's South Station, Nantao. Demonstrating the strength of public interest in the Sino-Japanese War, this famous photo was selected by US newsreaders and reproduced in *Life* early in 1938 to represent one of the top news stories of 1937.[68] In concert with such interest in the mainstream, on October 5, President Franklin D. Roosevelt gave what came to be called his "Quarantine Speech" in Chicago, calling for the international containment of aggressor nations guilty of spreading "the epidemic of world lawlessness"—thus taking a step away from the traditional US foreign policy of neutrality and nonintervention. In this speech, Roosevelt, obviously referring to Japan, described its war in criminal terms: "Without a declaration of war and without warning or justification of any kind, civilians, including vast numbers of women and children, are being ruthlessly murdered with bombs from the air."[69] In a survey conducted by the American Institute of Public Opinion (the Gallup poll) a month earlier, 43 percent had responded that they were "pro-China" as opposed to only 2 percent who were "pro-Japan." The "pro-China" figure rose to 59 percent in October.[70]

Du Bois resisted such a rising trend of public opinion. In his weekly column "Forum of Fact and Opinion," in the September 25, 1937, issue of the *Pittsburgh Courier*, he contended that "what we as American Negroes must understand is the broad outline of the whole thing, and not be unconsciously misled by the propaganda current in America."[71] In October, when Harry F. Ward, chairman of the American League against War and Fascism, wired an appeal to Du Bois to endorse the pro-China People's Congress for Democracy and Peace slated for Pittsburgh in November, Du Bois deliberately rejected it.[72] Du Bois did not accommodate himself to public opinion. Instead, in a column in the October 23 issue of the *Courier*, captioned "China and Japan," he wrote that "Japan fought China to save China from Europe, and fought Europe through China and tried to wade in blood toward Asiatic freedom. Negroes must think straight in this crisis."[73]

This seemingly proimperialist narrative of the Sino-Japanese War in Du Bois's *Courier* column has featured prominently in the scholarship as an illustration of his radical failure of vision with regard to Japanese imperialism. However, pending the eventual sublation of such a narrative, I would like to here examine what Du Bois called "the broader outline of the whole thing"—an outline by which he urged African Americans to make sense of the war and make political choices relating to it. From the perspective of Du Bois, an understanding of the war requires that African Americans move beyond the facile explanations of hostilities as fascism versus antifascism, or war versus pacifism, to take a broader, better-integrated historical view of modern regionalism in East Asia. In his *Courier* column of September 25, Du Bois observes that "it would have been magnificent providence of God if Russia and China could have made common ground for the emancipation of the working classes of the world." For Du Bois, the ideal scenario would have been that after the Chinese and Russian Revolutions to end the Chinese Empire and the Tsarist Russian Empire in 1911 and 1917, respectively, a new regional order emerges based on the continental contiguity and solidarity between the Soviet Union and the Republic of China. Such a union would have been possible, according to the black thinker, because the program of Sun Yat-sen, founder of the Republic of China, was essentially "Communism; not the complete Russian line, but an extreme socialism which envisaged division of the land, control of industry, ownership of capital in heavy industry, and the welfare state" (RA, 142). If a Sino-Soviet alliance had come to pass, Du Bois claims in the same *Courier* column, "the salvation of China then would not have rested upon Japan, and two-thirds of the world would have been arrayed against the industrial imperialism of Europe." However, as Du Bois observes, "after losing her great and far-sighted leader, Sun Yat-sen" (who died in 1925), the Republic of China "turned in reality toward the leadership of modern industrial imperialism as represented in China, especially by England."[74] This happened in China under "a greedy, crafty man of no ideals or integrity"—namely, Chiang Kai-shek.[75] In accordance with this outline, Du Bois concluded that Japan hence "fought Europe by attacking China, and that is the reason of the present war."[76]

From our vantage point, East Asian regionalism in 1937 was indeed marked by intersecting developments: the crisis of the centuries-old Sinocentric world in continental Asia; the crisis of the international system in maritime Asia (that had occurred on Western terms, first under the British-led treaty ports system and then under the US-defined Washington system that affirmed the Open Door policy in China); and Japan's aspiration both to be "the middle" of the Sinocentric world and to break the international Anglo-American hegemony. Du Bois seems to have understood the Battle of Shanghai in this regional context. The root of the Sino-Japanese conflict, he explained to his *Courier* readers on October 23, lay in "a mad muddle of motives." As Du Bois explains, the Republic of China "preferred to be a coolie for England" (to remain integrated in the international system based on unequal treaties) rather than to "acknowledge . . . the leadership of Japan," thereby allowing Japan, a country that had long been on the periphery of the Sinocentric world, to take the place of the "middle kingdom" in East Asia. This political choice was, as Du Bois writes, motivated by the "supercilious disdain" that the Republic of China or "young China"—a modern state that denied the imperial past but inherited from it the sense of Sinocentricism—heaped on Japan, "a parvenu." Thus, "licking the European boots," China "taught her folk that Japanese are devils." Du Bois concludes that "the straight road to world dominance of the yellow race was ruined in Asia by the same spirit that animates the 'white folks' nigger' in the United States."[77]

Remarkably, the most important context in which Du Bois understood the Battle of Shanghai was during his recent trip to Manchuria. The seemingly proimperialist narrative of the conflict in his *Courier* column of October 23 was not only informed by his interview with Matsuoka and his approval of the Manchurian venture. (Du Bois defines Japan's mission as follows in "I Gird the Globe": "Japan is called . . . to lead world revolution, and lead it with the minimum of violence and upheaval. . . . In the twentieth century she is called to save the world from the slavery to capital" [RA, 146]). The column was also a supportive response to a public statement that Matsuoka had issued from Manchuria a fortnight previously. Published in the *New York Times* on October 10, Matsuoka's statement rebutted the anti-Japanese propaganda in America that was disseminating the claim that "Japan is fighting for loot and profit." According to the president of SMR, "this fight-for-loot theory" was "an insult to plain arithmetic," let alone to Japan, as the billions of yen that Japan was spending on the war in China would clearly yield no return, and Japan knew it. "No treasure trove is in her eyes, only sacrifices upon sacrifices," declared Matsuoka, because Japan was "fighting simply for her conception of her mission in Asia," that is, to keep Asia from turning into "a crazy quilt of European colonies" and "becoming another Africa."[78] Having walked out of the League of Nations to keep Manchuria from the international control the league proposed,[79] Matsuoka in his *New York Times* statement once again took a stand before the world to defend Japan's continental expansion as an attempt to reintegrate East Asia as a contiguous regional community. In this regard, Du Bois's *Courier* column of October 23 amounted to the African American intellectual's effort to stand with Matsuoka in Manchuria across the Pacific.

When Stalin Enters

Du Bois's black Manchurian narrative endorsed Matsuoka's vision of instituting a regionally integrated Asia. It represented the African American thinker's imagined socialist internationalism encompassing Japan's Manchurian venture. A challenge to Du Bois's internationalism soon came in December 1937, however, when the Sino-Japanese War's theater shifted to Nanking, about 170 miles inland from Shanghai on China's eastern coast, and the progress of the war apparently became derailed from Japan's war aim proclaimed by Matsuoka in the *New York Times*.

On December 13, 1937, the Japanese army seized Nanking, the capital of the Republic of China under the KMT. The central episode of the Sino-Japanese War, the Nanking Massacre or Rape of Nanking as it is commonly known, that followed the fall of Nanking, is the most potent symbol of the genocidal character of the conflict. (The incident has entered the political consciousness of Americans as a genocide recently with the success of Iris Chang's bestseller *The Rape of Nanking: The Forgotten Holocaust of World War II* [1997]. Chang claimed that the death toll in Nanking far exceeded that of atomic bomb victims in Hiroshima and Nagasaki.[80]) The atrocities perpetrated in China's Nationalist capital by Japanese troops became widely known almost immediately in the United States.

Firsthand reports of the massacre appeared in the US press less than a week after the fall of Nanking, dispatched by American journalists who remained in the city during the siege and the first few days of the Japanese occupation.[81] Under the headline "Nanking Massacre Story: Japanese Troops Kill Thousands" on the front page of the *Chicago Daily News* of December 15, 1937, Archibald T. Steele reported that "Japanese brutality at Nanking is costing them a golden opportunity to win the sympathy of the Chinese population, whose friendship they claim to be seeking."[82] Arthur Menken, a newsreel cameraman for Paramount, radioed an account of the capture of Nanking to the Associated Press (AP) in which he observed that the city was strewn with hundreds of uniforms shed by Chinese soldiers "substituting civilian garb" to escape death at the hands of the Japanese. Menken wrote, "All Chinese males found with any signs of having served in the army were herded together and executed."[83]

C. Yates McDaniel, an AP correspondent, wired a firsthand account, published in the *Chicago Daily Tribune* on December 18, of a Chinese man with his hands tied, who broke away from a long line of war prisoners en route to an execution ground to beg McDaniel to save him from death. "I could do nothing," wrote the AP correspondent. "My last remembrance of Nanking: Dead Chinese, dead Chinese, dead Chinese."[84] Frank Tillman Durdin, a correspondent for the *New York Times*, reported that slaughter, looting, and rape by the Japanese had "turned Nanking into a city of terror." After the fall of the city, according to Durdin, scattered crowds of civilians, relieved that the siege was over, cheered the columns of Japanese troops marching into the city. However, their "feelings of relief and of welcome soon gave up to terror." The "barbarities" of the Japanese had the effect of creating hatred of the Japanese among the Chinese population, Durdin observed, rather than of gaining the "'cooperation' for which [the Japanese] profess to be fighting China."[85]

Moreover, contemporary magazines carried images of the Japanese atrocities that matched the eyewitness accounts. The January 10, 1938, issue of *Life* magazine included a four-picture spread of "the worst holocaust in modern history" entitled "The Japanese Conqueror Brings 'A Week of Hell' to China's Nationalist Capital of Nanking." One image presented the decapitated head of an "incorrigibly anti-Japanese" Chinese man that had been mounted on a barbed-wire barricade—frightening evidence of Japanese cruelty.[86] With anti-Japanese sentiment rapidly mounting as a result of the Japanese sinking of the US Navy gunboat *Panay* on the Yangtze River on December 12, 1937, the sympathies of Americans clearly lay with the Chinese as the media coverage of the Sino-Japanese War unfolded.

Did the prevailing mood in the mainstream US media reflect the sentiments of black America? In December and throughout the first few months of 1938, the African American press actively promoted the debate over Japan's war in China. In its editorial (January 15, 1938), the Baltimore *Afro-American* issued an equivocal endorsement of Japanese continental expansion to "set up an Asiatic 'Monroe doctrine.'" The editorial declared, "The AFRO-AMERICAN believes that Japan is fully justified." It sparked a flurry of letters to the editor and heated exchanges between its readers over the ensuing weeks.[87] The contentious nature of the Sino-Japanese conflict made it also a topic of debate for African Americans in church and literary clubs as well.[88] The African American community sought out both sides of the story—Chinese and Japanese—in attempting to understand the true import of the war.[89]

The contrast between the representations of the Sino-Japanese War in the mainstream United States and those in black American forums underscores our need to consider the social significance and political implications of the diversity of frames of reference within which African Americans in general and Du Bois in particular addressed the conflict. Having moved beyond the binarisms of fascism versus antifascism and war versus pacifism, the African American community significantly situated the war in the interaction of regional and global processes. As we have seen, Du Bois based his argument on the case of Manchuria and East Asian regionalism. William Pickens, field secretary of the NAACP and contributing editor for the Associated Negro Press, who emerged in the vanguard of advocates of the pro-Japan position in the Sino-Japanese War, argued in the context of Ethiopia and the international security system that became increasingly volatile after the Italo-Ethiopian War (1935–1936).

Indeed, on both sides of the debate, the critical lens of Ethiopia afforded black America a view of the Sino-Japanese conflict as not just a regional process but part of a global process.[90] Cyril Briggs, a black member of the CPUSA, wrote in the January 20, 1938, issue of the *Philadelphia Tribune* that he regarded the wars in East Africa and East Asia as continuous. In Briggs's account, the two wars taken together constituted a narrative of how the Japanese Empire "joined with Europe's imperialistic nations." Briggs relates that in 1935, many African Americans "eagerly turned their eyes toward the Far East in the belief that Japan would aid, in one way or another, the beleaguered East African nation" against Mussolini's fascist aggression. However, "Japanese imperialism did not lift a finger to help the Ethiopian people, either materially or morally," but rather, as Briggs describes, Japan's rulers "treacherously stabbed [Ethiopia] in the back" by "extend[ing] diplomatic recognition in Italy's 'Ethiopian Empire.'" The Sino-Japanese War only brought into clearer focus what the war in Africa had revealed: that Japan's posture as the "champion" of the world's darker races was a facade.[91] Japan's recent signing of an anti-Comintern protocol with Italy and Germany on November 6, 1937, may have also offered more evidence, in Briggs's view, that Japan had joined the fascist ranks.

By contrast, in Pickens's view, published in the December 18, 1937, issue of the *Pittsburgh Courier*, it was not Japan that had "joined with Europe's imperialistic nations" in the present crisis but rather the Republic of China, in seeking Western aid and intervention by the League of Nations. Pickens observes that Ethiopian emperor Haile Selassie had pursued a similar course of action in the Ethiopian crisis, only to precipitate, rather than prevent, the fall of the Ethiopian Empire. Chiang Kai-shek, Pickens asserts, "ought to send for Haile Selassie," for the Ethiopian emperor "can give him some fine points on the matter of magnanimous and altruistic help from Europe and America." Pickens writes, "These [white] nations, with their own axes to grind, kept shouting for Selassie to 'hold Mussolini!' until they could make up their minds and pass a few more resolutions. 'Hold him, Selassie! We are standing at your back!' . . . Haile stood until it was almost too late to run away with a few personal belongings." Selassie's departure for exile in England as his nation fought on cleared the way for Mussolini to proclaim the Ethiopian Italian Empire in May 1936. The lesson of the Italo-Ethiopian War for Pickens is, then, that China should "deal directly with Japan . . . and settle their own differences" and "keep those European and American Lions and Eagles and Bears [England, the United States, France, Holland, and the USSR] out of the Oriental business."[92] Chiang, advises Pickens, "had better stop waitin' on de Lord and on the white folks and deal directly with Japan, or pretty soon he will be where Haile Selassie is, cooling his heels on the Thames, or on the Seine—or on the Potomac—or more riskily still on the Moscow river."[93]

The aforementioned editorial in the January 15, 1938, issue of the Baltimore *Afro-American* captured this perception succinctly in declaring, "The Chinese have become a kind of 'Uncle Tom' of Asia." The editorial concluded that the leaders of the Republic of China "have kow-towed to the white exploiters, licked their boots and allowed themselves to become the footstools of Western conquerors." In a cartoon accompanying the editorial, a man with an old Manchu queue labeled "China" is thus depicted kowtowing to the Western members of the Pacific Community (England, the United States, Holland, and the USSR) while a soldier in uniform labeled "Japan" is, as the editorial describes, "kicking China in the pants to make it stand up straight and be a man." Yet conspicuously absent from the cartoon depicting Japan standing alone are the figures of Mussolini and Hitler, the worst enemies of black people, with whom Japan chose to form the Anti-Comintern Pact. In trying to explain away this offensive alliance, the *Afro-American* editorial gave the following reason: "Since most of the democratic nations have their hands in China's pie, there were no other alliances for Japan to make."[94]

The Sino-Japanese War shuffled and reshuffled the partnering of nation-states across the color line in a manner that was, from a racialist perspective, unthinkable at the time of the Ethiopian crisis. China's partnering with Western powers in the Pacific Community (the United States and Great Britain) and Japan's partnering with fascist powers on continental Europe (Italy and Germany) during the Sino-Japanese War gave rise to coalitions that would eventually become the Allies and the Axis in World War II. With the Japanese attack on Pearl Harbor and America's entry into the war, the Chinese Nationalist government would issue a declaration of war on Japan on December 9, 1941, formally announcing that China, "a peace-loving nation," had been at war with Japan since 1937. The Sino-Japanese War, even as it was finally declared, was no longer simply a war between China and Japan. The declaration read, "After her long and fruitless attempt to conquer China, Japan . . . has treacherously launched an attack on China's friends, the United States and Great Britain," thereby "making herself the arch enemy of justice and world peace."⁹⁵

However, this reference in China's declaration of war to the United States and Great Britain as "friends" did not reflect a straightforward outcome of the long-term, deliberate coalition making through which the Republic of China sought victory in the Sino-Japanese War. The Soviet Union's involvement in the conflict created significant complications for both China and Japan. (Although the Soviet Union joined the Allied powers, it did not go to war against Japan in World War II until after an atomic bomb was dropped on Hiroshima, just before the end of the war.) On August 21, 1937, in the immediate wake of the outbreak of the Battle of Shanghai, the KMT government concluded the Sino-Soviet Nonaggression Pact with the Soviet Union, which provided a political basis for Stalin to supply material to Chiang Kai-shek and possibly to intervene directly in the war against Japan.⁹⁶ In response, on November 6, the Japanese imperial government signed the anti-Comintern protocol in Rome with Italy and Germany. This move increased the threat to the Soviet Union of a two-front war on its European and Far Eastern frontiers. In the Far East, in accordance with the Sino-Soviet pact, "Soviet pilots were fighting Japanese aircraft in China's skies, Soviet advisers [were] drafting military operations on Kuomintang staffs, [and] Soviet aircraft, tanks, artillery, small arms, ammunition and other military equipment [were] flowing into China in an unending stream," as historian Boris Slavinsky observed.⁹⁷ It was as if the Soviet Union and the Japanese Empire had undertaken a (proxy) war to compete for regional hegemony in East Asia. In the meantime, along both the Manchukuo-Soviet border and the border between Manchukuo and the Mongolian People's Republic, sharp military clashes between the Soviet Union and Japan were developing into the Battle of Lake Khasan (July–August 1938) and the Battle of Khalkhyn Gol or the Nomonhan Incident (May–September 1939), the latter evolving into a decisive (though undeclared) border war fought between the Soviet Union and the Mongolian People's Republic, on one side, and Japan and Manchukuo, on the other. For Du Bois, Stalin's entry into Asia's war threatened the integrity of his socialist Manchurian narrative, as I will discuss further below.

The Eurasian and the Pacific in World Geopolitics

As represented by its opponents such as black members of the CPUSA, the Japanese Empire's alliance with Hitler and Mussolini presented an antiblack pact "sealed upon the basis of predatory aims and hatred of democracy common to all three partners."[98] Yet Du Bois deliberately mapped the theme of Japan's alliance not onto antiblack race ideology but onto the modern regional system in the Pacific that had undergone a substantial change since World War I. In 1922, the Washington Naval Conference abrogated the Anglo-Japanese alliance, cornerstone of the international order in maritime Asia, and reintegrated the Pacific region instead under "US-British hegemony."[99] Du Bois contends, in his address entitled "The Meaning of Japan" delivered in black colleges in 1937, that when "the race prejudice of England and America . . . refuses Japan fellowship as an equal, she has been forced almost into the lap of Fascist Germany and Italy who represent today war, tyranny, reaction and race hate on the most dangerous scale."[100]

Not surprisingly, such criticism by Du Bois of the US-defined Washington system aroused suspicions in Congress that he was a paid propagandist for the Japanese imperial government, which had proclaimed a "New Order in East Asia" (November 1938) in defiance of the international Anglo-American hegemony. Du Bois received a letter dated February 13, 1939, from Waldo McNutt, a supporter of the NAACP's efforts to secure the passage of federal antilynching legislation. McNutt conveyed the concerns of a number of liberal members of Congress who were interested in the legislation that Du Bois was rumored to be "receiving funds for Japanese propaganda work" in the United States. The rumor did not seem groundless, McNutt put to Du Bois, in that Du Bois's utterances regarding the Sino-Japanese War "coincided with" the propaganda of official Japanese agencies. McNutt furthermore wrote that in China, the *China Weekly Review* had named Du Bois "a suspect in the dissemination of Japanese propaganda."[101] McNutt requested that Du Bois issue a statement indicating his "official position on the Sino-Japanese conflict" so as to put these "ugly rumors" to rest. Du Bois responded forthrightly, declaring, "I have never received a cent from Japan or from any Japanese and yet I believe in Japan." Du Bois did not falter in his belief in an East Asian regionalism, concluding, "I believe in Asia for the Asiatics and despite the hell of war and the fascism of capital, I see in Japan the best agent for this end."[102]

Du Bois also received a letter in January 1940 from Henry L. Stimson, former secretary of state, who was to be installed secretary of war in July. Stimson was mobilizing public opinion in support of economic sanctions against Japan, because Japan's intention of expanding into Southeast Asia under European and American colonial rule was now clear. In February 1939, Japanese troops fighting in China had moved down to take over the island of Hainan to strengthen the blockade of the South China Sea. In March, Japan assumed jurisdiction over the Spratly Islands that had formerly been claimed by France. The United States notified Japan in July 1939 that it would terminate the Japanese-American commercial treaty six months later. Stimson wrote that America's abrogation of the commercial treaty, which would take effect on January 26, 1940, would free the Roosevelt administration to take "prompt measures" but that such measures as the government could and would take in its foreign policy would be constrained by public opinion. As honorary chairman of the American Committee for Non-Participation in Japanese Aggression,[103] Stimson invited Du Bois to support the organization's campaign for an embargo on exports of use to the Japanese military machine. In Stimson's view, the Sino-Japanese conflict was essentially a clash of "two types of civilization," one "pacific and evolutionary" and the other "militaristic and aggressive," and the US regional policy in the Far East required a strong, independent China to ensure the stability and security of the Pacific Community, now under threat from Japanese expansion.[104] In a public reply to Stimson in his weekly column in the *New York Amsterdam News*, Du Bois voiced his suspicion—and indeed predicted correctly—that the measures short of war that Stimson was proposing for the United States would "lead to virtual and even open war with Japan," and the black thinker protested that, to achieve this end, Stimson "wishes my cooperation and support." Du Bois announced, "He will not get it."[105]

Beyond the Pacific, the Eurasian continent spanned a fault line in the shifting geopolitics of the world, providing Du Bois with another convoluted context. The diplomatic earthquake of the Nazi-Soviet Pact struck in Europe in August 1939, with aftershocks extending across the continent to the conflict in the Far East between the Soviet Union and the Japanese Empire; the latter had concluded the Anti-Comintern Pact with Germany against the Soviet Union three years previously. In a column in the *Amsterdam News* entitled "As the Crow Flies" (November 18, 1939), Du Bois responded to news of the Hitler-Stalin pact by forecasting an imminent international realignment of nation-states across the Eurasian continent. He entertained the possibility of a Nazi-Soviet-Japanese rapprochement across the continent arising from America's anti-Japan foreign policy in the Pacific area. As Du Bois writes, the United States once "broke" the Anglo-Japanese alliance in the Pacific and thereby "threw Japan into the arms of Germany and Italy" in Europe. Du Bois reasons that "analogous tactics today may bring Russia, Germany and Japan into a world-dominating position."[106]

The Nazi-Soviet-Japanese alliance across the Eurasian continent that Du Bois envisaged in his *Amsterdam News* column was precisely what Matsuoka worked to build in reality following his appointment as foreign minister of Japan in July 1940. When the news arrived that Matsuoka had been named to a new cabinet under Prince Konoye (who was also president of KBS), Du Bois welcomed the rise of the former president of the SMR Company to power. Recalling Matsuoka and Manchukuo in his *Amsterdam News* column of August 3, 1940, Du Bois wrote, "I know the Minister of Foreign Affairs of the new Konoye government of Japan. I remember the day, late in the year 1936, when he received me in his office in the capital of Manchukuo. We sat and talked together about the world and color prejudice. . . . That fall day in Singking [*sic*] we talked about democracy—that broader democracy that sees no color line. Such a democracy, said Matsuoka, only Japan could lead."[107] It would seem that Du Bois's black Manchurian narrative was moving out of the prolonged impasse precipitated by the Sino-Japanese War.

Shortly after assuming the post of foreign minister, Matsuoka proclaimed the Greater East Asia Co-Prosperity Sphere (August 1940) as a new regional system, placing a Japan-Manchukuo-China economic bloc at its core and extending to the Dutch East Indies and French Indochina in Southeast Asia.[108] The Greater East Asia Co-Prosperity Sphere was an expression of his aspiration for the Japanese Empire to be at once "the middle" in the long-established Sinocentric world in continental Asia and to challenge international Anglo-American hegemony in maritime Asia. Thereafter, Matsuoka drew up the preliminary arrangement for the Tripartite Pact with Germany and Italy to be signed in Berlin in September. This Axis Pact was a necessary step toward what Matsuoka conceived as the formation of a Eurasian Continental Bloc, comprising a Japanese-German-Italian-Soviet four-power entente as a deterrent against the international hegemony of Western maritime empires, in particular, the United States and Great Britain.[109] Based on this design, Matsuoka negotiated the Tripartite Pact and then turned to reaching an agreement with the Soviet Union.[110]

Hence, when Matsuoka departed from Manchuria by rail for Europe in March 1941—returning along the same transcontinental route taken by Du Bois in 1936—his real diplomatic mission lay in neither Germany nor Italy.[111] Ostensibly, the European tour was aimed at reaffirming the Axis alliance and demonstrating the solidarity of its partners to the world. However, the true purpose of Matsuoka's tour would be broached en route, when the train made stopovers on its outward and return journeys at the terminus of the Trans-Siberian Railway in Moscow and Matsuoka visited the Kremlin.

A striking aspect of the Matsuoka-Stalin talks in the Kremlin on March 24 and April 12, as recorded in declassified Soviet records,[112] is their resonance with the Du Bois–Matsuoka interview that took place in Dairen, Manchuria, in 1936. The records show that Matsuoka told Stalin, as mentioned above, that communism had long been practiced in Japan—as a credo that he called "moral communism"—but that this traditional aspect of Japanese society had been undermined by the "evils of capitalism." Matsuoka averred to Stalin that although "he did not agree with political and social communism," he "basically . . . adhered to communism" himself and "was decisively against Anglo-Saxon capital." In view of their commonalities—despite their more substantial differences in polities: the emperor system and the single-party communist state—Matsuoka proposed that the Japanese Empire and the Soviet Union cooperate to expel the baneful influence of Anglo-Saxon capitalism from Asia.[113]

With regard to the Sino-Japanese War, Matsuoka explained to Stalin that Japan was not at war with the Chinese people, "whom Japan does not want to fight." Rather, Japan's enemy was Chiang Kai-shek, "an agent of Anglo-American capital" whom Japan was determined to fight to the end. Matsuoka maintained to Stalin that the Sino-Japanese War "must be viewed from precisely that viewpoint," a perspective from which Soviet support for Chiang (required by the Sino-Soviet Nonaggression Pact of 1937) was not "sensible." In light of world history, Matsuoka argued, Japanese-Soviet cooperation was inevitable to "wipe out the Anglo-Saxons" from Asia.[114] Evidently, Matsuoka believed that the powerful pact of the Japanese Empire and the Soviet Union would ease Japanese negotiations with Chiang's China and the United States. For Stalin, a neutral treaty with Japan meant that the Soviet Union would be saved from the danger of a two-front war on its European and Far Eastern frontiers.[115] Stalin replied that "the Russians had never been [the Anglo-Saxons'] friends, and now were perhaps not very keen to befriend them."[116] After the signing of the Japanese-Soviet Neutrality Pact (April 13, 1941), Stalin reportedly told Matsuoka that Russians were "Asiatic."[117]

The result of Matsuoka's secret negotiations in the Kremlin was the "surprise agreement" of the Japanese-Soviet Neutrality Pact. It guaranteed peaceful and friendly relations between Japan and the Soviet Union, and an accompanying declaration that pledged mutual respect for the territorial integrity and inviolability of Manchukuo and the Mongolian People's Republic. News of this sudden accord resounded throughout the world, and it was not welcomed by the Western democracies that had Pacific possessions. As the *Washington Post* reported, "The world-shaking significance of this new reaching of hands from Rome to Berlin to Tokyo to Moscow"—a Eurasian power bloc—presented momentous dangers. The *Washington Post* story presented the conclusion of the pact as follows: "Russia and Japan, long-term dueling powers of the Far East, joined in a neutrality pact today that may be as portentous as the nonaggression accord between Berlin and Moscow in 1939, which preceded the German invasion of Poland."[118] Just as the Nazi-Soviet pact safeguarded Germany's eastern front to enable its southward advancement, the story suggests, the Japanese-Soviet pact could give Japan a free hand to move southward in the Pacific.

The signing of the pact came as a psychological blow to China. For China, it represented a betrayal by the Soviet Union, which had been aiding China's war effort against Japan based on the Sino-Soviet Nonaggression Pact of 1937. American novelist Ernest Hemingway, then a war correspondent in China, predicted that Russian aid would continue even after the new Soviet pact with Japan.[119] However, according to historian Boris Slavinsky, "In mid-1941 all Soviet volunteers were recalled from China, and supply of military power to that country practically ceased."[120]

Matsuoka, as Japan's foreign minister, thus instituted two new regional systems in Asia: the Greater East Asia Co-Prosperity Sphere and the Eurasian Continental Bloc. This specter posed a "revolutionary" challenge to the old order of Western imperialists. The Japanese-Soviet Neutrality Pact, in particular, was a diplomatic triumph for Matsuoka. With his triumph, the two foundational exemplars of Du Bois's internationalism, Soviet Russia and Japan—"the fountain of socialism and the first-born of budding 'colored' world powers"—seemed to converge in their ideological and historical trajectories.[121]

The prospect of a Eurasian Continental Bloc apparently dazzled Du Bois. It was, as he put it, a "world of singular beauty with the confusing tracery of patterns but echoing our world." It lasted only for a brief moment, though, for the outbreak of the German-Soviet war shattered the idyll. In his *Amsterdam News* column of July 12, 1941, Du Bois writes in blank surprise, "Out of another world of singular beauty . . . I come back to solid earth." Du Bois tells his readers the war "compels nearly all of us to rearrange our thoughts and forecasting." Hitler's attempt to "subdue Russia and to fight Communism with everything that Communism stands for except democracy," in Du Bois's words, left the thinker "puzzled and awhirl." Du Bois found Hitler's war even more puzzling when he pondered its implications for the destiny of Asia, as ironically the outbreak of the war seemed to link Asia's liberation from white dominance with Hitler's victory. "If the Fascists win" in Europe, Du Bois reasons, Japan would expand southward and "logically . . . dominate Dutch India, British East India and Australia" to fill the power vacuum in the Pacific left by the European colonial powers, especially Great Britain, defeated by Hitler. This assumption of hegemony in Asia, however, would leave "the puzzle of the relation of Japan to Hitler and Mussolini," in Du Bois's analysis, and "eventually Japan must make a tremendous choice." Du Bois asserts that Japan "has got to realize that the new industrial revolution which has already essentially transformed the Western World which she has been imitating, must be yielded to [communism]." However, this "will be easier than it appears," Du Bois concludes, for "as Matsuoka, himself, once told me: within and essentially, Japan is already Communistic."[122]

However, Du Bois was not to see Matsuoka transform Asia into a contiguous regional community that transcends nationalism, realizing the promise of the Co-Prosperity Sphere that is "communism." A week after Du Bois's column of July 12 appeared, the Japanese foreign minister was dismissed from Konoye's cabinet, and Matsuoka's Co-Prosperity Sphere became an autarchic regional empire that Japanese militarists dreamed of as industrially strong enough to wage total war. History also proved that Japanese-Soviet cooperation—and the Eurasian Continental Bloc that it enabled—could not work as a diplomatic deterrent against the international Anglo-American hegemony in maritime Asia. The United States, fearing that the Japanese-Soviet pact would embolden Japan to advance south against the British and American assets in Asia and the Pacific, "accelerated its own war preparations against Japan and adopted an even tougher stance in its negotiations with Tokyo," setting the stage for Pearl Harbor.[123] Ironically, the geopolitical vista that appeared on the Eurasian horizon in 1941—which briefly made Du Bois's socialist Manchurian narrative seem viable in its resonance with Matsuoka's foreign diplomacy—proved to be neither a deterrent to war nor an augury of a new international (and racial) order. Rather, it precipitated the Pacific War, merging the Sino-Japanese War into the greater conflict in the Pacific theater of World War II.

In this essay, I have delineated a black Eurasian Pacific geography that Du Bois charted and argued for the crucial—though rarely acknowledged—role that his Manchurian narrative played in it. In Du Bois's description, the communism that he imagined developing from Asia was "Marxian in its division of income according to need" but "distinctly Asiatic in its use of the vertical clan division and family tie, instead of reaction toward a new bourgeoisie along horizontal class layers" as in Europe. This communism afforded "vast hope," Du Bois writes in his travel manuscript. "With its Asiatic stress on character, on goodness, on spirit," it promised to avoid "the tendency of the Western socialistic state to freeze into bureaucracy," according to Du Bois. "Instead of socialism ever becoming a stark negation of the freedom of thought and a tyranny of action and propaganda of science and art," the black thinker posits, it might create "a great democracy of the spirit." Du Bois speculates that if the experiment had succeeded, it might have fulfilled Matsuoka's Greater East Asia Co-Prosperity Sphere; indeed, it might have "achieved a co-prosperity sphere with freedom of soul" (RA, 150–150A, 151). But the Japanese Empire was "under curious double control" (RA, 133). Eventually Japan's "headstrong leaders," writes Du Bois, "chose to apply Western imperialism to her domination of the East, and Western profit-making replaced Eastern idealism" (RA, 151).

After the Japanese Empire's capitulation in World War II, Matsuoka was judged on "Class A" charges of "crimes against peace" in the International Military Tribunal for the Far East. He died of tuberculosis before his trial was completed. Manchukuo vanished from the postwar world map; on August 8, 1945, two days after the atomic bomb was dropped on Hiroshima, the Soviet Union declared war on Japan, breaching the neutrality pact, whereupon Stalin broached the Manchurian frontier and placed Manchukuo under Soviet control.[124] Inspired by Matsuoka, Du Bois's Manchurian narrative demarcated the promise of Asian socialism that the Manchurian venture once seemed to furnish. This essay has attempted to convey this unique power of Manchuria to exercise the imagination of the African American leftist intellectual, who would evolve into a Maoist in the 1950s.

Notes

This chapter previously appeared in Etsuko Taketani's *The Black Pacific Narrative: Geographic Imaginings of Race and Empire between the World Wars,* published in 2014 by Dartmouth College Press. The chapter epigraph is from Henry L. Stimson, *On Active Service in Peace and War* (New York: Harper and Brothers, 1948).

1. Greil Marcus, *The Manchurian Candidate* (London: British Film Institute, 2002), 62; John Frankenheimer, dir., *The Manchurian Candidate* (1962; Century City, CA: Twentieth Century Fox Home Entertainment, 2002), DVD.

2. The state established in Manchuria was also spelled Manchoukuo.

3. Victor Shiu Chiang Cheng, "Imagining China's Madrid in Manchuria: The Communist Military Strategy at the Onset of the Chinese Civil War, 1945–1946," *Modern China* 31, no. 1 (2005): 77, 94, 103.

4. John K. Fairbank, "Born Too Late," in *Bertolucci's "The Last Emperor": Multiple Takes,* ed. Bruce H. Sklarew et al. (Detroit: Wayne State University Press, 1998), 203; Bernardo Bertolucci, dir., *The Last Emperor* (1987; Tokyo: Tohokushinsha Film Corporation, 2008), DVD.

5. As Arnold Rampersad observes, "Two concerns dominated [Du Bois's] analyses of international events in the 1930s and 1940s: the success of socialism, objectified in the fate of the USSR, and the rise of the darker races out of colonialism or, in the case of Japan, to the height of international power" (Rampersad, *The Art and Imagination of W. E. B. Du Bois* [Cambridge, MA: Harvard University Press, 1976], 225). In the phrasing of Francis L. Broderick, Du Bois's assessments of world powers were based on two criteria —"their sympathy for colored colonial peoples and their aversion to capitalism"—which

resulted in his championing of Soviet Russia and Japan (Broderick, *W. E. B. DuBois: Negro Leader in a Time of Crisis* [Stanford, CA: Stanford University Press, 1959], 196).

6. Gerald Horne, *Race War: White Supremacy and the Japanese Attack on the British Empire* (New York: New York University Press, 2004), 110.

7. Bill V. Mullen, *Afro-Orientalism* (Minneapolis: University of Minnesota Press, 2004), xvii, xxxvii, xxxviii.

8. While Du Bois's novel *Dark Princess* (New York: Harcourt, Brace, 1928) is a prime example of "Afro-Orientalism" that stresses Afro-Asian solidarity, I am interested in re-thinking black internationalism by linking it less to ideology and more to travel.

9. W. E. B. Du Bois, "As the Crow Flies," *Crisis* 41 (April 1934): 93. El Salvador was the first country in the Americas to recognize Manchukuo diplomatically, and the Dominican Republic also extended recognition.

10. See, for instance, Mullen, *Afro-Orientalism*; and Yuichiro Onishi, *Transpacific Antiracism: Afro-Asian Solidarity in Twentieth-Century Black America, Japan, and Okinawa* (New York: New York University Press, 2013).

11. David Levering Lewis, *W. E. B. Du Bois: The Fight for Equality and the American Century, 1919–1963* (New York: Henry Holt, 2000), 392, 419.

12. Report, Atlanta, Georgia, November 12, 1942, 1, William E. B. Du Bois, FBI file 100–99729; Kenneth O'Reilly, *Black Americans: The FBI Files*, ed. David Gallen (New York: Carroll and Graf, 1994), 83.

13. Report, New York City, May 1, 1942, 1, FBI file 100–99729.

14. Lewis, *W. E. B. Du Bois*, 390–91, 392.

15. See Langston Hughes, *I Wonder as I Wander: An Autobiographical Journey* (New York: Hill and Wang, 1993), chapter 6.

16. Travel itinerary, in "No. 5741, December 12, 1936, Visit of Professor Du Bois," Adjutant, Ministry of Navy, Ref. C05034825300, Japan Center for Asian Historical Records (hereafter cited as JACAR), National Archives of Japan, Tokyo. My translation.

17. W. E. B. Du Bois, "Forum of Fact and Opinion," *Pittsburgh Courier*, March 13, 1937, 15; W. E. B. Du Bois, *Newspaper Columns by W. E. B. Du Bois*, ed. Herbert Aptheker (White Plains, NY: Kraus-Thomson Organization, 1986), 1:180.

18. "No. 5741, December 12, 1936, Visit of Professor Du Bois." KBS requested permission for Du Bois to inspect the navy's battleship at Yokosuka.

19. Mark Stille, *Imperial Japanese Navy Battleships, 1941–45* (Oxford, UK: Osprey, 2008), 31–32, 34.

20. Du Bois, "Forum of Fact and Opinion," *Pittsburgh Courier*, March 20, 1937, 10; Du Bois, *Newspaper Columns*, 1:181–82. The "count" mentioned in Du Bois's dispatch was probably Count Ayske Kabayama, chairman of the board of directors of KBS and member of the House of Peers.

21. KBS did not "invite" Du Bois to Japan, though it significantly facilitated his planned visit. In 1936, KBS was "contemplat[ing]" extending an invitation to Zona Gale Breese, winner of the 1921 Pulitzer Prize, to visit Japan. She was indeed invited and vis-

ited Japan in the spring of 1937 ("Distinguished Visitors," *K.B.S. Quarterly* 3, nos. 1–4 [April 1937–March 1938]: 3).

22. "The Kokusai Bunka Shinkokai since Its Establishment," *K.B.S. Quarterly* 1, no. 1 (April–June 1935): 4. On KBS, see also *Kokusai Bunka Shinkokai (The Society for International Cultural Relations): Prospectus and Scheme* (Tokyo: Kokusai Bunka Shinkokai, 1934); and Atsushi Shibasaki, *Kindai Nihon to Kokusai Bunka Koryu: Kokusai Bunka Shinkokai no Sosetsu to Tenkai* [International Cultural Relations and Modern Japan: History of Kokusai Bunka Shinkokai, 1934–1945] (Tokyo: Yushin-do, 1999). The cultural activities of KBS included the production of films, lantern slides, gramophone records, and photographs; exchanges of professors and students; exhibitions; the establishment of contacts with overseas organizations; and the arrangement and sponsorship of visits by distinguished foreign guests. KBS also established the Japan Institute (1938–1941) in New York.

23. "Kokusai Bunka Shinkokai Jigyo Hokoku: Kokusai Bunka Jigyo no 7 ka nen" [Report on the Seven-Year Work of KBS's International Cultural Activities] (December 1940), 26, KBS Activities Collection, Japan Foundation Information Center Library, Tokyo (hereafter cited as KBS Collection).

24. "Kokusai Bunka Shinkokai Yakuin Meibo" [KBS: Directors, Advisers, Councilors List, as of September 1, 1936], KBS Collection. KBS's councilors included the director of the information department of the Foreign Office (which gave Du Bois a geisha party); the president of the Tokyo Pan-Pacific Club (which invited him to its monthly luncheon); the director of the Tokyo Imperial Household Museum (which he visited); the presidents of Tokyo Imperial University and Waseda University (at each of which he lectured); the director of the Tokyo Imperial University Library (which he inspected); the chairman of the board of directors of the *Osaka Mainichi*, a major newspaper company (at the hall of which he gave a lecture entitled "Message to Japan"); the executive director of Japan Broadcasting Corporation, Japan's national public broadcasting organization (which mentioned Du Bois's arrival in Japan "twice in nationwide radio hookups"); the mayor of Osaka (who "officially" received him); the vice minister of railways in the Japanese government (which provided him a free rail pass); the president of Nippon Yusen Kaisha (which provided passage on its ship *Tatsuta Maru* when he left Japan); and others (Du Bois, "Forum of Fact and Opinion," *Pittsburgh Courier*, March 13, 1937, 11; Du Bois, *Newspaper Columns*, 1:179).

25. "Purpose," *K.B.S. Quarterly* 1, no. 1 (April–June 1935): v.

26. Tomoko Akami, "The Emergence of International Public Opinion and the Origins of Public Diplomacy in Japan in the Inter-War Period," *Hague Journal of Diplomacy* 3, no. 2 (September 2008): 120.

27. Ramon H. Myers, "Japanese Imperialism in Manchuria: The South Manchuria Railway Company, 1906–1933," in *The Japanese Informal Empire in China, 1895–1937*, ed. Peter Duus, Ramon H. Myers, and Mark R. Peattie (Princeton, NJ: Princeton University Press, 1989), 119.

28. W. E. B. Du Bois to Chih Meng, May 15, 1936, reel 45, frame 494, Papers of W. E. B. Du Bois (microfilm), University of Massachusetts, Amherst, MA (hereafter cited as Du Bois Papers).

29. Chih Meng, *China Speaks: On the Conflict between China and Japan* (New York: Macmillan, 1932), 4–5.

30. M. [Matsuhei] Matsuo to W. E. B. Du Bois, June 4, 1936, reel 46, frames 129–30; Y. [Yoshiyasu] Kumazawa to W. E. B. Du Bois, July 29, 1936, reel 45, frame 946, Du Bois Papers. As a result of this change in itinerary, Du Bois reached Peking from the port of Dairen by steam, rather than from Mukden by rail.

31. W. E. B. Du Bois, "Russia and America: An Interpretation," draft manuscript, 132, reel 85, Du Bois Papers. All subsequent references to the work are cited as RA in the text. Page numbers for "Russia and America" are cited as they appear in the manuscript.

32. M. Matsuo to W. E. B. Du Bois, September 22, 1936, reel 46, frame 131, Du Bois Papers.

33. William C. Kirby, *Germany and Republican China* (Stanford, CA: Stanford University Press, 1984), 143–44.

34. For an account of border tension between the Soviet Union and Manchukuo, see Robert T. Pollard, "Russo-Japanese Tension," *Annals of the American Academy of Political and Social Science* 175 (September 1934): 101–9.

35. All foreign travelers through Manchukuo were required to obtain visas at the passport office in the compound of the Manchouli station.

36. On the city planning of Hsinking, see Akira Koshizawa, *Manshukoku no Shuto Keikaku* [Planning of Manchukuo's Capital] (Tokyo: Nihon Keizai Hyoron-sha, 1988); and Qinghua Guo, "Changchun: Unfinished Capital Planning of Manzhouguo, 1932–42," *Urban History* 31, no. 1 (May 2004): 100–117.

37. Du Bois notes that the Yamato Hotel at Hsinking was once "a Russian club . . . amid ancient acacias" (RA, 130), but he has probably confused the two Yamato hotels—both owned by SMR—at Harbin and at Hsinking.

38. Eri Hotta, *Pan-Asianism and Japan's War, 1931–1945* (New York: Palgrave Macmillan, 2007), 116.

39. Louise Young, *Japan's Total Empire: Manchuria and the Culture of Wartime Imperialism* (Berkeley: University of California Press, 1998), 250.

40. South Manchuria Railway Company, *Illustrated Guide Book for Travelling in Manchoukuo with Sketch Map* (Dairen, Manchukuo: Author, 1934), 45.

41. "Senman-nin 'Kokujin no Jifu': Dyuboisu hakase Sakuya Rairen" [Father of Ten Million Blacks: Dr. Du Bois Arrived at Dairen Last Night], *Manshu Nichi-Nichi*, November 18, 1936, 7.

42. "Kokujin no Jifu, Sakuya Koenkai" [Father of Blacks Lectured Last Night], *Manshu Nichi-Nichi*, November 19, 1936, 7.

43. Du Bois, "Forum of Fact and Opinion," *Pittsburgh Courier*, February 13, 1937, 15; Du Bois, *Newspaper Columns*, 1:168.

44. John J. Stephan, "Hijacked by Utopia: American Nikkei in Manchuria," *Amerasia Journal* 23, no. 3 (winter 1997–1998): 3.

45. "Manshukoku Kenkoku Sengen" [Declaration of Founding of Manchukuo], March 1, 1932, frame 0021, Ref. B02030709100, JACAR.

46. Stephan, "Hijacked by Utopia," 2, 15.

47. Du Bois, "Forum of Fact and Opinion," *Pittsburgh Courier*, February 13, 1937, 7; Du Bois, *Newspaper Columns*, 1:166; RA, 132.

48. "Manshukoku Kenkoku Sengen" [Declaration of Founding of Manchukuo], frame 0021.

49. For an analysis of the competing resistant nationalist and collaborative accommodationist discourses that developed on the Japanese Empire in Manchuria, see Rana Mitter, "Evil Empire? Competing Constructions of Japanese Imperialism in Manchuria, 1928–1937," in *Imperial Japan and National Identities in Asia, 1895–1945*, ed. Li Narangoa and Robert Cribb (London: RoutledgeCurzon, 2003), 146–68.

50. Du Bois, "Forum of Fact and Opinion," *Pittsburgh Courier*, February 13, 1937, 7; Du Bois, *Newspaper Columns*, 1:167; RA, 132.

51. Du Bois, "Forum of Fact and Opinion," *Pittsburgh Courier*, February 13, 1937, 7; Du Bois, *Newspaper Columns*, 1:167.

52. Du Bois, "Forum of Fact and Opinion," *Pittsburgh Courier*, February 13, 1937, 7, 15; Du Bois, *Newspaper Columns*, 1:167–68.

53. See Katsuji Nakagane, "Manchukuo and Economic Development," in Duus, Myers, and Peattie, *Japanese Informal Empire in China*, 141–46.

54. Young, *Japan's Total Empire*, 291.

55. Manchukuo, *Economic Construction Program of Manchukuo* (New York: New York Office of the South Manchuria Railway Company, 1933), 4.

56. Nagaharu Yasuo, "Manchukuo's New Economic Policy," *Pacific Affairs* 11, no. 3 (September 1938): 326.

57. See also Du Bois, "Forum of Fact and Opinion," *Pittsburgh Courier*, February 13, 1937, 7; Du Bois, *Newspaper Columns*, 1:167.

58. See also Du Bois, "Forum of Fact and Opinion," *Pittsburgh Courier*, February 13, 1937, 7; Du Bois, *Newspaper Columns*, 1:166.

59. Chih Meng to W. E. B. Du Bois, September 10, 1936, reel 45, frame 495; see also Poeliu Dai to W. E. B. Du Bois, November 27, 1936, reel 45, frame 496, Du Bois Papers.

60. Du Bois, "Forum of Fact and Opinion," *Pittsburgh Courier*, February 27, 1937, 15; Du Bois, *Newspaper Columns*, 1:174.

61. Roy Wilkins, "Watchtower," *New York Amsterdam News*, January 30, 1937, 12.

62. "Weekly Topics: Japan Gets Both Cheers and Boos," *New York Amsterdam News*, September 4, 1937, 14.

63. [George S. Schuyler], "The Far East and Us," *Pittsburgh Courier*, October 30, 1937, 10.

64. Langston Hughes, "Roar China!," in *The Collected Poems of Langston Hughes*, ed. Arnold Rampersad (New York: Vintage, 1994), 198.

65. Richard Wright, "Big Harlem Rally for China Tonight," *Daily Worker*, September 27, 1937, 4. In 1941, Wright applied to cover the Sino-Japanese War as a foreign correspondent for the Associated Negro Press (ANP). Wright sought this assignment out of envy of Ernest Hemingway, who had recently visited Chungking, the wartime capital of China's Nationalist government, as a correspondent for the New York leftist newspaper *PM*, along with his wife Martha Gellhorn, a war correspondent for *Collier's* magazine (Hazel Rowley, *Richard Wright: The Life and Times* [New York: Henry Holt, 2001], 235). Wright wanted "to see how men and women of color are living in other parts of the world" and became determined to go to the Far East (Richard Wright to Claude A. Barnett, March 4, 1941, box 93, folder 1187, Richard Wright Papers, Yale Collection of American Literature, Beinecke Rare Book and Manuscript Library, Yale University, New Haven, CT). However, Wright's application to the State Department for a passport to travel to China and the Soviet Union as a reporter for the ANP was denied (R. B. Shipley, Passport Division, to Richard Wright, June 24, 1941, box 107, folder 1645, Richard Wright Papers).

66. "Robeson to Help Chinese in War," *Pittsburgh Courier*, November 27, 1937, 1; "Paul Robeson Aiding China against Japan," *Chicago Defender*, November 27, 1937, 24.

67. *Chee Lai! (Arise!): Songs of New China* (New York: Keynote Recordings, 1941), 5.

68. "The Camera Overseas: 136,000,000 People See This Picture of Shanghai's South Station," *Life*, October 4, 1937, 102; "Ten Best News Stories of 1937 Are Picked by the Newsreaders," *Life*, January 3, 1938, 13.

69. Franklin D. Roosevelt, "Quarantine" speech at Chicago, in *The Public Papers and Addresses of Franklin D. Roosevelt, 1937* (New York: Macmillan, 1941), 407, 410.

70. George H. Gallup, *The Gallup Poll: Public Opinion, 1935–1971* (New York: Random House, 1972), 1:69, 72.

71. Du Bois, "Forum of Fact and Opinion," *Pittsburgh Courier*, September 25, 1937, 11; Du Bois, *Newspaper Columns*, 1:240.

72. Harry F. Ward to W. E. B. Du Bois, October 7, 1937; Du Bois to Ward, October 7, 1937, in W. E. B. Du Bois, *The Correspondence of W. E. B. Du Bois*, ed. Herbert Aptheker (Amherst: University of Massachusetts Press, 1973–1978), 2:147.

73. Du Bois, "Forum of Fact and Opinion," *Pittsburgh Courier*, October 23, 1937, 11; Du Bois, *Newspaper Columns*, 1:245.

74. Du Bois, "Forum of Fact and Opinion," *Pittsburgh Courier*, September 25, 1937, 11; Du Bois, *Newspaper Columns*, 1:240–41.

75. RA, 142. As Manning Marable observes, "Du Bois had been quite critical of the regime of Chiang Kai-Shek since 1928, primarily because of Chiang's anti-Marxist policies" (Marable, *W. E. B. Du Bois: Black Radical Democrat*, updated ed. [Boulder, CO: Paradigm, 2005], 156).

76. Du Bois, "Forum of Fact and Opinion," *Pittsburgh Courier*, September 25, 1937, 11; Du Bois, *Newspaper Columns*, 1:241.

77. Du Bois, "Forum of Fact and Opinion," *Pittsburgh Courier*, October 23, 1937, 11; Du Bois, *Newspaper Columns*, 1:245.

78. Yosuke Matsuoka, "A Knockout Blow Held Aim of Japan," *New York Times*, October 10, 1937, 12.

79. The league had proposed establishing international control of Manchuria. In speaking against this proposal, Matsuoka, Japan's chief delegate, asked rhetorically, "What justification is there for such an attempt on the part of the League of Nations? I cannot see. Would the American people agree to such control over the Panama Canal Zone? Would the British people permit it over Egypt?" (League of Nations, delegation from Japan, *Japan's Case in the Sino-Japanese Dispute as Presented before the Special Session of the Assembly of the League of Nations* [Geneva: Author, 1933], 60).

80. Iris Chang, *The Rape of Nanking: The Forgotten Holocaust of World War II* (1997; London: Penguin, 1998), 6.

81. On the American journalists who witnessed the massacre, see Takashi Yoshida, *The Making of the "Rape of Nanking": History and Memory in Japan, China, and the United States* (New York: Oxford University Press, 2006), 38–39.

82. A. T. Steele, "Nanking Massacre Story: Japanese Troops Kill Thousands," *Chicago Daily News*, December 15, 1937, 1.

83. Arthur Menken, "Witness Tells Nanking Horror as Chinese Flee," *Chicago Daily Tribune*, December 17, 1937, 4.

84. C. Yates McDaniel, "Nanking Horror Described in Diary of War Reporter," *Chicago Daily Tribune*, December 18, 1937, 8.

85. F. Tillman Durdin, "All Captives Slain: Civilians Also Killed as the Japanese Spread Terror in Nanking," *New York Times*, December 18, 1937, 1; F. Tillman Durdin, "Japanese Atrocities Marked Fall of Nanking after Chinese Command Fled," *New York Times*, January 9, 1938, 38. In addition to reports by US journalists, *Manchester Guardian* correspondent Harold John Timperley's stories became available to the American public in 1938 (H. J. Timperley, *Japanese Terror in China* [New York: Modern Age Books, 1938]).

86. "The Camera Overseas: The Japanese Conqueror Brings 'A Week of Hell' to China's Nationalist Capital of Nanking," *Life,* January 10, 1938, 51. Later in the year 1938, *Look* magazine carried shocking photos under the title "Killing for Fun!" which captured Japanese soldiers executing Chinese prisoners of war by bayonet and live burial. One picture showed a boy about to be beheaded "because he stepped on a telephone wire" ("Killing for Fun!," *Look*, November 22, 1938, 55).

87. "The Case for Japan," *Afro-American,* January 15, 1938, 4. A number of readers reacted negatively (see, for example, John Chen Tome, "Chinese Differs with Editorial on Japanese," *Afro-American*, January 22, 1938, 4; H. Baker, "Raps China Editorial," *Afro-American*, January 22, 1938, 4; and Louis W. Hann, "Dislikes Editorial," *Afro-American*, February 26, 1938, 4). Exchange and debate also took place in the *Philadelphia Tribune*, following Robert W. Bagnall's editorial (see Bagnall, "Bagnall: Sino-Japanese Situation," *Philadelphia Tribune*, November 25, 1937, 4; Bilal Farook, "Wants Japanese to Dominate

China," *Philadelphia Tribune*, December 9, 1937, 4; A. White, "Sino-Japanese War Is Fascism vs. Communism," *Philadelphia Tribune*, December 23, 1937, 4; and Bilal Farook, "Masses Treated Same under All Systems," *Philadelphia Tribune*, January 6, 1938, 4).

88. See, for instance, "Discuss Japanese in Chinese Intervention," *New York Amsterdam News*, March 19, 1938, 11; "Discussed Japs in China," *New York Amsterdam News*, April 9, 1938, 10; and "Brooklyn Debaters Meet Lincoln," *Afro-American*, April 9, 1938. 14.

89. See, for instance, "City-Wide Forum Hears America Is Headed for World Struggle," *Afro-American*, October 16, 1937, 22; "Sino-Jap Dispute Explained to Harlemites," *New York Amsterdam News*, February 5, 1938, 4; and Kaju Nakamura, "The Situation in the Far East—An Analysis," *New York Age*, April 16, 1938, 1–2. Du Bois arranged for Kiichi Miyake, a professor at Tokyo Imperial University and one of his KBS acquaintances, to give a talk on the Sino-Japanese War at Atlanta University in March 1938 (W. E. B. Du Bois to Yasuichi Hikida, March 11, 1938, reel 48, frame 1166; Kiichi Miyake to Du Bois, March 15, 1938, reel 49, frame 282, Du Bois Papers). The issue of propaganda in the China-Japan conflict is complex, for propaganda emanated from both Japan and China; see William E. Daugherty, "China's Official Publicity in the United States," *Public Opinion Quarterly* 6, no. 1 (spring 1942): 70–86.

90. That the Italo-Ethiopian War was one of the most important points of reference in the African American community is reflected by the invitation of Malaku E. Bayen, "representative of Emperor Haile Selassie" and founder of the Ethiopian World Federation in New York, to attend a debate on the Sino-Japanese conflict at the Dunbar Literary Club of Harlem in January 1938 ("Discuss Japan," *New York Amsterdam News*, January 29, 1938, 2).

91. Cyril Briggs, "Japan Proves Not to Be 'The Hope [of] Darker Races,'" *Philadelphia Tribune*, January 20, 1938, 2.

92. William Pickens, "Dean William Pickens Writes on Japan—'Masters of the Orient,'" *Pittsburgh Courier*, December 18, 1937, 14.

93. "The Week's Editorial," *Afro-American*, December 18, 1937, 1.

94. "The Case for Japan," 4.

95. "China Declares War on the Axis Powers: Declaration of War on Japan," *Contemporary China* 1, no. 15 (December 15, 1951): 1.

96. On Sino-Soviet relations, see John W. Garver, "Chiang Kai-shek's Quest for Soviet Entry into the Sino-Japanese War," *Political Science Quarterly* 102, no. 2 (summer 1987): 295–316.

97. Boris Slavinsky, *The Japanese-Soviet Neutrality Pact: A Diplomatic History, 1941–1945*, trans. Geoffrey Jukes (London: RoutledgeCurzon, 2004), 16.

98. Communist Party of the United States of America, *Is Japan the Champion of the Colored Races? The Negro's Stake in Democracy* (New York: Workers Library, 1938), 17.

99. Bruce Cumings, "Japan and Northeast Asia into the Twenty-first Century," in *Network Power: Japan and Asia*, ed. Peter J. Katzenstein and Takashi Shiraishi (Ithaca, NY: Cornell University Press, 1997), 146–47.

100. W. E. B. Du Bois, "The Meaning of Japan," speech, Morehouse College, Atlanta, GA, March 12, 1937, and Dillard University, New Orleans, LA, June 2, 1937, reel 80, frame 660, Du Bois Papers.

101. The *China Weekly Review* reported on a rumor circulating in China that Du Bois, "who recently toured the Orient, had expressed pro-Japanese sympathies" ("Serious Racial Element in the Sino-Japanese Struggle," *China Weekly Review*, December 10, 1938, 32).

102. Waldo McNutt to W. E. B. Du Bois, February 13, 1939; Du Bois to McNutt, February 25, 1939, in Du Bois, *Correspondence of W. E. B. Du Bois*, 2:184–85.

103. For an account of the committee, see Donald J. Friedman, *The Road from Isolation: The Campaign of the American Committee for Non-Participation in Japanese Aggression, 1938–1941* (Cambridge, MA: East Asian Research Center, Harvard University, 1968).

104. Henry L. Stimson to W. E. B. Du Bois, January 24, 1940, in Du Bois, *Correspondence of W. E. B. Du Bois*, 2:205.

105. W. E. B. Du Bois, "As the Crow Flies," *New York Amsterdam News*, February 24, 1940, 14; Du Bois, *Newspaper Columns*, 1:287.

106. Du Bois, "As the Crow Flies," *New York Amsterdam News*, November 18, 1939, 14; Du Bois, *Newspaper Columns*, 1:271.

107. Du Bois, "As the Crow Flies," *New York Amsterdam News*, August 3, 1940, 10. This column on Matsuoka is reprinted erroneously under the date of March 30, 1940, in Du Bois, *Newspaper Columns*, 1:292.

108. See Yosuke Matsuoka, "Proclamation of the Greater East Asia Co-Prosperity Sphere," in *Japan's Greater East Asia Co-Prosperity Sphere in World War II: Selected Readings and Documents*, ed. Joyce C. Lebra (Kuala Lumpur, Malaysia: Oxford University Press, 1975), 71–72.

109. On Matsuoka and the Eurasian Continental Bloc, see Chihiro Hosoya, "The Japanese-Soviet Neutrality Pact," trans. Peter A. Berton, in *The Fateful Choice: Japan's Advance into Southeast Asia, 1939–1941*, ed. James William Morley (New York: Columbia University Press, 1980), 44–85; and Yukiko Koshiro, "Eurasian Eclipse: Japan's End Game in World War II," *American Historical Review* 109, no. 2 (April 2004): 420–23.

110. Slavinsky, *Japanese-Soviet Neutrality Pact*, 7. Also, it is worth noting that Matsuoka's pro-Axis attitude did not entail anti-Semitism, although that charge has been leveled against him. As biographer David J. Lu notes, Matsuoka launched a rescue operation through SMR to render assistance to Jewish refugees from Nazi persecution. The operation provided refugees with shelter, visas for travel, passage to the United States and South America, or settlement in Manchuria and Shanghai (Lu, *Agony of Choice: Matsuoka Yōsuke and the Rise and Fall of the Japanese Empire, 1880–1946* [Lanham, MD: Lexington Books, 2002], 135–36).

111. In Rome, American modernist poet Ezra Pound welcomed Matsuoka in a letter to the foreign minister, in which he wrote, "No occidental decently aware of" the qual-

ities of Japanese civilization could be "infected with anti-japanese [*sic*] propaganda." In this letter, Pound also raised a proposal for peace directly with Matsuoka: "Men like myself would cheerfully give you Guam for a few sound films" of Noh drama (Ezra Pound to Yosuke Matsuoka, March 29, 1941, in Sanehide Kodama, ed., *Ezra Pound and Japan: Letters and Essays* [Redding Ridge, CT: Black Swan Books, 1987], 249).

112. The details of the Matsuoka-Stalin talks that transpired in the Kremlin on March 24 and April 12 were slow to emerge. Although an account of the first conversation as Matsuoka described it to Hitler was found in confiscated German Foreign Ministry files immediately after the war, and was in the hands of the Allied prosecutors in the Nuremberg and Tokyo Trials, official Soviet records of the conversations remained classified in the Russian Foreign Ministry archives until December 1994. The declassified records were fully brought into the public domain by Slavinsky's *Japanese-Soviet Neutrality Pact*.

113. "Record of Conversation of Comrade I V. Stalin with Minister of Foreign Affairs of Japan Matsuoka, 24 March 1941," and "Record of Conversation between Comrade J. V. Stalin and Foreign Minister of Japan Matsuoka, 12 April 1941," Russian Federation Foreign Ministry, quoted in Slavinsky, *Japanese-Soviet Neutrality Pact*, 37, 49.

114. Ibid.

115. Hosoya, "Japanese-Soviet Neutrality Pact," 79, 80–81.

116. "Record of Conversation of Comrade I. V. Stalin with Minister of Foreign Affairs of Japan Matsuoka, 24 March 1941," in Slavinsky, *Japanese-Soviet Neutrality Pact*, 37.

117. Otto D. Tolischus, "Victor's Welcome Given to Matsuoka," *New York Times*, April 23, 1941, 7; "Japan: Matsuoka Home with a Head," *Time*, May 5, 1941, 30; "Japan's Foreign Minister Does Grand Tour of Axis," *Life*, May 5, 1941, 40. According to John W. Dower, America's Cold War rhetoric of the Russians as an "Asian" people, the menace from the East, originated in this reported exchange (Dower, *War without Mercy: Race and Power in the Pacific War* [New York: Pantheon, 1986], 364n16). According to Yukiko Koshiro, in prewar Japan, the recasting of the Russians as Asians posed no problems; "the lesser 'whiteness' of the Russians facilitated their inclusion in Japan's pan-Asianist rhetoric" (Koshiro, "Eurasian Eclipse," 423).

118. "Accord Frees Tokyo's Hands in East, Soviet's in Europe," *Washington Post*, April 14, 1941, 1.

119. Ernest Hemingway, "Russia Still Aids China, despite Neutrality Pact with Japan," *Washington Post*, June 10, 1941, 1. For an account of Hemingway's trip to China as war correspondent, see Peter Moreira, *Hemingway on the China Front: His WWII Spy Mission with Martha Gellhorn* (Washington, DC: Potomac Books, 2006).

120. Slavinsky, *Japanese-Soviet Neutrality Pact*, 60.

121. Broderick, *W. E. B. DuBois*, 193.

122. Du Bois, "As the Crow Flies," *New York Amsterdam Star-News*, July 12, 1941, 1, 14; Du Bois, *Newspaper Columns*, 1:376.

123. Hosoya, "Japanese-Soviet Neutrality Pact," 85.

124. George S. Schuyler attributed the surprise attack of the Soviet Union on Man-

chukuo to the US dropping of the atomic bomb in Hiroshima. He editorialized in his *Pittsburgh Courier* column, "The dropping of the atom bomb did more than slaughter Japanese workers and their families. It spurred Russia to belatedly declare war on her erstwhile Japanese allies so that she would not be left out in the cold when the time came for distributing the Far Eastern swag" (Schuyler, "Views and Reviews," *Pittsburgh Courier*, August 18, 1945, 7).

[8]

ROB WILSON

TOWARD AN ECOPOETICS OF OCEANIA: WORLDING
THE ASIA-PACIFIC REGION AS SPACE-TIME ECUMENE

Counter-Conversions toward Oceania

This essay aims to invoke the emerging Pacific regional category and the global
and local vision of an ocean commons called Oceania to open the American
Pacific region—and American Studies—up to stronger modes of translocal
solidarity, ecological alliance, and world belonging. At the core will be the
projection of an environmental ecopoetics, here articulated via thinking
with and beyond the Pacific and Asia imaginary of Epeli Hau'ofa's works
in social theory and literature, as a means of overcoming nation-centric or
more absolutely racialized and bordered frameworks of Asian and Pacific
identity. This ecopoetics would reframe sites like California, Hawai'i, Taiwan, Fiji, and Okinawa and construct an affiliated poetics of transregional
worlding, bioregion, and translocal solidarity that has been long enacted in
"transpacific dharma wanderers" and writers like Albert Saijo, Gary Snyder,
Nanao Sakaki, Robert Sullivan, Susan Schultz, and Craig Santos Perez.[1]

This push toward an ecopoetics of Oceania will begin by invoking three
local images of the Pacific Ocean—"local" referring to Monterey Bay in
central coastal California, where I have lived and worked since moving from
Hawai'i in 2001. When I use the term "local," it should have the multiscalar
resonance of place-based specificity, agonistic struggle for social justice and
native recognition, and the globally entangled dialectics of world systems in
which I was immersed in Hawai'i and that I tried to theorize and enact in
Reimagining the American Pacific and later essays.[2]

The first image is that of the human-dwarfing sequoias in the mountains and
hills of Santa Cruz, which have survived for centuries partly on fogs that come
from as far as China and as near as Hawai'i—trees that shifting thermal patterns now threaten with drying needles and diminishing size. The second is of
the ocean floor at Monterey Bay, which is becoming a one-ton layer of military-

industrial and other human discards (like artillery shells, fishing lines, bottles, and plastic items) despite the vigilant efforts of many environmental forces and agencies. The third, and more apocalyptic, image, which many people are familiar with by now, forms a kind of collective work of global-capitalist postmodern art (so to speak): our global-waste installation in the transpacific ocean commons created by a hyperconsumerist ethos and ecological uncon- sciousness. The allusion here is to the Great Pacific Garbage Patch: a gyre of detritus twice the size of Texas and weighing some hundred million tons that lies just below the ocean's surface between California, Hawai'i, and Japan (the Northern Pacific Gyre) and is formed of plastic bottles, chemical sludge, non- biodegradable waste, and polymers harmful to marine wildlife.[3]

I invoke these three ecopoetic images, but there are many others: Tuvalu Island disappearing due to global warming and rising tides, the military buildup and resulting ongoing damage from Guam and Okinawa to the Persian Gulf, the melting Arctic, the increasingly numerous typhoons of Tai- wan and the Philippines. It is as if they are in some bleakly post-Whitmanic transnational catalogue aimed at converting you (as it were) to a vision of Oceania as a site of transpacific solidarity. This stance toward Oceania presumes a translocal regional formation of water-crossing linkages and multiscalar reimagining built up from field-imaginary works in literature and social science by the social scientist and fabulist Epeli Hau'ofa (1939– 2009), to whom so many of us across the Pacific region remain indebted.[4] But I would move Hau'ofa's islander-centric regional frame toward evoking a more capacious vision of alternative transnational belonging, ecological confederation, and transracial solidarity: Oceania as a performative speech act enacts what Arjun Appadurai has called "imagination as social prac- tice," a public form of intellectual labor and cultural practice that Hau'ofa was spectacular at doing in his own original, humorous, and visionary way.[5]

When I gesture toward that loaded verb "convert," this might well give the reader postcolonial pause, hearing in this performative verb quasi- imperialist echoes of some latter-day orientalist, that liberal scholar whom Edward Said memorably described in 1978 (as if echoing in ironic reversal the Puritan tonalities of Thomas Shepard across the "praying Indian" wilder- ness of colonial Massachusetts in the 1640s[6]): "Yet the Orientalist makes it his work to be always converting the Orient from something into something else: he does this for himself, for the sake of his culture, in some cases for what he believes is the sake of the Oriental."[7] Said's caustic elegance might be enough to scare off Saint Paul, the pluralist Pierre Hadot, or even the Jer- emaic Bob Dylan, from any such other-oriented benevolence.[8] When I gave a talk on my study *Be Always Converting, Be Always Converted* in 2010 at the Academia Sinica in Taipei, a young Taiwanese scholar of literary and psychoanalytical persuasion remarked, rightly to my mind, "your title must mean 'be always perverting' because . . . the meanings and forms of conversion change in these Pacific and Asia contact zones [like New Caledonia, Tonga, Hawai'i, and Taiwan]."[9]

The strongest postcolonial portrait of conversion, in my study of literary and theopoetic dynamics across the decolonizing Pacific, was drawn from Epeli Hau'ofa, for whom Christian conversion had become reborn, or transculturally mutated as cultural form or frame, via his place-based and ocean-affiliated metamorphosis of postcontact indigenous belief into what I called "counter-conversion" to Polynesian polytheism. This results for Hau'ofa in a large-scale "regoding" of the Native Pacific Ocean into the presencing of Pele and Maui as cultural, political, and environmental forces: in effect, Hau'ofa was enacting a turn away (or deconversion) from the conversion *telos* of capitalist hyperdevelopmentalism and its turbocharged work ethic of production and consumption that has gotten the ocean into the trouble it is now in, with its Great Pacific Garbage Patch ecoscape. I described this process of counter-converting in *Be Always Converting, Be Always Converted*:

> Oceania as such invokes this New Pacific ecumene, for Hau'ofa, a strategic mode of refiguring this Pauline universality of address for Pacific Islanders for whom globalization discourse would hail them into market dependency, subaltern labor, and secular difference. Oceania, vast, watery, evocative, at core mysterious (like the earlier PNG pidgin-vernacular term "wansolwara" for the Pacific as "one salt water" which can be translated into "one ocean, one people") becomes a strategic way of reframing and forming a critical regional identity. "South Seas," "Australasia," "South Pacific" (introduced via James Michener, Rodgers and Hammerstein et al. during the postwar American hegemony in the cold war ethnoscape of "militourism"), "Pacific Basin" and "Pacific Islands" all give way to Oceania as the self-identified signifier of Pacific choice.[10] But, in this turn, counter-conversion is generated from the volcanic earth and sea on the Big Island in Hau'ofa's "Our Sea of Islands." The new ecumene for Pacific Islander coalition-building is called "Oceania" and its capacious vagary of definition becomes a re-signifying identity of unity through which Polynesian, Micronesian, and Melanesian and all such colonial-imposed definitions of race or nationhood could be sloughed off, or cast away like dead boundary lines, false confinements into smallness, littleness, irrelevance, and global dependency.[11]

Hau'ofa framed his rebirth turn (in 1993) toward Oceania—it was originally a French geographical term—*l'Océanie*—coined in 1831 by the French explorer Dumont d'Urville, but it has become the name for one of eight ecozones on the planet—along a road leading from Damascus and Suva to Kona and Volcano on the Big Island. He went on writing and theorizing for nearly two decades, until his death in Fiji in 2009, about this hope-generating ecumenical turn back to native gods, goddesses, and art and away from what he saw as neodependency and globalization models of smallness, lack, or belatedness across the Pacific Islands.

Ecumene is a frame drawn from, and troped on here, the Greco-Roman world, where it meant the inhabited part of the earth. World geographers now use it to stand for populated sites. Similarly, "ecumenical" has been used by religious forces since 1545, the time of the Roman Catholic dispensation, to stand for a way of promoting unity and cooperation across divisions of faith: *ut unum sint*, as Norman Brown recapitulated this drive to unity beyond fractured differences in Pope John XXIII (as well as Marx and Freud).[12] But to be sure, Hau'ofa gives his "ecumene" a more water-based and oceanic way of belonging to the world: underspecified as to borders and mores, the term "Oceania" becomes a regional framework whose center we could say (echoing Emerson and Pascal on God) is everywhere in the interior Pacific and whose circumference is not fixed or certain, from its early use (which included Australia and New Zealand at the core) to Hau'ofa's later iterations (which can exclude all of Asia, as I will discuss below).[13]

Tellingly, Oceania remains one of the ecumenical categories of the Roman Catholic Church's global vision still used today. An early example of this would be the 1888 study written by the vicar apostolic of Western Oceania and the founder of the Catholic Church in Aotearoa in 1838, Jean Baptiste François Pompallier's *Early History of the Catholic Church in Oceania*.[14] There is a stained glass window of Bishop Pompallier in the church at Lapaha, Tonga, Hau'ofa's familial homeland, where Pompallier is called the first bishop of Central Oceania: in other words, Hau'ofa would have known such French and Roman Catholic usages. Pompallier wrote his own study in English and (in my view), Hau'ofa was troping on and mutating this prior theopoetic framework of Catholic Oceania.

"Ecumene," too, as we can learn from Gary Snyder's presciently ecopoetic usage, is related to the term "ecology,"[15] the very "earth household" (as Snyder tropes on its etymology in the essays and poetry collected in *Earth House Hold*) of water and land, economy and planet, that we have been reaching toward as a mode of more planetary belonging. As Snyder writes in "Notes on Poetry as an Ecological Survival Tool," in 1969 (just before ecology emerged as a global science in the 1970s), "Ecology: 'eco' (*oikos*) meaning 'house' (cf. 'ecumenical'): Housekeeping on Earth. Economics, which is merely the housekeeping of various social orders—taking out more than it puts back—must learn the rules of the greater [planetary] realm."[16] Hau'ofa's Oceania serves as his postcolonial catholic (with a small *c*) and boundary-shattering ecumene of Pacific Ocean belonging. Oceania, as materialized and envisioned in Hau'ofa's work, functions as "God-term" (as Kenneth Burke called the terminological end-term of such rhetorical persuasion), a grandly inclusive synecdoche of part-whole belonging that is all but visionary in its boundary-crossing capaciousness.[17]

Hau'ofa shows—in terms of myriad social-scientific and literary works as constructions of this interior Oceania in his *We Are the Ocean: Selected Works*—that a process of "world enlarging" occurs across diverse sites of pre- and postmodernity in five ways:[18]

1. Via processes of material and semiotic exchange based on an ethos of reciprocity
2. Via seafaring and jet travel interconnecting sites
3. Via myths and visions of gods, peoples, and sites
4. Via diasporic expansion and interconnection to great cities like Auckland, Honolulu, or those of the Bay Area in California
5. Via this vision of Oceania as a counter-converting trope turning the Pacific away from the *telos* of global domination and the ethos of disruptive developmentalism

More to the point, Hau'ofa's Oceania serves as an environmental framework of self-world interfusion and projects a regional configuration at once ancestral and postmodern or global, in which spaces of premodern and modern connection by sea voyage and jet travel are relinked across modern colonial maps that render island peoples as small, disconnected, and depleted, just the inhabitants of some "invisible vast wilderness of islands" flyspecked on a tourist map, as Mark Twain put it in *Following the Equator*.[19] Stories, images, art, dance, and legends perform a deep sense of Pacific sublimity; long-standing and tightly woven networks of interconnected reciprocity prove crucial to this formation, as islands and oceans are interconnected, move, link, flow across borders, and thus counter the late capitalist world from before, within, and after it. Hau'ofa, honored in life and death as the so-called Chief of Oceania, has—in the view of the Papua New Guinea poet Steven Edmund Winduo— opened a "school of thought," made a new beginning for Pacific cultural producers, and vibrantly reframed Oceania as a "spirit of relatedness" that we can (as I am doing here) build on in other disciplines and related sites.[20]

Transformations in Asian Pacific Knowledge Formations

Across emerging worlds and altered spatialities and knowledge formations, boundaries and study objects of areas and disciplines are being remade into frameworks like that of Hau'ofa and those gathered in this collection on transnational American studies. Regions and parts are being situated into different wholes and linked to differing social and ecological energies. Pedagogies push toward articulating counterworlds, and the forms of new spatiality that have emerged in literary, social-scientific, and cultural studies. Perhaps reflecting modes of technological interconnectivity and global mobility, from above and below, regions are becoming theorized as more open to fluid forms of relationality and interconnection—in frameworks like Oceania, Inter-Asia, Asia/Pacific, the so-called new Europe, and the circum-Mediterranean— than previous area studies had allowed.

In a 2005 essay titled "Asia Pacific Studies in an Age of Global Modernity" —published in *Inter-Asia Cultural Studies*, a journal in which this interdisciplinary work in field reshaping and multisited transformation of the Asia Pacific region has taken place since its first issue in 1999—Arif Dirlik, the postcolonial Marxist historian, provides an insightful overview of ongoing transformations of the Asia-Pacific field imaginaries as tied to areas and regions since the late 1980s.[21] Dirlik and I were coeditors of a special issue of *boundary* 2 called "Asia/Pacific as Space of Cultural Production," (including at its core Hau'ofa's frame-shattering "Our Sea of Islands"), wherein we aggravated discrepancies between these two Cold War areas, at the same time placing Asia and the Pacific in contentious, rhizomatic, interlinked, and ongoing transdisciplinary and transspatial dialogue.[22]

As the introduction to *Asia/Pacific as Space of Cultural Production*—a book based on the articles in the special issue of *boundary* 2—declared, "the all-but-reified 'Asia-Pacific' formulated by market planners and military strategists is inadequate to describe or explain the fluid and multiple 'Asia/Pacific.' . . . The slash would signify linkage yet difference."[23] The term "Asia-Pacific," more frequently referred to as APEC, weights the Pacific toward Asia as a site that controls motions in labor, capital, and culture as we surveyed in the book.[24] But Asia/Pacific can also mean opening up the Pacific to alternative formations, "as [the] Asia/Pacific region enacts the reconfigured space of nation-state deterritorialization, reinvention, struggle, and flight as power leaks out of the Cold War binary-machine."[25]

In the 2005 essay,[26] Dirlik reflects on such disciplinary transformations and points to what he calls five overlapping "trends" that have arisen across global academia, following on the crisis in area studies and the dismantling of Cold War rationales, or what Kuan-Hsing Chen calls the ongoing process of "de-Cold-Warization" across Asia and the Pacific.[27] Dirlik identifies these five trends as civilizational studies, the Asianization of Asian studies, indigenous studies, oceanic studies, and diasporic studies. While he sees the first three as still largely "continuous with [area studies and nation-based formations] in terms of fundamental spatial assumptions" of borders and fields via nations, he goes on to discuss oceanic and diasporic studies as representing "novel spatialities" that have arisen to challenge—and assert alternatives to—area- or nation-based models that had solidified during and after World War II (161). What Dirlik calls "the Asianization of Asian studies" as "directed against the hegemony of Eurocentric knowledge [of the area], especially United States domination of scholarship," as measured against the opposing turn to "insiders' views of Asian problems" and theories (164), however, might well be framed (in interior Pacific contexts) the "Pacific indigenization of Pacific studies." This would overlap with and complicate what he separates into the third trend, "indigenous studies" (wherein he draws on the work of Vilsoni Hereniko and others [162–63]), as this turn would often be directed against Australian or European claims to priority of perspective and would fit into "oceanic studies" as well.

"Oceanic studies," while related to Pacific Rim studies of transpacific capitalism in Asia-Pacific and other world ocean sites, can serve discrepant global, national, and local interests. As Dirlik phrases this contemporary dialectic, "Oceans may represent projections of place-based indigenous ideals into space, as they do for Epeli Hau'ofa, or they may be used in service of an APEC version of space in the service of capital and [transnationalizing] states" (167). Gazing across the Pacific to Japanese Zen and Chinese poetry as well as to communist movements in Russia and China, Kenneth Rexroth had noted this uneven possibility of linkage and difference in a 1971 interview on San Francisco as long connected to Asia Pacific by the transpacific ocean: "Oceans, like steppes, unite as well as separate. The West Coast is close to the Orient. It's the next thing out there. . . . SF is an international city and it has living contact with the Orient."[28]

Dirlik's five trends—what we might call, following Foucault, power/knowledge shifts in disciplinary paradigms—summarized as "civilizational revivals, the new attention to oceans, controversies over inside/outside forms of knowledge, diasporic motions and indigenous movements" (167) all point to transformations in the making of Asia Pacific and the Pacific region as such and need to be implemented with critical caution, lest we return (say) to the "The Glorious Pacific Way" of the neocolonizing "Forge Foundation," as Hau'ofa warned through the faux indigenizing character of Ole Pacifikiwei in his short story, who sells out oral histories of the area, as he becomes a "first-rate, expert beggar."[29]

Asia Sublates the Pacific

Unmaking and deworlding colonial modes with raucous satire, Hau'ofa's own poetic and fictional works are written in the post-British "many Englishes" of

Polynesia—sometimes called by Juliana Spahr and others "alter Englishes"[30]—
which are often creolized and pidginized in form. So pidgin artists (like Joe
Balaz, Wayne Westlake, and others) can and do figure in the remaking of
this reworlded Oceania, resisting the reign of what Hau'ofa's mocked as
World Bank English.[31] Yet Hau'ofa's works often demonize or mock contemporary Asians, or exclude them from having any affirmative claim on, or
role in, the construction of this alternative Oceania of ecological belonging
and cultural and political resistance. In his satirical Pacific novella, *Tales of
the Tikongs*,[32] Japanese corporate forces are linked to Pacific Rim operators
from Australia and New Zealand ("The Pacific Way belongs to regional
Elites . . ." [46]), building cars that are too small for hefty Tikong people
(12) and a tuna cannery that ends in disarray (19–21); and the gaming par-
lors of Taipei and sex shops of Tokyo and Sydney conspire to turn Tiko
into "the South Pacific Haven for Gambling and Prostitution" (81). Pacific
developers like Ole turn to "regional [money] laundry centers" in Bangkok,
Kuala Lumpur, Manila, Suva, and Moumea to learn how to do this sub-
limated mode of Asia-Pacific exploitation (92). In a related carnivalesque
vision of Asians in the Pacific, *Kisses in the Nederends* centers on New Age
modes of duping, tranquilizing, and conning the indigenous Pacific body of
Oilei Bomboki via that sage, yogi, and con man of Asian capitalist yoga and
libidinal love, Babu Vivekanand.[33]

This subaltern interior Pacific is staged in contrast with the more instru-
mentalizing and expansionist Asia as figured forth in Hau'ofa's fictional
works as just described—as well as in his Pacific-based turn against Asia in
his essay "The Ocean in Us"—as *not* part of this newly emerging Oceania,
suggesting instead the cognitive mapping of US and Asian commercial forces
aligned in hegemony over the interior Pacific. In this imaginary of Asia-
Pacific, Asia sublates the Pacific into neo-imperialist dynamics, with the sea
becoming capital's element of expansion across East and West: the Pacific is
a transnational space of sea power and ocean commerce, just "liquid capital" coming and going from Asia, as Christopher Connery summarized this
telos of Pacific Rim forces.[34]

At several points in "The Ocean in Us"—an essay based on the Oceania
lecture delivered at the University of the South Pacific in Suva in 1997 that
was published in *Dreadlocks in Oceania*[35] and served as the ecological manifesto in *We Are the Ocean*[36]—Hau'ofa moves toward forms of ecological
solidarity. "And for a new Oceania to take hold," he writes, "it must have
a solid dimension of commonality that we can perceive with our senses.
Culture and nature are inseparable. The Oceania that I see is a creation of
people in all walks of life" (56). Earlier in the same essay, discussing who
belongs to this new Oceania, Hau'ofa observes that "Oceania refers to a

world of people connected to each other. . . . As far as I am concerned, anyone who has lived in our region and is committed to Oceania is an Oceanian" (50–51). Belonging to Oceania, in this formulation, is a matter of ethical, political, and cultural commitment. Being Oceanian involves not only having a sense of history and cultivating a set of attitudes and beliefs, it also involves a sense of belonging to the earth and ocean as a biological and regional horizon of care.

But later in the same essay, Hau'ofa goes on to claim that in this Oceania "Asian mainland influences were largely absent in the modern era," and that more specifically speaking, "Pacific Ocean islands, from Japan through the Philippines and Indonesia, which are adjacent to the Asian mainland, do not have oceanic cultures and are therefore not part of Oceania" (53). In other words, Asians are excluded by history, tradition, and territorial site from belonging to this new Oceania. Questions haunt such sites in the Pacific and Asia: can Asia ever become (a past or present) part of Oceania, can Oceania become the basis of a broader environmental collation, and how can Oceania alter the hegemonic "Pacific Rim" or "Asia Pacific" frameworks?[37]

This view of Asia as sublating the interior or subaltern Pacific or being excluded from belonging to Oceania as a political ecoscape is understandable in historical terms and not uncommon in a range of works and genres. Teresia Teaiwa, in her song "Amnesia" from *Tereneisa*, performed with the Samoan novelist Sia Figiel, captures such a Pacific-evacuating Asia-Pacific, when she writes: "They're after American Pie in the East and some kind of Zen in the West. . . . So it's easy to forget that there's life and love and learning between Asia and America."[38] In *The Shark That Ate the Sun*, John Pule sees this American navy's Asian base–linked Pacific turn into an "American Lake," as linking "ships in Samoa / Hawai'i, Taiwan, the Philippines, / Belau, Kwajelein, Truk / The Marianas, the Carolines" and as forming a security chain across Oceania in which "the dead [as at the Bikini Atoll] are louder in protest than the living."[39]

Technological reformations of Asian and Pacific spaces and bodies are dystopically figured in Karen Tei Yamashita's "A Cyber Asian Odyssey"—a theatrical performance piece of technological orientalism in her *Anime Wong: Fictions of Performance*—and transpacific Maoist links are forged between China and Asian American struggles for Bay Area multicultural decolonization in her novel of transpacific and trans-Americas revolutionary heritage, *I-Hotel*.[40] In "Shrinking the Pacific," the Japanese American poet Lawson Inada imagines a shrunken, water-displaced Pacific Rim across which global travelers can "take the gleaming bridge / and bop into and around Hokkaido for lunch. / Maybe stay the night, or come back to Oregon, / which, by now is full of Hokkaido tourists" or neighbors—it is hard to tell

the difference in this unified Asia-Pacific.[41] Joe Balaz, in a poem published
in the online journal *Otoliths*, depicts the Hawaiian watershed at Waikiki
as having become a shopping-mall carnival of fake cultures and clownish
versions of indigeneity, commodified into what he calls (in the title) a "Polynesian Hong Kong":

> it's a hootenanny
> and a hoedown
> if you're on da top
>
> and you pull da strings
> on all da puppet clowns.[42]

This presumes a global capitalist framework spun around the making of
Asia-Pacific that I had circulated in cultural studies venues and poems, with
Asians on the Pacific Rim portrayed as not really part of the forging of
alternative frameworks (like Oceania) or claims (like those of indigeneity).
Instead, this Pacific Rim Asia was aligned with the transnational cultural
class, with its tactics of domination and simulation: a kind of "Disneyfication" writ large for global tourist consumption (as Fredric Jameson alle-
gorizes this postmodern "ethnicity-effect").[43] In essays such as "Imagining
Asia-Pacific"[44] and the chapter on Hau'ofa's carnivalesque Asia-Pacific in
Be Always Converting, Be Always Converted, I resorted to antagonistic formulations such as: "*Asia/Pacific* and *inter-Asia* do not just belong to the
'imagined community' of transnational capital and the astronaut class of
[Asian] frequent flyers; they cannot just sublate Pacific into Asia."[45] But
much more is taking place in and hold on the Asian and Pacific dynamics of
cultural production and site-based work across decolonizing Oceania.

In postcolonial Taiwan, to invoke a strong counterexample in the northern Pacific, a school of cultural studies work is arising that links Taiwan
native studies to Native American transnational frameworks of extranational and transindigenous belonging on the one hand, and on the other
hand that forges a primordial and contemporary connection with oceanic
frameworks that would unsettle territorial ties to the Chinese mainland and
reframe this decentered island site as long connected to the Pacific Ocean.
In an essay on these oceanic ties in Taiwan as refracted through the works
of Shyman Raporgan, a Tau poet from Orchid Island (long part of Austronesian culture and site of antinuclear protests in the 1980s), Hsinya Huang
writes: "Through their own lived experience, as well as that of their island
kin, Hau'ofa and Raporgan conceive of Oceania as a communal (sea) body,
through which they can ultimately resist the imaginary political lines drawn
by colonial powers. Their narratives turn hyper-modernized Pacific islanders

(like themselves) back towards a perception of bodily identities as individual projects in intimate connection with Oceania." Huang notes that Raporgan, like Hau'ofa, "represents Oceanic peoples as custodians of the sea, who 'reach out to similar people elsewhere in the common task of protecting the seas for the general welfare of all living things.'" Huang invokes Raporgan's reading of Oceania in the northeastern Pacific as an archipelagic region reshaping Taiwan as transindigenous nation-space linked to Austronesian (if not Polynesian) modes of language, space, body, and culture: "What does the 'world atlas' mean? A chain of islands in Oceania. The islanders share common ideals, savoring a freedom on the sea. On their own sea and the sea of other neighboring islands, they are in quest of the unspoken and unspeakable passion toward the ocean or maybe in quest of the words passed down from their ancestors."[46]

In *Earth House Hold*, Snyder ends his poetic and didactic journey out of Cold War US formations and into alternative worlding constructions of place, self, and community in Asia and the Pacific (linking sites in Japan, India, Tonga, "Cold Mountain" China, and the Pacific Northwest) by building up the Banyan Ashram on Suwa-No-Se Island in the Amami groups of islands that continue from Okinawa and the Ryukyus to Taiwan. This ashram, led by the amazing poet and transpacific dharma Buddhist wanderer Nanao Sakaki of works like *Break the Mirror*, cultivates ties to place and ocean through small-scale farming and fishing, "offering shochu to the gods of the volcano, the ocean, and the sky" and oceanic bonding for nourishment: "For some fish you must become one with the sea and consider yourself a fish among fish."[47]

Meditating, farming, fishing, dancing, chanting, getting married to person and place, Snyder, his wife, Masa; and their mentor, Sakaki, push their transpacific journey toward an ontology of wider world belonging, situating Japan in an Oceanic framework: "It is possible at last for Masa and me to imagine a little of what the ancient—archaic—mind and life of Japan were. And to see what could be restored to the life today."[48] Snyder brought the ecological and political stance I have been calling ecopoetics back across the Pacific in works of global and local ecological affects like *Turtle Island*, *Regarding Wave*, and *Mountains and Rivers without End* and in a work of ecological and poetic essays, *A Place in Space*.[49]

Albert Saijo's wondrously post-Beat, pidginized, "vandalized," Zen-and-Emerson-haunted ecological rhapsody, OUTSPEAKS forges what he calls an alternative "cosmovision" of place, ocean, and planet from his home on the edge of the Pacific near Hapu'u Forest in Volcano on the Big Island.[50] The kolea, or golden plover, becomes his figure of an oceanic traveler living on scraps and edges, who forges at once a line of flight and a mode of frugal inhabiting in "A Kona" (139–45). Identifying himself not as an ethnic or abjected Asian settler but as a "REBORN HUMAN" (197) of world ecology— the whole book is written in the declamatory capital letters of the manifesto ("I WANT TO OUSPEAK" forces of capitalist domination like a "FIELD PREACHER" [17]) or trans-species rant, as in an "Animal Rhapsode" (18)— Saijo presents his view of the small and caring life in hiking and sustenance living as beautiful. He summarizes his poetics and life close to the wilderness and his poetic and Buddhist quest (in the mode of Gary Snyder and Lew Welch) for embodied beatitude in self and world this way: "EDGING AN ACTIVE VOLCANO—LIKE THEY SAY IF YER NOT LIVIN ON THE EDGE YER TAKIN UP TOO MUCH SPACE" (199). Saijo's poems like "O Muse" invoke and honor this "RADIONCARBONIC" and "BIOLUMINESCENT" oneness of body with the radio waves, carbonic presence, and light of world (13). In *Jan Ken Po: Live in Honolulu*, 'Elepaio Press and Hawai'i Dub Machine productions (in the Dharma Brothers Studio) put together a CD of the 2000 poetry reading of these "transpacific dharma wanderers," Gary Snyder, Albert Saijo, and Nanao Sakaki, whose work from the 1950s to the present has forged an alternative vision of Asia and the Pacific tied to ecopoetic modes of planetary belonging, linking the human to other animals and the Buddha.

Three book-length contemporary poems by Craig Santos Perez perform the hugely innovative, serial, and historically informed feat of repossessing Oceania and the Marianas, a mode of world belonging in which Guam (or Guahan) can never be named (or forgotten as) just another unincorporated territory of the post-1898 American Pacific.[51] Resisting Guam's being just another "Pacific hub to Asia" (*hacha*, 30) and US "jurisdiction" (*saina*, 101), or its being referred to as "USS Guam" (*hacha*, 11) in the Pacific, to use a powerful example of Asia and Pacific remapping, Santos Perez also resists the centuries-long Spanish and US "reduction" process of "subduing, converting, and gathering natives through the establishment of missions and the stationing of soldiers to protect those missions" (*hacha*, 11).

Guam can no longer be taken as just a militarized island with "planes [forever] roaring out from Guam over Asia" and turning the Americanized Pacific into "a sea of toiling men," "a bloated thing" of war, dispossession, and exploitation (*hacha*, 10). These poems (tied in transpacific tidelands to the experimental writings of Tinfish in Honolulu and the Bay Area open poetics of Robert Duncan, Rob Halpern, Barbara Jane Reyes, and others) would proliferate counternamings and trace precarious routes and roots on Guahan, resulting in a whole countergeography of archipelagic belonging to Oceania and the Marianas as more than an act "to prove the ocean / was once a flag" (*hacha*, 47). Dispossessed by the Spanish of native seafaring tools and boats of "tasi" (the ocean or sea) like the flying proas or the sak-

man (long-voyaging canoe) and thus prevented from traveling between islands, "the chamorros themselves were by this time [1780s] no longer a people of the sea" (*hacha*, 74), and in World War II Guam was called an "omiya
jima" (great shrine island) by the Japanese (*hacha*, 76). All this process of
dispossession leads to the poet using Chamorro as a "drowned language"
(*hacha*, 78), returning in fragments and broken phrases and the renaming of
plants, history, and other things. At the same time, eight thousand marines
will be transferred to Guam from Okinawa by 2014 through a joint effort
of the United States and Japan (*hacha*, 91). And an ecological miscreant,
the brown tree snake that reached war-torn Guam as a stowaway in World
War II cargo ships (*hacha*, 87) has expanded its population exponentially
and led to declining numbers of birds and losses of native animals, as illegal
dumpsites proliferate as well.

Santos Perez "convenes," as the poet Aaron Shurin puts it, "an oceanic
poetics"[52]: the poems, like its rooted and routed people, must begin again in
salt water and subsurface groundings and waterings, tracing one salt water
across different parts of the Pacific. "What the map cuts up," as Michel de
Certau refers to this quest,[53] "the story cuts across" (*saina*, 44), as the poet
works in a diaspora of open-field or circumoceanic poetics (Santos Perez
has lived in Northern California since his family moved there in 1995) to
tell the broken story in shards; remainders; and space-time constellations of
place, family, and handed down stories. Oceania is reconvened to put the
water-land nexus back into pre- and postcolonial focus, via a resurrected
spatiality of four languages.

As the poet writes, acknowledging intertexual borrowings from Charles
Olson as well as from Hau'ofa in his oceanic "field composition" poems,
"Hau'ofa draws our attention to an oceania, preoceania, and transoceania
surrounding islands, below the waves, and in the sky—a deeper geography
and mythology" (*saina*, 63). Santos Perez does not just use the term "New
Oceania," he enacts this region in performative worlding. He also quotes
from Robert Sullivan's waka, "Ocean Birth": "every song to remind us / we
are skin of the ocean" (*saina*, 113). And he quotes the fluid documentary
poet Muriel Rukeyser, from "The Outer Banks": "All is open. / Open water.
Open I" (*saina*, 113), making fixities break down, fuse, and link across
imposed divides of subjected verbs; making "open" into world-making and
I-breaking action.[54]

The Asia of these poems by Santos Perez is an exploitative one as well, in
which well-off pregnant South Koreans arrive in us territories to give birth
to children who thereby become us citizens as promoted by "birth tour
agencies" (*saina*, 47). And the postwar tourists begin to pour in from the
Pacific Rim, particularly Japan, with its ties of war and colonial settlement:

"1967: 109 passengers on pan am flight 801 from haneda, japan arrive; 'japanese rediscover guam'" as "ginen sourcings" grimly puts the timeline (*saina*, 87). Since 1973 a quarter of a million tourists—70 percent of them Japanese—have been coming to Guam each year. The sections of the poem all have Japanese numbers embedded in them, along with English, Chamorro, and Spanish numbers. The rebranding of Guam as a "world class tourist destination" with hotels "all with ocean views" continues (*saina*, 115), as a function of what Teresia Teaiwa calls the "militourist" mode of space production of the Pacific for Asian and Euro-American fulfillment.[55] Even as the grandmother's Catholic rosary ties the Pacific together in grass-roots beatitude and oceanic crossings, "when I say rosary [in Chamorro] I think I can hear her voice / even here in California" (*saina*, 119). The *guma* collection continues to extend and enrich the historical, linguistic, and formal range of Santos Perez's ongoing serial poem, in effect pushing this fatal impact narrative into quasi-epic scope as a portrayal of Guam in all its indigenous, colonial, modern, and contemporary complexity. The contradictory island site is portrayed as at once hybrid, assimilated, and decolonizing. Ethnography, autobiography, history, geography, literary criticism, journalism, ecology, the fascist writings of Ezra Pound, the spectral figure of Juan Malo, dietary regimes of junk food, and poems by other contemporary Chamorro poets all collide with and are woven into this seriocomic intertextual mix of oceanic convening.

No Asian or Pacific region-making framework can remain innocent these days of uneven power dynamics, historical elisions, bordered exclusions, internal discrepancies, or aporias of place making. Postmodern Oceania (full of Sullivan's Maori wakas and Santos Perez's Chamorro sakman as well as 350-meter-long diesel-powered ships from Matson and Evergreen to STX, some of which lose 10,100 containers at sea each year) offers no ecological cure or postcolonial kava pill for the Cold War hangovers of war, post-9/11 remilitarization, racial tension, or the dynamics of neoliberal globalization that are reshaping space, time, self, and world.[56]

We cannot forget war, racism, colonialism, and neocolonial economic disparities in the magical waters of the Pacific as Oceania. Still, as I urged in my study of Hau'ofa, affiliation to Oceania can become not just a matter of heritage or blood but can help forge "a trope of commitment, vision, and will" in the remaking of Asia and the Pacific.[57] As Gayatri Spivak reminds us, reading literature from such discrepant spaces and the clashing of cultures, "the old postcolonial model—very much India plus the Sartrian Fanon—will not serve now as the master model for transnational to global cultural studies on the way to planetarity."[58] For we are dealing with heterogeneity, as she argues of sites like post-Soviet Russia and other Asias

or decolonizing Oceania; new paradigms are emerging on a scale of intervention and responsibility that are more than just the same old global and
postcolonial ones.

Toward an Ecopoetics of Asia-Pacific Solidarity in Oceania

Across six postwar decades and transpacific contexts, Snyder has forged
a coherent and consistent ecopoetics from *Earth House Hold* to *A Place
in Space*. As I suggested above, Snyder is a poet activist from the Beat era
who has long advocated the regenerative power of wilderness, what he calls
"the practice of the wild," and enacted the deep ties of the Pacific Rim to
the powers of emplaced consciousness and reinhabitory energies in the wilderness. In Snyder's geographical and poetic reframing of the coastal Pacific
into what he calls in his 1992 essay "Coming into the Watershed"—which
has become crucial to the field of American ecological criticism and was
reprinted in *A Place in Space*—"the San Francisco / valley rivers / Shasta
headwaters bio-city region" are all interconnected (by slashes here) and lead
to modes of gratitude and planetary care for "Turtle Island" as an ethical
attitude.[59] Snyder renames this biological community from his home in the
Kitkitdizze Sierras biological region the "Shasta Nation" (*A Place in Space*,
255), where the regenerative energies of the wild and the sense of primordial
planetary belonging can lead Euro-Americans, Asian Americans, African
Americans, and North Beach dharma bums on the reworlding path to "become 'born-again' natives of Turtle Island" ("Coming into the Watershed,"
234). Snyder's ecumene is an ecologically interconnected, planetary, and re-
nativized counter-conversion to place.

In Snyder's earlier essay on urban place, "North Beach" (reprinted in
The Old Ways), the poet enacts an uncanny biopoetics of the region as con-
tado and as counterhistory and counterculture. North Beach is portrayed
as a "non-Anglo" multicultural habitat where the Costanoan peoples had
lived for over five thousand years in the Bay; it later became a place of Alta
Californian dairy farms, before waves of Irish, Italian, Sicilian, Portuguese,
Chinese (Cantonese and Hakka) and "even Basque sheepherders down from
Nevada" settled in.[60] Beneath the Transamerica Pyramid, Snyder conjures
up "a tiny watershed divide at the corner of Green and Columbus," where
"northward a creek flowed" toward Fisherman's Wharf, all covered by
oblivious landfill now.[61] By evoking remnants of the Pacific bioregion and
the occluded history of settlement, Snyder aims at "hatching something else
in America; pray it cracks the shell in time." That something else is a vision
of the bioregion that would connect place to living watersheds, a sense of
bioregional belonging, and the influx of place-tied values that abide and

have come down to ecopoetics from Native America and global cultures of Asia and the Pacific.

In a much-cited essay called "Indigenous Articulations," James Clifford applies the "articulation" theories of Stuart Hall and Antonio Gramsci on the coalitional forging of counterhegemony to offer a multiple-edged model of Pacific region making that he calls "subaltern region-making."[62] Pacific indigenous peoples can creatively compose in this process "a region cobbled together, articulated [with global forces], from the inside out, based on everyday practices that link islands with each other and with mainland diasporas" (22–23). As in his early work on the Melanesian world, Clifford turns back to the work of Jean-Marie Tjibaou in New Caledonia and the Loyalty Islands, "where a composite 'Kanak' identity was emerging in political struggle" (31). Such a vision of place, land, and identity as "interdependent" would "also embrace the Pacific sea of islands—a wider world of cultural exchange and alliances that were always crucial for Tjibaou's thinking about independence as inter-dependence" (ibid.), as Clifford summarizes Tjibaou's gesture toward the island land and sea as world home in Oceania.

We can also thicken the meanings and tactics of Oceania via a well-situated anthology called *Whetu Moana*, in which ten Hawai'ian poets figure prominently. Many of the poems are concerned with links not just to the people of "the 'āina" but also to sustenance from, connections to, and wayfaring across Oceania—including ecologically oriented poems based in Hawaiian waters like "Spear Fisher" and "Da Last Squid" by Joe Balaz and poems of Native Hawaiian ecological recovery by Brandy Nalani McDougall.[63] Crucially in 1976, and in waves of Pacific-crossing voyages afterward, the Hawaiian voyaging project Hoku'leia began to remap the Polynesian triangle across Oceania and helped create this interconnected ocean of stars via native knowledge, techniques, and community-building forms cutting across nations and colonizing prejudices, as in Robert Sullivan's eclectic waka assemblages in *Star Waka* and the countergeographies and indigenous ocean-sailing tactics of Santos Perez that I have touched on above.

If we think with and beyond Hau'ofa's crucial new vision of the Pacific, Oceania can become the framework for the forging of ecological solidarity; the site of alternative modes of Asian and Pacific, or Pacific and Asian, linkage and knowledge formation; and a mode of transforming social and regional practices and helping prod the making, shaping, and gathering of what I have been calling ecopoetics. Literature, as I have been arguing, can help us see such links and affects between ocean, self, and planet. Like geographical cultural studies, poetics can thus help us overcome and reframe what Lawrence Buell has called "the foreshortened or inertial aspect of [the] environmental unconscious," so that we can develop better modes of rein-habitation and a "watershed consciousness" of an Oceanian ethos that is aware of our ties to rivers, shores, and the global commons of the ocean.[64]

Taking Care of the Body in Oceania: Olap's Canoe

Citing Clifford's evocation of New Caledonia as a connecting place to the ocean world, Snyder's oceanic ashram in Japan with Nanao Sakaki in *Earth House Hold* and *Jan Ken Po*, Saijo's ocean-facing Big Island in OUTSPEAKS, Sullivan's waka assemblages; and renativizing Taiwan's turn into a coun-termainland site aligned to Oceania, as in the work of Hsinya Huang and others, I have (here and elsewhere) been trying to overcome the taken-for-granted view of an Asia/Pacific imaginary with Asian cultures and sites cast as transnational capital forces of globalization and set relentlessly against the interior Pacific—which is figured as a raw resource, fantasy site, va-cancy, and/or source of subaltern or diasporic labor. I have aimed to pro-duce a multiple-edged vision of ecological solidarity in the region: "We [cul-ture workers, critical theorists, teachers] can seek the antagonistic synergy of Asia/Pacific forces, flows, linkages, and networks."[65] With wry wit and capacious-hearted humor Hau'ofa often implied that this was possible in his own first-person-plural evocations, as when he left that catholic "we" of oceanic solidarity open and underspecified in the title *We Are the Ocean*, thus making us capable of expansive coalition building inside and across the Pacific and the world: we are the ocean indeed, in some fundamental ecological sense of body and world.[66]

As Sylvia Earle wrote in *Time* magazine in 1996 (in an article Hau'ofa was fond of citing), "every breath we take is possible because of the life-filled life-giving sea; oxygen is generated there, carbon dioxide absorbed. . . . Most of Earth's living space [its ecumene], the biosphere, is ocean—about 97%. And not so coincidentally 97% of Earth's water is Ocean."[67] We know from effects like El Niño and polar melting that the sea shapes weather and climate patterns, and its moisture stabilizes and replenishes the fresh water in rivers, lakes, and streams. We are the Ocean in our very bod-ies as well, since each living person is some 60–70 percent water. As Milton Murayama, a Japanese author from Maui, memorably advised, "take care da body," and you may just take care of the place, soul, and other creatures on earth as well.[68]

The aim of this essay has been to open Oceania up to a Pacific-affiliated ecopoetics of translocal solidarity, place, and bioregional worlding that is being built up across the Pacific Ocean and that writers like Sakaki, Snyder, Westlake, Richard Hamasaki (who sometimes uses the pen name red flea) and Saijo have long stood for in their "transpacific dharma wanderings."[69] Whether I have succeeded or not, the ocean that we are part of will long know and the planet will feel the consequences of our ecopoetic gestures and activities for generations to come. One last ecopoetic image: in a section called "Flows" in *Asia/Pacific as Space of Cultural Production* collection, Dirlik and I included a translation by Theophil Saret Reuney of an ocean-based aboriginal work from Truk (in the Federated States of Micronesia) called "The Pulling of Olap's Canoe." The work and its elaborate footnotes, with untranslatable coinages and unfillable gaps, are full of names for places, birds, whales, plants, waves, rocks, navigation customs, islands, and species of Oceania, as in lines like "The whale whose names are Urasa and Pwourasa / They guard those pompano fish which belong to wasofo [a name for the new canoe, and by extension the new navigator]."[70]

Reuney, like the beloved Epeli Hau'ofa, has passed away. But Reuney's works are being used by linguists and biologists (like Alan Davis in his compilation of a Chuuk lexicon at a University of Guam archive site)[71] to compile Chuukese names for plants and animals, some of which are now extinct, and by the cultural studies scholar Joachim Peter to forge an oceanic-based vision of horizon, world, and place. Let us hope that these names and these creatures can survive our own planetary plundering across the Anthropocene. Clearly the world of Olap's ocean is endangered and full of ecological pathos, as when Reuney's footnote 48, to the line "You delve deeply into the fish of mataw anu," records that for the name *mataw anu*, the "meaning is ambiguous, especially since the type of fish is unknown."[72]

Notes

1. The trope of "transpacific dharma wanderers" (reflecting shared interests in ecology, Buddhism, and the environment as discussed below) alludes to the title of a poetry reading given by Gary Snyder, Nanao Sakaki, and Albert Saijo at the University of Hawai'i at Manoa on March 2, 2000, organized by Richard Hamasaki and others. See Burl Burlingame, "Wanderers Find Poetry in the Environment," *Honolulu Star-Bulletin*, March 1, 2000.

2. See Rob Wilson, *Reimagining the American Pacific: From "South Pacific" to Bamboo Ridge and Beyond* (Durham, NC: Duke University Press, 2000) and "Reframing Global/Local Poetics in the Post-Imperial Pacific: Meditations on 'Displacement,' Indigeneity, and the Misrecognitions of US Area Studies," in *World Writing: Poetics, Ethics, Globalization*, ed. Mary Gallagher (Toronto: University of Toronto Press, 2009), 224–45.

3. This paragraph draws on Paul Simons, "Weather Eye: Disappearing Fogs of the Pacific Coast," *London Times*, February 25, 2010; Jane Palmer, "Junk Accumulating on Monterey Bay Ocean Floors: Scientists Find Iincreasing Levels of Debris in the Deep Sea,"

Santa Cruz Sentinel, February 2, 2010; Maggie Shiels, "Boat Made of Trash [The Plastiki] Prepares to Set Sail," *BBC News*, March 3, 2010.

4. See, for example, James Clifford, *Returns: Becoming Indigenous in the Twenty-First Century* (Cambridge, MA: Harvard University Press, 2013), with its chapter on "Hau'ofa's Hope" as a quasi-utopic vision of the reindigenizing Pacific "necessarily entangled with other, more ambivalent, scenarios and dystopias" (212).

5. Arjun Appadurai writes: "The image, the imagined, the imaginary—these are all terms which direct us to something critical and new in global cultural processes: *the imagination as social practice*. No longer mere fantasy (opium for the masses whose real work is elsewhere), no longer simple escape (from a world defined principally by more concrete purposes and structures), no longer elite pastime (thus not relevant to the lives of ordinary people) and no longer mere contemplation (irrelevant for new forms of desire and subjectivity), the imagination has become an organized field of social practices, a form of work (both in the sense of labor and of culturally organized practice) and a form of negotiation between sites of agency ('individuals') and globally defined fields of possibility" ("Disjuncture and Difference in the Global Capitalist System," *Public Culture* 2, no. 2 [1990]: 5).

6. Thomas Shepard, *God's Plot; the Paradoxes of Puritan Piety; Being the Autobiography and Journal of Thomas Shepard*, ed. Michael McGiffert (Amherst: University of Massachusetts Press, 1972), 67.

7. Edward Said, *Orientalism* (New York: Vintage, 1994), 6.

8. See Pierre Hadot, "Conversion" (in *Encyclopaedia Universalis*, ed. Claude Grégory [Paris: Encyclopaedia Universalis France, 1968], 4:979–81), in which he elaborates the many classical and post-Christian meanings of conversion from *epistrophe* (return of self to an origin) to the more radical version of *metanoia* (mutation and rebirth).

9. Rob Wilson, *Be Always Converting, Be Always Converted: An American Poetics* (Cambridge, MA: Harvard University Press, 2009).

10. Meditating on the semiotics and politics of "Oceania," Hau'ofa admits having in mind the Pacific pidgin term "Wansolwara," the name of a newspaper produced by Pacific Islander journalism students at the University of South Pacific in Fiji, when he founded the Oceania Centre for Arts and Culture (in 1997). See "The Ocean in Us," 114–17.

11. Wilson, *Be Always Converting, Be Always Converted*, 126.

12. Norman O. Brown, *Love's Body* (Berkeley: University of California Press, 1966), 81.

13. From Saint Augustine to Ralph Waldo Emerson and Marshall McLuhan (as in his televised talk with Father Patrick Peyton), God was commonly defined as "a circle whose center is everywhere and whose circumference is nowhere."

14. Jean Baptiste François Pompallier, *Early History of the Catholic Church in Oceania* (Auckland: H. Brett, 1888).

15. As Felix Guattari elaborates on the Greek origin of the term, "ecology" derives from a complex of "house, domestic property, habitat, natural milieu," meaning the geo-

graphical place where interactions and encounters take place(*The Three Ecologies*, trans. Gary Genosko (London: Athlone Press, 2000), 91 note 52).

16. Gary Snyder, *Earth House Hold: Technical Notes and Queries to Fellow Dharma Revolutionaries* (New York: New Directions, 1969), 127.

17. See Kenneth Burke, *A Grammar of Motives* (Berkeley: University of California Press, 1969), 355–365, on a God-term (like money) designating the ultimate motivation or substance of a given rhetorical or constitutional frame.

18. Epeli Hau'ofa, *We Are the Ocean: Selected Works* (Honolulu: University of Hawai'i Press, 2008), 30–188.

19. Mark Twain wrote: "For a day or two we have been plowing [in the Pacific near Fiji] among an invisible vast wilderness of islands, catching now and then a shadowy glimpse of a member of it. There does seem to be a prodigious lot of islands this year; the map of this region is freckled and fly-specked all over with them" (*Following the Equator: A Journey around the World* [New York: P. F. Collier and Sons, 1899], 72).

20. Steven Edmund Winduo, "Chief of Oceania," in "Epeli's Quest: Essays in Honor of Epeli Hau'ofa," ed. Terence Wesley-Smith, *Contemporary Pacific* 22, no. 1 (2010): 114–116.

21. Arif Dirlik, "Asia Pacific Studies in an Age of Global Modernity," *Inter-Asia Cultural Studies* 6, no. 2 (2005): 158–70.

22. Arif Dirlik and Rob Wilson, eds., "Asia/Pacific as Space of Cultural Production," special issue of *boundary 2* 21, no. 1 (1995). On related modes of regional transformation and cultural studies, see Laura Lyons, "American Pacific Culture and Theory," *The Year's Work in Critical and Cultural Theory* 6, no. 1 (1996): 315–24; Houston Wood, "Cultural Studies for Oceania," *Contemporary Pacific* 15, no. 2 (2003): 340–74.

23. Rob Wilson and Arif Dirlik, "Introduction: Asia/Pacific as Space of Cultural Production," in *Asia/Pacific as Space of Cultural Production*, ed. Rob Wilson and Arif Dirlik (Durham, NC: Duke University Press, 1995), 6.

24. For related interventions into refigurations of the Pacific, see also Arif Dirlik, ed., *What Is in a Rim? Critical Perspectives on the Pacific Region Idea*, 2nd ed. (Lanham, MD: Rowman and Littlefield, 1998); Vilsoni Hereniko and Rob Wilson, eds., *Inside Out: Literature, Cultural Politics, and Identity in the New Pacific* (Lanham, MD: Rowman and Littlefield, 1999). For a technological and cyberspace take on the region that draws on such work, see Larissa Hjorth and Dean Chan, eds., *Gaming Culture and Place in Asia-Pacific* (London: Routledge, 2009).

25. Wilson and Dirlik, "Introduction," 13.

26. Dirlik, "Asia Pacific Studies in an Age of Global Modernity." For further references to this work, I will provide page numbers in parentheses in the text.

27. Kuan-Hsing Chen, "Taiwan as Club 51: On the Culture of US Imperialism," in *The Worlding Project: Doing Cultural Studies in the Era of Globalization*, ed. Christopher Leigh Connery and Rob Wilson (Berkeley, CA: North Atlantic, 2007), 111.

28. Interview with Kenneth Rexroth, in *The San Francisco Poets*, comp. David Meltzer (New York: Ballantine, 1971), 30.

29. Epeli Hau'ofa, "The Glorious Pacific Way," in *We Are the Ocean*, 118.

30. Juliana Spahr, "Connected Disconnection and Localized Globalism in Pacific Multilingual Literature, *boundary* 2 31, no. 3 (2004): 75–100.

31. For previous historical and aesthetic contexts for such experimental and local work, see Rob Wilson, "Pacific Postmodern: From the Sublime to the Devious," *boundary* 2 28, no. 1 (2001): 121–51.

32. Epeli Hau'ofa, *Tales of the Tikongs* (Honolulu: University of Hawai'i Press, 1994). For further references to this work, I will provide page numbers in parentheses in the text.

33. Epeli Hau'ofa, *Kisses in the Nederends* (Honolulu: University of Hawai'i Press, 1995). For further references to this work, I will provide page numbers in parentheses in the text.

34. Christopher L. Connery, "Pacific Rim Discourse: The U.S. Global Imaginary in the Late Cold War Years," in *Asia/Pacific as Space of Cultural Production*, 40.

35. Sudesh Mishra and Elizabeth Guy, eds., *Dreadlocks in Oceania* (Fiji: University of the South Pacific Press, 1997), vol. 1.

36. For further references to Hau'ofa, *We Are the Ocean*, I will provide page numbers in parentheses in the text.

37. Vilsoni Hereniko, an ally of Hau'ofa's in Pacific literary and cultural studies, director of the Pacific Studies Center at the University of Hawai'i, and successor to Hau'ofa as director of the Oceanian arts center at the University of the South Pacific in Suva, offered me astute feedback on the issue of how, and to what extent, Hau'ofa excluded Asians from Oceania and the material national history of the Pacific. Hereniko pointed out, at my keynote talk at the 2010 School of Pacific and Asian Studies Conference at the University of Hawai'i at Manoa, through historical anecdote and critical reflection, that Hau'ofa did more than anyone to support the Indian settlers in Fiji at a time when other Pacific writers were more on the side of keeping Fiji for Fijians and supporting the nativist-based hegemony and regime changes there. Thus, too, less capacious forms of Pacific- and Oceania-based identity had often become a way of including or excluding "Asia" (another vague term) and Asians (like those Indo-Fijians whose families had labored in Fiji for four and five generations) from linking the subaltern regional Pacific to art, culture, social vision, ecology and so on.

38. Teresia Teaiwa, "Amnesia," in *Terenesia* (Honolulu: Eleipaio, 2000).

39. John Pule, *The Shark That Ate the Sun* (Auckland: Penguin, 1992), 73–75. For ongoing struggles against this militarized archipelago of US bases across the Pacific, see Setsu Shigematsu and Keith L. Camacho, eds., *Militarized Currents: Toward a Decolonized Future in Asia and the Pacific* (Minneapolis: University of Minnesota Press, 2010).

40. Karen Tei Yamashita, *Anime Wong: Fictions of Performance*, afterword by Stephen Hong Sohn (Minneapolis: Coffee House, 2014), and *I-Hotel* (Minneapolis: Coffee House, 2010).

41. Lawson Inada, "Shrinking the Pacific," in *Asia/Pacific as Space of Cultural Production*, 80–81.

42. Joe Balaz, "Polynesian Hong Kong," *Otoliths*, 2010, http://the-otolith.blogspot .com/2010/01/joe-balaz-polynesian-hong-kong-its.html, accessed February 12, 2015. For a broader discussion of Balaz, see Rob Wilson, "On the Creolized Hawaiian Poetics of Joseph Puna Balaz: Draft," https://www.academia.edu/1394774/On_the_Creolized_Ha waiian_Poetics_of_Joseph_Puna_Balaz_DRAFT, accessed February 12, 2015.

43. Fredric Jameson, "New Literary History after the End of the New," *New Literary History* 39, no. 3 (2008): 375–387. For example, Jameson writes: "In globalization, there are no cultures, but only nostalgic images of national cultures: in postmodernity we cannot appeal back to the fetish of national culture and cultural authenticity. Our object of study is rather Disneyfication, the production of simulacra of national cultures; and tourism, the industry that organizes the consumption of those simulacra and those spectacles or images" (ibid., 379).

44. Rob Wilson, "Imagining Asia-Pacific: Forgetting Politics and Colonialism in the Magical Waters of the Pacific," *Cultural Studies* 14, nos. 3–4 (2000): 562–592. See also Rob Wilson, "Imagining Asia-Pacific Today: Forgetting Colonialism in the Magical Free Markets of the American Pacific," in *Learning Places: The Afterlives of Area Studies*, ed. Masao Miyoshi and Harry Harootunian (Durham, NC: Duke University Press, 2002), 231–60.

45. Wilson, *Be Always Converting, Be Always Converted*, 139.

46. Hsinya Huang, "Representing Indigenous Bodies in Epeli Hau'ofa and Shyman Raporgan," in *Indigenous Bodies: Reviewing, Relocating, Reclaiming*, eds. Jacqueline Fear-Segal and Rebecca Tillet (Albany, NY: SUNY Press, 2013), 163–178. On this multisited transindigenous work, see also Hsinya Huang, Philip Deloria, Laura Furlan, and John Gamber, "Special Forum: Charting Transnational Native American Studies," *Journal of Transnational American Studies* 4, no. 1 (2012), https://escholarship.org/uc/item/3w4347p6, accessed February 12, 2015; Hsinya Huang, "Towards Transnational Native American Literary Studies," *CLC Web: Comparative Literature and Culture* 13, no. 2 (2011), http://docs.lib.purdue.edu/clcweb/vol13/iss2/6/, accessed May 5, 2015.

47. Gary Snyder, *Earth House Hold* (New York: New Directions, 1969), 140–42. See also Nanao Sakaki, *Break the Mirror*, foreword by Gary Snyder (Nobleboro, ME: Blackberry, 1996), and *How to Live on Planet Earth: Collected Poems* (Nobleboro, ME: Blackberry, 2013).

48. Snyder, *Earth House Hold*, 142.

49. Gary Snyder, *Turtle Island* (New York: New Dimensions, 1974), *Regarding Wave: Poetry* (New York: New Directions, 1970), *Mountains and Rivers without End* (Washington: Counterpoint, 1997), *A Place in Space: Ethics, Aesthetics, and Watersheds* (Berkeley, CA: Counterpoint, 1995).

50. Albert Saijo, *OUTSPEAKS: A Rhapsody* (Honolulu: Bamboo Ridge, 1997), 73–74, 163. For further references to this work, I will provide page numbers in parentheses in the text.

51. Craig Santos Perez, *from Unincorporated Territory [hacha]* (Honolulu: Tinfish,

2008), *from Unincorporated Territory [saina]* (Richmond, CA: Omindawn, 2010), and *from Unincorporated Territory [guma]* (Richmond, CA: Omindawn, 2014). For further references to these works, I will provide short titles and page numbers in parentheses in the text.

52. Aaron Shurin's remark on "oceanic poetics" is taken from his endorsement on the back cover of Santos Perez, *Unincorporated Territory [saina]*.

53. Santos Perez's "map" passage (*saina*, 44) alludes to Michel de Certau, *The Practice of Everyday Life*, trans. by Steven Rendall (Berkeley: University of California Press, 2011), 129.

54. Santos Perez is quoting from Robert Sullivan, *Star Waka: Poems* (Auckland: Auckland University Press, 1999), a related book-length poem that inventively recreates Maori Oceania, and Muriel Rukeyser, *Outer Banks* (Greensboro, NC: Unicorn, 1980).

55. Teresia K. Teaiwa, "On Analogies: Rethinking the Pacific in a Global Context," *Contemporary Pacific*, 18, no. 1 (2006): 75.

56. If globalization discourse presumes that world space is at the mercy of market norms promulgated by neoliberal policies reshaping the world from Beijing to Paris, this can lead to what Jean-Luc Nancy calls the earth-shattering values of the *immonde* or "glomus" (*The Creation of the World, or Globalization*, trans. Francois Raffoul and David Pettigrew [Minneapolis: University of Minnesota Press, 2007], 117 and 37) delivered to the planet by this world-becoming-market. Worlding—as a critical practice that my own work is affiliated to via this region making of Oceania—enacts the opening up of space, time, and consciousness to other values and modes of being. Spatially, a worlded criticism seeks to disclose altered connections and articulations that cut across place (such as an area or city) and given regional forms. The term "worlding" implies a fully culture-drenched and being-haunted process of dedistancing the ever-globalizing world of technological domination and its badly managed nuclearized standing reserve troops. As a gerund, "worlding" turns a noun (world) into a verb, thus shifting the taken-for-granted forms of the market and war into yet-to-be-generated and remade forms. As such a gerundive process of situated articulation and world making, worlding helps show how modes and texts of contemporary being and uncanny worldly dwelling (as in reading the language of first-world novels against the imperial grain, for that matter) can become a historical process of taking care and setting limits, entering into, and making the world's horizon come near and become local, informed, situated, and instantiated as an uneven or incomplete material process of world becoming. See Rob Wilson, "Worlding as Future Tactic," in *The Worlding Project*, 211–12.

57. Wilson, *Be Always Converting, Be Always Converted*, 15.

58. Gayatri Spivak, *Death of a Discipline* (New York: Columbia University Press, 2005), 85.

59. Snyder, *A Place in Space*, 233.

60. Gary Snyder, *The Old Ways: Six Essays* (San Francisco: City Lights, 1977), 4.

61. Ibid., 6.

62. James Clifford, "Indigenous Articulations," in *The Worlding Project*, 23. For further references to this work, I will provide page numbers in parentheses in the text.

63. Albert Wendt, Reina Whaitiri, and Robert Sullivan, eds., *Whetu Moana: Contemporary Polynesian Poems in English* (Honolulu: University of Hawai'i Press, 2003), 6–10 and 122–25.

64. Lawrence Buell, *Writing for an Endangered World: Literature, Culture, and Environment in the U.S. and Beyond* (Cambridge, MA: Harvard University Press, 2001), 22. For more on oceanic and riverine ecopoetics, see especially chapters 6 and 8.

65. Wilson, *Be Always Converting, Be Always Converted*, 139.

66. I. Frazer from Dunedin, New Zealand, captures this implicit sense of coalition building in *We Are the Ocean* in a customer review on Amazon.com: "[This collection] will be of interest to everyone who knows his [Hau'ofa's] work and who shares his optimism and passion for the Pacific—which he preferred to call, in the spirit of *pan-Pacific co-operation and inclusiveness*, Oceania" ("Valuable Collection from Famous Pacific Academic and Writer," March 19, 2009, Amazon.com, http://www.amazon.com/We-Are-Ocean-Selected-Works/dp/082483173X/ref=sr_1_2?ie=UTF8&qid=1432441609&sr=8-2&keywords=We+Are+the+Ocean, accessed May 27, 2015; emphasis mine).

67. Quoted in Hau'ofa, *We Are the Ocean*, 52.

68. Milton Murayama, *All I Asking for Is My Body* (Honolulu: University of Hawaii Press, 1988), 3. See also Rob Wilson, "Milton Murayama's Working Class Diaspora across the Japanese/Hawaiian Pacific," *Postcolonial Studies* 11, no. 4 (2008): 475–79.

69. For Asian-affiliated formal and conceptual dimensions of Richard Hamasaki's work as a poet, see Rob Wilson, review of *From the Spider Bone Diaries: Poems and Songs* (2000), in *Contemporary Pacific* 14, no. 2 (2002): 511–13.

70. "The Pulling of Olap's Canoe," trans. Theophil Saret Reuney, in "Flows," in *Asia/Pacific as Space of Cultural Production*, 347. For a related approach to Reuney's cultural poetics, see Joachim Peter, "Chuukese Travellers and the Idea of Horizon," *Asia Pacific Viewpoints* 41, no. 3 (2002): 253–67.

71. Alan E. Davis, "Chuuk Lexicon," http://university.uog.edu/up/micronesica/chuuk_lexicon.htm, accessed February 13, 2015. See also Alan E. Davis, "A Preliminary List of Animal Names in the Chuuk District, with Notes on Plant Names," *Micronesica* 31, no.1 (1999): 1–245. Chuukese is an Austronesian language in the branch of the Malayo-Polynesian family that is dispersed across the Pacific islands, Indonesia, Malaysia, and the Philippines, and thus far more widely dispersed than the related yet Taiwan-concentrated branch of the Austronesian language that contains the Formosan languages used by the pre-Han peoples of Taiwan.

72. "The Pulling of Olap's Canoe," 349.

[9]

ANTIPODEAN TRANSNATIONALISM: THE EMPIRE LIES ATHWART

WHILE DEFINITIONS OF "TRANSNATIONALISM" remain contested, one relatively common thread among the various conceptual approaches involves an interrogation of the idea of universalism, the idea of there being only one true center of gravity. This involves a skepticism, as Naoki Sakai puts it, about Jürgen Habermas's equation in *The Theory of Communicative Action* of the "claim to *universality* with our *Occidental understanding of the world*" (1984, 44), something that, in Sakai's eyes, characterizes Habermas's predominantly Eurocentric intellectual project (Sakai, 1998, 477). Pointing out how "the relationship between the West and the non-West seems to follow the old and familiar formula of master/slave" (ibid., 487), Sakai notes that until the late nineteenth century, "it was understandable and partially inevitable to conceive of history simply as the process of Westernization (Europeanization)," in which "the entire world was viewed from the top" (ibid., 488). The "top," in this case, was of course Europe, and the rest of the world was supposed to acknowledge that continent's historical sense of its own primacy, a position assumed in the twentieth century more by America. Harry Harootunian, whose particular interest is in Japan, writes cogently of how "one of the more remarkable but unobserved occurrences invariably effaced by area studies is the obvious fact that the peoples of the world outside of Euro-America have been forced to live lives *comparatively* by virtue of experiencing some form of colonization or subjection enforced by the specter of imperialism" (2005, 26). Harootunian's understanding of how the Japanese in recent times "were compelled to live comparatively—life in double time—as a condition of their modern transformation" (ibid.) might be extended to the principles of transnationalism more generally, to which double perspectives, reflecting how "comparison always involves relations of power," as Pheng Cheah puts it (2009, 531), are endemic. This is different in kind both from the radically decontextualized world of comparative literature in its more traditional forms, and also from the threat of homogeneity that Gayatri Spivak associates with globalization, whose financial apparatus involves "the imposition of the same system of exchange everywhere" (2012, 338).[1] Instead, transnationalism involves at the very least some kind of structural reciprocity, not merely adding to international influences that have had an impact on Europe and the United States or charting America's role in the wider world, but rather challenging the categories that consolidated particular versions of national identity in the first place.

Werner Sollors referred back in 1998 to "an age of transnationalism" (1998, 3), one that he associated in a US institutional context with a gradual movement away from monolingualism under the pressure of greater visibility for diverse ethnic cultures, even though Sollors noted that the "blind spot of language is shared by the 'conservative' and 'radical' sides in the multiculturalism debate" (ibid., 5). Sollors's point was that a simple incapacity on the part of scholars to read anything other than English had unduly stunted critical accounts of American literature, whose development has in fact since its earliest days been intertwined with an "impressive" range of different languages (ibid., 2). Since the time Sollors was writing, both the trauma of 9/11 and radical shifts in the world economy have rendered the position of the United States at the center of its own imaginary universe still more precarious. Judith Butler's analysis of the "heightened vulnerability" (2006, xi) of the United States after 9/11, when both the literal and symbolic breach of its borders involved the crucial "loss of a certain horizon of experience, a certain sense of the world itself as a national entitlement" (ibid., 39), has been matched by hardheaded economic analyses from more conservative perspectives that corroborates what Butler calls this "decentering of First Worldism" (ibid., 8). According to Adam Garfinkle, a former speechwriter for both of George W. Bush's secretaries of state, Colin Powell and Condoleezza Rice, the twenty-first century will mark the first time in four hundred years that the globe has had a "normative environment" that is "non-Western," and this is likely to have a profound impact on how American studies comes to be reconceived in transnational terms (2011, n.p.). Shadowed by the consolidation of the North Atlantic Treaty Organization, in the middle years of the twentieth century American studies operated as an intellectual field that extended American cultural influence into beleaguered Europe, beset as that continent then was by threats from a divided Germany and Warsaw Pact countries more generally. But in future decades, as President Barack Obama acknowledged during a trip to Australia in 2012, the strategic focus of the United States is likely to turn more toward Asia, for both military and economic reasons.

This in turn will position Australia in particular as a potential American intermediary and ally against China, much as Britain was positioned against the Soviet Union in the 1950s. At the time of Obama's Australian visit, the *Washington Post* quoted an anonymous source as saying that "Australia did not look all that important during the Cold War. But Australia looks much more important if your fascination is really with the Southeast Asia archipelago" (Uren 2012). This is not, of course, to advocate a simple replication of the old dynamics of Cold War American studies, organized as the field was around surreptitious government funding and the indirect influence of the Central Intelligence Agency, in a different geographical setting. But academic subjects are always interwoven in complex ways with a variety of theoretical and material infrastructures, and part of the remit of transnational American studies involves acknowledging how these political dynamics necessarily enter into the construction of the subject. Harootunian's "double time" might thus be understood as a methodological as well as a contextual aspect of transnationalism: not only does this more materialistic kind of comparative approach juxtapose different national formations, but it also seeks to elucidate the messy terrain where abstract formulations intersect and collide with the more obdurate compulsions of political history. "History," as Fredric Jameson reminds us, "is what hurts. It is what refuses desire and sets inexorable limits to individual as well as collective praxis," for which it operates as "ground and untranscendable horizon" (1981, 102).

Such a sobering formulation carries particular relevance to transnational American studies, which has on occasions been hindered by a weightless utopian rhetoric, particularly in transpacific horizons that have not been as "untranscendable" as Jameson envisaged. It is, of course, easy enough to understand how such radically idealistic agendas have emerged, often as deliberately counterpointed critiques of U.S. imperialism. Paul Lyons, for example, punningly describes "American Pacifism" as forms of pacification or "structured ignorances" (2005, 10), in which US theories of "sexuality, masculinity, race, nation, or ecological movements" (ibid., 8) are simply imposed on the Pacific region without sufficient respect for native source materials, and in a way that is "damagingly unmindful of Oceanian epistemologies" (ibid., 9). Similarly, Yunte Huang reads nineteenth-century American authors such as Ralph Waldo Emerson, Herman Melville, Mark Twain, and Henry Adams as "spokespersons for the nineteenth-century U.S. imperial vision" (2008, 7), arguing that they were concerned above all with imaginatively colonizing the Pacific as a natural extension, in transnational terms, of the westward domestic movement associated with Manifest Destiny. But, as Butler has remarked, to assume such a "single subject" of "US omnipotence" is to encode the kind of familiar political paranoia that "is fed by the fantasy of omnipotence" (2006, 9). US excursions across the Pacific in the nineteenth century were complicated not only by encounters with native peoples but also by sporadic conflicts with the rival imperial power of Britain, which used its base in Australia to exert influence over large sections of Pacific island space. Melville in *Typee* chronicles not only issues of indigenous language but also the stand-off in the 1840s between Britain and America for control of the Sandwich Islands, now Hawaii, while the narrator of Melville's subsequent novel, *Omoo*, chronicles how he spends time on an Australian whaling ship, the fictional *Julia*—mirroring the author's adventures on an actual Australian whaler, the *Lucy Ann*, in 1842. The *Julia* is said to have been "fitted for a privateer out of a New England port during the War of 1812" before being "captured at sea by a British cruiser," and at the time the narrative takes place, it is being "employed as a government packet in the Australian seas" ([1849] 1968, 9). The ship's mixed provenance, moving from America to Australia via England, thus epitomizes the colonial *métissage* that structures Melville's novel, enhancing the confusions that surround the very idea of national identity in Melville's seafaring fiction. In this sense, Melville does not represent the Pacific Ocean as any kind of tabula rasa on which can be readily imposed the all-encompassing designs of US hegemony; instead, he superimposes turbulent Atlantic currents on Pacific waters to produce a more elusive *mise-en-abîme*, a space in which physical geography and political history do not entirely coincide with each other. The Pacific, according to this perspective, becomes an always already colonized expanse, where autochthonous cultures find themselves caught up in others' struggles for power and dominion. The transpacific circuit has always been made up of imperial crosscurrents as well as aquatic flows and island domains, with these imperial pressures flowing back across the Pacific, from Britain's settlement of Australia and New Zealand and from Germany's involvement in New Guinea and Samoa. It is much too one-dimensional, in every sense of that word, to suggest that such imperializing narratives have only ever extended westward from California.

    Arguing on principle against such impositions of external constraints on native peoples, the Tongan scholar Epeli Hau'ofa produced in 1993 a celebrated essay, "Our Sea of Islands," in which he sought intellectually to justify an oceanic space "that had been boundless for ages before Captain Cook's apotheosis" ([1993] 1999, 30). Hau'ofa argued against "derogatory and belittling views of indigenous cultures" (ibid., 28) imposed by a series of missionary and imperial forces, and he concluded optimistically that "we must not allow anyone to belittle us again and take away our freedom" (ibid., 37). Hau'ofa's attempt to reclaim a romantic, mythological register for Oceania, one dominated by deterritorializing flows of water rather than the reified constructions of a land-based continent, has been influential in the postmodern reinscription of Pacific island space as means of shattering what the University of Cyprus scholar Antonis Balasopoulos calls "the territorial cognitive map of imperial high modernity" (2008, 19). Balasopoulos links "postcolonial geopoetics" (ibid., 9) with what he calls an "islandness to come" (ibid., 23), a way of escaping "monological containment" through the geographical expropriation of "island form" (ibid., 23). Similarly, Elizabeth DeLoughrey undertakes a comparative study of Caribbean and Pacific islands to construct a "transoceanic imaginary" (2007, 37), extrapolating from the Pacific a sense of "our own location on a terraqueous globe, a watery planet that renders all landmasses into islands surrounded by sea" (ibid., 2). This version of "a tidalectic between land and sea" (ibid., 45) enables DeLoughrey to position the Pacific as a kind of pastoral space in which key political and ecological issues, such as nuclear fallout and environmental pollution, can be properly illuminated and clarified. While DeLoughrey carefully chronicles the ways in which "peoples of the sea" should be historicized (ibid., 26), there is still a predilection in her work and that of other California-based critics—Rob Wilson (2009) and Christopher Connery (1994 and 2012), for example—for using the Pacific as an exemplary or regenerative space. Arguing that "the rise in naturalized images of transoceanic diaspora derives from increased maritime territorialism" (2007, 30), DeLoughrey draws on Hau'ofa's work to describe this ever-elusive sea as offering "new ways to destabilize natural and ethnic boundaries by drawing upon a transoceanic imaginary that reflects the origins of island cultures as well as their imbrications in the fluid trajectories of globalization" (ibid., 37). Connery, from his base in Santa Cruz, finds the whole agenda of transnationalism to be compliant with the ideologies of neoliberalism, associated in his mind with "symbolic analysts" (2012, 56) in the mold of Robert Reich, secretary of labor in the administration of President Bill Clinton, eager to transfer and exchange capital across national frontiers. In Connery's eyes, Pacific studies should operate primarily as a form of resistance, a way of countering US hegemony by playing the neoliberal assumptions associated with "Pacific Rim discourse" (1994) off against alternative cultural vistas. For Connery, as for Whitman and Thoreau 150 years earlier, Asia functions as an apotheosized idea, a way of rendering corrupt landlocked regimes more open to a distant fluidity of spirit.

Connery also cites "Australian cultural studies" as an example of local resistance to American global hegemony (2012, 52), and it is true that this field as it emerged in Australia in the early 1990s defined itself, at least in part, in contrast to the kind of "neoliberal rhetoric" associated in the eyes of John Frow and Meaghan Morris with attempts on the part of Rupert Murdoch to fold Australia further into a US-based corporate culture (1993, vii). Over a longer historical trajectory, however, antipodean transnationalism has always encompassed a much more extensive historical and geographical trajectory, involving pressures of British as well as American colonialism and the complications incumbent upon various forms of exchange between indigenous and white settler cultures. In 1989, *The Empire Writes Back*, a formative critical intervention in the field of postcolonial studies, was published by three Australian scholars—Bill Ashcroft, Gareth Griffiths, and Helen Tiffin —who sought to encompass within a postcolonial framework all countries whose literatures had characteristically "emerged in their present form out of the experience of colonization," while emphasizing "their differences from the assumptions of the imperial centre" (2002, 2). In this configuration, which included the literatures of African and Caribbean countries as well as those of India, Australia, and New Zealand, Britain (rather than America) became the whipping boy for its attempt universally to impose "Eurocentric standards of judgment" (ibid., 7), and indeed the United States was defined as one of the countries falling under this postcolonial rubric since, despite "its current position of power, and the neo-colonizing role it has played . . . its relationship with the metropolitan centre as it evolved over the last two centuries has been paradigmatic for post-colonial literatures everywhere" (ibid., 2). However, the actual treatment of American literature in this book was nugatory, with the narratives of Charles Brockden Brown and James Fenimore Cooper being recognized only as "an important site of conflict within post-colonial literary cultures," where "the desire of early American writers to compete on equal terms with their British counterparts clashed with the desire to repudiate borrowed models and follow an independent path" (ibid., 135).

Such a reductive binary opposition—between "borrowed models" on the one hand and an "independent path" on the other—does not speak aptly to the cultural complications framing the works of Brown, whose texts mediate German romanticism and American Federalist party politics in their attempts to repudiate the pastoral utopianism that he associated with Thomas Jefferson's Republican party in the first decade of the nineteenth century. In his characteristically double-voiced narratives, Brown sought to chart new directions for American literature that were cognizant of their necessary overlap with the cultural freight of the British Empire. He wrote pamphlets addressing the recent British colonization of "New Holland," as Australia was then called, while recommending that the new United States should abandon its exceptionalist and isolationist policy, grounded on Jefferson's vision of the desirability of an "ocean of fire" between the United States and the rest of the world (Jefferson 1904, 287), and engage instead with the realpolitik of imperial affairs.[2] Indeed, in Brown's unfinished *Memoirs of Carwin the Biloquist*, written in 1798 as a sequel to his novel *Wieland*, the hero's "perverse and pernicious curiosity" (1977, 251) leads him into the orbit of the radical visionary Ludloe, who is committed to the kind of "scheme of Utopian felicity" (ibid., 277) that became associated with Louis Antoine de Bougainville and other Pacific explorers of the eighteenth century. Since it is "plain" to Ludloe that "the nations of Europe were tending to greater depravity" (ibid.), he plans to look elsewhere to execute his "plan of colonization" (ibid., 278), and Carwin subsequently discovers in Ludloe's atlas a mysterious hand-drawn chart that, from the latitude and longitude specified there, can readily be identified as a map of Australia. Although Carwin infers that Ludloe's "geographical secret" had involved putting his "plans for civilization . . . into practice in some unvisited corner of the world" (ibid., 301), these precise spatial coordinates drag this hypothetical realm—utopia as "no place"—back into the land of the actual, where the bonds of British imperial authority hold sway. By February 1805, when this work was written (Cowie 1977, 336–37), these antipodean islands were no longer an empty space for the projection of transcendent visions, as Ludloe fondly imagines, but formed another part of the cyclic pattern of imperial time and space. As Hsuan Hsu observes, *Memoirs of Carwin* is thus "a fragment in which both the forgotten voice of the colonized" and the repressed fact of America's continuation of Britain's imperial policy "return with a vengeance" (2000, 154). *Memoirs of Carwin* thus actually foregrounds the geographical *mise-en-abîme* whereby British colonial developments in Australasia echo British colonial practices in Ireland and America, which were themselves echoed by the growth of an American empire in the 1790s.[3] For all of the ways in which, as Nigel Leask says, the "late-eighteenth-century Atlantic imagination was thoroughly seduced by the utopian promise of a Pacific *Terra Australis*" (2000, 348), Brown was enough of a hardheaded Federalist skeptic to doubt that any new world, either in pastoral America or the more distant antipodes, might effectively position itself beyond the circumference of colonial power.

The point here is simply that Brown's geographical materialism, encompassing as it does recent explorations in the South Pacific as well as the legacies of Europe, makes it impossible to resolve his narratives into the binary model of postcolonialism outlined by Ashcroft, Griffiths, and Tiffin. Although Brown's texts engage with colonialism, they do so in convoluted and multifaceted ways, where attitudes toward dominant powers carry psychological as well as political implications. The title of *The Empire Writes Back* was taken from an article written in 1982 by Salman Rushdie, "The Empire Writes back with a Vengeance," which argued how "Anglo-Saxon attitudes" were being reinvigorated by "new literatures" beginning to manifest themselves in the wake of British immigration policies of the 1950s and 1960s (1982). But Rushdie's theme turned on a paradox rather than a simple opposition: noting how "Britain needs decolonising, too," he argued for the rhetorical style of this new literature as being necessarily hybrid and "unwashed," rather than any kind of pure phenomenon (ibid.). Indeed, the title of Rushdie's piece was itself a punning play on George Lucas's 1980 American epic film, *Star Wars Episode V: The Empire Strikes Back*. Ashcroft, Griffiths, and Tiffin themselves acknowledged that "post-colonial culture is inevitably a hybridized phenomenon" (2002, 220), and, like Rushdie, they saw part of their impetus as involving a "counter-discursive" practice (ibid., 221) designed to unmask hegemonic assumptions and thus to destabilize the canonical constructions associated with them. But these Australian critics also expressed reservations, particularly in the book's second (2002) edition, about how the term "postcolonial" had been "adopted by so many fields and in so many different ways that we are in danger of altogether losing sight of its actual provenance" (ibid., 194), a threat of vitiation the authors associated particularly with "metropolitan-based exponents such as Said, Bhabha and Spivak who have gained most attention in the rarefied air of high theory" (2002, 196). Said's version of "Orientalism" (1978) was similarly critiqued by the Australian anthropologist Nicholas Thomas, who argued that such a notion of colonial discourse as "an enduring and self-authorizing set of ideas," however valuable it might be in relation to "representations of Islam and the Middle East," is "not helpful for the Pacific" (1997, 16–17). What we find here in general terms is a complicated situation, in which the more abstract dimensions of postcolonial theory collide with more grounded political aspects of regional geography.

As an extension of this Pacific praxis, the notion promoted by Ashcroft, Griffiths, and Tiffin of the empire writing back might more usefully be recast in antipodean terms as the empire lying athwart. Positioned as it has always been at the intersection of competing imperial and indigenous interests, antipodean transnationalism is not easily resolved into any clearly unilateral or oppositional perspective. In this light, the conceptual matrix of transnationalism may speak more appositely than that of postcolonialism to the variegated, multidirectional nature of colonial legacies and crosscurrents. Kuan-Hsing Chen has promulgated the working hypothesis of "Asia as Method," drawing on the "far-reaching psychic and cultural effects of colonialism" (2010, 121) to propose a decathected resignification of the imperial imaginary, and it might be possible to suggest an analogous version of "Australia as method" that would work in similarly deterritorialized terms. Given the extensive history of US engagement with Taiwan since World War II, and arguing that the more amorphous process of "deimperialization is theoretically a much wider movement" than the simpler possessive issue of "decolonization" (ibid., 6), Chen talks of the psychological difficulty contemporary Taiwanese have in engaging critically with the United States, since "being anti-American is like opposing ourselves" (ibid., 186). Along similar lines, we might suggest that both the dilemma and the challenge for antipodean transnationalism is to navigate among competing psychological and political positions, in a situation where mutual engagements of colonizer and colonized operate across a ubiquitous but amorphous force field in a state of constant transposition, rather than being confined to any kind of singular position susceptible of resolution within a conventional postcolonial or area studies framework.

One of the most valuable aspects of antipodean transnationalism in this regard is the way it effectively foregrounds the kinds of spatial power relations that are inherent, if customarily suppressed, in any kind of area studies dynamic. The most distinguished precursor of this theoretical approach in the second half of the twentieth century was the Australian art historian and cultural critic Bernard Smith, who explicitly used the word "trans-national" as early as 1986, in his foreword to Peter Fuller's *The Australian Scapegoat*. Smith praised Fuller for being "the first person to grasp the trans-national implications of the Antipodean intervention of 1959" (1986, xiii), referring to the "Antipodean Manifesto" drafted by Smith and published as a foreword to the catalogue for the Antipodean Exhibition held in Melbourne in 1959. Smith was one of eight signatories to this manifesto, which claimed that "it is natural . . . we should see and experience nature differently in some degree from the artists of the northern hemisphere" (1976, 166).[4] This intervention was not so much a justification of local or national culture per se; instead, it emphasized that the reception of art was always interwoven with power relations, testifying to what Peter Beilharz has called Smith's fascination with "peripheral vision, and dual vision" (1997, 99), along with his "lifelong interest in unequal cultural exchange" (ibid., 94). This arose to some extent from his radical political affiliations: Smith was, of course, steeped in Marxist cultural theory, and he also participated in the debates about surrealism that flourished in Australian art circles during the 1940s. But this countersuggestible tendency was also rooted in his ethnic provenance: the illegitimate son of a young Irish immigrant woman, Smith was baptized a Roman Catholic and indeed specified at the end of his life that he wanted a Catholic funeral service, even while insisting that he would "die an atheist" (Palmer 2011). He frequently found himself at odds with the Anglo-Australian establishment, specifically expressing resentment in his autobiography "against the legitimate ones who ruled the world and taught you what you should do" (1984, 187). Yet such heterodox psychological impulses also informed a more broadly based antipodean methodology, since Smith's work sets itself deliberately to overthrow what he regarded as supine conventions, drawing intellectual sustenance from an antagonistic approach to hegemonic cultures of all kinds and from the intellectual pleasure of turning things around the other way. Many of his most famous works, notably *European Vision and the South Pacific*, take delight in juxtaposing apparently disparate categories and in complicating established hierarchies by suggesting ways in which top and bottom become mutually defining. In his preface to the second edition of this book, in fact, Smith claimed it was not so much about the "fatal impact of Europe on the Pacific" but "precisely the opposite: the impact of the Pacific upon Europe" (1985, vii).

Rather than being organized merely around geographical location or benign forms of open transaction, then, Smith's version of the antipodean imaginary involves a circuit in which contrary impulses are held in tension while dominant and subordinate impulses are contained paradoxically, and sometimes pathologically, in the same spectrum. Indeed, it was the very lopsided nature of this antipodean matrix, and the heft of the institutional forces contributing to its consolidation, that fired Smith's deliberately provocative scholarship. In a late work, *Modernism's History*, Smith describes how as an "Australian art historian" he sees "Europe as my antipodes" since "antipodes is not a place but a relationship" (1998, 7). In this sense the antipodean or transnational dynamic becomes for him a more materialist, historicized version of international engagement, in which the emphasis is not on abstract global flows of either a financial or a watery nature, but on the unequal exchanges of money, power, and prestige across national and hemispheric borders. There have been subsequent challenges—by Margaret Jolly, Raewyn Connell (2007), and others—from a combative Australian perspective to the domination of social theory by those in what Jolly has called "the metropoles of Europe and North America" (2008, 75). However, the heterodox nature of Smith's work remains unusual in the way it does not seek simply to justify the culture of the Southern Hemisphere in an oppositional spirit, but aspires more broadly to reinterpret Western traditions in the light of antipodean perspectives. In his recent work on "archipelagic diaspora," the American critic Brian Russell Roberts develops his focus on "the planet's material geography" (2013, 122) to project the idea of an antipodean imaginary in a similar kind of way, describing for instance "the East Indies and West Indies, Haiti and Tahiti, Caledonia and New Caledonia" as "antipodal island-spaces" (ibid., 144), while inferring from this term that "antipodal [is] . . . a site of unpresentable distance from the known world, and . . . a site of emancipatory inversion in relation to that world" (ibid., 128).

The other key area where antipodean transnationalism is contributing to a broader elucidation of Western culture's planetary dimensions is in relation to the legacy of indigenous cultures. In *Trans-Indigenous*, Chadwick Allen productively aligns "purposeful indigenous juxtapositions" (2012, xx) of "Native North American, New Zealand Māori, Hawaiian, Indigenous Australian" cultures across a global compass (ibid., xvii). Specifically rejecting the proposition that the prefix "trans" involves simply recapitulating US power, while suggesting that through its commitment to "paradoxes of simultaneity, contradiction, coexistence" (ibid., xxxii) the hybrid term "*Trans-* could be the next *post-*" (ibid., xv), Allen goes on to consider ways in which the progressive nature of Māori art and race relations might open up the wider field of inquiry in a more enlightening way. He discusses, for example, the mixed-media sculpture *Whakamatunga* (Metamorphosis) by the Māori artist Fred Graham, installed as part of a transindigenous exhibit on Māori and Pacific Northwest Coast Art staged in Vancouver, Canada, in 2006, where the chameleonic variations of this sculpture drew on the whale's iconic status in Māori culture to exemplify how, in Graham's words, "the whale is a frequent traveller between the Northern and Southern Hemispheres. In my sculpture, as the whale crosses the equator it changes both in shape and in body design, from Northwest Coast Indian to Maori. Day changes to night" (quoted in Allen 2012, xxiv). If we place this alongside the famous representation of the whale in Melville's *Moby-Dick* ([1851] 1987), it becomes easy enough to see how the latter has too often been circumscribed in US literary criticism either by abstract universalist typologies or by the localized concerns of domestic politics. By contrast, a broader understanding of how the whale functions in Māori lore as an epitome of transhemispheric transposition can potentially open a reader's eyes to the self-consciously planetary dimensions of Melville's oceanic epic, specifically the way it projects the white whale as an image of nature's inverse, antipodean properties. Geoffrey Sanborn has showed how Melville drew heavily on George Lillie Craik's *The New Zealanders* (1830) for his portrait of Queequeg, and how Melville revised *Moby-Dick* during its composition to take account of Craik's representation of the magnanimous Māori chief Te Pehi Kupe, thereby making Queequeg less "the native of an unspecified south-western island" and more specifically "a Maori" (Sanborn 2011, 106), a tribe that by the 1830s was beginning to be described, according to Sanborn, "as the most impressive tribal people that Europeans had ever encountered" (ibid., 6). Huang describes *Moby-Dick* as "the first canonical American literary text dealing with the transpacific" (2008, 53), but the novel also deliberately displaces its focus from the Northern to the Southern Hemisphere, something equally important to both the path of the *Pequod* and the construction of Melville's novel. Anticipating the voyage around the Cape of Good Hope and across the Indian Ocean, Ishmael envisages "many long night-watches in the remotest waters, and beneath constellations never seen here at the north" (Melville [1851] 1987, 73).

Allen also describes how new technologies of aerial photography and computer modeling have helped elucidate the complex and elaborate patterns of Native American structures across North America, revealing that these Indian earthworks were constructed to mirror the trajectories of equinox, solstice, and other perceived patterns in the sky. This again evokes the notion of a "watery planet . . . an abstract model for our world conceived from the perspective of Oceania" (Allen 2012, 233), since the process of planetary rotation necessarily foregrounded by antipodean transnationalism —predicated as it is on a geography of cosmic distance—finds its correlative in the relationship of Native American settlements to celestial astronomy. This serves to detach the study of Native American culture from the more stifling ethnographic and anthropological typologies within which it was incarcerated throughout most of the twentieth century, and it reflects back in turn on the planetary dimensions that have always been implicit, if generally suppressed, in the field of American literature. By rotating its conceptual axis toward Oceania, in other words, the methodology of antipodean transnationalism not only illuminatingly juxtaposes Native American and Māori culture but also opens up Western culture more generally to the trajectory of planetary orbits. Insofar as the conceptualization of "indigenous philosophy . . . is a way of recasting contemporary thinking," as Stephen Muecke argues (2004, 176), this is another example of the empire not so much writing back but lying athwart: rather than operating unilaterally or antithetically, the positional politics of antipodean transnationalism lie across the social dynamics of power in a crosswise, reversible direction.

Such structural reciprocity serves also to hollow out the metaphysics of authenticity with which the study of Australian Aboriginal culture, in particular, has been institutionally encumbered. Elizabeth Povinelli refers scathingly to "contemporary pageants of atonement" such as Australia's National Sorry Day in May 1998 (2002, 43–44), commenting on how these became accommodated to a glossy, sentimentalized version of national reconciliation under the banner of liberal multiculturalism as a way of avoiding the harsher economic demands of social justice. While Nancy Munn has usefully commented from a legal perspective on how the boundaries (both spatial and legal) of Aboriginal and Euro-Australian customs diverge and overlap, creating in effect a "hybrid type of space" (1996, 449–50) where different national territories are superimposed on each other, one general characteristic of antipodean transnationalism is its refusal to apotheosize

Australian Aboriginal culture as a metaphysical end in itself—a refusal that creates a distance from the kind of "poetics of the sacred" or "wave of connection" that has featured heavily in anthropological approaches to indigenous cultures (Rose 2000, 287, 292). Smith, whose primary interest was in aesthetics rather than the more reified constructions of anthropology, focused in his critiques of Aboriginal culture on its ontologies of alienation, its structurally embedded forms of doubling, and its sites of political intersection with or crossing over more established domains. In his 1980 Boyer lectures for the Australian Broadcasting Commission, subsequently published as *The Spectre of Truganini*, Smith discussed Aboriginal culture in terms of how it had been repressed by white Australia, but his methodology was more Freudian—or "psycho-cultural," as he put it (1980, 16)—than phenomenological, and his aim there was not so much to present any kind of authentic account, but rather to discuss how patterns of "cultural convergence" (ibid., 44) had induced white Australian artists to move away from "narrow Europeanism" (ibid., 51), in the poetry of Les Murray and the music of Peter Sculthorpe, for example. As in work on Native American culture, the risk here of appropriation is the price necessarily paid for engaging with the inherently alien dimensions of recuperative scholarship.

One of the paradoxes associated with the study of Australian Aboriginal culture is that its proposition of "deep time" for Australian history is such a recent event, arising, as Tom Griffiths notes, out of "the twin revolutions of professional archaeology and radiocarbon dating, both of which emerged in local practice in the 1950s and 60s" (2011, 20). Through this renewed legitimation of Aboriginal communities, the institutional ascription of a *longue durée* for Australian history—one predating by some 50,000 years the arrival of Captain James Cook in the 1770s—has consequently involved a back projection stemming from twentieth-century technological perspectives, just as the strange ambience of Sidney Nolan's surrealist paintings of the Australian desert in the 1950s derived in part from his being the first painter to see these expansive landscapes from the air. Indeed, Nolan's wife somewhat comically described how "Sidney gazed with his mouth open and his tongue pushed between his teeth, as he does when painting with the greatest intensity," during an air trip across Australia in 1948 (quoted in Haynes 1998, 172). Nolan, who was born in Melbourne in 1917, first visited the United States on a Harkness Fellowship in 1958. Stephen Spender in Santa Barbara introduced him at that point to Robert Lowell's *Life Studies* (1959), to which Nolan responded with various original drawings (Adams 1987, 141), and Nolan got to know Lowell well during the 1960s, contributing illustrations for Lowell's 1967 book of poems, *Near the Ocean*. This volume consists of translations from Dante, Horace, Juvenal, and other classical writers set alongside more typical Lowell poems evoking life in contemporary Boston. According to Lowell's prefatory note to *Near the Ocean:* "The theme that connects my translations is Rome, the greatness and horror of her Empire. . . . How one jumps from Rome to the America of my own poems is something of a mystery to me. Perhaps the bridge is made by the brilliant drawings of Sidney Nolan. May my lines throw some light on his!" (1967, 9). Lowell's choice of the word "lines" here is a deliberate pun, since Nolan's illustrations are indeed line drawings, characteristic of the artist's style in being, as Andrew Sayers observes, "non-figurative" and with a disarming "lightness of touch" (1989, 5), such that they delineate human figures cavorting in acts of fellatio, buggery, and various other inebriated conjunctions in a deliberately sketchy manner. Oil paintings of such lecherous classical scenes would probably have seemed too heavy-handed and literal, but, by reducing the human form to its barest outline in a style both elemental and cartoonlike, Nolan captures a sense of both the frailty and the tenuous nature of corporeal desire, and indeed of human life in general.

Such frailties comprise a central theme of Lowell's volume, as epitomized in his poem "The Vanity of Human Wishes," described in its subtitle as "A Version of Juvenal's Tenth Satire":

> Now only fevers warm the thinning blood,
> diseases of all kinds lock hands and dance,
> even their names escape you—let me list
> the many lechers Oppia will love,
> slow-coming Maura drain a day, how many
> schoolboys Hamillus will crouch on, the partners
> Hirrus will swindle, the sick men Themiston will kill
> this autumn—I could more easily count
> the villas bought up by the barber whose
> razor once grated on my stiff young beard. . . .
> One man has a sagging shoulder, one a hernia,
> another has a softening hipbone, and another
> has cataracts; another's spoonfed; listen,
> they yawn like baby swallows for their swill! (1967, 89–90)

Nolan's sketch of the lines "how many / schoolboys Hamillus will crouch on" presents the copulating protagonists in a grotesque, inverted position (ibid., 91), and it is curiously reminiscent of his other drawings around this time, particularly the Ned Kelly sequence, that link the dehumanized protagonist to bleak late modernist landscapes: the figure of Kelly, for instance, is portrayed in an Australian desert framed by emaciated signs of crucifixes and smoking chimneys redolent of Auschwitz (Sayers 1989, 8). This in turn is reminiscent of the crucifixion jest in Samuel Beckett's *Waiting for Godot*, where one of the tramps, Vladimir, remarks that "one of the thieves was saved," calmly observing: "It's a reasonable percentage" (1965, 11). Nolan, in other words, picks up on and illuminates the more alien and modernist aspects of *Near the Ocean*, that more austere part of Lowell's style that is too often obscured by his garrulous, colloquial domesticity. In an interview in which he discussed "The Vanity of Human Wishes," Lowell drew attention to the way in which, in Samuel Johnson's 1749 reworking of Juvenal's poem, "the framework doesn't quite fit," since "eighteenth-century London wasn't as awful as Juvenal's Rome . . . and yet he's forced to say that it was." At the same time, Lowell recognizes how "off key" elements in Johnson's "way of transforming the poem" lend it a particular mode of artistic innovation: "While I just try to give an accurate, eloquent photograph of the original, he did something much more avant-garde" (Carne-Ross [1968] 1988, 138). Yet Nolan's illustrations effectively foreground the idiom of displacement at work in these temporal shifts from Juvenal to Johnson and then to Lowell, restoring that etymological sense of translation as a carrying across, something that Lowell's more down-to-earth "photograph" tended, for its own artistic reasons, to downplay. Commenting on this poem, Vereen Bell argued that the "difference between Juvenal's formalized identity and Lowell's is that the Lowell in the poems is implicated in the subject matter, cannot remain a displaced observer" (1983, 100); yet the Nolan sketches provide precisely the kind of alternative perspective that highlights the "displaced" aspects of Lowell's inherently estranged, transnational position. Whereas Lowell's poem emphasizes the quotidian stuff of human comedy, Nolan's pictorial frame illustrates more abstract dimensions of corporeal embodiment and decomposition.

Moving thus between the familiar and the cosmic, between a confessional idiom and the toils of the *longue durée*, Lowell's work traverses different spatial and temporal measures, evoking ways in which sex, power, and appetite lead inexorably to corruption and death. Lowell majored in classics at Kenyon College, and he proposes here a scenario in which the ancient world exposes the kind of knowledge of corruption to which the American Transcendentalists, Lowell's Bostonian ancestors, were blind: "Do Rome and Carthage know what we deny?" he asks in the book's last poem, "The Ruins of Time" (1967, 124). The very title of this collection, *Near the Ocean*, speaks to a sense of liminality that runs through these works: "For Theodore Roethke" describes Lowell's fellow poet as "the ocean's anchor" (ibid., 52) in the way he "honoured nature, / helpless, elemental creature" (ibid., 51), and *Near the Ocean* similarly positions itself as adjacent or "near" to the "ele-

FIGURE 9.1. Cover illustration by Sidney Nolan for Robert Lowell, *Near the Ocean* (New York: Farrar, Straus and Giroux, 1967). Courtesy of the Sidney Nolan Trust

mental" but not fully immersed within it, thereby giving the poet scope to play with a dialectic between human language and physical deliquescence.

Wai Chee Dimock has suggested that Lowell in these poems undertakes a "yoking together of ancient and modern history" (2006, 141), and that the poet gains an alternative angle on the politics of the Vietnam war by relating it to the trials and tribulations of first-century Rome. While this is true, it involves on Dimock's part a reading outward from Vietnam to the more distant Roman analogy, whereas the Nolan illustrations serve to highlight more overtly the late modernist dimensions implicit in *Near the Ocean*: the uneasy link between twentieth-century America and elemental oceans or deserts, and the radically decontextualized association of human sexuality with the prospect of universal corruption, such as we see, albeit in more ascetic forms, in the narratives of Beckett or Franz Kafka. Though the inclusion of Nolan's illustrations led some American literary critics to deride Lowell's book as a pretentious coffee-table item on its first appearance in 1967 (Hamilton 1982, 348), it is arguable that Nolan's drawings lend *Near the Ocean* a specifically antipodean inflection, since Lowell used a transnational dynamic to link not only Boston and ancient Rome but also the

United States and Australia. Nolan's drawings speak to the kind of interest in deep time that he explored aesthetically in his Australian desert paintings of the 1940s and 1950s, and to which he also gave expression in his jacket illustrations, again in the barest line drawing form, for editions of various novels by Patrick White, including *The Tree of Man* ([1956] 1961) and *Voss* ([1957] 1960). White, who had a long and tempestuous friendship with Nolan, correlates in *The Tree of Man* the cycle of generations in a small Australian bush community with a sense of deep, elemental time: one of the characters wonders "if this town will still be here in a thousand years" (1961, 22), while White embeds his characters in the landscape to such an extent that we are told the Quigleys "could have been carved from wood" (ibid., 51).⁵ This is a late modernist, minimalist style given a specifically antipodean dimension, linking the remote nature of this bush community to a sense of metaphysical stasis, with the "slow time" of "hot summer days" (ibid., 104) conjuring up a planetary sphere where the "whole earth was in motion, a motion of wind and streaming trees, and he was in danger of being carried with it" (ibid., 47). Such atavistic proximity is precisely what we find in *Near the Ocean*, where Nolan's drawings, transposing men into animals and generally inverting the human proprieties, realign American poetry with the sense of comic degradation and the demystification of liberal humanist sensibility under the force of a radically inhumane environment that developed in Australian modernism after World War II out of the country's new technological engagement with the ancient spirit of the land.

In relation to American studies as transnational practice, then, it might be argued that it only ever works as a mode of practice, as a nuanced and necessarily detailed account of the complex issues associated with points of intersection between different national formations. Methodologically, it involves various forms of reciprocity and exchange, in which us culture becomes susceptible to the circulation of global forces rather than being merely their malign, all-powerful agent. The antipodean version of transnationalism, through its historical tendency (as in Smith's work) to foreground power relations and the politics of geospatial position, is an apt measure of how such dynamics might work in the twenty-first century. The transnational turn in American studies has already produced a more finely calibrated account of the complicated place of the United States in the world, and to outline some of the frailties addressed by Lowell in *Near the Ocean*, under the influence of antipodean modernism, is to illuminate ways in which aspects of what Butler called "precarious life" (2006) that were symbolically magnified in us consciousness after 9/11 have, in fact, been always already implicit in the field, from the nineteenth-century engagements of Brown with the British Empire and the passage of Melville's white whale into the Southern Hemisphere. Whereas in the second half of the twentieth century the institutional parameters and voluble rhetoric of American exceptionalism kept the subject in a relatively sequestered state, the new conditions of precarious life in the twenty-first century—"America's Pacific century," as Obama's Secretary of State Hillary Clinton rhetorically called it (2011)—are extending the horizons of the field not only geographically but also chronologically, with antipodean transnationalism producing new backward accounts of American studies across colonial time as well as across planetary space.

Notes

1. On comparative literature, Susan Stanford Friedman writes that "comparison decontextualizes: that is, it dehistoricizes and deterritorializes; it removes what are being compared from their local and geohistorical specificity" (2011, 754–55).

2. Jefferson expressed the wish that "there were an ocean of fire between us and the old world" in a letter to Elbridge Gerry, 13 May 1797 (1904, 287).

3. On the significance of Ireland in Brown's representation of colonialism, see Gibbons 2004. For a more extended discussion of Brown's engagement with "New Holland," see Giles 2013, chapter 3.

4. In addition to Smith, the manifesto was signed by Charles Blackman, Arthur Boyd, David Boyd, John Brack, Bob Dickerson, John Perceval, and Clifton Pugh.

5. White's portrayal of the painter Hurtle Duffield in his novel *The Vivisector* is based in part on Nolan. The book is dedicated "to Cynthia and Sidney Nolan" ([1970] 2008, v).

Works Cited

Adams, Brian. 1987. *Sidney Nolan: Such Is Life*. Hawthorn, Victoria, Australia: Century Hutchinson.

Allen, Chadwick. 2012. *Trans-Indigenous: Methodologies for Global Native Literary Studies*. Minneapolis: University of Minnesota Press.

Ashcroft, Bill, Gareth Griffiths, and Helen Tiffin. 2002. *The Empire Writes Back: Theory and Practice in Post-Colonial Literatures*. 2nd ed. London: Routledge.

Balasopoulos, Antonis. 2008. "Nesologies: Island Form and Postcolonial Geopoetics." *Postcolonial Studies* 11 (1): 9–26.

Beckett, Samuel. 1965. *Waiting for Godot*. 2nd ed. London: Faber.

Beilharz, Peter. 1997. *Imagining the Antipodes: Culture, Theory and the Visual in the Work of Bernard Smith*. Cambridge: Cambridge University Press.

Bell, Vereen M. 1983. *Robert Lowell, Nihilist as Hero*. Cambridge, MA: Harvard University Press.

Brown, Charles Brockden. 1977. *Wieland, or The Transformation: An American Tale; Memoirs of Carwin the Biloquist*, edited by Sydney J. Krause. Vol. 1 of *The Novels and Related Works of Charles Brockden Brown*. Bicentennial ed. Kent, OH: Kent State University Press.

Butler, Judith. 2006. *Precarious Life: The Powers of Mourning and Violence*. Rev. ed. London: Verso.

Carne-Ross, D. S. [1968] 1988. "Conversation with Robert Lowell." In *Robert Lowell: Interviews and Memoirs*, edited by Jeffrey Meyers, 129–40. Ann Arbor: University of Michigan Press.

Cheah, Pheng. 2009. "The Material World of Comparison." *New Literary History* 40, no. 3: 523–45.

Chen, Kuan-Hsing. 2010. *Asia as Method: Toward Deimperialization*. Durham, NC: Duke University Press.

Clinton, Hillary. 2011. "America's Pacific Century." *Foreign Policy*, November, 56-63.

Connell, Raewyn. 2007. *Southern Theory: The Global Dynamics of Knowledge in Social Science*. Crows Nest, Australia: Allen and Unwin.

Connery, Christopher L. 1994. "Pacific Rim Discourse: The U.S. Global Imaginary in the Late Cold War Years." *boundary 2* 21 (1): 30–56.

———. 2012. "Reflections on the Politics and Location of Knowledge Making in a Time of Crisis." *Concentric* 38 (2): 45–63.

Cowie, Alexander. 1977. "Historical Essay." In Charles Brockden Brown, *Wieland, or The Transformation: An American Tale; Memoirs of Carwin the Biloquist*, edited by Sydney J. Krause, 311–48. Vol. 1 of *The Novels and Related Works of Charles Brockden Brown*. Bicentennial ed. Kent, OH: Kent State University Press.

Craik, George Lillie. 1830. *The New Zealanders*. London: Knight.

DeLoughrey, Elizabeth. 2007. *Routes and Roots: Navigating Caribbean and Pacific Island Literatures*. Honolulu: University of Hawaii Press.

Dimock, Wai Chee. 2006. *Through Other Continents: American Literature across Deep Time*. Princeton, NJ: Princeton University Press.

Friedman, Susan Stanford. 2011. "Why Not Compare?" *PMLA* 126 (3): 753–62.

Frow, John, and Meaghan Morris. 1993. Introduction to *Australian Cultural Studies: A Reader*, edited by John Frow and Meaghan Morris, vii–xxxii. St. Leonards, Australia: Allen and Unwin.

Fuller, Peter. 1986. *The Australian Scapegoat: Towards an Antipodean Aesthetic*. Nedlands: University of Western Australia Press.

Garfinkle, Adam. 2011. "The Decade Ahead." Paper presented at "The 9/11 Decade: How Everything Changed" conference, US Studies Centre, University of Sydney, June 7.

Gibbons, Luke. 2004. "Ireland, America, and Gothic Memory: Transatlantic Terror in the Early Republic." *boundary 2* 31 (1): 25–47.

Giles, Paul. 2013. *Antipodean America: Australasia and the Constitution of U.S. Literature*. New York: Oxford University Press.

Griffiths, Tom. 2011. "Deep Time and Australian History." *History Today* 51 (11): 20–25.

Habermas, Jürgen. 1984. *The Theory of Communicative Action*. Translated by Thomas McCarthy. Vol. 1. Boston: Beacon.

Hamilton, Ian. 1982. *Robert Lowell: A Biography*. London: Faber.

Harootunian, Harry. 2005. "Some Thoughts on Comparability and the Space-Time Problem." *boundary 2* 32 (2): 23–52.

Hau'ofa, Epeli. "Our Sea of Islands." [1993] 1999. In *Inside Out: Literature, Cultural Politics, and Identity in the New Pacific*, edited by Vilsoni Hereniko and Rob Wilson, 27–38. Lanham, MD: Rowan and Littlefield.

Haynes, Roslynn D. 1998. *Seeking the Centre: The Australian Desert in Literature, Art and Film*. Cambridge: Cambridge University Press.

Hsu, Hsuan L. 2000. "Democratic Expansionism in 'Memoirs of Carwin.'" *Early American Literature* 35 (2): 137–56.

Huang, Yunte. 2008. *Transpacific Imaginations: History, Literature, Counterpoetics*. Cambridge, MA: Harvard University Press.

Jameson, Fredric. 1981. *The Political Unconscious: Narrative as a Socially Symbolic Act*. Ithaca, NY: Cornell University Press.

Jefferson, Thomas. 1904. *The Works of Thomas Jefferson*. Edited by Paul Leicester Ford. Vol. 8. New York: G. P. Putnam's Sons.

Jolly, Margaret. 2008. "The South in *Southern Theory*: Antipodean Reflections on the Pacific." *Australian Humanities Review*, no. 44:75–99.

Leask, Nigel. 2000. "Irish Republicans and Gothic Eleutherarchs: Pacific Utopias in the Writings of Theobald Wolfe Tone and Charles Brockden Brown." *Huntington Library Quarterly* 63 (3): 347–67.

Lowell, Robert. 1959. *Life Studies*. New York: Farrar, Straus and Giroux, 1959.

———. 1967. *Near the Ocean*. Drawings by Sidney Nolan. New York: Farrar, Straus and Giroux.

Lyons, Paul. 2005. *American Pacifism: Oceania in the U.S. Imagination*. New York: Routledge.

Melville, Herman. [1846] 1968. *Typee: A Peep at Polynesian Life*, edited by Harrison Hayford, Hershel Parker, and G. Thomas Tanselle. Evanston, IL: Northwestern University Press.

———. [1849] 1968. *Omoo: A Narrative of Adventures in the South Seas*, edited by Harrison Hayford, Hershel Parker, and G. Thomas Tanselle. Evanston, IL: Northwestern University Press.

———. [1851] 1987. *Moby-Dick; or, The Whale*, edited by Harrison Hayford, Hershel Parker, and G. Thomas Tanselle. Evanston, IL: Northwestern University Press.

Muecke, Stephen. 2004. *Ancient and Modern: Time, Culture and Indigenous Philosophy*. Sydney, Australia: University of New South Wales Press.

Munn, Nancy D. 1996. "Excluded Spaces: The Figure in the Australian Aboriginal Landscape." *Critical Inquiry* 22 (3): 446–65.

Palmer, Sheridan. 2011. "Father of Art History Had Far-Reaching Influence." *Sydney Morning Herald*, September 8.

Povinelli, Elizabeth E. 2002. *The Cunning of Recognition: Indigenous Alterities and the Making of Australian Multiculturalism*. Durham, NC: Duke University Press.

Roberts, Brian Russell. 2013. "Archipelagic Discourse: Geographical Form, and Hurston's *Their Eyes Were Watching God*." *American Literature* 85 (1): 121–49.

Rose, Deborah Bird. 2000. "To Dance with Time: A Victorian River Aboriginal Study." *Australian Journal of Anthropology* 11 (3): 287–96.

Rushdie, Salman, 1982. "The Empire Writes back with a Vengeance." *Times* (London), July 3.

Said, Edward. 1978. *Orientalism*. London: Routledge and Kegan Paul.

Sakai, Naoki. 1988. "Modernity and Its Critique: The Problem of Universalism and Particularism." *South Atlantic Quarterly* 87 (3): 475–504.

Sanborn, Geoffrey. 2011. *Whipscars and Tattoos: The Last of the Mohicans, Moby-Dick, and the Maori*. New York: Oxford University Press.

Sayers, Andrew. 1989. *Sidney Nolan Drawings*. Canberra, Australia: Australian National Gallery.

Smith, Bernard. 1976. *The Antipodean Manifesto: Essays in Art and History*. Melbourne, Australia: Oxford University Press.

———. 1980. *The Spectre of Truganini*. Sydney, Australia: Australian Broadcasting Commission.

———. 1984. *The Boy Adeodatus: The Portrait of a Lucky Young Bastard*. Ringwood, Australia: Allen Lane.

———. 1985. *European Vision and the South Pacific*. 2nd ed. Sydney, Australia: Harper and Row.

———. 1986. Foreword to Peter Fuller, *The Australian Scapegoat: Towards an Antipodean Aesthetic*, ix–xv. Nedlands: University of Western Australia Press.

———. 1998. *Modernism's History: A Study in Twentieth-Century Art and Ideas*. New Haven, CT: Yale University Press.

Sollors, Werner. 1998. "Introduction: After the Culture Wars; or, From 'English Only' to 'English Plus.'" In *Multilingual America: Transnationalism, Ethnicity, and the Languages of American Literature*, edited by Werner Sollors, 1–16. New York: New York University Press.

Spivak, Gayatri Chakravorty. 2012. *An Aesthetic Education in the Era of Globalization*. Cambridge, MA: Harvard University Press.

Thomas, Nicholas. 1997. *In Oceania: Visions, Artifacts, Histories*. Durham, NC: Duke University Press.

Uren, David. 2012. "US Seeks Deeper Military Ties." *Australian* (Sydney), March 28.

White, Patrick. [1957] 1960. *Voss*. Paperback ed. London: Penguin.

———. [1956] 1961. *The Tree of Man*. Paperback ed. London: Penguin.

———. [1970] 2008. *The Vivisector*. With an introduction by J. M. Coetzee. New York: Penguin.

Wilson, Rob. *Be Always Converting, Be Always Converted: An American Poetics*. Cambridge, MA: Harvard University Press, 2009.

10

JOHN CARLOS ROWE

TRANSPACIFIC STUDIES AND THE CULTURES OF US IMPERIALISM

WE HAVE ENTERED A new stage of scholarship of what was previously designated as "the Pacific Rim," even though the precise boundaries of the region remain as contested as ever. In my view, this new stage can be characterized as predominantly postcolonial, in which interests revolve around efforts by formerly colonized states to achieve cultural, economic, and political sovereignty in their relation to the Pacific region both as a geographical site and as a series of commercial, military, and cultural routes. Despite the familiar criticism of postcolonial studies as "presentist," we know that the best work in postcolonial studies never forgets the imperial legacies so many have worked to overcome. The academic field itself is tied profoundly to these anticolonial struggles, even when it is critical of specific postcolonial state formations in which the imperial heritage is still operative.

Area studies specialists in the Pacific have done very substantial work on the diverse indigenous communities of this vast oceanic and insular region, as well as its contact zones with other oceans and seas and their bordering communities. Their archive is too vast to be summarized here, although I will try to include relevant scholars in what follows, but I want to acknowledge from the beginning that Pacific studies is usually postcolonial in its outlook. In many cases, scholarly studies of the Pacific are closely connected with political and civil rights movements led by native peoples in demographically and territorially small communities that are further "minoritized" by the global interests of first-world powers like the United States, the People's Republic of China, Japan, and Russia. The recent turn in Pacific studies toward the affirmation of indigenous and other local communities strengthened by their histories of resisting imperialism is evident in such collections as *Inside Out* and *Militarized Currents*.[1] Rob Wilson's *Reimagining the American Pacific* focuses on both the imperial realities and postcolonial utopia other scholars identify with the "new Pacific," and such work is complemented by Keith Camacho's recent *Cultures of Commemoration*.[2] Scholar-activist poets like the Chamoru writer Craig Santos Perez have contributed to coalitions of political and cultural activists with poetry like his *From Unincorporated Territory* and spoken-word performances on Guahan (Guam) and elsewhere in the Pacific, Asia, and the United States.[3]

These scholars are just a few of the many who are working today at the intersections of Asian, Pacific, postcolonial, and Asian American studies and who remain attentive to the continuing effects of global imperialism in these regions. I cannot pretend to possess their expertise or to command these large, overlapping fields, but I do think much of their work has been marginalized in American studies, even the new American studies whose adoption I strongly advocate for its hemispheric scope, its attention to the consequences of imperialist expansion, its respect for cultural and linguistic diversity, and its concern with transcultural and transnational relations. My effort in this essay, then, is to identify some of the ways in which the new American studies might more positively address the issues raised by the new Pacific and Asian studies. I recognize that my approach risks an incorporation of the work of such area studies of the Pacific into an enveloping American studies, which might itself be understood as cultural imperialism. But I think this risk is worthwhile if it will help us distinguish cultural inclusiveness and attention from neo-imperialist appropriation. My goal, then, is to find ways for the new Pacific studies to influence the new American studies, as well as to identify some common concerns.

The editors of this volume and the other contributors will offer their own interpretations of the term "transpacific" as a replacement of the older, now outmoded "Pacific Rim," but I want to offer my own understanding of how the use of the new term changes the scholarly study of US imperialism. In addition to treating reductively a complex series of regions and routes in the Pacific, the term "Pacific Rim" employed a visual metaphor suggesting an emphasis on the horizon of East Asia. The Pacific Ocean and its diverse island cultures signified as means of transport—way stations in the journey between West and East. Unquestionably European and US relations with East Asia were shaped by an Orientalism specific to Japan, Korea, China, and the border regions in South and Southeast Asia. Of course, there is a great deal of work still to be done to understand and challenge such Orientalism, but we must also recognize that the central attention paid to its critique in Asian studies has often resulted in another, unintentional Orientalist effect: the neglect of the multiple imperialist activities that have reshaped the Pacific island communities from the United States and nations in Europe and Asia.

Edward Said's adaptation of the European term for the Middle East is today overused and not entirely appropriate to either East Asia or the Pacific.[4] My intention is not to debate terminology, but instead to call attention to the insular communities otherwise overlooked as we cast our gaze toward that distant horizon of the Pacific Rim. The transpacific perspective would bring into view these different human and natural communities by first addressing the multiple colonial inscriptions of them, treating both the hybridized postcolonial societies and recovering their indigenous or migratory histories. We should not abandon too hastily this critical study of colonialism in the Pacific, because many of its communities are so shaped by these different colonial influences as to be no longer recuperable in their traditional or indigenous forms. To be sure, independence and sovereignty movements throughout the Pacific suggest diverse agency on the part of the Pacific's traditional inhabitants, but in many cases such political activism is still engaged with oppressive colonial and neocolonial practices that are often ignored by the wider world.

New postcolonial scholarship in the transpacific area will thus be concerned primarily with a continuation of the work initiated by the Asian and African nations meeting at the Bandung Conference in Indonesia in 1955. That celebrated post–World War II gathering of so-called nonaligned nations recalled longer legacies of anticolonial struggles, including the Pan-African congresses of the early twentieth century, to pursue postcolonial goals independent of the Big Three's one-sided declaration of decolonization. Indeed, Great Britain, the Soviet Union, and the United States had barely announced the project of decolonization before they began to divide up the world again according to their own neo-imperial ambitions. Sixty-five years after the Yalta and Potsdam conferences in which this postwar redistribution began, scholars have so thoroughly criticized such imperialism as to warrant new directions more in keeping with the agencies of the peoples once struggling as subalterns under colonial and neocolonial domination.

Valuable as I consider this new scholarship, I also am convinced we must continue to study the still operative legacies of imperialism and neo-imperialism in the Pacific. Unlike the Atlantic, which at least since Paul Gilroy's *The Black Atlantic* has been reinterpreted in terms of several counternarratives to the dominant North Atlantic narrative, the Pacific has remained relatively undertheorized in terms of the imperial narrative.[5] First, the transpacific region is far more difficult to conceptualize than the Atlantic, both because of the Pacific's immense size and its complex borders. Does the Pacific end at the Coral and Tasman Seas' borders with the Indian Ocean, thus excluding Australia from consideration, but retaining New Zealand? Are there primary transpacific routes, such as those defining the conventional Pacific Rim of Japan, Korea, and China by way of economic relations with the west coasts of the United States and Canada? How should we consider the North Pacific routes of Asian peoples who historically migrated by sea, Bering land bridge, or a combination of the two to North America millennia before European contact, thus connecting indigenous peoples on both sides of the Pacific, however distantly in historical terms? Second, such examples of the different borders involved in any study of the Pacific region are rendered even more complex when we consider the remappings produced by imperial contestation among European, Asian, and Creole nationalists from the Western Hemisphere from the seventeenth-century voyages of global exploration to eighteenth- and early nineteenth-century colonization efforts in Asia and the Pacific to twentieth-century independence movements in the region.

The reconceptualization of the Atlantic as a series of flows and circulations, rather than a specific geography or region, has been made explicit in recent years by cultural geographers interested in maritime contact zones. Martin Lewis and Kären Wigen argue in *The Myth of Continents* that the "Continental" model for understanding the different regions of the globe has tended to reify geopolitical boundaries and neglected "the complex webs of capital and commodity exchange" that become visible when we think in terms of "oceans and bays," rather than "continents" or "cultural blocs."[6] Since 1998, these authors have conducted a multidisciplinary research project at Duke called Oceans Connect: Culture, Capital, and Commodity Flows across Basins. Interestingly, their argument in *The Myth of Continents* tends to rely heavily on the Atlantic, even though Lewis began his career with a scholarly study of Luzon in the Philippines and Wigen is a specialist in Japanese studies.[7]

In many respects, the idea of theorizing regions in oceanic terms finds its most interesting applicability in the Pacific, where so many different insular communities have traditionally defined themselves and been defined by outside forces, often imperialist, in terms of the economic, cultural, political, military, and other flows they facilitate. Indeed, oceanic thinking encourages connections between indigenous and imperial contacts in ways that I think might avoid some of the potential binaries we risk in postcolonial work that tends to forget its anticolonial origins. Although I disagree with several of Lewis and Wigen's claims in *The Myth of Continents* and in some of the work that has come out of the Oceans Connect project, I want to draw on the broad conception of oceanic thinking to explain how my own work on Euro-American imperialism in the Pacific may have continuing relevance to transpacific scholarship.

My interests in transpacific studies focus on the rise of the United States as an imperial power in its nineteenth-century contestation with European powers in the Pacific. Trained as a literary and cultural historian, I am interested most in how US imperialism was understood culturally between the War of 1812 and the Spanish-American (1898) and Philippine-American (1899–1902) Wars. All of my previous work on US neo-imperialism in the period after World War II, which has focused on the cultural responses to the Vietnam War and to post-9/11 military missions in Iraq and Afghanistan, follows my initial interest in US imperialism in the formative years of the US nation, which I wrote about in *Literary Culture and U.S. Imperialism*.[8]

I understand nineteenth-century US expansion in and across the Pacific in terms of the expanded notion of Manifest Destiny elaborated by Richard Drinnon in *Facing West*, which remains one of the key works in American studies to articulate the relationship between internal and external colonialism.[9] Drinnon is particularly persuasive in his critical account of Henry Adams, the well-connected American historian who seems to have little to do with the Pacific, but who actually has much to say about the proper path of US expansion across the Pacific, with the primary goal of gaining a US "foothold in Asia," as he put it in a letter to his brother, Brooks Adams, on November 3, 1901.[10] Every student who has read *The Education of Henry Adams* knows how deeply invested in European culture and politics Henry Adams was. His famous meditation on the steps of the Church of Santa Maria di Ara Coeli (a Christian church built on the foundation of an ancient Roman temple) traces all modern history back to classical Rome. Despite Adams's famous declaration of confusion and despair in not understanding what that history meant, his Eurocentrism is unavoidable and urgent: "Rome was actual; it was England; it was going to be America."[11]

But ancient Rome had not expanded across the Pacific, as England had done in the eighteenth and nineteenth centuries with the United States following, annexing extensive territory from the Philippines to Hawai'i, American Samoa, and Guam in the late nineteenth and early twentieth centuries. Adams was by no means naïve or even just old-fashioned. His close relationship with Secretary of State John Hay, Adams's close friend and neighbor (they occupied two semi-detached mansions designed by the famed architect Henry Hobson Richardson, located just across the street from the White House, where today's Hay-Adams Hotel stands) put him in direct, daily conversations with the architect of US foreign policy in the Pacific and Asia in the late nineteenth and early twentieth centuries. There is little question that Adams clearly understood the importance of the Pacific Rim to what he considered the British and US inheritance of the Roman legacy: an imperial destiny, after all.[12]

Traditional scholars of Henry Adams had little to say about his travels to the South Pacific and Japan in 1890–91 with his close friend, the artist

John La Farge, except to comment on Adams's flight from the tragic suicide of his wife, Marion Hooper Adams, in 1885. But the trip that produced Adams's odd, privately printed *Memoirs of Maura Taaroa* and La Farge's exquisitely illustrated and Orientalist *An Artist's Letters from Japan* was more than just some junket for wealthy Americans, but part of the developing US foreign policy narrative that would lead through Tahiti to Japan and then to the colonial wars in Vietnam so many years later.[13] Adams's memoir is a fictionalized autobiography that betrays his deeply ethnocentric assumptions about Pacific primitivism and the need for the enlightenment Anglo-American civilization would bring. With its anxieties about mixed-race genealogies and its reliance on European heritage and values, Adams's family history is a small, but important, testament to the Pacific's role in US expansionism in the period culminating in the Spanish-American and Philippine-American Wars.

What Hay advocated was free trade, and his brand of modern US imperialism depended on the argument that all foreign policy decisions should be shaped by free-trade ideology. Nearly a century before Hay formulated US foreign policy in these terms, Captain David Porter had attempted to annex the Marquesas Islands—he would have renamed them the Washington Islands —for the United States while he cruised the Pacific with the goal of harassing British shipping during the War of 1812. His effort was nearly the first US extraterritorial annexation by legal fiat, but President James Madison and other government officials missed his dispatch because they were fleeing British forces that set the White House on fire. What Porter wanted in the Marquesas was only nominally a naval station, a foothold in Polynesia, or even trade with the local Happar and Taipi peoples. He wanted most of all some symbolic status in the ongoing struggle between the European and Russian powers for colonial influence in the transpacific region, already imagining that the next great stage of colonial contestation would be Asia. Melville's *Typee* is a wonderful nineteenth-century account of how Porter's Marquesan misadventures were linked with European and US colonialism at home.[14] Many have read Melville's novel as an allegory of the fugitive slave narrative, and still others have interpreted it as a thinly disguised criticism of US policies toward Native Americans.[15]

Less frequently remarked on is Melville's connection of the Marquesas with the growing US involvement in the Hawai'ian Islands in the 1840s, a subject Mark Twain would take up more vigorously in the concluding sections of *Roughing It*, as the United States meddled more directly in the colonial instabilities and internal politics of Hawai'i as it moved toward annexation of the islands.[16] I will not recount here the complex use Melville makes in *Typee* of Captain James Cook's fate—both his death and the much-debated fate of his body—to offer what seems to me a very profound indictment of how the United States would imitate and improve on the cultural arguments used to justify British colonialism, except to note that this transformation of traditional imperialism (exemplified by the British) into neo-imperialism (exemplified by the Americans) is extremely evident in the nineteenth-century transpacific and still relatively understudied. Reenacted in several nineteenth-century theatrical productions, Cook's death was quickly mythologized in Great Britain and the United States as a tragic encounter between the modern explorer and the primitive native, even though the most likely explanation of Cook's death is his ignorance of Hawai'ian cultural and religious practices.[17]

In *Island World*, Gary Okihiro provides a counternarrative that gives priority to the Hawai'ian influences on the shaping of the US nation.[18] In many respects, Okihiro provides a theoretical model for further studies of the transpacific, insofar as he reads the continental United States from the perspectives of the maritime and the Pacific islands, stressing the impact the latter have had on the US nation. Recovering the history of how Hawai'ian immigrants lived in nineteenth-century California, fought in the Civil War, served as sailors on nineteenth-century New England whalers and other commercial vessels, Okihiro emphasizes what Sara Johnson terms the "transcolonial imagination" at the height of Western nationalism.[19] We should not forget, however, that the history Okihiro recounts cannot be separated from its imperial entanglements. Hawai'ans traveled more widely in the United States as American economic, political, and religious interests in the islands grew; the dialectical relationship must be understood to avoid a simple interpretation of the evils of Western imperialism and the victimization of Pacific islanders.

The annexation of the Hawai'ian islands by the United States in 1898 was motivated in part by the desire to control commercial routes that would serve, among other far-flung enterprises, the ill-fated Klondike Gold Rush. In *China Men*, Maxine Hong Kingston links "The Great Grandfather of the Sandalwood Mountains" with "Alaska China Men," reminding us that the geographically disparate ventures of sugar-cane and pineapple agribusiness in Hawai'i and the Yukon Gold Rush are linked not only by way of Chinese workers, but also by the logic of US neo-imperialism.[20] Much as Kingston condemns the mistreatment of Chinese immigrants in the United States during the period of Chinese exclusion, she also recognizes the complicity of these same Chinese workers in the sorts of racial marginalization that would condemn Native Americans and African Americans to subaltern positions, subject not only to economic and social exploitation but often to social death and outright murder. Witnessing executions of Native Americans in Dawson on Douglas Island, Chinese miners were expelled from the Yukon by the judgment of the miners' meetings, then rowed out by local Native Americans to a ship in the harbor, where the captain of the ship promised to "take them home," only to have them agree: "'Yes, . . . Take us home . . . to Douglas Island,'" where they would ignore their exploitation, their conflicts with other radicalized and excluded minorities, Native Americans, and still look, as their fathers had hunted in the Sierra, for the yellow metal that makes men crazy, to paraphrase Nick Black Elk (*CM*, 161).

Kingston's fictional reconstruction of Chinese immigration to the United States complicates further Okihiro's efforts to recognize Hawai'ian contributions to US nationalism and modernity. Oppressed by the Manchu dynasty in China, worked as virtual slaves by colonial agribusiness in Hawai'i, legally excluded from citizenship and basic civil liberties in the United States, nineteenth-century Chinese immigrants nonetheless contributed importantly to US modernization, whose expansionist logic also rendered them legally invisible and economically poor. The history of Hawai'i is one important example of how our study of the transpacific often involves multiple imperialisms and thus several distinctly exploited groups.

Three other issues in transpacific studies are of both historical and continuing relevance when viewed in terms of the cultural history of US imperialism. The Philippine-American War is still neglected in American studies, despite wonderful new work on Philippine-American writers and culture from Carlos Bulosan to Jessica Hagedorn. Students do not even know we fought such a war against republican insurgents encouraged by the US defeat of the Spanish Empire. Philippine scholars like Dylan Rodriguez and Susan Harris have done remarkable work, but American studies continues to pay only the vaguest lip service to this unrecognized war and the postcolonial situation of the Philippines, from the capture of Emilio Aguinaldo to the exile of Ferdinand and Imelda Marcos.[21] The extent to which the Philippines remain a US client state is still neglected in scholarly debates. In the US healthcare industry alone, Philippine immigrants, many with medical degrees from Philippine universities, are denied certification, forced to retake courses of study in US institutions, and often relegated to positions as part-time "home care" givers who have far more expertise than their native-born equivalents. Today's Philippine-American healthcare workers are in many respects the late-modern heirs of the Piñoy agricultural workers whose exploitation Bulosan famously criticizes in *America Is in the Heart*.[22] Public debates in the United States regarding immigration reform hardly ever address these crises facing middle-class, well-educated Philippine immigrants, reinforcing the impression that immigration issues revolve around unskilled laborers from Mexico, Central America, and China.

What Chalmers Johnson has termed the US "empire of bases" needs to be expanded to include specific studies of the Mariana Islands (Guam, Saipan, Tinian, and so on), American Samoa, and other US military bases in the Pacific and Asia that serve the larger colonial purposes Johnson limits to what is inside the legal, territorial, and social boundaries established by the US military.[23] US military zones surrounding US bases in Japan, for example, are outside Japanese jurisdiction and governed by the US Military Command through its military police and judge adjutant general. Workers in bars, restaurants, houses of prostitution, and other enterprises flourishing on the edges of US military bases are thus protected not by Japanese law, but by US military law. Immigrants to Japan who often work in such poorly paid, easily exploited jobs are thus doubly mistreated in this shadow economy and have little recourse in the US military legal system, which certainly favors its own personnel and those who are fluent in English.[24] Many of these migrant workers in the sex and entertainment industries come from other Pacific regions, such as the Philippines, and can thus be legally and economically marginalized both by the Japanese and US governments. In addition, some immigrants are often caught between the cultural and social conventions of the host country and those of the US military.[25]

The long history of different colonial conflicts in the Pacific—from Porter's excursion in the Marquesas during the War of 1812 to the present— have usually included US participation, despite our tendency to think of US neo-imperialism as a recent phenomenon, developed primarily in the aftermath of the Cold War. Saipan was the principal airbase for the US Air Force bombers that targeted Japanese cities during World War II, and the *Enola Gay* took off from Tinian Island on August 6, 1945, on its mission to drop an atomic bomb on Hiroshima at the end of the war, as did another B-29, *Bockscar*, which three days later dropped an atomic bomb on Nagasaki. Guam became a US territory at the end of the Spanish-American War and was occupied by the Japanese in 1914 and during World War II, until US troops reoccupied the island in 1944 after fierce fighting.

Following the Gilbert and Marshall Islands campaign, also in 1944, the US military established a large military base on Wake Island (Enen-kio) in the Marshall Islands. Atomic testing on Bikini (Pikinni) Atoll in the Marshall Islands from 1946 to 1958 contaminated the atoll with cesium-123. In 1979, the Republic of the Marshall Islands (RMI) achieved its independence from the United States, operating from 1979 to 1986 under a "Compact of Free Association" with the United States. It was accepted by the United Nations as an independent republic in 1990. Nevertheless, the US military still occupies Wake Island, despite the RMI's claim to it. And despite international appeals that the toxic waste on Bikini Atoll be cleaned up, the United States has done nothing to repair the environmental and human damage left from the detonation of twenty-three nuclear devices there. In addition to its military base on Wake Island, the United States maintains a missile testing range on Kwajalein Atoll within sovereign RMI territory.

The transpacific can thus not be imagined apart from this long, continuing use of the Pacific islands by diverse imperial interests, which stretch from Spanish, Portuguese, French, and Dutch ventures in the region from the seventeenth to the end of the nineteenth century and include German, Japanese, and US claims in the later nineteenth century to the first half of the twentieth. More careful scholarly accounts would include contested claims by South American nations to Pacific islands, such as Chile's military occupation of Juan Fernandez and Ecuador's annexation of the Galápagos Islands in 1832 (they became a UNESCO World Heritage Site in 1978). Modern nations, territories, protectorates, and other geopolitical designations in the Pacific may in many cases have achieved postcolonial status of various kinds, but the legacies of imperial definition are profound and not easily dismissed. From the Spanish, English, French, and other imperial names given to islands that often had their own indigenous names to the development of economies and political processes deeply dependent on their previous colonial rulers, many islands in the Pacific are the means of broader military and commercial ventures across the Pacific, rather than ends in themselves.

I have only briefly alluded to the much more complex history of US annexation of the Hawai'ian Islands and US involvement in modern Philippine politics, in part to stress how these smaller, usually forgotten insular ventures are part of the larger history in which the United States has been involved since its inception. When considered merely as discrete entities, small, underpopulated islands like the Marshall Islands hardly deserve our attention in the already crowded liberal arts curriculum. But when understood as crucial parts in the larger movement of the United States across the Pacific to gain a "foothold in Asia," these neglected areas gain significance not only in the study of US imperialism but also in terms of their own struggles for cultural identity and geopolitical sovereignty. There is a historical continuity linking the Plains Wars in the late nineteenth century with the US role in the Philippine-American War and the Taiping and Boxer Rebellions in China, as Drinnon has pointed out.[26] Of course, if we equate the indigenous revolts of the Lakota Sioux (among others) with those of Aguinaldo in the Philippines or Hong Xiuquan—the Christian mystic who led the Taiping Rebellion—we will repeat the racist rhetoric of US troops who called Philippine insurgents "Indians" in the Philippine-American War.

But the connections established by US imperialism have had real consequences on colonized and postcolonial communities across the Pacific. The US decision to use nuclear weapons to defeat the Japanese in World War II not only is related to later atomic testing in the Marshall Islands in Americans' Cold War struggle for military supremacy over the Soviet Union, but it also perversely connects the Marianas (to which Guam and Saipan belong) with the Marshall Islands' Bikini Atoll. Environmental damage from military testing or occupation alone also gives the inhabitants on these islands common cause to protest and work toward reform, reparation, and environmental restoration. European, Asian, and US imperialist ventures in the Pacific not only provide a shared history of oppression and desire for postcolonial independence, but they have also created shared conditions that can enable such coordinated, transnational organization for reform. Thus local struggles against US military imperialism in Japan and on the Korean Peninsula inevitably are connected with similar efforts in the Philippines and the smaller Pacific island republics hosting US military bases.

Such coalitions of nonaligned nations were the goals of the Bandung Conference and remain worthy purposes in today's inequitable processes of globalization. Understanding the specific complaints and thus histories of colonized and occupied communities across the Pacific should include our broader interpretation of how such imperial and neo-imperial practices have contributed to the long history of European, Asian, and US expansionism. As I have suggested in this essay, there is a direct historical line connecting US involvement in the Taiping and Boxer Rebellions, the Chinese exclusion laws, the Spanish-American and Philippine-American Wars, the Portsmouth (New Hampshire) Treaty that concluded the Russo-Japanese War, World Wars I and II, the postwar occupation of Japan, the Korean War, support of the French in the Indochina wars, the Vietnam War, the US invasion of and ongoing military presence in Iraq, and the current US military intervention in Afghanistan and deep involvement in Pakistan's politics and military campaigns against dissidents. When connected with this larger history, the people and ecosystems of the Pacific islands become visible and relevant, as do their challenges to such alternative forms of imperialism as the operation of foreign military bases in their territory, often with questionable or outdated authority.

Indeed, the general issue of how and when the US government acquired leases to land and facilities for military uses needs to be studied in detail. From Guantanamo in Cuba to Clark Airforce Base and the US Naval Station in Subic Bay in the Philippines, US military installations have been contested and challenged by local political leaders. In the Philippines, the nearly century-old US military bases were closed in 1991, although US efforts to establish new military bases have led to US political interference between the Philippine government and the dissident Moro Islamic Liberation Front (MILF). Since 2006, rumors have circulated that the United States has been in negotiations with the MILF to trade rights to military bases in territory it controls with help in concluding a favorable peace treaty with the Philippine government.[27] Not until the US military base at Guantanamo Bay, Cuba, was used for terrorist detainees—to avoid Geneva Convention provisions requiring legal due process for such prisoners of war held within the United States—did the American public pay much attention to this long-established lease agreement between the US and Cuban governments. The lease can be traced back to US efforts in the late nineteenth century to acquire a naval base in the Caribbean to control shipping in the region in anticipation of the construction of the Panama Canal. Rejected by the Haitian government in its efforts to lease, buy, or simply "annex" Môle St. Nicolas, the large natural harbor on the Northwest coast of Haiti, the United States looked to Cuba for a military base in the Caribbean.

In 2009, six Uighur men who were held in Guantanamo as Chinese dissidents, having been charged along with other Uighurs in terrorist acts in China, were sent by the administration of President Barack Obama to the tiny island nation of Palau, composed of two hundred islands (only ten of which are inhabited) about four hundred miles southeast of the Philippines. Other Uighur detainees in Guantanamo have balked at being relocated to Palau, but the Obama administration paid Palau $200 million to house these six detainees.[28] Viewed by most Americans as simply another instance of how difficult it would be to relocate the Guantanamo detainees, the removal of the Uighurs to Palau is by no means an exceptional path of migration between the Caribbean and Pacific. Nineteenth-century Chinese immigrants, often drawn from those who had already worked in Hawai'i, were imported to work as virtual slaves on the uninhabited guano islands of the Caribbean. The rich deposits of bird guano were a valuable fertilizer in the nineteenth century, but the working conditions and life in general on these islands for imported Chinese laborers were at the very limits of human existence. In short, migrations and diasporas from the Caribbean to the Pacific are stark reminders of the consequences of Euro-American imperialism in the Western Hemisphere and the Pacific.

Finally, the comparative cultural, political, and legal study of the Maori (New Zealand), Aboriginal peoples and Torres Straits' Islanders (Australia), and North American Native Americans needs to be included in any theorization of transpacific studies and our continuing work on the consequences of modern imperialism. Considered in oceanic rather than continental terms, indigenous rights in New Zealand, Australia, and North America are closely related not only by respective appeals to legal precedents but also by shared indigenous arguments regarding their original rights to land ownership. In the United States, the 1831 decision *Cherokee Nation v. Georgia* of the John

Marshall Supreme Court declared that Native American tribes were "domestic dependent nations." In its earlier decision in *Johnson v. McIntosh* (1823), the Supreme Court attempted to solve the problem of who owned the land by declaring native peoples mere "occupants" whose claims had been replaced by European "ownership" established by conquest and use, effectively converting indigenous "owners of discovered lands into tenants on those lands."[29]

In Australia, the British used the legal doctrine of *terra nullius*—Latin for "no land"—to contend that the Aboriginal inhabitants of the continent did not own the land because they did not enclose it and thus use it productively, despite evidence that different Aboriginal communities traditionally granted each other seasonal access to their lands for purposes of hunting and gathering. Indeed, many Aboriginal leaders assumed that British settlers who requested land for farming and grazing were merely doing so on such unpaid lease arrangements, rather than settling permanently on Aboriginal lands. *Terra nullius* prevailed as a legal doctrine until 1992, when the celebrated Eddie Mabo case, first brought in the 1950s against the Australian government, was finally settled in favor of Mabo, who had died in the meantime. Even that case depended on establishing very clear indigenous claims to enclosed property, thus affirming the British principle of land ownership, because Mabo was a Murray Islander in the Torres Straits Islands, where islanders had for millennia enclosed land. In fact, Mabo's lawsuit was based on the enclosure of his kitchen garden, but it did at least establish the concept of indigenous enclosure, even if the larger issue that different land uses than European enclosure might establish property rights was ignored in the final decision. Nevertheless, the Mabo victory in 1992 effectively overturned *terra nullius*, although only after more than two centuries of devastation of Australian aboriginal cultures, including the forced removal of Aboriginals and Torres Strait Islanders from their traditional homelands and the imprisonment of many of them in remote internment camps—often on inhospitable islands, like Flinders Island in the Bass Straits (between Tasmania and Australia)—or the concerted efforts to exterminate Aboriginals as the Tasmanians did in the so-called Black War of the 1830s.[30] *Terra nullius* probably influenced John Marshall as he framed his Supreme Court decisions in the 1820s and 1830s regarding Native American land rights; North American legal precedents and treaties justifying indigenous removal certainly influenced subsequent Australian decisions regarding the civil, economic, and legal rights of Aboriginal peoples and Torres Strait Islanders. Yet Australia barely figures in most US university curricula and is rarely discussed in American studies scholarship, except as a distant analogy or comparison state.

There are, of course, countless other equally complex indigenous rights issues to be studied in transpacific terms, including not just the many different insular peoples of the Pacific but also indigenous peoples of Japan, China, Korea, Tibet, Nepal, Mongolia, and other regions in Asia with historical, legal, or just universal ties to the indigenous rights of those living in Canada and the Americas. Indeed, those six Uighurs languishing now on Palau and their comrades in Guantanamo are cases of indigenous rights dissidents cast far and wide across the Pacific and the Western Hemisphere as a consequence of the displacements of Euro-American imperialism. In particular, then, transpacific studies should centrally include indigenous rights. How we read the rights and cultural issues of the indigenous peoples who were in the way of European and US imperialism will tell the real story of our research in the coming years.

The differences among indigenous peoples in the Pacific region should also remind us that oceans disconnect even more than they connect. Thinking in oceanic rather than continental terms should also encourage us to articulate social, political, environmental, and human differences sustained by the separation of landmasses by the oceans. Lewis and Wigen are thus not entirely correct to stress the contact zones of the world's oceans while ignoring the ineluctable fact that oceans disconnect in ways that produce dramatically different ecosystems. In *Following the Equator*, Twain notes how the Australian platypus "was never in the Ark," and thus the animal makes a hash of Darwinian theories of evolution.[31] The platypus's status as a monotreme (neither fish nor fowl!) threw nineteenth-century European natural science into such disarray that some naturalists insisted the creature must be a hoax, and not a real animal. Scientific efforts to study *Ornithorhynchus anatinus* almost drove the shy creature to extinction in the nineteenth century, as the wry Twain himself acknowledges when he notes that while in New Zealand his host "gave me an ornithorhyncus [*sic*], and I am taming it," a considerable challenge even for this great satirist (*FE*, 301).

Some scholars might argue that in the era of air travel, satellites, and such related technologies as the Internet, oceanic thinking, whether focused on contacts in maritime flows or on the differences such distances between communities create, is archaic and easily ignored. But when considered in ecological and cultural terms, oceanic thinking stresses our profound dependence on the health of oceans, the different global environments those maritime zones nurture, and the common debt we have to the entire system of natural differences that is the true source of productivity, wealth, and health. We live in an era in which overfishing and climate change have threatened the health of our oceans. At the Summit on Climate Change in Copenhagen in 2009, the Fijian government argued that the rising level of the Pacific threatened the very existence of its nation. In the same year, the Alliance of Small Island States (AOSIS) joined the Group of Least Developed Countries to create a coalition of some eighty countries advocating that the United Nations set a limit of 1.5 degrees centigrade for global warming annually—a limit so far ignored by most first-world highly industrialized nations. AOSIS includes such small island states as the Seychelles Islands in the Indian Ocean and the Marianas and Fiji Islands in the Pacific. Yet the history and contemporary global concerns of these island states hardly figure in US liberal education, except as the conventional Pacific Rim that has traditionally designated one-way globalization and the seemingly ceaseless upward spiral of capitalist need. One way to resist such a limited conception of the Pacific is to understand the many different ways the communities of the Pacific have affirmed their cultural, political, and economic identities, and a related critical part of that counternarrative is our scholarly articulation of the ongoing European, Asian, and US imperialism in the transpacific region.

In conclusion, we should not assume that the disappearance of overt institutions and practices of imperial domination from the Pacific leaves us simply with postcolonial struggles for sovereignty and cultural self-representation. Decolonization is still an activist agenda, which depends on alliances among activists around the globe. Commercial exploitation of minerals and other natural resources on the floor of the Pacific threatens not only the Pacific islands but the continental mainlands. The legacies of imperialism are historically long and culturally deep; they are as visible in the tattooing practices of Samoan Christians as they are in the tourism of Waikiki Beach and the Uighurs wandering a bit bewildered on the shores of Palau. Imperialism, indigeneity, and migration or diaspora all must be read together in their layered simultaneity; they are the currents of the transpacific region.

Notes

1. Vilson Hereniko, Rob Wilson, and Patricia Grace, eds., *Inside Out: Literature, Cultural Politics and the New Pacific* (London: Rowman and Littlefield, 2012); Keith L. Camacho, Cynthia Enloe, and Setsu Shigematsu, eds., *Militarized Currents: Toward a Decolonized Future in Asia and the Pacific* (Minneapolis: University of Minnesota Press, 2010).

2. Rob Wilson, *Reimagining the American Pacific: From "South Pacific" to Bamboo Ridge and Beyond* (Durham, NC: Duke University Press, 2000); Keith L. Camacho, *Cultures of Commemoration: The Politics of War, Memory and History in the Mariana Islands* (Honolulu: University of Hawai'i Press, 2011).

3. Craig Santos Perez, *from Unincorporated Territory [saina]* (Richmond, CA: Omnidawn, 2010).

4. Edward Said, *Orientalism* (New York: Random House, 1978), 1–3.

5. Paul Gilroy, *The Black Atlantic: Modernity and Double Consciousness* (Cambridge, MA: Harvard University Press, 1993).

6. Martin Lewis and Kären Wigen, *The Myth of Continents: A Critique of Metageography* (Berkeley: University of California Press, 1997), 1.

7. The Oceans Connect project is part of the Center for International Studies at Duke University.

8. John Carlos Rowe, *Literary Culture and U.S. Imperialism: From the Revolution to World War II* (New York: Oxford University Press, 2000). See also John Carlos Rowe and Rick Berg, eds., *The Vietnam War and American Culture* (New York: Columbia University Press, 1991); John Carlos Rowe, *The Cultural Politics of the New American Studies* (London: Open Humanities Press, 2011).

9. Richard Drinnon, *Facing West: The Metaphysics of Indian-Hating and Empire-Building* (Minneapolis: University of Minnesota Press, 1980), 268–74.

10. Henry Adams to Brooks Adams, November 3, 1901, *The Letters of Henry Adams*, ed. J. C. Levenson, Ernest Samuels, Charles Vandersee, and Viola Hopkins Winner, with the assistance of Jayne N. Samuels and Eleanor Pearre Abbott (Cambridge, MA: Harvard University Press, 1988), 5:306.

11. Henry Adams, *The Education of Henry Adams*, ed. Ernest Samuels and Jayne N. Samuels (Boston: Houghton Mifflin, 1973), 91.

12. Rowe, *Literary Culture and U.S. Imperialism*, 165–76.

13. Henry Adams, *Memoirs of Marau Taaroa, Last Queen of Tahiti* (Washington: n.p., 1893); John La Farge, *An Artist's Letters from Japan* (New York: Century, 1897). Although technically an autobiography, *Memoirs of Marau Taaroa* was printed under Adams's authorship, as if he were the Western anthropologist recording the testimony of his native informant.

14. Herman Melville, *Typee, or a Peep at Polynesian Life* (New York: Wiley and Putnam, 1846).

15. See Rowe, *Literary Culture and U.S. Imperialism*, 77–96.

16. Mark Twain, *Roughing It* (Hartford, CT: American Publishing Company, 1872).

17. Richard Hough, *Captain James Cook: A Biography* (New York: W. W. Norton, 1997), 341–55 and 365.

18. Gary Y. Okihiro, *Island World: A History of Hawai'i and the United States* (Berkeley: University of California Press, 2008).

19. Sara E. Johnson, *The Fear of French Negroes: Transcolonial Collaboration in the Revolutionary Americas* (Berkeley: University of California Press, 2012). A similar conception of colonial subjects writing back informs Anna Brickhouse's *Transamerican Literary Relations and the Nineteenth-Century Public Sphere* (New York: Cambridge University Press, 2004).

20. Maxine Hong Kinston, *China Men* (New York: Random House, 1980), 121–49, 159–62. Further references to this book in the text are to *CM*.

21. Dylan Rodriguez, *Suspended Apocalypse: White Supremacy, Genocide, and the Filipino Condition* (Minneapolis: University of Minnesota Press, 2009); Susan K. Harris, *God's Arbiters: Americans and the Philippines, 1898–1902* (New York: Oxford University Press, 2011).

22. Carlos Bulosan, *America Is in the Heart: A Personal History* (New York: Harcourt, Brace and Co., 1946).

23. Chalmers Johnson, *The Sorrows of Empire: Militarism, Secrecy, and the End of the Republic* (New York: Henry Holt, 2004), 151–86.

24. Ibid., 137–43.

25. See Rhacel Parreñas, *The Force of Domesticity: Filipina Migrants and Globalization* (New York: New York University Press, 2008).

26. Drinnon, *Facing West*, 250–58.

27. Fabio Scarpello, "US, Philippines Weigh New Military Marriage," *Asia Times online*, August 23, 2006, http://atimes.com/atimes/Southeast_Asia/HH23Aeo1.html, accessed May 18, 2015.

28. Mary Kay Magistad, "Life in Palau after Guantanamo," *PRI's The World*, March 10, 2010, http://www.pri.org/stories/2010-03-10/life-palau-after-guantanamo, accessed May 18, 2015.

29. Lindsay Robertson, quoted in Colin G. Calloway, *First Peoples: A Documentary Survey of American Indian History*, 3rd ed. (Boston: Bedford, 2008), 268.

30. Henry Reynolds, *Why Weren't We Told? A Personal Search for the Truth about Our History* (Victoria, Australia: Penguin Books Australia, 2000), 186–89.

31. Mark Twain, *Following the Equator: A Journey around the World* (Hartford, CT: American Publishing Company, 1897), 105. Further references to this book in the text are to: *FE*.

[IV]

DECOLONIZING KNOWLEDGE PRODUCTION FOR THE PACIFIC CENTURY

11

WALTER D. MIGNOLO

GEOPOLITICS OF KNOWING/UNDERSTANDING AND
AMERICAN STUDIES: A DECOLONIAL ARGUMENT OR
VIEW FROM THE GLOBAL SOUTH

When one says Eurocentrism, *every self-respecting postmodern leftist intellectual has vio-lent a reaction as Joseph Goebbels had to culture—to reach for a gun, hurling accusations of proto-fascist Eurocentrist cultural imperialism. However, is it possible to imagine a leftist appropriation of the European political legacy?*
        —Slavoj Žižek, "A Leftist Plea for Eurocentrism" (emphasis added)

When one says Eurocentrism, *every self-respecting decolonial intellectual has not violent a reaction as Joseph Goebbels had to culture—to reach for a gun, hurling accusations of proto-fascist Eurocentrist cultural imperialism.* Instead, a self-respecting decolo-nial intellectual will reach for the light and will find Frantz Fanon instead of Joseph Goebbels: "Now, comrades, now is the time to decide to change sides. *We must shake off the great mantle of night which has enveloped us, and reach for the light.* The new day which is dawning must find us determined, enlightened and resolute. . . . So, my brothers, how could we fail to understand that we have better things to do than follow in that Europe's footsteps?"
        —Walter Mignolo, "Geopolitics of Knowing and Understanding,"
        quoting Frantz Fanon (emphasis added)

I

In my presentation at the symposium on American Studies as Transnational Practice (quoted in the epigraph above), I intended to play devil's advocate. Properly speaking, I am not an expert in American studies, although I have some knowledge of the historical foundation of the Americas much before the United States of America was founded and its history since. I suppose I was invited to participate in the symposium because I have something to say about América in general, as the fourth continent in the European con-sciousness. Thus my presentation explored the meaning of the title of the symposium and by doing so intended to take American studies as an object studied from a perspective outside the American imaginary in which is grounded "American" as both an object of study and a locus of enunciation. In other words, my argument was formulated outside the domain of American studies as a locus of enunciation and focused on American studies as an object to be analyzed.

What I have to say about América comes from my memories, subjectivities, and disciplinary training (in literature, semiotics, anthropology, and philosophy) in the South. That is, from my experiences of the imaginary of América with an accent. By "the South" I mean here South and Central Spanish and Luso América, as well as the Caribbean in its variegated colonial legacies (English, French, Dutch, and Spanish). Spanish and Luso América joined forces with imperial France in the nineteenth century to confront the imperial ambitions of the United States, shown in the 1848 Treaty of Guadalupe Hidalgo that allowed the United States to move its frontier miles to the south, appropriating a vast expanse of Mexican territory. That forgotten history is particularly relevant today when conservative forces in Arizona want to keep so-called Mexican illegal immigrants out of the territory of which they, as Mexican nationals, have been dispossessed. But I think this set of events is also relevant to think about in considering American studies as transnational practice.

To what America does the term "American studies" refer? And what does it mean? Is the point that American studies is a project of American scholars or that America is the domain of investigations of any scholar, American or not, who is trained in the discipline? In other words, does American studies refer to the locus of enunciation or to America as a complex domain of investigation, both national and transnational? In this sense too, America could be transnationally studied and not only be the place where transnational practices are enacted.

With my oral presentation at the symposium, I showed a mixture of images and texts. Oral and written media are different in nature. In addition, I do not read papers and instead organize my talks following a handwritten script, I did not have a written version of my presentation to submit for publication in this volume. What I have to do here is provide a written version with illustrations of what I did at the symposium with a combination of sounds (my voice) and images. Thus, what I will do is tell the story of what I said.

What I said started with my showing on the screen a quotation from the symposium statement overlaid on Pedro Lasch's map of Latino/a America.

The map has been exhibited in many places; in galleries and books and on the walls of public buildings and walls that look like a border between the two Américas, like the one shown in figure 11.1.

FIGURE 11.1. Pedro Lasch map of Latino/a America, visualized in diverse outlets, is a floating statement revealing the fictional ontology of the Western Hemisphere. Latino/a America. Series begun in 2003, ongoing. Time based, social and multimedia.

The quotation from the symposium statement that I presented in tandem with Lasch's map is the following:

American Studies as transnational practice not only raises questions on the changing roles that the United States has played as a superpower in the global arena since the late nineteenth century, but also calls attention to its own disciplinary premises, interests, and imaginaries in relation to area studies and comparative literature. As American Studies has recently intervened in us exceptionalism and neoliberal capitalism in its critique of discourses that vary from "manifest destiny" to "market democracy," it also foregrounds its own formation as a product of the Cold War and its renewed influence in the post-socialist regimes in China, Russia, and East Europe. Meanwhile, with new paradigm shifts in transnational and global studies that encompass transoceanic, hemispheric, and planetary consciousness, how does American Studies negotiate and reconfigure its own field imaginaries and boundaries? If Hemispheric Studies foregrounds the issue of "the Americas," how would its critical disposition "provincialize" American Studies? If the westward movement was central to us nation-building and the national imaginary, how would the northward movement of Mexicans and Latino/as reconstitute the US consciousness as new national narratives? If Trans-Pacific Studies has marked a new moment in transoceanic studies, how would the Pacific pose as a new dimension of American Studies in interaction with the Atlantic? If we reconsider US literature as global literature and US history as global history, what are the critical implications and cultural incentives?[1]

The quotation is long, but it is important to keep it in mind since my argument attempts to change the geography of reasoning that the symposium's statement proposes. Lasch's map is a first step: what America are we talking about in "Latino/a America"?

2

I said above that I would like to look at American (US) studies from the perspective of the other América, the América with an accent. American studies, in the sense that the expression had in the symposium, is not very common in South América and the Caribbean. I heard that there is some use of the term in that sense in México, but in general, in South America and the Caribbean the tendency is to delink rather than to have a branch of American studies. By raising these issues I hope to engage in transnational practice that takes American studies as an object of investigation and reflection rather than as a locus of enunciation from which to understand the world and to understand the United States in the world. My locus of enunciation is geopolitically elsewhere, tangentially related to the discipline—in its exteriority, to be more precise: América with an accent is outside the purview of American studies, but it is also inside it, for without its difference from the South, the North could not have its identity. Exteriority is the outside defined by the inside in the process of defining itself as inside. Being able to decide what is outside presupposes the control of knowledge and the capacity to endow meaning. Hemispheric American studies is attempting to overcome the historical difference between the two Americas and the differential of epistemic power implied in the difference, but the epistemic colonial difference between the two Américas remains.

All practitioners of American studies know very well the landmark of the discipline. Those of you who are reading this volume and are American studies scholars could skip to the next section of this essay. Those of you who are not practitioners or well acquainted with the discipline may not be aware of one of its key historical moments: on May 8, 1928, an English professor at the University of Washington, Vernon Parrington, received a telegram from the Pulitzer Prize Committee announcing that he had won the historical writing award for the first two volumes in his *Main Currents in American Thought*.[2]

Institutionally the American Studies Association was founded in 1951 and provided the basis for the creation of American studies as a discipline in colleges and universities. During the Cold War it provided the platform for promoting Western civilization values and American culture. Shortly after the Cold War, a shift in the discipline took place. The culture of Western imperialism took center stage. If up to that point American studies was the platform to promote Westernization, after the Cold War American studies became also a place to denounce and unveil the darker side of Westernization: imperialism.[3] The two volumes of Parrington's *Main Currents of American Thoughts* that had been published in 1927 had much to do with the field's orientation. That is, the institutionalization of the discipline took place about two decades after the publication of Parrington's landmark text. Now, let's take a look at the dates Parrington used to trace the historical moments in American thought. The title of the first volume is very revealing: *The Colonial Mind, 1620–1800.* The history of American thought begins about 130 years after the date that people in Anáhuac and Tawantinsuyu were surprised by the arrival of strangers to their land, without passports or invitations.

The title of the second volume is less relevant to my argument, but just to complete the picture here it is: *The Romantic Revolution in America, 1800–1860.* This volume has been perceived as tracing the optimistic mood of a country eager for land and new opportunities embodied by Andrew Jackson and Abraham Lincoln. A third volume of *Main Currents of American Thoughts*, published after Parrington's death and titled *The Beginnings of Critical Realism in America*, covered the period from 1860 to 1920.[4] Readers who are not in the discipline should be informed that the journal *American Quarterly* was founded in 1949 and the American Studies Association in 1951. Obviously, the field of American studies was considered to include everything concerning American history and cultures and contributing to the consolidation of the idea of American civilization as understood in and by the history of the United States.

I am retelling this story, so well known to American studies practitioners, for several reasons. One of them is a concern for transnational practices. The term "Americanists"—which may refer to the practitioners of the discipline labeled American studies—has various genealogies. The term first appeared in 1875 in the inauguration of the Congrès international des Américanistes in France. Notice that the congress was inaugurated in the period when the French government and some of its "organic intellectuals" (in Antonio Gramsci's sense) were attempting to add "Latin" to América, that is, they wanted to stop the United States from moving its frontier southward after the 1848 Treaty of Guadalupe Hidalgo. Furthermore, the intent was explicit: France was already looking into the globalization of French history and culture—in other words, seeking the global control of knowledge—in a way that was also transnational. The first article of the charter of the congress states: "Le Congrès internationale des Américanistes a pour objet contribuer au progrès des études ethnographiques, linguistiques et histori-ques relatives aux deux Amériques, spécialement pour les temps antérieurs à Christophe Colomb, et de mettre en rapport les personnes qui s'intéressent à ces études."[5]

Parrington's America was indeed an object of study for European Amer-icanists. The word "transnational" was not in use at the time, but "interna-tional" is quite explicit of the goals of the congress. "Americanism" means first of all a European (particularly French) imperial enterprise through the mediation of knowledge. This story may be useful to think about when con-sidering what American studies as transnational practice may mean today. Is it not the turn of the United States to do what France did, or intended to do, in the second half of the nineteenth century? Thus, we can say in retro-spect that American studies institutionalized as a discipline belongs to the line of thought that started with the idea of the Western Hemisphere, the idea that is an implicit frame in Parrington's trilogy. If the term "Western Hemisphere" was telling Europeans that there was a line that could not be crossed, but Europeans crossed that line epistemically with the creation of the congress, then the creation of American studies was asserting that there was no need for French Americanists to study us, for we Americans are ca-pable of studying ourselves and the world.[6] Thus, the institutionalization of American studies materialized during the Cold War, simultaneously with the creation of area studies that consisted of US scholars in social sciences and the humanities studying the world. There was then a totality in the control of knowledge: American studies took care of building knowledge about us, and area studies took care of building knowledge about them.

The preceding considerations were necessary to clarify two points:

(A) There is a distinction between US studies and American studies. Now, I can say that while I am not a practitioner of US studies, I certainly am engaged in Américan studies in the general sense of the term that goes back to Martin Waldseemüller's *Cosmographia Introductio*, where the name "America" first appeared.[7] I have been studying the history of the term since it emerged in European consciousness, and I have been studying globalization from the perspective of the invention of the word América to name a continent that Europeans believed they had discovered. If this is what we understand by American studies, the field is not only transna-tional but global. Thus, to study America means to ask these fundamental questions first: when and why did the name "America" appear in the human imaginary, and what were the consequences of that appearance? (B) In this perspective, the emergence of new republic of the United States in 1776 and, after that date, the emergence of a historical consciousness that traces the history of American thought to 1620 is only a national history within the larger picture of the continental and hemispheric American continent, the fourth continent in the European consciousness, as I noted above. And I emphasize here that in spite of the European consciousness of China and the Arabo-Islamic region (what we refer to today as the Middle East), for example, Western Christians divided the world into three continents and attributed them to Noah's three sons. There was no Asia either for people living in what Christians named Asia. For people in China and Japan did not know they had lived in Asia (not yet quite Europeans) until they received that news from Western Christian cartographers, travelers, historians, theologians, and philosophers.

In terms of US studies, Parrington's two initial volumes were very important in that they changed the geography of reasoning, and although his conception of the field was provincial (limited to the United States and the colonial period in 1620), it was indeed a strong manifestation of the appropriation of the word "America" from its European genealogy. That move was already taking place with the invention of the idea of the Western hemisphere, which occurred almost a century before Parrington's work. The idea of the Western hemisphere emerged during the years that Parrington identified as the end of the colonial period. That is what the idea of the Western Hemisphere does: it closes imperial linear thinking and changes the geography of reasoning. But of course, Parrington's use of "America" instead of "the United States" is a problem not because he misidentifies US intellectual history but because it mutated into an institution: American studies. This mutation raises the following questions from the American South: when and why did the United States appropriate the name "America" and naturalize it?

3

In my oral presentation I referred to the Venezuelan philosopher Enzo Del Bufalo, author of a book titled *Americanismo y democracia*.[8] In a nutshell, his argument is as follows: The American Revolution was indeed the realization of the European modern dream that began during the Renaissance with the invention of the secular idea of man (humanism), an idea that would gain ground in the late seventeenth century (particularly in the Glorious

Revolution in England) and that would be complemented with the idea of freedom, but that could not be achieved in a Europe divided by constant wars and interstate imperial conflicts. When Georg Wilhelm Friedrich Hegel saw in America the next stop of the spirit, and Alexis de Tocqueville discovered democracy in America, "America" mutated from being a European invention proposed by Waldseemüller into the actualization of the project of modernity that was already prefigured in Immanuel Kant's idea of the Enlightenment. That the continental America invented by Europeans became "America" to signify the United States that prompted the conditions to make the claim, a few decades after the American Revolution, that America (the continent) is for the American (the United States of America). The Western Hemisphere shrank: it was no longer Waldseemüller's continent of America, but Kant's and Hegel's America (North America) stolen from the European imaginary and planted in the land of the United States.

The problem for scholars in and from the South emerges when the new nation-state, the United States, appropriated the meaning of *Americanidad* and, by con-fusing the political and philosophical spheres, transformed the United States into the guardian of freedom. Here is where Del Bufalo's argument gains its force. The appropriation by the United States of the idea of freedom and democracy was the first step in the transformation of a postcolonial state into an imperial state that became the guardian of freedom and democracy. In the process, US Americanism became un-American. That means that while America was the dream of freedom and democracy in the European imagination, the actual independence of the United States made the American ideal a tool of imperial expansion. Therefore, Americanism in the hands of the United States became un-American in the precise sense that it negated what the dream offered. But since it negated the dream in a positive way (becoming the model and leader of world democracy), Americanism became an anchor for the rhetoric of modernity while at the same time hiding its undemocratic and imperial project—that is, hiding coloniality, the darker side of Western modernity.

This turn of events (the process that led to the evolution of the United States from a postcolonial formation into an imperial player and finally a global leader), was introduced into American studies in the already classic volume edited by Amy Kaplan and Donald Pease, *Cultures of United States Imperialism*.[9] In that genealogy of thoughts, American Studies as transnational practice—both the symposium held at Lubbock, Texas, where I presented the preliminary ideas in this essay, and the volume are embedded in the mutations of American studies as an association and a disciplinary field from 1951 to the last decade of the twentieth century. That is, from the initial goals of American studies to consolidate and promote the culture and civilization of the United States (the decade of the 1950s, when the United States was on its way to assume global leadership) to the "end of history" announced after the end of the Cold War, an inversion of the principles upon which the United States was founded in 1776 was taking place. That inversion consisted of the imperial imposition (by diplomacy, international relations, or force) of freedom and democracy that Kaplan and Pease denounced. In my view, Kaplan and Pease's volume planted the seeds for a de-imperial line of reflection,—neither postcolonial nor decolonial, but de-imperial.

What do I mean by that? The concept of imperialization was explored by Leo Ching in his superb reflections on "becoming Japanese."[10] A US citizen of Taiwanese descent, Ching is sensitive to the problem of coloniality, not only because of his connection to Taiwan but also because of his membership in one of the ethnic minorities in the United States. By imperialization, Ching means that for a state to fulfill its imperial designs, it must do more than subjugate the colonial population: it also must convince the citizens of the imperial state to support imperial projects. Thus, imperialization works at both ends of the spectrum: to incorporate colonial subjects within imperial management and to convince imperial subjects of the legitimacy of colonization for the good of both the colonial subject and the subject of the imperial monarchy or nation-state. That is what imperialization is to Ching, and that is how he reads Japan's internal politics while the Japanese made imperial advances in Taiwan. Ching's imperialization was taken up by another Taiwanese based in Taiwan—Kuan-Hsing Chen, in his controversial and groundbreaking book *Asia as Method*.[11] If imperialization is the politics of the state toward its citizens and its attempts to integrate its colonial subjects (for example, Japanese policies toward the Taiwanese), then de-imperialization is the work that has to be done by the political society (including intellectuals) to unveil the crooked rationality used to justify any imperial takeover or overruling. In contrast, decoloniality signals the work that has to be done to liberate the colonial subjects subjected to imperial rules by dominance and hegemony. Needless to say, colonial subjects are no longer just in the colonies or former colonies but in the heart of Western Europe and the United States—they are called immigrants. This would certainly be one of the lines of work that could be entertained under the banner of American studies as transnational practice. Migration is a transnational phenomenon, and much of the migration from the former Third World to the United States was precisely because the United States was the leading nation-state of the First World. However, decoloniality is mainly the project and the task of colonial subjects, who need to recover their memories and their dignity and to liberate themselves from the chains of state politics and corporative economy and values. De-imperialization and decolonialization complement each other as projects oriented toward building nonimperial and, therefore, noncolonial futures. The two projects work at the opposite ends of the spectrum, on the imperial and the colonial subjects. I will come back to this issue in the closing section below.

The word "transnational" was not in use at the time of the *Congrès international des Américanistes*. The organization's use of "international" makes its goals quite explicit. To think in parallel terms, the United States would need not an international association of Americanists but an international association of Europeanists. But instead of that, what emerged and flourished in the United States during the Cold War was area studies—which mean that the disciplines (knowledge) were in the United States and the object to be studied in the Second and Third Worlds. It is not by coincidence that area studies (the control of meaning), on the one hand, and the World Bank and the International Monetary Fund (the control of money), on the other hand, were created during the same period—the march of the United States toward leadership of the world controlled meaning (knowledge) and money (the economy). It was in that context that "globalization" became the buzzword of US academic and nonacademic imperial designs. It is in the same context that Kaplan and Pease's volume made a signal political intervention, in both the academe and the public sphere. And that is precisely the context that demands de-imperial responses.

4

The analytical narrative I am building could be used to think about what American studies as transnational practice might mean today.[12] Take, for example, the social sciences, and take sociology instead of American studies. The example of sociology is appropriate because, like American studies, it came into being as a discipline devoted to understanding the societies in which it emerged: the civilized societies of the British Empire and French colonialism, and later the developed societies of US imperial designs. But sociologists soon realized that their domain of inquiry was too narrow, and with globalization, sociology went transnational. By the end of the twentieth century, sociology had branches in dozens of non-European countries. It was then the moment to evaluate the present and the future of the discipline. Out of this evaluation came the Gulbenkian report.[13]

The Gulbenkian report confronted, among many issues, one similar to the issue that now faced American studies as transnational practice. While sociology was born to study modern European societies, while the rest of the world was taken up by anthropology, at the end of the twentieth century sociology became a transnational practice focusing on globalization and having branches in many countries. But once sociology had migrated from its point of origin (Europe and then the United States), the problem became what to do with sociology when it is practiced in non-European nation-states (beyond, of course, the United States, for the reasons alluded to above), most of which were the domain of anthropology. But above all, what happens when the object of study of anthropology is also part of the domain of sociology, and the Third World anthropologist becomes a sort of native informant? In other words, the issues confronted by a Third World sociologist when the discipline lands in his or her territory is the question confronted in the last part of the story of the Gulbenkian report, prepared during the 1990s.

What happens with sociology in the non-European world? What is its function? Who is eager to introduce it, and why? What is the justification for such an imperial exportation of a knowledge-making institution–cum-discipline? Who accepts the offer as a sign of modernization, and who challenges it as a sign of imperialization? Remember that the point of origin of sociology was the heart of Europe: France, England, and Germany—which is where you have hard-core sociologists, notably Émile Durkheim in France, Max Weber in Germany, and Herbert Spencer in Britain. The non-European world became the point of arrival of many routes of dispersion from Western Europe and the United States. Europe has knowledge; the rest of the world has cultures that have to catch up with the train of modernity, science, and progress. Once sociology is installed in a given country, sociologists in that country, have at least three options. One is to serve as local agents of civilization by helping their country engage a Western discipline in the social sciences. A second option is to use sociology as a tool to reflect on and understand the social structures, changes, and tensions of their nation-state or region. Here, sociology becomes an instrument of local nationalism. There is nothing wrong with that. Sociology in Europe was part of the national formation of England, Germany, and France. However, the colonial epistemic difference now comes into play: sociology outside of the First World is looked at as second-class sociology. There is here an epistemic dependency parallel to the political and economic dependency that was theorized in the 1960s in Latin America. The third option is to use the tools of sociology to engage in a political critique of imperial designs, including sociology as an institution, a discipline, and an instrument of civilization. We have entered the terrain of de-imperial and decolonial projects. Now think of American studies in parallel with sociology.

Can we think of similar scenarios for American studies as transnational practice? I think we can. American studies in China or Japan, for example, could follow any and all of the three previous trajectories.

However, American studies as transnational practice and sociology are similar in one way and different in another. Like sociology, American studies has expanded to many centers and departments outside the United States. What is at stake, for instance, for a US-based scholar and practitioner of American studies and what is at stake for a Hungary- based scholar and practitioner of the same discipline? The reasons for engaging in American studies in the United States and in Hungary are, I suspect, quite different. The problem is not the enunciated reasons (which will be the same in both countries). The question lies in the enunciation—why and what does it mean to engage American studies within the United States, which is part of global designs, and within Hungary—which lost the potential of imagining global designs at the time of the Austro-Hungarian Empire. If we remain at the level of the enunciated reasons, we can say that American studies is American studies no matter where it is practiced. Or we can move to the level of the enunciation and say that it is one thing to practice American studies in the United States and another thing to do so in Hungary. The question is then the geopolitics of knowing rather than the universality of the domain to be known. Some of these questions are addressed in Eva Cherniavsky's essay in this volume.

Now, imagine that a report similar to that of the Gulbenkian Commission on the Restructuring of the Social Sciences was to be prepared for American studies (in the sense of US studies) and that the same kind of questions were being asked: What happens when the discipline migrates outside of the United States? Why would Hungarian, Bolivian, Tanzanian, Korean, or Chinese scholars and intellectuals be interested in having a branch of US studies in their countries? Of course, the answers will vary. China may be more interested in housing US studies than Bolivia, for example. But in any case, to have US studies outside of the United States, we must deal with transnational power relations and power differentials.

At this point, we arrive at the crucial issue of the geopolitics, that of knowing the basic questions that prompt geopolitical epistemic inquiries: Who intends to study what, when, why, where, and to what ends? The focus is on the enunciation, not in the enunciated, although the only way to get to the former is through the latter.

5

My goal is to query the role of the discipline once we understand (and/or accept the fact) that the denomination American/US studies (or US critical studies) of the program created at Duke University intended to make explicit that "America" doesn't equal "the United States." This is also one of my arguments here. Shall we distinguish between US studies as transnational practice and American studies as transnational practice? Engaging in one or the other project has different import and consequences.

If we engage in US studies (critical or not), we engage in a discipline whose primary focus is the history and culture of a nation-state and its influence around the world. At this point, US studies becomes part of a larger issue, which is globalization—or, better yet, globalism—as the general frame for the project of modernity. Are not modernity and globalism since the sixteenth century a happy marriage, with capitalism as the party officiating at the wedding? By engaging in investigating the intricacies and consequences of globalism, we are already engaged in a transnational practice. And if we do that, then the question about what is at stake for a scholar in Hungary or China who engages in American or US studies could have any one of series of answers between two ends of the spectrum. At one end, a Chinese or Hungarian scholar could contribute to the dissemination of US cultures and values in his or her country; at the other end, a Chinese or Hungarian scholar could contribute to the understanding of the role of the United States in the history of Western global expansion. The goals are not exclusive; they just have different focuses.

To engage in American studies—understanding Americanness, rather than America, as the ideal of freedom and democracy—would mean to work not with the history of the United States but with the emergence of the idea of America in the sixteenth-century Europe and its avatars since. The United States is a nation-state, perhaps the first of the modern or colonial world. America is a continent that became part of the European imaginary at the beginning of the sixteenth century. And in this case American studies would be very different from US studies, for the issues in American studies would be nothing less than focusing on the formation and transformations of the modern or colonial world since the sixteenth century. In a nutshell, there is no Western civilization before the European Renaissance. The invention of America is a fundamental component in the making of the idea of Western civilization. The invention of the Americas went hand in hand with a double genocide, that of the indigenous population and enslaved Africans. It was promoted for the glories of Europe while the genocides were hidden or justified for the advance of civilization. Consequently, the mutation of America into Americanness (the United States equaling America) established the United States as the locus of freedom and democracy.

6

Let s keep on walking in the same direction although we now take a different path. In the European imagination of the eighteenth century, Iberian

América had already failed to catch the train of modernity. This downgrading was a logical consequence of the "black legend," the English demonization of the brutality with which the Spaniards treated the Indians in order to displace Spain's imperial role so that England could occupy the vacuum.[14] Hegel, who was aligned with the legacies of the "black legend" (even if he was not aware of it), was very explicit about downgrading the part of America formerly colonized by the Spanish and Portuguese (which was the goal of the black legend).[15] However, since the nineteenth century Spanish Creoles have appropriated the name "America" as their own and in doing so have replaced the name "Indias Occidentales," which had been the name of the Spanish territories in the New World. Spanish and Portuguese possessions were divided between Indias Occidentales (the Treaty of Tordesilla, 1494) and Indias Orientales (the Treaty of Zaragosa, 1529). The Treaty of Tordesillas divided Indias Occidentlaes (later America) between the two crowns. The Treaty of Zaragosa divided Indias Occidentales (Asia) between them.[16] Before the French interventions in the Americas and the invention of the name "Latin America" (which I discussed in detail in my monograph on the topic)[17] French imperial officers in complicity with the elite Creoles (those born in America of Spanish descent) began to use "America" to identify their own territory (what today we know as Central and South America). In the second half of the nineteenth century, however, "Latin America" was invented by French imperial agents in complicity with local Creoles, to stop the advance of the United States toward the South which was already evident in the Guadalupe-Hidalgo Treaty of 1848.

In 1958 Edmundo O'Gorman, a Mexican philosopher and historian of Irish descent, published a groundbreaking book, *La invención de América. El universalismo en la cultura occidental* (The invention of America. universalism in Western culture).[18] It was translated into English in 1960 with a different subtitle: *The Invention of America: An Inquiry into the Historical Nature of the New World and the Meaning of Its History.*[19] The fact that this book is not included in the bibliography of American studies is another example of the fact that American studies really means US studies, and that the term "US studies" maintains the semantic appropriation (which also has implications in the economic and political spheres) of a continent by one nation. And it maintains the confusion of US imperial designs with the utopian dreams named "America," dreams that every US president seems to invoke in their speeches. But let s return to the story from the South.

O'Gorman's inquiry goes back to Waldseedmüller's introduction of the name "America" and traces its avatars to the present history of the United States. O'Gorman's thesis is similar to the one that Del Bufalo advanced about forty years later. O'Gorman's book was published at a time when the Spanish American intelligentsia was concerned with exploring national and subcontinental identities. Interestingly enough, América—not "Latin" America—is O'Gorman's concern. However, he is not dealing with or participating in American studies (still less, Latin American studies). And he is not concerned with the formation of a discipline but with the transformation of already existing ones: history and the philosophy of history. What is unique about O'Gorman's explorations is that he couched the question of the invention of América as a global (or universal) problem of meaning in history and philosophy. By the same token, he was asking about meaning in the foundation of the modern or colonial world. Thus, América becomes a complex node with different meanings for Europeans, the aboriginal population, and the massive contingent of enslaved Africans transported to a continent newly named and integrated into the European geopolitical imagination.

American studies as transnational practice should indeed include the historical foundation of America, with all its transnational complexities— indigenous populations, enslaved Africans, the first European diaspora of the modern or colonial world, migrations from around the world since the nineteenth century, and the formation of Latinos (both the Mexicanos trapped in the United States when the US frontier moved south and people who migrated from South and Central America and the Caribbean).

About the same time that O'Gorman published *La invención de América*, another Mexican philosopher, Leopoldo Zea, published a landmark book titled *América en la historia*, followed a decade later by *El pensamiento latinoamericano*.[20] The topic of the first was the emergence of América in the history of humankind. In the second, Zea reduced the scope of his investigation to Latin American thought. In a sense, Zea's project was similar to Parrington's, except that Parrington focused on a nation-state while Zea focused on a subcontinent. In retrospect, one can see that Parrington's domain was Anglo-America and Zea's was Ibero (that is, Spanish and Portuguese) America. However, in terms of institutionalization, their goals were dissimilar. While Parrington's work became a standard reference in American studies, Zea's did not serve a similar purpose in Latin American studies. Instead, the work of Zea and O'Gorman was used to reconceptualize America in history and to offer another option to the canonical European and Anglo-American narratives. Curiously enough, the Latin American Studies Association was founded around the time of publication of *La invención de América*, but in the United States rather than in Latin America. Thus, American studies and Latin American studies were founded during the same period and in the United Studies. The geopolitics of knowing and understanding comes into full force here: while American studies helped consolidate a sense of national being and memories, Latin American studies helped reunite a series of disciplines, particularly social sciences, for which Latin America was a reality out there, while the disciplines and the locus of enunciation was in here.

In 1962 and 1970 Rodolfo Kusch, an Argentinian philosopher of German descent, published two books exploring similar issues. The first one was *América profunda*, and the second one *Pensamiento indígena y pensamiento popular en América*.[21] Thus, there was a sustained concern about América, and all of these works were transnational or global, since none of them was limited to the image of an enclosed "Latin América" that was the object of the Latin American Studies Association. And they were not limited to the Latin America of people of European descent, including *pueblos originarios* as well. The Afro population was indeed invisible in the case of O'Gorman and only briefly mentioned in the case of Kusch. But we can doubtless add many people, projects, and events that will fill the space of Afro South America to be comparable to the Afro Caribbean and Afro North America (including Canada, of course). The fact remains that the generalization involved in the "Latin América" has much to do with the foundation of Latin American studies.

I would just mention in the context of our concerns here the influential Caribbean politico-economic think tank that formed around the journal *New World*, which began publishing around 1964 when the group was created and is now being revamped. The group was truly transnational, for its focus was to understand plantation economy as an economy in the Caribbean specifically in the five hundred years since the Caribbean was captured by European powers and integrated into the world economy. Lloyd Best's "Independent Thought and Caribbean Freedom" was and still is one of the most distinctive statements.[22] That indeed was America-Caribbean studies as transnational practice.

There was properly speaking the germination of thoughts in a region that global forces in complicity with local Creole elites in the South appropriated the name "América" and then "Latin América." All of these work and debates are not of course part of America or US studies as understood in the United States, but these work and debates are nonetheless crucial reflections on América (with an accent) and the Caribbean. if such a distinction needs to be made. This brings another issue into the debate: the extent to which the Caribbean (insular and continental) as an entity is or is not part of América. That is why it is common to find expressions such as "America and the Caribbean" and "Latin America and the Caribbean."

This riddle cannot be explained by looking objectively at a map, measuring distances and examining political and geographical borders. It should be explained instead through the locus of enunciation (who is describing the continent and the island and with what purpose, who controls meaning, and who disputes the control of meaning) and the epistemic power differential. In other words, it is a problem of geopolitics of knowledge, not one of empirical or objective continental divides. The ontological continental divides are not dictated by the continent itself, but they lies in the locus of enunciation, in the control and dispute of meaning and, thus, in the geopolitics of knowing and understanding. While the locus of enunciation of American studies has been construed as part of us national imperial ideology, reflections on the Américas in the South were construed as part of a subcontinental ideology aware of the fact that América is not the marked (or privileged) term of American studies as far as the United States and America are taken as synonymous. This, again, is a reflection that addresses both American studies as transnational practice and the global philosophical meaning of América in the imaginary of the modern or colonial world.

Kusch's reflections on *América profunda* rely on the enormous relevance of the ancient civilizations that, to simplify matters, I will refer to as those of the Mayas, Aztecs, and Incas. After Kusch's work one could say that these civilizations are to the historical foundation of América and to the present what Greece and Rome are to the history of Europe and to Western civilization. However, while Europeans and people identified with Western civilization are proud of their past, the past of América was relegated to museums: dead civilizations to be admired and at the same time kept in the past.

Kusch's arguments run parallel to the strong revival and radical transformation of historical consciousness in the United States and in South and Central América (particularly in the Andes, the southern part of Mexico, and Guatemala) by scholars, other thinkers, and activists identified with *pueblos originarios* rather than of European descent. Certainly, you are right if you are jumping ahead and objecting that there are no pure Natives or pure Europeans. Kusch and I are not talking about blood but about memories and cultural and epistemic power differentials. As always, biology doesn't determine education (in the family, school, or street). On the contrary, it is education in a racially divided world that sets the stage for us to see the biological in certain ways. But the biological does not carry its own meaning. Ontology is always framed by epistemology. However, what remains rather clear is who runs and controls meaning, who manipulates the rules, and what are the norms and rules that guide and legitimize interpretations and decisions.

Kusch uses the word "América" in all of his work. Why is he concerned with América? For the same reasons that Samuel Huntington later was concerned about it in *Who Are We? The Challenges of America's Identity*,[23] and for the same reasons that Rémi Brague later wrote *Europe: La voie romaine* to deal with exactly the same problem: that of national or continental identities.[24] The difference is that people dwelling in the memories of colonial legacies were concerned with identity much earlier than people dwelling in imperial countries, for whom the question of identity knocked at their door when immigration became a particular concern in the United States (in the case of Huntington) or when the emergence of the European Union, coupled with immigration from the former Third World forced people in the heart of Europe (France, England, and Germany) to addresses the question of their own identities.

For Kusch, América is—like for Parrington's United States—a geohistorical location in world history that transcends the particularly history of an ethnicity or class, the people of European descent—be they Latin from southern Europe or Anglos from northern Europe. But, in contrast to Parrington, Kusch engages in a search for *América profunda*—the América that has been buried by the people of European descent—that could be felt and sensed in indigenous and popular thought next to the legacies of Euro-American thought that were anchored, for him, in the urban centers along the Atlantic coast, from Buenos Aires to New York.

I am bringing Kusch into the conversation because his relentless explorations (from *Seduccion de la barbarie*[25] to *Geocultura del hombre americano* 1978)[26] are indeed transnational rather than translate reflections: he explored the difficulties of understanding across nations and languages in América. By "nation" I do not mean the state, as in the modern and secular illusion that one nation corresponds to one state. During the past ten years, Ecuador and Bolivia, including the rewriting of their constitutions, have initiated a new path toward the future: if the state survives as the hegemonic institution for governing, it will be plurinational. This is a guide-line that has emerged not from the needs of Western Europe or the United States, but from the need of regions with long-lasting colonial histories. However, the modern state makes us believe that there is a one-to-one correspondence between state and nation. That illusion may prevail once we talk about transnational practice and if we assume that transnational means transstate. If we do, we will blind ourselves to the urgent need to direct our attention to the transnational within a single state, like the United States, Ecuador, or Bolivia.

Sun Yat-sen, a somehow forgotten (in the West) intellectual and political powerhouse, in contrast to more familiar names such as Chiang Kai-shek and Mao Zedong, made an interesting observation that I discuss below about the equation between nation and state in his famous *Three Principles of Livelihood*.[27] And if we are to talk about transnational practices, we should pay attention to what "nation" means beyond Western concepts of "nation-state" and "nationalism." Briefly, nation-state and nationalism are not universal but local and regional Western European concepts put forward in the late eighteenth century and the early nineteenth. What "nation" means outside of the West is obviously entangled with Western European history and invention since it was Western Europeans who constructed the concept of nation and coupled it with the state. Kusch was a philosopher in the south of América, and Sun a thinker and politician in East Asia, far apart in terms of geography, history, language, religion, and ethnicity. But the two were at different ends of the same spectrum and connected in the colonial matrix of power by the tentacles of Western modernity. Although Europeans' and non-Europeans' local histories were far apart before the sixteenth century, the same colonial matrix that had emerged in the Atlantic and shaped the history of América disrupted the history of China (first through England and the United States, and later France) in the middle of the nineteenth century. Thus, Kusch and Sun were responding to the same problems. They were thinking transnationally simply because they had no other choice: Western Europe and the United States were dictating the destinies of both South America and East Asia.

For Sun, China was in need of salvation, but he did not see Western modernity as the savior. He left for us a very interesting observation on the relationship between nation and state, an observation that could have been made only by someone who could look at the European nation-state from outside its own history. Sun was working on what he called the principles of national salvation, which he connected to the principle of nationalism, equivalent to the doctrine of the state. Clearly, Sun was trying to incorporate the long history of China into an idea of nation-cum-state that did not emerge naturally from the history of China as it did from the history of the West. That is, he wanted to adapt to the disrupted history of China what had grown naturally in the history of the West. However, he was thinking of how to subsume Western ideas into the history of China rather than to subsume the history of China into Western ideals. He wrote:

My statement that the principle of nationality is equivalent to the doctrine of the state is applicable in China but not in the West. For the reason that China, since the Ch'in and Han dynasties, has been developing a single state out of a single race, while foreign countries have developed many states from one race and have included many nationalities within one state. For example, England, now the world's most powerful state, has, upon the foundation of the white race, added brown, black and other races to form the British Empire; hence, to say that the race of nation is the state [sic] is not true of England. We all know that the original stock of England was the Anglo-Saxon race, but it is not limited to England; the United States, too, has a large portion of such stock. So in regard to the other countries we cannot say that the race and the state are identical; there is a definite line between them.[28]

You can parse this statement and make many objections to it. First of all, Sun identifies "nations" (*natio*, communities of birth or ethnicity) with "race." But do not jump too quickly into critiques of nationalism encouraged by the postmodern and neoliberal celebrations of globalization. Look first who is benefiting from globalization and who is benefiting from nationalism, and then you can make up your mind and cast your vote. Neoliberals who support globalization and cosmopolitan liberal and Marxist intellectuals are sometimes too quick to dismiss nationalism, without thinking that although nationalism may be a nuisance for them, it is a way for non-Western people to be saved from them. And you would be right to point out that in China, where the majority of the population is of Han ethnicity, there are other nations as well, and that one cannot avoid perceiving the racism of the Han ethnic group, both in Sun's day and now.[29] That is true, but it is also true that we find white racism among globalizers and cosmopolitans. The bottom line is that in the modern or colonial world order (1500–2000), "transnational" means the entanglement of imperial local designs and colonial local histories. They are entangled through imperial and colonial differences, which are the two basic categories of racial classification.

Whatever you may make of these observations, and as much as you can question that in China "the principle of nationality is equivalent to the doctrine of the state," you cannot question either that Sun believed that the correlation applied to China or that there is not a one-to-one relation between nation and state. The formula "nation-state" is a European myth that secured the state in the hands of one ethnic-based class, the class that defined the state, defined itself as nation, and kept both state and nation under its control. That myth was translated to other regions of the world. Today Bolivia has a majority of indigenous nations (the Aymara nation, Quechua nation, Chiquitanos nation, and so on). The idea of the plurinational state emerges precisely from the awareness that the state cannot belong to one nation and that the very idea of nation should be revised—hence, the idea of the transnational. Peasant organizations that are not nations in the sense of indigenous nations are making organized claims about the plurinational state. In that sense, if peasants are not a nation, nor are they part of the nation that founded the Bolivian state and has managed it since its inception.

Much the same can be said about the United States. The historical foundation of the United States by people of European descent left out of consideration Native American nations and people of African descent. By the time of the foundation of the United States, both groups of foreigners (those of European and those of African descent) had already produced three or four generations in America, next to *pueblos originarios* who became Native Americans in the United States. Today, the plurinationality of the United States is becoming increasingly apparent, above all due to the numerical and political presence of Latino/as. It is true that from the early nineteenth century to the end of World War II, two types of immigrants transformed the landscape of the country: migrants from Asia, including the Middle East (which was thus named toward the beginning of the twentieth century), and those from several states of Europe—among them, Jewish nations coming from different states. Thus, transnational explorations and understanding are not the same as transstate explorations and understanding. American studies as transnational practice become, at this point, a very complex proposition. What do we do with plurinational states in transnational studies?

7

I have been listening lately to people who belong to the nation of *pueblos originarios* (and who have been divided by states among, for example, the Mapuches in Chile, the Aymaras in Bolivia, the Osages in the United States, the First Nations in Canada, and the Maori in New Zealand) and who care for their histories and situations. From the perspective of the Quichua in Ecuador, the question is not so much transnational as it is intercultural. That is, their goal is to reach a situation in which the many nations in the State of Ecuador could work together to form a plurinational state. "Intercultural" should not be confused with "multicultural," although the meaning of the words changes when the locus of enunciation changes. When discourses pronounced in the name of the state use the concept of interculturalism, its meaning is similar to that of multiculturalism in the United States: the meaning is that one ethnic group manages the state and allows the others to do their things but not to change the mononational state into a plurinational one. I would like to highlight two relevant issues here. One comes from US Native Americans and the other from Indians (scholars, other intellectuals, and activists) in the South American Andes. Not all Native Americans and Indians are scholars, intellectuals, or activists; and Indian scholars and other intellectuals do not represent all the Indians in the same way that white or female intellectuals do not represent all whites or all women. But it so happens that a topic such as American studies as transnational practice is not a topic in which white farmers from Iowa or Aymara and Quechua people from El Alto, in Bolivia, would find their place. What, then, is the meaning of "transnational" in "American transnational studies"?

Within the sphere in which our discussion takes place, one issue that could serve as a foundation for reflections on American studies as transnational practice is discussed in the following short passage from George Tinker:

> In 1803 the United States purchased the entirety of Osage land—from France. Osages yet today are trying to figure that one out. It had to do with something called the Louisiana Purchase and something having to do with some obscure European legal doctrine called the "right of discovery." What it ever had to do with the Osage people, who were never privy to this doctrine or included in the negotiations, leading to the purchase, is still a mystery. It was nevertheless a powerful intellectual idea, mere words in a sense that enabled Mr. Jefferson to double the size of his country over night.[30]

"His country"—that is, Jefferson's at that time and, in general, the Anglo-white nation-state—is seen and understood through the eyes and the skin of a Native American whose relation with the state is ambiguous and with the Anglo-nation tense. The negotiations between France (a country seeking to rise to global domination) and the United States (seeking to consolidate its position after its revolution) refer to negotiations between two states ruled by the two nations, the Anglos and the Franks (French-speaking Western Christians). Why was the Osage nation left out of the negotiations between the Anglos in the recently formed United States and the Franks in the recently formed French Republic—which in 1789 had transformed its political system into one largely modeled on the American Constitution and Bill of Rights? The American Constitution? Isn't it that the "constitution that owes a debt not only to the European legal system but also to the organization of the Iroquois? In such a way the foundation of the United States, on which American studies via Parrington's work was structured, rests on two silenced pillars: the massive appropriation of the land of Osage nation and the sociological and juridical organization of the Iroquois nation. Thus, American studies as transnational practice should take into account the need to decolonize its own foundation. It is not specifically American studies that I am targeting. My argument goes beyond specific disciplines and points toward the coloniality of knowledge.

Thus, in this domain decolonization means, above all, decoloniality of knowledge and understanding. And here we are again in the heart of the geopolitics of knowing and understanding. Who produces knowledge, why, when, what knowledge, and what for? Both versions of American studies have pretty much operated with their back toward Native Americans. For that reason, Native Americans in the United States have created their own Native American and Indigenous Studies Association.[31] There is no such thing in the South for reasons related to the very structure of the university system. But there is instead, for example, the II Cumbre Continental de Pueblos y Naciones Indígenas, formed as part of the Foro Social de las América, whose first meeting took place in Quito, Ecuador, in July 2004. Although the creation of the Foro Social de las América was a consequence of the Foro Social Mundial (World Social Forum), it has its singular profile. First of all, the reason why the first forum took place in Quito was due to the confluence of neoliberal tendencies in the region at that time and the strength of the indigenous political society that has been radically transforming the history of the region in the past four decades.

During the II Cumbre Continental a resolution was passed to protest the Pope's decision in 1493 to distribute lands between the Spanish and the Portuguese without the consent of indigenous nations. Those lands today are named Abya Yala, which in the language of the Kuna Indians (in what is now Panama) means "land in its full maturity." Notice that we are talking here about Indias Occidentales, which is the entire continent of South America. Since 1786 a small portion became part of the United States and appropriated the name "America" in the same way that the United States appropriated Osage lands and the Iroquois sociolegal system.

Abya Yala instead of America has been adopted as the name from the perspective of all indigenous peoples of the continent, from the Mapuches in Chile to the First Nations of Canada.[32] What may seem arbitrary is nonetheless useful in understanding that the names "América" and "America" are equally arbitrary, since both were chosen by people of European descent without consultation with the indigenous people and the enslaved Africans who became citizen" of Abya-Yala. Once again, all these considerations make sense when we place them in the context of the geopolitics of knowing and understanding, which means epistemic power differentials and producing silence by celebrating achievements: América and America are both imperial names that make sense for those who invented and adopted them. Thus when we engage in American studies as transnational practice, we should be aware that American studies cannot be taken as the totality of Abya-Yala. Or, looked at in another way, transnational investigations from the perspective of the historical foundation of the Americas in the sixteenth century and the erasure of Abya Yala are necessary to prevent imperial tendencies in critical disciplinary formations.

Today the aboriginal population classified as Indians live in Abya-Yala and no longer in América, Latin America, or America. They are also building their own university as well as a scholarly association. I already mentioned the Native American and Indigenous Studies Association. Here I will devote some space to the Amawtay Wasi (which means the house of wis-

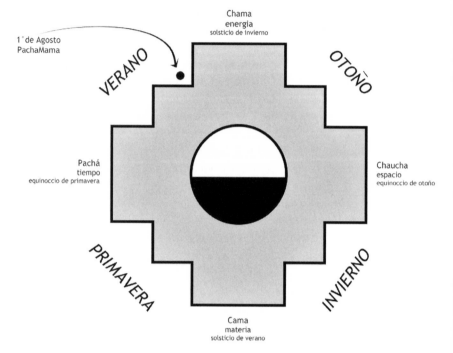

FIGURE 11.2. The *chakana* is a multifaceted Andean symbol for the energy of the creation and regeneration of life. It was modeled on the Southern Cross constellation.

dom).[33] When you to go to the organization's website, you find a sign that you may not immediately recognize. It is the *chakana* (figure 11.2), a sacred icon in Andean cosmology and philosophy. Inside the square you see the earth, in the sense of life (*vida*) or energy.

The *chakana* is a "translation" of the Southern Cross constellation, which is clearly seen in the Southern Hemisphere but completely invisible from the Northern Hemisphere. Although it has a totally different symbolic meaning, the *chakana* is to Andean cosmology what the cross is to Christian cosmology. The *chakana* embodies duality, not dichotomy (of the sun and moon, masculine and feminine, time and space, and matter and energy); it also embodies the trilogy (the sacred, or the world above; living beings, or the world where we are; and the world below). At the same time it embodies a fourfold partition, that of Tawantinsuyu (the incarnate divided into the four seasons).[34] Three points are of interest here:

A) The organization of Tawantinsuyu, the world divided into four parts, is a consequence of the correlation in Andean thoughts between the cosmos and society. Greek thinkers came to the same conclusion when

TAWA = QUATRE
INTI = SOLEIL
SUYU = REGION

TAWANTINSUYU
LES 4 REGIONS DU SOLEIL

FIGURE 11.3. In the geographical extension of Tawantinsuyu, Cuzco was the center of the four seasons.

they introduced the word "cosmopolis." And one can surmise that all existing civilizations found a similar principle of organization. Western civilization is not a privileged one. It is just the hegemonic one at this point in history.

B) The extension of Tawantinsuyu is seen in a current cartographic representation of South America, as shown in figure 11.3.

C) The Amawtay Wasi is structured on the *chakana* rather than the genealogy of the European university from the Renaissance to today.

8

With this context in mind, let us return to the Amawtay Wasi and its relevance for changing the geography of knowing and understanding. The university curriculum has four nodes, and each node has been modeled according to the *chakana*. The center is *kawsay* (origination, life), surrounded by *yachay* (to know), *munay* (to love), *ruray* (to do), and *ushay* (to be able to). Each node has a specific goal, and the curriculum is the medium used to achieve these goals.

I have done some research to understand how the Amawtay Wasi works to help me argue for the decolonization of education and explain that the

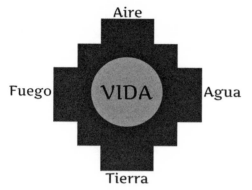

FIGURE 11.4. The *chakana* is organized according to the four basic elements of life (*vida*): *aire* (air), *agua* (water), *fuego* (fire), and *tierra* (earth). The basic diagram of Amawtay Wasi pedagogical philosophy correlates with the *chakana* and the map of Tawantinsuyu. At the center is life, or *kawsay* (in Quichua), which also could be translated as knowledge. The four elements are arranged according to Andean cosmology. Colors have a logical place in that cosmology.

Amawtay Wasi is a clear case of delinking education from the history of Western university and the goals of Western education. Why? One of the fundamental goals of the Amawtay Wasi is learning to be. When such a statement is pronounced by an indigenous person, it brings a full existential issue to the foreground and reminds us that colonial history convinced Indians that they were not people. Furthermore, if the plurinational state is an indigenous project, that project cannot be carried out through the education provided by national schooling and universities. The Western university, as we know, was of the state, be it monarchic and theological or secular and bourgeois. And there is nothing wrong with that. Every civilization organized its schools and education in relation to its history and social organization. Problems arise when the education of one state is presented as the universal way and used to devalue all other forms of education and the people educated by them.

What is of interest for our argument is that the organization's overall concept of education and curricular structure were based on the derivation from the Southern Cross that was also the model for the organization of Tawantinsuyu.

Kawsay is the center, and the point of arrival at the educational process is through one of the four nodes. It is not knowledge that is at the end of the road, but wisdom, and wisdom means that the four nodes have been integrated. In the process, the students are never in just one node at a time. Suppose you spend one year in the node of *ruray*, and with four others you are learning to build in the engineering and architectural sense of the word; some of you are learning advanced technology, and some of you are learning

YACHAY
Saber / Conocer / Manejar Epistemologia

USHAY
Potencia Enegria
Poder

KAWSAY
Sabiduria

MUNAY
Amar Pasion
Intuicion

RURAY
Hacer / Vivenciar / Construir

FIGURE 11.5. In the conceptual organization of the Amawtay Wasi, the center is occupied by *kawsay* (knowledge or wisdom). Each of the four sides of the curricular structure is designated by one of the four aspects of life's extension: *yachay* (knowledge, wisdom, epistemology), *munay* (love, passion, intuition), *ruray* (to do, experience life, build), and *ushay* (potency, energy, power).

about the generation and the regeneration of items necessary for survival, from food to herbal medicine. Remember, the goal of this education is not to succeed by being number one and making money. The education is oriented toward service, not personal benefit. This may seem romantic in comparison to the education of current Western university. From the perspective of corporate values and the state of Ecuador Amawtay Wasi was not academic enough to be accredited for its excellence. That is why Rafael Correa closed Amawtay Wasi in 2014. From the perspective of the Amawtay Wasi's values, Western and corporate universities and state universities are unethical, for their education promotes success and reproduces inequalities, and it encourages competition instead of cooperation. The Amawtay Wasi's education and nurturing promote the fullness of life and living in harmony, not increasing gains and wealth, with the wisdom to live the plenitude of life. In the last analysis, what is wrong with it? Why is the Amawtay Wasi not having the support that Harvard University, for example, has? Harvard and similar institutions today are run by corporate values. Doesn't the Amawtay Wasi have the right do what it does and be supported by the state for that and not be closed because it does not provide the education the state wants but the education that indigenous and nonindigenous people need, an education based on values that the state and the corporations deny?

9

This is the point I was trying to get at: the Amawtay Wasi is moving us away from America, with or without an accent. Once we take a step away and look at America, and once we ask again what American means in American studies, two aspects come into focus: First, American studies basically means the study of America, without an accent and within a self-fashioned narrative of what America is—that is, the United States. And second, American studies as transnational practice thus means that now the United States means more than just the country. Thus, to engage in American studies as transnational practice means to expand the study of the history of a nation-state and its role in the world. In this regard, it is tantamount to studying the global role of the United States since World War II, from the Cold War to neoliberal globalization.

The last question I would like to ask is this: Since American studies and American studies as transnational practice imply that the locus of enunciation belongs to the self-fashioning narrative of America, what would be the consequences if we displaced the locus of enunciation so that America became an object of transnational studies but from a locus of enunciation that was no longer located in the imaginary of the Americas but somewhere else? Say, for instance, in the narrative of the Amawtay Wasi or that of Asia as method, as Chen has recently argued?

This is the argument: Asia as method is based on the following observation by a Chinese intellectual, Wang Hui: "The notion of Asia is colonial, and it is also anti-colonial; it is nationalist and it is also internationalist; it is European, also in turn has shaped the self-understanding of Europe; it is tightly connected to the question of the nation-state, and is overlapping with the perspective of the empire; it is a civilizational concept in relation to Europe, but is also a geographical category established in geo-political relations."[35] Elaborating on this observation, Chen states: "Asia as method recognizes the need to keep a critical distance from uninterrogated notions of Asia, just as one has to maintain a critical distance from uninterrogated notions of the nation-state. It [the method] sees Asia as a product of history, and realizes that Asia has been an active participant in historical processes."[36]

The statement is a corollary of a shift in the geography of knowledge that Chen's book's argument proposes: Asian studies in its several forms has been mainly carried out in the First World as part of area studies. This division of scientific labor presupposed that knowledge was in the First World, while cultures were in the Third World, and Asia was part of that. Now that Asians are doing Asian studies, Asia is no longer an object but a method, a way of looking at and understanding the world. Chen asserts:

The implication of Asian studies in Asia is clear. If "we" have been doing Asian studies, Europeans, North Americans, Latin Americans, and Africans have also been doing studies in relation to their own living spaces. That is, Martin Heidegger was actually doing European studies, as were Michel Foucault, Pierre Bourdieu and Jürgen Habermas. European experiences were their system of reference. Once we recognize how extremely limited the current conditions of knowledge are, we learn to be humble about knowledge claims. The universalist assertions of theory are premature, for theory too must be deimperialized.[37]

What does Chen mean by decolonization and de-imperialization, two concepts that are crucial to understanding the significance of the two previous statements? He writes:

> By decolonization, I do not simply mean modes of anticolonialism that are expressed mainly through the building of a sovereign nation-state. Instead, decolonization is the attempt of the previously colonized to reflectively work out a historical relation with the former colonizer, culturally, politically and economically. . . .
>
> If decolonization is mainly active work carried out on the terrain of the colonized, then deimperialization, which is no less painful and reflexive, is work that must be performed by the colonized first, and then on the colonizer's relation with its former colonies.[38]

Making a jump from *Asia as Method* to American studies as transnational practice, it becomes evident that the first question to be asked is what we might mean as method if we were to say "America as method"? Since America was, like Asia, a knowledge construction (as noted by O'Gorman), it is relevant to question America—a place that is understood as the solid ground of a disciplinary locus of enunciation (American) that constitutes itself as an object of studies (America) but that now transcends itself as an object and finds itself out there in the transnational world. America then becomes part of that transnational object. However, once we start reasoning from *Asia as Method*, all geohistorical locations should be seen as method—that is, as the locus of interrogation of this formation and its coming into being.

10

In closing, I would say that the entire argument is organized around the facts that I was born and educated in South America, and hence I am following the teaching of Rodolfo Kusch, and that I have lived in the United States for more than thirty years. Hence, I am reasoning from what I have learned from being Latino in the United States and Latin American at the same time. My reflections are existential, referring to my transnational existence, and transdisciplinary, for I am not a practitioner of American studies or of Latin American or Latino/a studies. It is my conviction that we should use disciplinary formations to solve problems and understand experiences rather than trying to encapsulate experiences and existences into disciplinary formations.

Notes

The epigraphs are from Slavoj Žižek, "A Leftist Plea for Eurocentrism," *Critical Inquiry* 94, no. 4 (1998): 988; and Walter Mignolo, "Geopolitics of Knowing and Understanding," keynote address at the American Studies as Transnational Practice symposium, Lubbock, Texas, April 10, 2010, quoting Frantz Fanon, *The Wretched of the Earth*.

    1. Yuan Shu, "The 2010 Texas Tech University Comparative Literature Symposium on 'American Studies as Transnational Practice,'" http://call-for-papers.sas.upenn.edu/ node/35308, accessed May 19, 2015.

    2. Vernon Louis Parrington, *Main Currents in American Thought*, vols. 1–2 (New York: Harcourt Brace, 1927).

    3. Amy Kaplan, "Left Alone with America: The Absence of Empire in the Study of American Culture," in *Cultures of United States Imperialism*, edited by Amy Kaplan and Donald E. Pease (Durham, NC: Duke University Press, 1993), 3–21.

    4. Vernon Louis Parrington, *Main Currents in American Thought* (New York: Harcourt Brace, 1954), vol. 3.

    5. Congrès internationale des Américanistes, *Congrès Internationale des Américanistes: Compte-rendu de la première session* (Paris: Maisonneuve, 1875), 3.

    6. See Walter D. Mignolo, "The Western Hemisphere in the Colonial Horizon of Modernity," *New Centennial Review* 1, no. 2 (2001): 19–54.

    7. See Raquel Urroz's review of J. W. Hessler's *The Naming of America: Martin Waldseemüller's 1507 World Map and The Cosmographie Introductio*, *Investigaciones Geogr'aficas* 69 (2009): 143–48.

    8. Enzo Del Bufalo, *Americanismo y democracia* (Caracas: Monte Avila, 1992).

    9. Amy Kaplan and Donald E. Pease, eds., *Cultures of United States Imperialism* (Durham, NC: Duke University Press, 1993).

    10. Leo T. S. Ching, *Becoming Japanese: Colonial Taiwan and the Politics of Identity Formation* (Berkeley: University of California Press, 2001).

    11. Kuan-Hsing Chen, *Asia as Method: Toward Deimperialization* (Durham, NC: Duke University Press, 2010).

    12. An important frame to use in speculating about this question is *The Future of American Studies*, ed. Donald E. Pease and Robyn Wiegman (Durham, NC: Duke University Press, 2002).

13. Gulbenkian Commission on the Restructuring of the Social Sciences, *Open the Social Sciences* (Stanford, CA: Stanford University Press, 1996).

14. Margaret Greer, Walter Mignolo, and Maureen Quilligan, *Rereading the Black Legend: Discourses of Race and Religion in the Renaissance Empire* (Chicago: Chicago University Press, 2007).

15. Margaret Greer, Walter Mignolo, and Maureen Quilligan, eds., *Re-Reading the Black Legend: The Discourses of Racial and Religious Differences in the Renaissance Empires* (Chicago: Chicago University Press, 2007).

16. To understand both partitions, see "Colonial Demarcation Lines between Castille/Spain and Portugal in the 15th and 16th Centuries," http://upload.wikimedia.org/wikipedia/commons/2/21/Spain_and_Portugal.png, accessed May 22, 2015.

17. Walter D Mignolo, *The Idea of Latin America* (London: Blackwell, 2005).

18. Edmundo O'Gorman, *La invención de América. El universalismo en la cultura occidental* (Mexico City: Universidad Nacional de México, 1958).

19. Edmundo O'Gorman, *The Invention of America: An Inquiry into the Historical Nature of the New World and the Meaning of Its History*, trans. Terry Smith (Bloomington: Indiana University Press, 1960).

20. Leopoldo Zea, *América en la historia* (Mexico City: Universidad Autónoma de México, 1956), and *El pensamiento latinoamericano* (Mexico City: Universidad Autónoma de México, 1965).

21. Rodolfo Kusch, *América profunda* (Buenos Aires: Hachette, 1962), and *Pensamiento indígena y pensamiento popular en América* (Buenos Aires: Hachette, 1970). The second was recently translated into English: Rodolfo Kusch, *Indigenous and Popular Thinking in America*, trans. María Lugones and Joshua Price (Durham, NC: Duke University Press, 2009).

22. Lloyd Best, "Independent Thought and Caribbean Freedom: Thirty Years Later," *Caribbean Quarterly* 43, nos. 1–2 (1997): 16–24. The essay was originally published in 1967.

23. Samuel Huntington, *Who Are We? The Challenges of America's Identity* (New York: Simon and Schuster, 2004).

24. Rémi Brague, *Europe: La voie romaine* (Paris: Gallimard, 1992).

25. Rodolfo Kusch, *Seduccion de la barbarie* (Buenos Aires: Raigal, 1953).

26. Rodolfo Kusch, *Geocultura del hombre americano* (Buenos Aires: Garcia Cambeiro, 1978).

27. Sun Yat-sen, *Three Principles of Livelihood*, translated by Frank W. Price and edited by L. T. Chen (New York: Da Capo, 1975).

28. Ibid., 2.

29. Chen, *Asia as Method*, chapter 2.

30. George T. Tinker, *Spirit and Resistance: Political Theology and American Indian Liberation* (Minneapolis, MN: Fortress, 2004), 4–5.

31. See Department of American Indian Studies, University of Minnesota, "Native

American & Indigenous Studies Association (NAISA) May 21–23, 2009," http://amin .umn.edu/naisa2009/, accessed February 16, 2015.

32. Segunda Cumbre Continental de los Pueblos y Nacionalidades Indígenas de Abya Yala, "Declaración de Kito," March 2007, http://www.cumbreindigenabyayala.org/, accessed February 16, 2015.

33. Amawtay Wasi, Universidad Intercultural de las nacionalidades y Pueblos Indígenas del Ecuador, http://pluriversidadamawtaywasi.org/, accessed May 19, 2015. A full description and explanation of the Amawtay Wasi can be found in a book in three languages (Kichwa, Spanish, and English): Universidad Intercultural Awatay Wasi, *Sumak Yachaypi, Alli Kawsaypipash Yachakuna* (Paris: UNESCO), 2004.

34. For more details on the complexity of the chakana, see "Chakana," http://en.wiki pedia.org/wiki/Chakana, accessed May 22, 2015.

35. Wang Hui, "The Politics of Imagining Asia: A Genealogical Analysis," translated by Matthew A. Hale, *Inter-Asia Cultural Studies* 8, no. 1 (2007): 12.

36. Chen, *Asia as Method*, 214–15.

37. Ibid., 3.

38. Ibid., 3–4.

12

VIET THANH NGUYEN

INDUSTRIES OF MEMORY: THE VIỆT NAM WAR IN ART

FOR MANY AMERICANS, THE war in Việt Nam is more than just an object in the rearview mirror of the fabled American automobile, aimed always toward progress and intent on leaving behind a past that is closer than it appears. Wars in Iraq and Afghanistan have compelled Americans to look in the mirror, checking to see whether that object is a ghost from a horror movie of their own making or something that is safely dead, autopsied repeatedly by academics, journalists, politicians, and generals hoping to extract useful lessons for current campaigns. The war's first impressions in American memory remain mostly visual, as seen on television, in the movies, in photographs, and in high art, morphing to such an extent that the war lives again through parody and pastiche, through repetition and invocation. These visual resurrections range from big-budget comedies like *Tropic Thunder* that assume no knowledge of either the war's real or cinematic history to the passionate guerrilla art of Martha Rosler, whose contemporary Iraq War collages quote her Việt Nam–era antiwar collages, with their graphic scenes of war and human damage inserted into the manicured domestic propaganda of fashion and beauty ads. The war is over, but its visual images live on.

As America remembers, so to some extent does the world. Even if the United States is a reduced industrial base, it is still a superpower in the globalization of its own memories. The American memory industry is on a par with the American arms industry, outpacing Detroit with its exports and compelling other countries, regardless of their own memories of the war, to cope with Hollywood goods and the instantly infamous snapshots that struck viewers between the eyes. There was Colonel Nguyễn Ngọc Loan, shooting a Viet Cong suspect in the head (captured by the camera of Eddie Adams), or Phan Thị Kim Phúc running naked and screaming down a road after being flayed by an airborne napalm strike (framed by Nick Ut).[1] These shots were seen around the world because American media possessed the apparatus to helicopter journalists into and out of battlefields with endless film rolls, processing their negatives almost immediately and printing them globally. In contrast, North Vietnamese photographers lived in the jungles, hoarded their handfuls of film rolls, and dispatched their negatives over treacherous land routes to Hà Nội via messengers who risked death—some of whom were indeed killed in bombardments. These circumstances limited what was seen by North Vietnamese eyes.[2] Even nearly forty years after the war's end, Việt Nam's premier film director, Đặng Nhật Minh, acknowledges Hollywood's influence with his last film, *Don't Burn*, which gestures explicitly at the helicopter assaults and peasant massacres of *Platoon* and *Apocalypse Now*. *Don't Burn* tells the true story of a heroic young North Vietnamese doctor, slain in her prime by American troops in 1972. Đặng Thùy Trâm's recovered diary became a Vietnamese publishing sensation in 2005, but the movie based on her words opened in Việt Nam during the same week as *Transformers 2*. While the American blockbuster was a monster truck crushing all competition, his film, the director said, "was a bicycle."[3]

In short, memory is the outcome of an industry in which the individual who remembers, feels, or propagates a memory is only a pieceworker on an assembly line. The individual's memory matters to the individual, but the real matter of memory for the world is determined by the industry of memory, by which I mean something more than a set of technologies through which memories are fashioned, or the network of professionals who curate, design, and study memories.[4] The industry of memory includes both of these and also incorporates the processes of individual memory, the collective nature of its making, and the social contexts of its meanings; in addition, it acknowledges memory's means of production. These are the possibilities that determine how memories are made, whose memories get made, in what quantities, and the extent of their distribution. Mass memory's impact depends on vertical integration and economies of scale, with those who control the most significant means of production seeing their memories exported to the world's far corners. This industry of memory cannot be considered separately from other industries, as the case of the United States and Việt Nam makes especially clear. Wealthy and powerful countries can export their memories more effectively than poorer ones, and war only exacerbates this inequality. Countries with more massive war machines can not only do more human damage than weaker countries, but they can also justify that damage through the manufactured memories of the related industry of memory.

So, in Việt Nam, memories are peddled in ways that differ from the American manner, both for the Vietnamese and their visitors. As industrial and postindustrial products, memories are a form of transportation to the past and a form of transportation in the present, if we believe that the past is what propels us ever forward (if we stopped remembering, we would be dead). Đặng Nhật Minh's metaphor is therefore an appropriate one, for if America is dominated by four-wheeled machines, Việt Nam is a two-wheeled country, characterized first by precious Chinese-made bicycles during the war and its aftermath and now by Japanese-made motorbikes as the sign of middle-class prosperity. While America had the Model T Ford, Việt Nam had the Honda Dream, these vehicles symbolizing the differences in the ways that people travel, enabled by their nations' wealth and correlating directly to the ways their memories circulate both domestically and abroad. Memories are not merely personal, even if they begin and end that way. Rather, as industrial and postindustrial products once they enter the public sphere, memories are as anemically or as aggressively manufactured, branded, sold, and exported as the rest of a nation's goods under globalization, which means that the industry of memory is structured through relations of exploitation and inequality. Memories exist for fun and as fetishes, but they also exist for profit.

As feelings and as products, memories circulate not just in social, personal, or aesthetic worlds, but also in political and economic ones. So, after the shooting war, the United States continued a quiet war, effectively embargoing for twenty years not just Việt Nam but also Vietnamese memories, allowing only a few token imports past American borders—a handful of novels by the celebrity dissidents Dương Thu Hương and Bảo Ninh, a clutch of other literary works translated and published by independent presses, brief exhibitions of art, and films for niche audiences. The Vietnamese have their own memories, of course, but these home-grown products must contend with American ones, so much so that Vietnamese are more aware of what Americans think and feel about their shared past than Americans are. This inequity shapes the public presentation of Vietnamese memories in a doubly conscious fashion. The memories are addressed to locals but also to others, articulated specifically with Americans in mind or with the awareness that visitors from other countries will come bearing American memories like lint in their pockets. The French, Japanese, and Koreans—other peoples who have had American soldiers fighting wars on their territory—do not face the same situation. France and Japan are large, wealthy nations with considerable memory industries of their own, while the Korean War is a forgotten conflict that left few memories behind, outside of Korea, for the world to ponder. But the American output of memory on the Việt Nam War is impressive, the prodigiousness of it equivalent to the rage of loss that Americans felt. While visitors of all nations are likely to have bumped into an

American rememory somewhere in the world, these visitors are unlikely to have seen, read, or heard the Vietnamese-language documentaries, feature films, novels, memoirs, short stories, speeches, and ceremonies commemorating the war, or to witness the private and public rituals that Vietnamese have to honor the dead, almost all of which recount a mostly heroic legend of the warrior past.[5]

This is hardly a surprise, since many Vietnamese themselves are not eager to undertake the drudgery of dredging up the past. The historical ignorance of the young that is periodically bemoaned in the United States is hardly an isolated American phenomenon. Vietnamese youth must be reminded that the war was sacrosanct and that the terrible human toll of the war was justified. One way this reminder is delivered is through Hồ Chí Minh's omnipresent slogan, "Nothing is more precious than independence and freedom." But in visiting Việt Nam at the beginning of the millennium, I knew Uncle Hồ's words had taken on an ironic cast when I heard the popular joke about his slogan: *What's more precious than independence and freedom? Nothing!* In other words, independence and freedom are worth less than nothing, and revolutionary ideology is bankrupt in a postrevolutionary society interested less in justice and equality and more in turning the đồng into a dollar. Since Việt Nam does not seem free to many people inside or outside of the country, memorializing the costly struggle for independence as a necessary war is crucial for the Communist Party, which grinds away at its own industry of memory, mostly a domestic affair.

Contemporary art has been key to these memory industries in both countries. If memory is an industry, art is one of its machines. What concerns me are nationalist ways of commemoration, in which art occupies a sanctified place, as well as the antinationalism of many artists whose works are not mass-produced on the assembly lines of memory but instead handcrafted in studios, garrets, and workshops—experimental, avant-garde, and artisanal one-offs in comparison to a Hollywood blockbuster or a state-sponsored museum. The negotiation and tensions between nationalism and its critics lead some of these artists and their audiences to jury-rig another kind of memory machine, an ethical one. Even as an ethical memory calls on its users to remember both sides, it acknowledges memory's inevitable elusiveness, the fact that something is always forgotten. An ethical memory remembers both sides of a battle over the past, but it is also dissatisfied with that gesture and its implication of reconciliation, which many (although far from all) Vietnamese and Americans profess they want in the postwar era. What gets left out in reconciliation? What does it enable and what does it foreclose? Instead of being locked into the gears of either mourning or melancholy, or seeking reconciliation and closure at all costs, ethical memory is constantly in motion, craning to look over its shoulder at the blind spot where danger lurks, or at that spot between the shoulder blades that cannot be seen and cannot be scratched, and in so turning nags at us, asking us what we should we do with these memories for the future as it also reminds us that no one is innocent in the war over remembrance.

State of the Art, or the Artist as Weapon

Not everyone remembers in the same way, and not everyone values art in the same way. In the United States, art that critics consider to be important is usually oppositional in one fashion or another, resisting capitalist values, depicting alienation, confronting the state, deriding bourgeois tastes, or criticizing itself or its artistic forebears. The war in Việt Nam was a focal point for a small group of artists who were determined to make art that was explicitly political and antiwar, a movement in which art was a weapon against the state and its war that these artists saw as unjust, brutal, racist, and sexist. Until very recently, Vietnamese art generally worked in exactly the opposite fashion, with art stressing harmony, beauty, and tradition, even when it comes to war. The art historian Bùi Như Hương notes drily that even though the Vietnamese experienced a thousand years of war, few images of death, pain, brutality, or trauma can be found in Vietnamese art, despite Western assumptions that art should confront those experiences, which feature heavily in antiwar American art. The absence of such images is not due to the restrictions of a political system but rather is evidence of a Vietnamese "national identity" that is found in "racial origins," "inherent in the nation's subconscious" (Bùi 86). The claim of a unified national and racial identity is doubtful, particularly if we remember that Việt Nam has fifty-three ethnic minorities that are not easily included in the nation despite the state's best efforts, as a memorial mosaic at the Củ Chi tunnels shows (figure 12.1). Here minorities are marshaled as part of the revolutionary effort to defeat American occupiers, liberate the South, and unite the country (a depiction that conveniently forgets how the contemporary Communist Party periodically suppresses minority groups when their members clamor for their economic, political, or religious rights). Here and elsewhere in Việt Nam, art works in service of the state, with art being a weapon wielded by and for the state as it stresses unity and solidarity rather than individuality and opposition.

Thus, the repeated themes of the war art exhibited in Vietnamese museums and at memorials are heroic struggle; military and peasant life; the glory of labor; revolutionary heroes; and women at work, war, and mourning. Such works of art are found at the Fine Arts Museums, Revolution

FIGURE 12.1. Mosaic depicting soldiers of the People's Army of Việt Nam and ethnic minorities at the Củ Chi tunnels. All photographs taken by the author except otherwise noted.

Museums, and History Museums of Hà Nội and Hồ Chí Minh City, as well as numerous smaller museums and memorials.[6] Among these, the Fine Arts Museum of Hà Nội is the country's best art museum, if by best we mean one that follows most closely Western standards of exhibition, display, lighting, and captioning, and one in which art is hallowed work. The war art in this museum occupies perhaps a third of the space, with the texture of the art similar to the texture of the other art on display. Both types of art are outcomes of the country's colonial history, in which France introduced the concept of Western art to its Indochinese colonies in the early twentieth century. Prior to the establishment of the Ecole des Beaux-Arts de l'Indochine (EBAI) in Hà Nội in 1925, artistic practices in Việt Nam were artisanal and crafts-oriented, based in villages and with anonymous creators. With the EBAI, an artistic tradition was created by French teachers and their Indochinese students, with auteurs steeped in impressionism and romanticism, trained in Western aesthetic techniques and media such as oil painting and gouache on paper, and ready to transform indigenous practices like lacquer and silk painting with these techniques.[7] The war against the French (1945–

54) put an end to the EBAI. This war plus the subsequent one against the Americans and South Vietnamese (1961–75), followed by a period of isolation abetted by an American embargo (1975–86), effectively froze dominant Vietnamese art in a moment of aesthetic and political stasis. In this period of nearly half a century, Vietnamese art became a partner with the state's military efforts, expressing itself via an appropriated Western aesthetics from the early twentieth century.

The Fine Arts Museum of Hà Nội and the other state-sanctioned museums are thus time capsules of a certain kind of art, blending state memory with aesthetic nostalgia, the fervor of the revolutionary expressed through the assimilated techniques of the colonizer. These museums are among the state's strongholds of memory, where art is on a pedestal, as long as it expresses the correct sentiment regarding the nation and revolution. Since the state exerts a powerful grip on art production through sponsoring and approving exhibitions and awarding prizes, the place of art in the public spaces controlled by the state is not merely ornamental and official. State-sponsored art was dominant in Việt Nam's art world, but its decline in importance began in 1986 with the introduction of Đổi Mới, the economic renovation policy of the Communist Party that slowly opened the doors of the nation to capitalism. After a decade of disastrous inflation, failed collective economic policies, nationwide rationing, and American embargoing, the postrevolutionary phase that began with Đổi Mới brought forces of change that affected the art world. The most visible effect was the influx of tourists eager to buy high-quality facsimiles of Western masterpieces or lush, romantic renditions of Vietnamese life—bucolic scenes of the countryside and its rural inhabitants and creatures or idealized sightings of willowy women in flowing áo dài, the national fetish outfit that every Western male visitor feels obliged to compliment and comment upon, from the average sex tourist to the iconic Graham Greene. Following these tourists, however, came collectors looking for higher-quality and more expensive artwork.

The Vietnamese art world is now split into at least three parts: the commercialized art market with low and high price levels; the state-sponsored world of ceremony and commemoration; and the emerging, energetic independent art scene that foreign artists and curators are most comfortable with. This scene speaks in the language of the avant-garde, Master of Fine Arts programs, the Venice Biennale, the art gallery, the international art circuit, and Western tastes and values imported into Việt Nam to create a fusion art that is undoubtedly exciting but perhaps not appealing to local and foreign cosmopolitan classes. These divisions in the art world resemble the divisions in Vietnamese society as it becomes a market economy. The country is assimilating capitalist practices while attempting to maintain an

official Communist ideology; in a similarly hybrid fashion, the art establishment has used Western techniques to describe native life and transform
indigenous art practices. The paradox is that the politically dominant art
commemorating war is not the economically dominant one. The political
art is major in one sense but minor in another, playing the role of the revolutionary grandfather espousing Communist ideology at a time when only
a very small minority of the population belongs to the Party (about two
million people out of over ninety million). The lack of participation in the
Party finds its art world corollary in the fact that the halls of state-sponsored
museums are mostly empty of local visitors, while the local artists are attentive to the commercial market or the independent art scene, where the war
is barely recalled—if it is acknowledged at all.

To the extent that the state makes any concession to the present in the
official memory of the war, it is in the acknowledgment that the war was not
only a just and heroic one, but one that occasioned great mourning, as
shown in a sculpture by Nguyễn Phú Cường of a mourning mother who is
literally hollowed out by loss as she cradles the helmet of an absent, dead
soldier (figure 12.2). In dominant Vietnamese culture, the dead soldier is
commemorated as a heroic martyr, paired with the heroic mother in a relationship that leads to the soldier's continual infantilization, as Hue-Tam
Ho Tai points out. This infantilization is matched by the mother's eternal
maternalization, in which sacrifice is prized above all—especially the sacrifice of sons for the revolutionary cause, with more dead sons leading to
more glory. The idealized image of this mourning, heroic mother resonates
both with the aesthetic tradition of Vietnamese fine art and with dominant
social mores about the importance of the family; filial piety; sacrifice; and
the proper roles of men and women, young and old. These images continue
in the postwar era, with sculptures of mourning mothers and heroic martyrs
flooding the urban and rural landscape, from memorials in city centers to
remote martyrs' graveyards, commemorating revolutionary heroes and forgetting everyone else, aimed primarily at Vietnamese who would come to
mourn or remember the revolutionary dead (figure 12.3).

While mourning is a crucial register for state-sponsored art, another public face of art exists as well, a more provocative and confrontational one
that belies the local and Western perception that Vietnamese art does not
deal with death and pain. These images appear at sites remembering the war
where local and foreign tourists are not only likely to come but do in fact
visit in significant numbers. At the museum in Sơn Mỹ commemorating the
Mỹ Lai massacre, a diorama uses sculptures of American soldiers shooting
and stabbing Vietnamese women and children against a painted backdrop
of dead bodies and burning homes (figure 12.4). On Côn Sơn Island, where

FIGURE 12.2. Nguyễn Phú Cường,
Tưởng Niệm (Commemoration).
Bronze sculpture, 160 cm, 2000.
Fine Arts Museum, Hà Nội.
Photo by Sam Sweezy.

over ten thousand political prisoners died in French, South Vietnamese, and American prisons, several restored jails house scenes of torture and imprisonment staged with hundreds of life-sized sculptures (figure 12.5). For a Western visitor, these scenes may evoke American horror movies and torture porn such as the butcher-shop franchises of *Saw* or *Hostel*. But perhaps those horror movies and torture porn so in fashion today recall indirectly the actual horrors committed during war and lurking in the American conscience.

These memorials and monuments are typical, not exceptional, in Việt Nam, trafficking not in fine art but in a low art of the kind that is not discussed by either Vietnamese or American critics. This art of anger and atrocity is not high-minded like state art, romantic like commercial art, or edgy like independent art; instead it is profane and crudely done, and it takes on itself the documentary impulse of Western photography. This art of anger and atrocity is the other side of the propaganda poster used by the revolution to bolster morale during the war, encouraging people to work hard and fight hard against foreign aggression. Ironically, propaganda posters are now revolutionary chic, with entire shops devoted to the sale of originals and

FIGURE 12.3. Statue of a mourning, heroic mother at the Martyrs Cemetery of Hồ Chí Minh City.

FIGURE 12.4. Diorama of the Mỹ Lai massacre, Sơn Mỹ museum, central Việt Nam, 2010. Photo by Sam Sweezy.

reproductions, purchased mostly by foreigners. But I find it hard to imagine anyone wanting to purchase the images of atrocity. The art of anger and atrocity, like the independent art that privileges performance, installation, and the ephemeral, resists the invisible hand of the market by not turning pain into entertainment. Instead, this art uses pain as pedagogy for tourists, both foreign and local. The written narratives that usually frame these images of anger and atrocity blame American soldiers and French colonizers, and as a result stir up either guilt or loathing on the part of foreigners.[8] For them, war art, whether high or low, induces memories of a past that is not theirs and a historical narrative that they may or may not agree with. The art also has a contradictory effect on the Vietnamese. The narrative offered by museums and tour guides is usually one of national pride and anticolonial resistance, which explicitly serves to reaffirm the story of the state. Implicitly, however, a narrative that recalls the glories of the revolutionary past may also remind the Vietnamese that the present ruled by the Party has not lived up to the sacrifices of the martyred. For either foreigners or locals, the art of the war is at base ambiguous, even if on the surface the meaning seems to be clear—the low art of anger and atrocity seeming to demand acknowledgment of guilt by association from Americans, the high art in state-sponsored museums seeming to demand loyalty to the Communist Party.

FIGURE 12.5. Torture scene, Côn Sơn Island prison.

One last kind of art exists that the critics have not commented on: the genre of captured war materiel displayed at various battlefield sites and museums. In most cases, the war materiel is merely a tank or a cannon, and its display is not ironically repurposed as art in the way that Marcel Duchamp christened a urinal as art. In at least one memorable instance, however, the sheer scale and style of the display qualifies as art—a remarkable monument of airplanes and their remains shot down by Vietnamese antiaircraft gunners, many of them women. This is the detritus of what the Vietnamese called the "Điện Biên Phủ of the Air" for American bombers, and it looms in the courtyard of Hà Nội's Military History Museum, the Vietnamese military itself a sponsor of art during wartime and afterward, unlike the American military (figure 12.6). Fashioning art from junk is a common Western gesture, and while the technique of the monument is not much different, its spirit is grander and more historical, and it is displayed at a military museum instead of a fine art museum.[9] This artistic integration of the remains of a war machine and of memory work as an industrial practice expresses absolute triumph on a massive scale, with an unnamed collective of artists instead of the individual artist transforming weapons into art. In its form and its content, this mass of metal is an expression of how revolution can fuse art and politics together.

FIGURE 12.6. Display of American and French warplanes, Military History Museum, Hà Nội. Photo by Sam Sweezy.

An Eye for an Eye, or the Art of Anger

American and Vietnamese societies share two features in their remembrance of the war: one is to remember their own dead, and the other is to re-member in anger, usually expressed through what Lucy Lippard calls "gore galore" (62). Recalling one's own dead is a mark of the dominant way of remembering, expressed most vividly and memorably in Maya Lin's Viet-nam Veterans Memorial. The powerful abstraction of the wall—with over 58,000 names of the American dead on black granite—takes place against an implied backdrop of figurative representation, in which the most pow-erful American images of the war, from mainstream print journalism to op-positional art, focus on the pain, suffering, and sorrow of human beings and bodies. The function of a war memorial usually is to remember only one's own, as is the case with the Trường Sơn Martyrs Cemetery in Quảng Trị, the largest martyrs cemetery in Việt Nam and one that shares the idea of listing the names of the dead. But it is also often the case that war me-morials will list the names of dead allies, as the War Memorial of Korea does for Americans and many others from countries in the United Nations. This acknowledgment of allies and friends is something not done by the Vietnam Veterans Memorial, despite the fact that the United States called on many of its allies to send soldiers to Việt Nam. Thousands of Korean, Australian, Cambodian, Laotian, and Hmong soldiers and smaller numbers of soldiers from several other countries also died, not to mention over two hundred thousand South Vietnamese soldiers, who were not allies inasmuch as they were the principal fighters for their own country. The absence of these non-American names is an aesthetic feature of the memorial just as the presence of American names is an aesthetic feature, marking the Việt Nam War as an American war rather than an international one in which the numbers of non-American military dead greatly outnumbered American military losses. Much of the discussion about Lin's wall remarks on the power of those names emerging from the black granite of the wall, merging with the reflection of visitors' faces in the granite and generating a communion between visitor and veteran, living and dead. But if American names are in the foreground, then the unseen names of others compose the dark matter of this wall, the invisible substance against which American mourning and healing shines.[10]

While Lin's wall has not been without controversy, it has triumphed as the most memorable memorial to war or its afterlife in the United States, and it stands as the major work of art about the war—perhaps even the only major work of art about the war, if by that we mean something most Americans would recognize. It is an industrial product, the effort of a state and a movement of veterans and citizens, and it is the manifestation of an entire society's bureaucratic and technological prowess, channeled through the vision of the individual artist, who herself is the outcome of an American program of immigration that funneled some of Asia's best and brightest (and their children) into American higher education. In contrast to her wall, the minor art about the war is marked by its much smaller scale, its methods considerably more modest than the industrial methods required by the wall. Minor in this sense does not mean lesser in terms of artistic accomplishment, but it does mean being overshadowed, harder to find, and less known to the general public. But the most significant difference is that this minor work is signed in anger and rage, premised as it is on opposing either the war or neutral stances to the war like Lin's. This oppositional stance is most explicit in Chris Burden's "The Other Vietnam Memorial," printed with three million Vietnamese names. Burden is a major artist, and this work is housed in Chicago's Museum of Contemporary Art. Nonetheless, I call it minor because it speaks in opposition to the majority, nationalist impulses evident in American film, TV, pop culture, and political discourse on the war, most of which is narrowly focused on American experiences. In contrast, many American artists in their minor role not only oppose the war but ask audiences to commemorate the dead of the other side or the dead of both sides, a gesture that is certainly antipatriotic and, in some cases and at some times, potentially treasonous.

Perhaps the most famous of these artists are Nancy Spero and Martha Rosler, who fuse antiwar critique with feminist politics. Spero's works from the time of the war and afterward are ghastly, graphic permutations of the war's horror into sketches and drawings of insect-like helicopters, bombs spewing pus, deformed body parts, and monstrous bodies. She treats combat not just as blood sport but gender clash, with phallic instruments of war and feminized victims (figure 12.7). Rosler likewise sees the war as an extension of deeply held gendered feelings. Whereas many Americans prefer to think of their wars as distant affairs being fought by their men, out of sight and out of mind, Rosler literally brings the war home in her collages, inserting wounded Vietnamese women and children into high-gloss living rooms, or having smiling American housewives open their curtains to scenes of warfare in Việt Nam (figure 12.8). For Rosler, the human and financial costs of war are hidden in the very fabric of American décor, domesticity, and bliss, leaving blood on all American hands, including those of women and consumers—haunted houses, indeed. Rosler's collages force viewers to notice what they do not want to see and remember what they do not want to recall by taking images from far away and bringing them very close. This spatial move is characteristic of antiwar art, which not only makes the world smaller but also conversely engages in a widening of the field of memory, working directly against the narrowness of vision that characterizes the nationalist memory of Lin's wall. Even as that wall has been seen as a statement against war, it is first and foremost a demand to remember dead American soldiers (almost all of whom were male), which Spero and Rosler refuse to do, including in their work instead the images of civilians, women, the mutilated and the disabled, and the enemy dead. By nationalism's standards, which are premised on refusing to remember the enemy, refusing to remember civilians, refusing to remember shattered bodies, and refusing to acknowledge war's gendered drive, this is perverse memory work, which is also an ethical memory that stands against the patriotic ethics of nationalism.

While major memory of the nationalist kind has the resources to be expansive, to see and recall widely, it refuses to do so, preferring the narrow focus of remembering one's own. In striking contrast, the minor art of war memory is committed to using its resources not just to expand memory across national boundaries (a move that is premised on resemblance, implying that the enemy is not so different from us) but also to expanding it across time (mostly through the act of repetition, implying that what happened before can happen again, or that what is happening now has already happened). Thus, Rosler repeats herself with her Iraq War collages, where

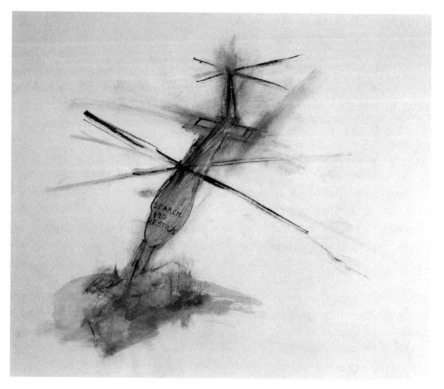

FIGURE 12.7. Nancy Spero, "Search and Destroy," gouache and ink on paper, 24 x 36 inches, 1967. Photo by David Reynolds. Courtesy of the Nancy Spero and Leon Golub Foundation for the Arts. Art © Estate of Nancy Spero/Licensed by VAGA, New York, NY.

she uses the same method as in her Việt Nam War collages to say that nothing much has changed. Sam Wiener's "45,391 . . . and counting" from 1970 makes the point of repetition explicit in its content, a phalanx of coffins draped in American flags whose images are repeated endlessly in a box of mirrors. Later Wiener turned the repetition of the dead into the repetition of the war when he retitled his work "Those Who Fail to Remember the Past Are Condemned to Repeat It," referring to US involvement in Central America and perhaps, Lippard thinks, to American wars in the Mideast in 1991 and 2003.[11] The theme of repetition deals with more than just history. Repetition is also enacted formally, as evidenced in Wiener's endless coffins and in Burden's asking us to remember the Vietnamese dead, a task premised on impossibility. Unable to find three million genuine Vietnamese names, Burden repeated four thousand Vietnamese names he found in a phone book (belonging to people who were obviously not dead). What also

FIGURE 12.8. Martha Rosler, "Cleaning the Drapes," pigmented inkjet print (photo-montage), 17 ⁵⁄₁₆ x 23 ¾ inches, 1967. Courtesy of the artist.

marks Burden's art as minor, especially in contrast to Lin's, is that neither he nor the Vietnamese state had the resources to find those three million names, whereas Lin and the United States did have the resources to remember the much smaller number of American dead. This capacity is also part of the industry of memory from which art about the war begins: the memory of the state itself, which, in keeping track of its citizens, can enable their memorialization or their erasure through its ability to archive. In contrast, one marker of the minority, to paraphrase James Baldwin, is that nobody knows their names.

Perhaps the ultimate act of repetition and memory in American art about the war is Harrell Fletcher's "The Art of War" exhibition. Here he photographs the exhibits of Hồ Chí Minh City's most popular tourist site, the War Remnants Museum, a substantial portion of which is a series of reproductions of Western journalistic photographs recording war atrocities. Many rooms in the museum are dedicated to more mundane matters—international antiwar movements, the history of colonization, postwar reconstruction, and so on—but without a doubt, most visitors remember the atrocities. I saw an abbreviated portion of Fletcher's exhibition when it came to Los Angeles, for which he had chosen to cut down his show to focus on the atrocities, even though he had photographed many of the mundane exhibits as well. Like Wiener's work, Fletcher's exhibit amounts to a house of mirrors in its concept. Fletcher has photographed reproductions of photographs recording horrendous history, and in so doing both replicates one purpose of the museum—to treat photographs as transparent windows onto factual atrocities—and also reminds us that what we are seeing is not transparent but is instead an aesthetic of brutality, fashioned to respond to the outrageous brutality of an American war machine, as Molotov cocktails might be thrown against an M-60 tank. In Fletcher's exhibit, the viewer encounters not the museum but framed photographs of photographs, in which—by the simple gestures of reproduction, repetition, and framing—he has turned documentary and journalism into (good or bad) art. Thus, instead of offering a cropped image of Fletcher's work, I include here my photograph of his book of photographs recording the photographs of the museum's exhibit (figure 12.9).[12]

Fletcher's work reminds viewers that when they look at photographs of atrocities or human damage, they are looking at representations and not just reproductions. They are seeing art in addition to photography, and they are encouraged to remember that photography is art, not just a capturing of reality. That is a generous reading about the power of repetition in Fletcher's work. A less generous reading arises from my memory of visiting the museum for the first time in 2002, when I was so deeply disturbed by what I saw that I could not bring myself to take a photograph. Was nothing sacred, was nothing private? (No, says Salman Rushdie.)[13] I sympathized with the mission of the War Remnants Museum but felt brutalized at the same time, for while I recognized the need to call up the memory of the victims, I felt that they were being violated yet again through another exposure of their dead, tortured, naked, or massacred bodies. Since the museum had already done this, then of course Fletcher himself could do so, too, and thus it is the Vietnamese curators who authorized the repetitions. The dead, violated once through their murder, are violated again in the repetition of their images, even for a supposedly good purpose. For Fletcher, this purpose is twofold: first to force Americans to confront a difficult history, and second to remind them, by analogy, that the war in Iraq has an American prequel in Việt Nam. Likewise, Burden was intent on signaling obliquely about Iraq in his "The Other Vietnam Memorial." We've done this before, the artists are saying, and we're doing it again. (Same-same but different, the Vietnamese supposedly said during the war.) Even the dead must be marshaled to fight in the war against war. Eventually I submitted to this message and its political imperative, as well as to the fear of not remembering what I was

44   45

FIGURE 12.9. Two pages from Harrell Fletcher's *The American War*. Harrell Fletcher's "The Art of War" exhibition.

seeing—the fear that the museum's memories themselves would change over the years without my knowing, as evidenced by how the bottled, deformed fetuses of Agent Orange victims, an apparently permanent part of the exhibit, disappeared. I could barely look at them in 2002 and had a graduate student take pictures of them for me in 2008; by the time I visited again in 2009, they were gone. So then I took pictures of everything—the mundane and the horrifying, the machinery and the humanity, the living and the dead—furiously.

Vietnamese American Art, or Somewhere between Triumph and Trauma

If the war in Việt Nam was a total war, then must the war in art be a total war? So it would seem in Vietnamese war art, where the entire population of the north and the patriotic south are depicted, not just fighting soldiers: women, children, the elderly, the militia, civilians, laborers, and party leaders, all cast visually in one way or another as part of a massive liberation campaign. From art museum to history museum and from historical site to memorial park, the ideological messages and images of war and revolution tend to be repetitive, working in either the high mode of celebrating state, soldier, and supporter or the low mode of tattooing atrocity onto the visitor's eyeball. Trauma turns into triumph through the therapeutic narrative of revolution as closure to a history of French colonialism and American occupation. The closure is far from complete, however, as the insistent images of death and destruction remain visible, raising other ways of interpreting revolutionary history through the haunting presence of the unspeakable and the dead.

Repetition is at work in American art as well, although for different purposes, where the difference is not so much between high and low as between state art and private art. In American state art, all the forces of American society were required for the creation of the Vietnam Veterans Memorial, a massive work chiseled into the American earth where the American dead are recalled repetitively, via their names. In antiwar American art, imaginative reach and commemorative desire become global even if the formal scale is small—the artists link past to present and future through repetition, connecting the war in Việt Nam to other wars and wars abroad to conflicts at home about race, poverty, and inequality. In state art, therapy is done via the citizen's and the survivor's patriotic communion with the heroic military dead. But in antiwar art, the intent is to prevent therapy, closure, and reconciliation; to prevent the viewer from moving on; to jam a stick into the gears of the war machine. In all these cases, artists are aware that confronting or acknowledging the awesomeness of the American war machine calls for a memory machine. In this memory machine, the artist and her product are only part of something larger, an effort by the state or a movement of like-minded artists, curators, and activists. Each of these memory machines needs an ethics to guide it—software or a set of decisions about who or what to remember, and who or what to forget.

Like the digital language of software, memory works as an endless set of binary decisions about remembering and forgetting, with an implied, mysterious third term—the "and" or the gap between a one and a zero. The filmmaker Chris Marker uses a different metaphor in his film *Sans Soleil* to suggest the same outcome when he says that the "function of remembering is not the opposite of forgetting, but rather its lining." A garment and its lining, the outside and the inside, the face and the back—all are joined together rather than remaining simply one or the other. As remembering and forgetting are entwined together, so are the histories of Việt Nam and the United States. An ethical memory does not condemn forgetting for forgetting's sake, since forgetting is necessary for memory, clearing the ground to let memory happen. Instead, ethical memory points to the most grievous of errors in forgetting—usually the forgetting of those whose memories contest our own—while also acknowledging that those we choose to forget commit those same errors. In their own ways, Vietnamese and American cultures have made efforts to remember the other side. Perhaps because those are mostly minor efforts on the American side, the Vietnamese do not notice them, and perhaps because Americans who visit Việt Nam tend to see what they want to see—a repressive society hung up on war trauma—they do not notice the Vietnamese efforts. Thus, visitors remark on the uniformity of war representation and the oppressiveness of state memory, without noticing how Americans are acknowledged, as shown in the War Remnants Museum's exhibits on the American antiwar movement and on Agent Orange's effects on Americans. Is Vietnamese memory selective? Yes. Amnesiac? Not completely. Racist, as is the usual dominant American version of the Vietnamese? Rarely.

Given the one-sidedness and dominance of nationalist memory, however, efforts to be judicious and to remember both sides are notable even when they are flawed. The war comic *The Other Side* by Jason Aaron and Cameron Stewart is a radical departure from the war comics of my youth, in which the Japanese of World War II, the Chinese and North Koreans of the Korean War, and the Vietnamese were interchangeable yellow-skinned little men screaming "Aiiieeeee!!!" *The Other Side* cuts between the story of an American soldier and a humanly rendered North Vietnamese soldier, both enduring horrific combat until their fateful confrontation. The American kills the Vietnamese and returns home, where he is haunted not only by images of dead friends and dead enemies but by visions of his family and neighbors with their heads blown off, as were the heads of Vietnamese villagers. *The Other Side* is a remarkable work of popular art, but in retrospect, it is no accident that the Vietnamese has to die and the American has to be haunted. Hollywood film has already established the narrative about the person of color whose suffering serves the white man, who is traumatized but nevertheless survives. Beyond this problem, however, what the comic displays very graphically is the problem of duality, of the limits of lending memory to the enemy, for one thing that is forgotten is the South Vietnamese who fought with the Americans. They are never shown.

Thus I give equal weight here not just to the art of Vietnamese and Americans but to the often overlooked South Vietnamese Americans who fled their lost war and came to the United States, where they found that no one likes losers. Their stories fit into neither the triumphant national narrative of Việt Nam nor the sorrowful one of the United States. Ironically, to the extent that Americans want to remember Việt Nam and reconcile with it, they are mostly interested in their former Vietnamese enemies, not their former allies who have settled in their own country. It is likewise the case with the Vietnamese that they are more interested in the memories of their American

enemy than in the memories of their evicted cousins in the Vietnamese diaspora. But these Vietnamese American cousins are not just victims or saints.
Even as they clamor to be remembered by both Americans and Vietnamese,
they are hardly immune themselves to amnesia. It is this triangulation of
memory that concerns me, rather than the bifurcation of memory between
two sides, so suggestively alluded to in the usual dichotomies of remembering and forgetting, memory and amnesia, and history and the present, in
which what is almost always privileged is everything associated with recall,
particularly for members of the minority whose names no one knows. But
recalling the past and remembering injustice is not as uncomplicated a good
as it may seem, as Vietnamese American art shows.

Vietnamese American artwork expresses and reflects the tensions of being
in between opposing sides and of being an aspiring minority in the United
States, framed by the history of the war and by the cultural politics of art
markets.[14] These tensions and aspirations lead to contrasting tendencies,
depending on whether Vietnamese American artists are participating in a
minor aesthetic oriented toward their ethnic community or a major aesthetic targeted at national and international audiences, particularly when
the topic is war and memory. The minor aesthetic and the discourse through
which it is received are shown most clearly in the case of controversial
works that supposedly deal with communism. One of the best-known examples is the controversial FOB II art exhibit of 2009, organized by Orange
County's Vietnamese American Arts and Letters Association and staged in
the largest Vietnamese diasporic community in the world (FOB stands for
"fresh off the boat," an ethnic slur against refugees that refugees sometimes
use against each other, maliciously or humorously). The exhibit featured
over fifty artists from Việt Nam and its diaspora, most of whom did not
deal with communism or the war, and many of whom showed sophisticated
work. But a handful of pieces that foregrounded communist imagery drew
the ire of the community, most notably Brian Doan's "Thu Duc" (2008).
"Thu Duc" features a young woman wearing a tank top with the Communist flag and a small bust of Ho Chi Minh. Community protestors defaced
the image during a significant and vocal demonstration against the exhibit,
charging that it showed sympathy toward communism. The protestors were
ultimately successful in making the exhibit a citywide issue and forcing it
to close. The controversial artwork was nowhere near as interesting as the
protests it provoked and the questions protestors raised concerning artistic
freedom, censorship, filial piety, respect for the community, and the politics
of representation.[15] In this case, the artwork and the debates about it are
minor because the discourse addressing them exemplifies how the space of

FIGURE 12.10. Dinh Q. Lê, "Doi Moi (Napalmed Girl)," C-print and linen tape, 48 ¼ x 70 inches, 2006. Courtesy of the artist.

the minority is one in which everything is political, becomes political, or is perceived as political, with the political defined in rigid ways—in this case, communist or not communist, the only distinction that matters in Little Saigon, Orange County. Representational art of the kind that sparked the protest against the FOB II exhibit speaks to memory explicitly, and in minor discourse, memory is one of the most dangerous of battlegrounds.

The Vietnamese American artwork that is major negotiates this battleground more successfully in the sense of not being as provocative, and of having aesthetic features that are more refined and political sentiments that are more ambiguous. The result is reward outside of the ethnic community, both for the artists and their works. Dinh Q. Lê is perhaps the best known Vietnamese American artist, and his work exemplifies the strategy of negotiation, ambiguity, and refinement characteristic of the major discourse in Vietnamese American art. His most famous body of work weaves iconic American images of the war together with anonymous Vietnamese photographs, the method of his work literally being a form of reconciliation (figure 12.10). As I have discussed his work in greater detail elsewhere, I focus here on two other artists who have achieved some significant recognition in the mainstream art world, Binh Danh and An-My Lê.[16] In all three cases, what is notable is how the artists have been recognized not only for the content of their work but also for

FIGURE 12.11. Binh Danh, "Mothers and Children," chlorophyll prints and resin, 12 x 20 inches, 2001. Courtesy of the artist.

their technical precision and formal achievements. Thus, in Danh's work, what strikes his critics is his use of wartime photographs combined with an innovative approach in which he imprints the images of the photographs with chlorophyll on leaves (figure 12.11). Photography and its evocation of death and haunting are well known, and Danh takes that formal element of photography; selects photographs that are often explicitly about combat, pain, trauma, or the dead; and layers the photographic medium on the medium of leaves, which evoke nature and the cycle of life, death, and regeneration. The blending of media, as in Lê's case, is harmonious, while at the same time gesturing at the discordant—the legacy of war and death in memory.

In contrast, minor art work gestures at the discordant without at the same time finding a method that allows the viewer a moment of communion with the pain being displayed. The distinction between major and minor speaks to the way the work is received by critics and mainstream audiences, not necessarily to the inherent value of the work itself. In some contexts, the minor is necessary, a needle in the eye of the person who would rather look away from the horror of the past, and who will respond in kind to such provocation. But the pleasures of major work such that of Lê or Danh comes with a cost, both for the viewer who must pay the requisite price for owning such popular work and potentially for other artists and viewers. Viewers are spared the discomfort of confrontation, not necessarily in the work itself, but through the transformation of pain into art. The making of trauma into something beautiful reduces the likelihood that communities outside of the art world will respond negatively to the work. Focusing on American soldiers or on the Vietnamese as victims, the work of Lê and Danh avoids dealing with the symbols most likely to inflame the Vietnamese American community—flags, Hồ Chí Minh, communist images, and anything else that could evoke communist representation or the idea of the South Vietnamese as being anything but victims. Where Lê and Danh's work is potentially most controversial is where it approaches those who cannot speak back, the dead—in this case their use of photographs from Tuol Sleng. These are photographs of the Cambodian victims of the Khmer Rouge, taken by the Khmer Rouge themselves, who stole not just the lives of their victims but also their images. These photographs are powerful in both their muteness and in their presentation by Lê and Danh (figure 12.12). But the beauty of the works and the use of images of the dead inevitably raises the question of the artists' ethical obligations to the dead, which is different from the ethical obligations of documentarians and photojournalists. Is there another way for artists to picture the dead without using their images?

Lê's book *Small Wars* responds to this problem by implication. *Small Wars* contains three of her photographic exhibits, and in the title exhibit she photographs Americans who reenact the Việt Nam War. Absent from these images are the blood, death, trauma, and pain of war photography, particularly Việt Nam War photography. She is cognizant of such images, as are her subjects, as is clear in a photograph for which the war reenactors asked her to play the role of a Viet Cong sniper (figure 12.13). American war photographers never captured such an image, which is more comparable to what North Vietnamese photographers shot. The framer is framed here, which brings attention not only to Lê's status as a Vietnamese shooting these Americans in more ways than one, but also to the history of posed scenes in war photography. Most infamously, it is the dead who are repositioned by the photographer, as in Matthew Brady's Civil War photographs, but here it is the living, playing out images already seen in photographic history. Instead of simply looking at photographs and identifying with their subjects, these reenactors literally embody the past, as does the photographer in this instance. Lê's photograph suggests the intensity of identification for both Americans and Vietnamese who have seen war photographs, either as viewers or as photographers themselves. This intensity of identification is also possible for the viewers of Lê's photographs, which are ultimately less about the history of the war than about our relationship to the memory of that history.

The absence of the dead in Lê's photographs and in the reenactment she records signals at least two things. One is that we should leave the dead

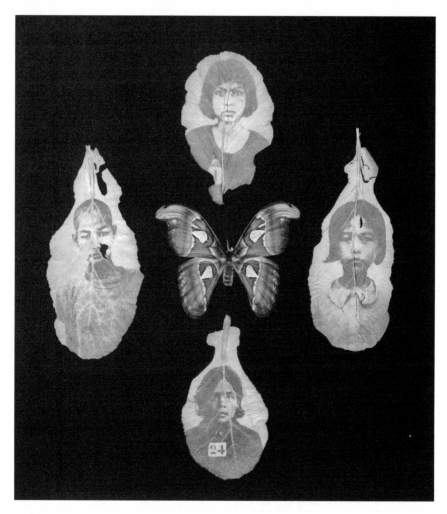

FIGURE 12.12. Binh Danh, "Ancestral Altar #20," chlorophyll prints, butterfly specimen, and resin, 32 x 27.5 inches, 2006. Courtesy of the artist.

alone: they have suffered enough already. But the other is that the absence of the dead allows war's reenactment, both in the playful sense that is recorded in Lê's photograph and in the more troubling sense of war's repetition on real battlefields. The Việt Nam War continues to have meaning for many in this sense of repetition, found in the debates over the wars in Iraq and Afghanistan. Are they repetitions of the previous tragedy of the Việt Nam War, or are they repetitions with a difference, new wars that can be won through having learned the lessons of the lost war? The paradox in writing about the memories of this war is that I may reinforce the tendency for Americans,

FIGURE 12.13. An-My Lê, "Small Wars (Sniper 1)," gelatin silver print, 26 x 37 ½ inches, 1999–2002. Courtesy of the artist.

and many people elsewhere, to remember Việt Nam as a war rather than a country. But my purpose is not to argue that we should remember the war for its own sake or even for the purpose of mourning the four million dead of the many countries involved, since the war was but one conflict in a long line of horrific wars. Instead, the most important reason to remember is the fear of repetition. As Freud said, what we do not remember, we will repeat. What we do not work through, we will act out. Both Việt Nam and the United States, and their diverse populations, share this problem posed by amnesia. The war remains important because we have more to fear from consigning it to the past than from confronting its continuing relevance, this war that remains impossible to forget, yet difficult to remember.

Notes

1. I use Vietnamese diacritics in Vietnamese personal and place names, with exceptions for those Vietnamese Americans who generally do not use those diacritics in describing themselves.

2. For a valuable study of North Vietnamese visual and war memories, see Schwenkel.

3. Đặng Nhật Minh, remarks delivered at "Dreaming of Peace: Vietnamese Filmmakers Move from War to Reconciliation," University of Southern California, Los Angeles, CA, January 23, 2010.

4. On technologies of memory and the Việt Nam War, see Sturken.

5. On Vietnamese memorial practices, see Malarney and the essays in Ho Tai, *The Country of Memory*.

6. Since the first draft of this essay was written, the Revolution Museum of Hồ Chí Minh City changed its name to the Museum of Hồ Chí Minh City.

7. For a more detailed exploration of the painting tradition in Vietnamese art, see Taylor.

8. Many of these tourists have recorded their sentiments in the comment books that are a common feature of Vietnamese museums, as Laderman documents.

9. For an example of junk repurposed as art, see Nancy Rubins's sculpture *Airplane Parts* in the courtyard of the Los Angeles Museum of Contemporary Art.

10. Sturken provides an excellent reading of Lin's memorial. For additional criticism and context, see Hass.

11. The art of Weiner, Rosler, and Spero, as well as that of many other artists dealing with the war, are found in Lippard.

12. Fletcher's exhibit was called "The Art of War," but his book was titled *The American War*.

13. Rushdie's answer is found in his essay "Is Nothing Sacred?," in *Imaginary Homelands*.

14. For a very useful account of Vietnamese American art, see Lê.

15. For an account of the FOB II controversy, see Duong and Pelaud.

16. For more on Dinh's artwork, see Nguyen.

Works Cited

Aaron, Jason, and Cameron Stewart. 2007. *The Other Side*. New York: Vertigo.

Bùi, Như Hương. 2009. "Modern Vietnamese Art: Process and Identity." In *Essays on Modern and Contemporary Vietnamese Art*, edited by Sarah Lee and Nhu Huy Nguyen, 78–86. Singapore: Singapore Art Museum.

Duong, Lan, and Isabelle Thuy Pelaud. 2012. "Vietnamese American Art and Community Politics: An Engaged Feminist Perspective." *Journal of Asian American Studies* 15 (3): 241–69.

Fletcher, Harrell. 2007. *The American War*. New York: J and L.

Freud, Sigmund. 1958. "Remembering, Repeating, and Working-Through." In Sigmund Freud, *The Standard Edition of the Complete Works of Sigmund Freud*, trans. James Stracey, 12:147–56. London: Hogarth.

Hass, Kristin. 1998. *Carried to the Wall: American Memory and the Vietnam Veterans Memorial*. Berkeley: University of California Press.

Ho Tai, Hue-Tam, ed. 2001a. *The Country of Memory: Remaking the Past in Late Socialist Vietnam*. Berkeley: University of California Press.

———. 2001b. "Faces of Remembering and Forgetting." In *The Country of Memory:*

Remaking the Past in Late Socialist Vietnam, ed. Hue-Tam Ho Tai, 167–95. Berkeley: University of California Press.

Laderman, Scott. 2009. *Tours of Vietnam: War, Travel Guides, and Memory*. Durham, NC: Duke University Press.

Lê, An-My. *Small Wars*. New York: Aperture, 2005.

Lê, Việt. 2005. "The Art of War: Vietnamese American Visual Artists Đinh Q. Lê, Ann Phông and Nguyễn Tân Hoàng." *Amerasia Journal* 31 (2): 21–35.

Lippard, Lucy. 1990. *A Different War: Vietnam in Art*. Bellingham, WA: Whatcom Museum of History and Art.

Malarney, Shaun. 2002. *Culture, Ritual and Revolution in Vietnam*. London: Routledge.

Marker, Chris, dir. 1983. *Sans Soleil*. New York: Criterion Collection.

Nguyen, Viet Thanh. 2007. "Impossible to Forget, Difficult to Remember: Việt Nam and the Art of Dinh Q. Lê." In *A Tapestry of Memories: The Art of Dinh Q. Le*, ed. Stefano Catalani, 19–29. Bellevue, WA: Bellevue Arts Museum.

Rushdie, Salman. 1991. *Imaginary Homelands: Essays and Criticism, 1981–1991*. London: Granta.

Schwenkel, Christina. 2009. *The American War in Contemporary Vietnam: Transnational Remembrance and Representation*. Bloomington: Indiana University Press.

Sturken, Marita. 1997. *Tangled Memories: The Vietnam War, the AIDS Epidemic, and the Politics of Remembering*. Berkeley: University of California Press.

Taylor, Nora. 2009. *Painters in Hanoi: An Ethnography of Vietnamese Art*. Honolulu: University of Hawaii Press.

13

ALFRED HORNUNG

CHINAMERICA: GLOBAL AFFAIRS AND
PLANETARY CONSCIOUSNESS

IN THIS ESSAY I will focus on the evolution of intercultural relations between China and America since the second half of the nineteenth century.
Against the background of major political developments, I will trace the history of cultural interactions at three decisive moments, which correspond to
three major movements in literature and the arts of the twentieth century: modernism, postmodernism, and neorealism. It is my assumption that coincidental
cultural movements and planned actions of cultural agents have prepared the
way for a close cooperation of the two countries constituting what I call Chin-
America. This transcultural constellation will potentially serve as a basis for a
new arrangement of global affairs between the two major global players in the
twenty-first century and for the establishment of a new transnational consciousness, which includes a concern for the preservation of the planet.

The three periods in the cultural and political interactions of China and
America, which will exemplify and prefigure the emergence of a new transcultural and transnational constellation of ChinAmerica for the twenty-first
century, range from the innovations of modernism via the ludic mode of
postmodernism to neorealism and the recent pictorial turn of popular culture. At each cultural moment the interaction of cultural agents takes on
different forms that point to the nature of ideological positions and attempt
to surpass them artistically. In *On China* former US Secretary of State Henry
Kissinger uses his extensive experience of fifty visits to the People's Republic of China to state important differences between the two countries and
to project a vision for a common collaborative future of the two nations,
which resembles my ChinAmerica project. As an American politician with
a European background, Kissinger looks at both countries from an Archi-
medean point of view and argues that the "relationship between China and
the United States has become a central element in the quest for world peace
and global well-being" (2011, xvi). What is necessary is to reconcile the

different sets of beliefs in exceptionalism held in both societies: "American exceptionalism is missionary. It holds that the United States has an obligation to spread its values to every part of the world. China's exceptionalism is cultural. China does not proselytize; it does not claim that its contemporary institutions are relevant outside of China. But it is heir of the Middle Kingdom tradition, which formally graded all other states at various levels of tributaries based on their approximation to Chinese cultural and political forms; in other words, a kind of cultural universality" (ibid., xvi).

Kissinger's close friend Helmut Schmidt similarly evokes the eminence of the Middle Kingdom and its 4,000-year civilization in recording his last visit to China in 2012. Recollecting previous conversations with Chinese politicians, the former German chancellor reiterates his long-held belief that China would emerge as an important world power after the turmoil of Mao's regime (Schmidt 2013, 10).

Following Kissinger's distinction between the American and the Chinese form of exceptionalism, I would like to argue for a merger of both nations for which I have coined the term "ChinAmerica." This neologism differs fundamentally from the term "Chimerica," used by the historian Niall Ferguson in *The Ascent of Money* (2008) to describe the economic interdependence of the two countries. The popularization of the latter term in a 2007 *Wall Street Journal* article written by Ferguson and the economist Moritz Schularick was seen both as a reaction to the negotiations between Presidents George W. Bush and Hu Jintao and as an outlook to Barack Obama's presidential candidacy—as far as regards the collaboration of the two countries in the twenty-first century. But it immediately evoked the criticism of political scientists in Beijing, who interpreted "Chimerica" as a new variation of the "yellow peril." Although my term "ChinAmerica" is also not immune to ideological criticism, I want to use it to analyze the intercultural relations between the two countries that may eventually lead to a transcultural and a transnational level of interaction. In my assessment this transnational horizon transcends mere economic relations or commercial interests and includes ecological concerns and a planetary consciousness, as suggested by postcolonial critics.

In her reconceptualization of comparative literature studies, Gayatri Spivak proposes to abolish disciplinary boundaries and political areas drawn up after World War II for the sake of her concept of planetarity. This new concept is motivated by her serious belief in and concern for a new humanist attitude toward the less fortunate people on earth. "Planetary" as "an alternate term for continental, global, worldly" differs decisively from those terms since it encapsulates the human concern. "The globe is on our computers," Spivak writes. "The planet is in the species of alterity, belonging to another system" (2003, 72). "To be human is to be intended toward the other," an ethical position which she also locates in such "transcendental figurations [as]—mother, nation, god, nature," which for her are "names of alterity, planetary subjects rather than global agents" (ibid., 73). Following Spivak I therefore differentiate between the digitalization of the world, as we know it from Google Earth, and a planetary awareness, which advocates alterity and the creation of a humanitarian network for the preservation of the planet. From a position of racial considerations, in *Postcolonial Melancholia* Paul Gilroy introduces the notion of "conviviality" for intercultural encounters and promotes "cosmopolitan solidarity and moral agency" (2006, xv). Like Spivak and Gilroy, the ecocritic Ursula Heise highlights these concepts of alterity and planetarity in *Sense of Place and Sense of Planet* (2008). More recently, Elizabeth DeLoughrey and George B. Handley have assembled articles in *Postcolonial Ecologies* (2011) that relate local ecological issues to a planetary scale.

This approach of a transnational cooperation—based on planetary ideas that have become increasingly common concerns of Chinese and American scholars in the twenty-first century (see Yang 2013)—goes beyond the one-sided traditional analyses of Chinese-American relations, summed up in John King Fairbank's authoritative *The United States and China*. The first edition, published in 1948, reflected the author's fascination with the country that began during his stay as a graduate student in Beijing in the 1930s and developed further while he worked at the US embassy in China in the 1940s. Fairbank's intention in the fourth edition "to explain China to Americans so we could live in peace and friendship" (1983, xiii) marks the one-sided perspective of conventional studies of the relationship between China and America. Likewise, the first Chinese accounts of America are based on personal experiences of graduate students in the United States. The autobiographies written from an American perspective by Yan Phou Lee (1887) and Yung Wing (1909) are cases in point. American studies scholars interested in China and America have used sources by Chinese immigrants in the United States for their critical studies. Thus the story of Chinese immigration to the United States has been analyzed politically and culturally since the days of the Californian Gold Rush in the second half of the nineteenth century, and numerous studies exist on the history of Chinese American literature (Meissenburg 1987). More recently, Sau-ling Wong, formerly at the University of California, Berkeley, has written one of the standard works in regard to the interpretation of Chinese-American literature (1993), which was later translated into Chinese (2007; see also Tunc, Marino, and Kim 2012). Xiao-huang Yin (2000) discovered new early examples of Chinese American literature, and Chinese American literature in Chinese has been collected by Him Mark Lai, Genny Lim and Judy Yung (1991). Mita Banerjee, Carmen Birkle, and Wilfried Raussert (2006) dedicated a thematic issue of *Amerikastudien/American Studies* to the European view of Asian American literature. And Brigitte Capelle (2011, 2013) has focused on the Japanese and Chinese interactions with American transcendentalism and pragmatism, including Asian perceptions of nature.

The engagements of Chinese scholars with American studies have long been determined by the political climate of dissent and have been subject to the waves of anti-Americanism flaring up sporadically after Deng Xiaoping's opening up of China and reforms in the 1980s. The contributions to Priscilla Roberts's edited volume *Bridging the Sino-American Divide* (2007) clearly demonstrates this ideological bias. More valuable studies have been undertaken by Chinese students of American studies abroad, such as Shanshan Yan's dissertation, "Americanization in China" (2010). Shelley Fisher Fishkin is collaborating with Gordon Chang in the Stanford Chinese Railroad Workers in North America Project to collect documents on the many thousands of Chinese laborers in the United States and China (G. Chang and Fishkin. n.d.). In similarly innovative work, the German Americanists Vanessa Künnemann and Ruth Mayer have put together two volumes that assemble original articles by European, American, and Chinese scholars, one volume with a focus on pre-communist China (2009) and the other comparing the architecture and culture of Chinese neighborhoods in the United States and Europe (2011). Künnemann and Mayer's triangular approach corresponds to my own conception of ChinAmerica—which, however, also includes the notion of the planetary perspective and is an instructive study object that demonstrates the values of a transnational American studies approach that supersedes existing binational studies. In his description of the Dartmouth Series in American Studies, "Remapping the Transnational," Donald Pease rightly states that "the emergence of Transnational American Studies in the wake of the Cold War marks the most significant reconfiguration of American Studies since its inception" (2011). Following moves toward internationalization of American studies research and comparatist methods, this new transnational approach provides an effective methodology appropriate for the analysis of transcultural and transnational developments.

Although the status of the "American" contained in this approach points in the direction of the United States and was seen by critics as a new version of American exceptionalism in scholarship (Pease 2009), the egalitarian collaboration of American studies scholars worldwide in drafting and launching the transnational American studies approach transcends the danger of national bias (Fishkin 2005; Hornung 2005). Thus it implies an extension of the field of research beyond the geographical boundaries of the United

States to areas where aspects of Americanness exist. Leaving behind the earlier conflation of the term with the international, the multinational, the global, and the diasporic (see Vertovec 2009), transnational American studies is now increasingly recognized as a discipline in academic institutions both in the United States and abroad. It builds on and expands regional concepts, such as European American studies or Asian American studies, and it transcends these principally dialogical interrelations multilaterally (see Tunc, Marino, and Kim 2012). The underlying common denominator is the direct or indirect presence of aspects of Americanness that are embraced, critiqued, or rejected in different parts of the world (Hornung 2011b; Robinson 2011; Rowe 2011). Methodologically, transnational American studies provides new approaches to correlate the local and the national to American phenomena in a process of mutual enhancement, in which the perspectives of American studies scholars outside of the United States can also prove to be more important than the ones of American scholars based in the United States. After years of claiming a superior status for their scholarship, us Americanists have recognized the quality and importance of the new insights of American studies scholars abroad (see Fluck, Brandt, and Thaler 2007; Ostendorf 2002). This common methodological basis also allows scholars in countries critical of the United States to surpass conventional ideological positions and to engage in new areas of research beyond the traditional canon of American studies. Hence my application of the transnational American studies approach seeks to include non-American positions and to create a balance between two national cultures captured in the term ChinAmerica. The three phases of the political and cultural relations between China and America span the range of the twentieth century from binational exchanges via intercultural manifestations to transnational achievements at the beginning of the twenty-first century, and they describe the trajectory from modernism through postmodernism to neorealism. Each of the three stages features key figures—such as Sun Yat-sen and Ezra Pound, Mao Tse-tung and Andy Warhol, and Mao Tse-tung and Barack Obama—in politics and popular culture to examine the correlation of Chinese and American cultural work for the creation of common political and ecological interests. Transnational American studies, hence, also contributes to the formation of a planetary consciousness (see Hornung 2014).

Modernity and Modernism 1912: The Interaction between Politics and Culture

The first period of my transnational analysis of ChinAmerica marks a significant revolutionary moment in Chinese politics and Western culture. The end of the dynasties of Chinese emperors in 1911 and the foundation of the Republic of China in 1912 coincide with the international movement of modernism. These events constitute a radical break with Chinese and Western traditions, respectively, for the sake of innovation in terms of politics and culture. In the same way in which modern Chinese turned to Western forms of government, modern artists in the West discovered newness in Eastern cultures. This cross-fertilization also seemed evident in the economic relations between China and the United States at the turn of the nineteenth to the twentieth century. The construction of railroads in the United States and in China on the one hand linked the imperialistic American interests and expansion with the Chinese interests in technological advancement. On the other hand, that construction juxtaposed President Theodore Roosevelt's open door policy, described in his 1908 address "The Awakening of China" (see Künnemann and Mayer 2009, 5 and 8) with the drastic constraint on Chinese immigration and the Qing dynasty's claim to represent overseas Chinese in the New World. On different levels, these are cross-cultural processes of modernization. Employing my transnational American studies approach, I would like to illustrate a more productive interaction of politics and culture with regard to Sun Yat-sen, the founder of the Chinese Republic in 1912, and Ezra Pound, the founder of modern poetry, as encapsulated in his famous slogan "MAKE IT NEW" (1935).

A crucial point in my analysis is Sun's evolution from his origin in the rural southern Chinese province of Canton to his eminent political position by way of his experience in Hawai'i. The sojourn of Chinese in the United States or on the islands of Hawai'i toward the end of the nineteenth century is part of the migration of young men either to pursue a Western education or to find work to alleviate economic hardship back in China. In either case, the men intended to return to their homeland. Sun joined his brother in Hawai'i, attended Iolani School, an Anglican-run boarding school, and matriculated in 1878 at Oahu College—coincidentally the same institution, later renamed Punahou School, where Barack Obama was a student almost a century later. Even before the annexation of the Polynesian archipelago by the United States in 1898, the kingdom of Hawai'i was under American and Christian influence. Afraid of Sun's leanings toward Christianity, his brother sent him back to China, where he earned a medical degree in Hong Kong, converted to Christianity, and eventually became a politician. Further stays abroad—such as his exile in Japan after the first Sino-Japanese war in 1895; fundraising tours to Europe and North America; and two more stays in Hawai'i in 1894 and 1904, when he enlisted the help of Chinese guest workers to promote his republican ideas (see Schiffrin 1968)—shaped his political career and revolutionary spirit. With the foundation of the Chinese Republic in 1912, based on the Western principles of nationalism, democracy, and the well-being of the people, Sun contributed to the promotion of China's opening to the West, counteracting Roosevelt's imperialistic mission. The combination of Sun's English and American formal education, exposure to Christian religion, and Western political ideas constituted the platform for his political career. The end to China's long imperial history and the subsequent creation of the Chinese Republic also redefined the role of the European colonial powers in China and revealed the imperialistic efforts of Japan and the United States (see Teng and Fairbank 1972). In my examination I correlate these changes to the radical innovations of modern poetics as embodied by the American poet Ezra Pound.

Pound's revolutionary impact on the formation of modern poetics is similar to the impact of Sun on Chinese politics. Furthermore, both men developed their new ideas as expatriates in a cultural environment different from their home. Pound's move from a provincial background in Idaho and education at the University of Pennsylvania to an international career in Europe with a focus on Euro-American literatures included an interest in Asian languages, particularly Japanese and Chinese. In 1908, at the beginning of the imagist movement, Pound received a manuscript written by the late Harvard professor Ernest Fenollosa; Pound edited the manuscript, which was published as *The Chinese Written Character as a Medium for Poetry* in 1918 (see Fenollosa and Pound 2008).[1] The series of essays that Pound started writing in 1912, published as MAKE IT NEW, relate directly to Chinese ideograms and the long tradition of the Chinese empire (Pound 1935; Symons 1987). Pound actually finds the source of his modernist credo "MAKE IT NEW" on the bathtub of Emperor Tching Tang (Qianlong; 1711–1799, ruled officially 1735–96) from the Qing dynasty and incorporates it into his *Cantos* (figure 13.1). It is the central theme in Canto 53 (1957, 274–75).

After seven years of drought, the Chinese famine cannot be ended by money but only by the emperor's prayer for rain. This story is related to the legendary book by Kao-Yao, in which the common people are endowed with great power: "Heaven can see and hear and that through the eyes and ears of the people; heaven rewards the people of virtue and punishes the wicked ones and that through the people" (Qu 1969, 22).[2] Pound uses the reinstatement of this interpretation in Confucian philosophy and transforms it into the poetological principle of creativity to revitalize the sterility of modern art in the West with spiritual values from the East. Thus he counteracts the attempts of intellectuals in the new Chinese Republic to turn against the cultural achievements of China. Against the anti-Confucian stance of his acquaintance F. T. Song, Pound sets the Western appreciation of Chinese culture: "At a time when China has replaced Greece in the intellectual life of

KAO-YAO

abundance.
Then an Empress fled with Chao Kang in her belly.
Fou-hi by virtue of wood;
Ching-nong, of fire; Hoang Ti ruled by the earth,
Chun by metal.
Tchuen was lord, as is water.
CHUN, govern
YU, cultivate,
The surface is not enough,
    from Chang Ti nothing is hidden.
For years no waters came, no rain fell
    for the Emperor Tching Tang
grain scarce, prices rising
so that in 1766 Tching Tang opened the copper mine (ante
                                        Christum)
made discs with square holes in their middles
    and gave these to the people
wherewith they might buy grain
                where there was grain
The silos were emptied
7 years of sterility
            der im Baluba das Gewitter gemacht hat
Tching prayed on the mountain and
                274

wrote MAKE IT NEW
on his bath tub
        Day by day make it new
cut underbrush,
pile the logs
keep it growing.
Died Tching aged years an hundred,
in the 13th of his reign.
        'We are up, Hia is down.'
Immoderate love of women
Immoderate love of riches,
Cared for parades and huntin'.
        Chang Ti above alone rules.
Tang not stinting of praise:
        Consider their sweats, the people's
If you wd/ sit calm on throne.

Hia! Hia is fallen
    for offence to the spirits
For sweats of the people.
        Not by your virtue
        but by virtue of Tching Tang
Honour to YU, converter of waters
Honour Tching Tang
Honour to YN
seek old men and new tools
                275

FIGURE 13.1. Ezra Pound, *The Cantos of Ezra Pound* (London: Faber, 1957) 274–75.

so many occidentals, it is interesting to see in what way the occidental ideas
are percolating into the orient" (quoted in Qian 2009, 132).

Pound's reception of the creative principle of "MAKE IT NEW" on the emperor's bathtub in Chinese ideograms, transmitted by way of Confucius,
takes on an additional meaning when seen in the contextual arrangement
of Canto 53 as part of a series of twenty cantos on Chinese and American
history first published in 1940 (Cantos 52–71 in Pound 1957; see also Hornung 1994, 308). It is the second of ten cantos on the succession of Chinese
dynasties, which are followed by ten cantos on John Adams and the early
American republic. The contrast between the old Chinese tradition of imperial rule and the young American democracy is part of how Pound shows
the influence of Chinese ideas on Western thinking, which he also treats in
the series of cantos *Jefferson—Nuevo Mundo* (Cantos 31–41). In these cantos,
Pound relates the correspondence of John Adams and Thomas Jefferson to
Confucian philosophy in an attempt "to measure the letters against the teachings of Confucius" and to reveal that "throughout the correspondence"
both presidents "are concerned with the precise definition of terms, which
lies at the heart of the Confucian ethic" (Kearns 1980, 80).

The application of a transnational American studies approach makes it
possible to correlate Sun's politics with Pound's poetics at the beginning of

the twentieth century in this first example of ChinAmerica. Pound's trans-national mediation between the teachings of Confucian ethics in the Chinese monarchy and American democratic ideas can be compared to Sun's appli-cation of democratic principles in the constitution of the Chinese Repub-lic and the end of the monarchy. Both transnational achievements coincide with the ideas of the Jewish American cultural critic Randolph Bourne, who dismisses the melting pot idea and uses his essay "Trans-National America" (1916) to shape the concept of a new America, which reaches out for other cultures and ideas. It is the beginning of a transnational spirit and increas-ing exchanges, most prominently represented by the pragmatic philosopher John Dewey, whose stay in China from 1919 to 1921 became the basis for an intensive ChinAmerican process of mutual teaching and learning (see Wang 2007).

Maoism and Postmodernism: Cultural Revolutions of the 1960s and 1970s

In line with Chinese tradition, Mao also embraced Kao-Yao's legendary mes-sage, which invests sovereign power in the people to execute a divine will (see J. Chang and Halliday 2007, 5–6). In this sense Mao, like Sun, le-gitimizes the Chinese revolution and appears as the representative of the people's rights. In the Western world a versatile Mao cult developed during the course of the 1960s. It was part of a youth protest culture in North America and Europe against the hierarchical structures of the parent gener-ation and expressed the search for alternative philosophies of life. Mao and the *Quotations from Chairman Mao Tse-tung* (1966), known in the West as the Little Red Book, become powerful symbols of resistance against the capitalist system and military interventions such as the war in Vietnam. At the same time, the juvenile enthusiasm for Maoism reflected the revolution-ary spirit of the time and can easily be related to the culture of postmod-ernism. Jan Wong, a Canadian student of Chinese descent, captures this postmodern Maoist spirit—which motivated her to become one of the first two North Americans accepted as exchange students at Peking University in 1972—in her autobiography *Red China Blues* (1996). Her classification as an overseas Chinese was only the beginning of a general disillusionment that culminated in her rejection of China's political system during her later visits to the country.

While the foundation of the People's Republic of China in 1949 was based on the erection of Mao's rigid regime and the radical transformation of Chinese society, the reception of Mao's teachings in the West for Marxist activism gradually turned into the popular fashion of radical chic (Wolfe 1970). In the United States prominent postmodernists like the pop artist

Andy Warhol and the playwright Edward Albee stand for a playful engagement with the Mao cult. Albee uses his short play *Quotations from Chairman Mao Tse-tung* (1971), first performed in 1968, for postmodern alienation effects. While Albee wants the Mao figure on stage to possess Asian features, he gives the figure the role of a teacher whose lessons—directly taken from the Little Red Book—are not heard. The other three characters in the play are a Long-Winded Lady, an Old Woman, and a Minister. Except for the Minister, who does not have a speaking part, all other characters recite their texts without communicating with each other. According to Chris Bigsby, the play is "a collage of words and images; it uses surrealistic methods not to reveal the marvellous but to penetrate the bland façade of modern reality—personal, religious, and political" (1975, 157). The play takes place on a steamboat in the middle of the ocean, a location that emphasizes the emptiness of the political jargon without an audience. While this playful deconstruction of the referential quality of words serves Albee's intention to stage experimental theatre, it also serves his purpose to reject "escapist romances," such as Maoism. "A playwright," Albee writes in the introduction, "has two obligations: first, to make some statement about the condition of 'man' (as it is put) and, second, to make some statement about the nature of the art form with which he is working. In both instances he must attempt change. In the first instance . . . the playwright must try to alter his society; in the second instance . . . the playwright must try to alter the forms within which his precursors have had to work" (1971, 124).

Both objectives are part of Albee's project to work for change. The frequent references by Chairman Mao in the play to the ideological struggle of the Chinese Communist Party against American imperialism is early on connected to the divine power invested in the people: "Today, two big mountains lie like a dead weight on the Chinese people. One is imperialism, the other is feudalism. The Chinese Communist Party has long made up its mind to dig them up. We must persevere and work unceasingly, and we, too, will touch God's heart. Our God is none other than the masses of the Chinese people" (Albee 1971, 138).

Albee's intention to deconstruct Mao's political rhetoric as empty phraseology also refers to Mao's evocation of Kao-Yao's legend about the power of the people. Mao's definition of his position as the servant of the people is as elusive as the "escapist romances" of Western Maoists.

Andy Warhol also takes up the Mao cult. In an analogy to his Marilyn Monroe silk-screen prints of the 1960s, Warhol created a series of Mao prints starting in 1972, probably in response to the new diplomatic ties between China and the United States (figure 13.2). Similar to the glamor of Monroe, the quintessential American sex symbol of the 1950s, the political

FIGURE 13.2. Andy Warhol, "Mao Portrait." © 2012. The Andy Warhol Foundation for the Visual Arts, Inc. / Artists Rights Society (ARS), New York.

glamor of Chairman Mao was being deconstructed by Warhol. Compared with Mao's official state portrait overlooking Tiananmen Square, which holds the Great Hall of the People and Mao's mausoleum, and which Warhol visited in the fall of 1982, Warhol's postmodern representation disfigures the eminent leader and reduces him to a series of small figures.

According to Jean-François Lyotard's classic study *The Postmodern Condition* (1984), Mao's master narrative dissolves into many small anecdotes, similar to the staging in Albee's experimental play.[3] To what extent the so-called ping-pong diplomacy by US Secretary of State Henry Kissinger can also be related to the playfulness of postmodern art as a prelude to the transnational resolution of political differences is still subject to analysis (see Kissinger 2011, 232–35).[4] But without a doubt, the conversations between President Richard Nixon and Chairman Mao in 1972 reestablished the diplomatic ties between their respective countries after years of ideological opposition and meant the beginning of economic cooperation (see ibid.).

Similar to my first example of ChinAmerica, in the case of the postmodern reception of the Mao cult, the transnational American studies approach relates the events of cultural revolutions in China, North America, and Europe and reveals their common objective of deconstructing authority figures and bourgeois conventions. The approach also goes beyond the one-sided Western scholarship on postmodernism and its analysis of decorative innovations in the 1960s by focusing on the neglected operations of underground activities as the source of cultural revolutions and the underlying political meaning of a romanticized reception of Maoism (cf. Hornung 2015). Paul Clark's history of the Chinese Cultural Revolution (2008) is a first attempt to take account of neglected sources and their influence on the formation of contemporary Chinese culture. New forms of literature and culture emerge from the new political situation, but they are usually omitted from the political account of the Cultural Revolution.

Pop Culture and Neorealism

The transnational reach of pop culture as exemplified in Warhol's series of Mao silk-screen prints relates directly to the current state of cultural interaction at the turn of the twentieth century. Don DeLillo, an American writer of Italian descent, saw these reproductions of Mao in the New York Museum of Modern Art in 1989 as part of an Andy Warhol retrospective. They inspired him to write his novel *Mao II* (1991; see figure 13.3), but in that work he moved away from his earlier postmodern fiction.

Having lived through the period of the Mao cult and postmodernism in the 1960s and 1970s, DeLillo links Warhol's Mao figure in *Mao II* to the reality of terrorism and political violence that operate on a global scale. Hence critics have read this neorealist novel as an account of increasing terrorism and have stressed the interrelation between the media and fiction, especially the visual poetics of DeLillo's fiction (see Ickstadt 2002). The connection between Warhol's pop art and the inclusion of Mao in DeLillo's novel has not received much attention (see Karnicky 2001; Olster 2011). The juxtaposition of the Mao figure with the fictional writer Bill Gray, who eventually becomes a victim of terrorism in Lebanon, seems to be part of DeLillo's "strategy of initial contrast and increasing convergence" (Schneck 2007, 117). Contrast and convergence seem to underlie DeLillo's representation of the commercialized Mao cult of the 1960s, and they form part of a revisionist perspective of the period, including ideological reinterpretations.

FIGURE 13.3. Cover of Don DeLillo, *Mao II*.

While Chinese scholars like Mobo Gao (2008) attempt to counteract the demonizing perception of Mao and the Cultural Revolution in the West by pointing to the benefits of Maoism for the rural poor and the urban working class, DeLillo takes Mao and his political inheritance to task. Hence the Mao references, including the quotation "Our god is none other than the masses of the Chinese people" from the Little Red Book and mentions of the Cultural Revolution (DeLillo 1991, 162–63), are set against depictions of the television coverage of student demonstrations in Tiananmen Square on June 4, 1989 (ibid., 176–78). The depoliticized Mao poster contrasts with the reincarnation of Mao as a technologically reproduced *Mao II*, who has to account for the massacre, even though it was Deng Xiaoping whose policies of reform and opening China up to the West (that is, his idea of a socialism with Chinese characteristics), begun in 1978, had fostered democratic yearnings among the young generation squashed in the military repression (see Kissinger 2011, 335–36). DeLillo's alignment of these televised pictures with Warhol's Mao stands for the transformation of political contrast through the mediation of pop art into the transcultural convergence of a transnational world.

This aspect of convergence was the subject of an exhibition organized by Britta Erickson in 2005 at the Cantor Center for Visual Arts at Stanford University, titled "On the Edge: Contemporary Chinese Artists Encounter the West." Erickson assembled works by "Political Pop" artists of the 1980s and 1990s in China "who '[defuse] potent political imagery' by fusing it with 'an American pop sensibility' indebted to Andy Warhol, Roy Lichtenstein and others to critique the 'current condition of Chinese culture'" (quoted in Fishkin 2006, 23–24). Erickson's intent to exhibit the encounter of Chinese artists with the West can also be seen as a form of convergence of pop culture. Warhol's deconstruction of the Mao portrait is also the subject of many Chinese pop artists, particularly those who lived in exile in the United States. In his "Long Live Chairman Mao" series, Zhang Hongtu reproduces the omnipresent picture of Mao on an ordinary Quaker Oats container. The eerie resemblance between the communist leader and the Quaker farmer mixes propaganda, religion, and ideology with commercial kitsch and celebrity cult. Yu Youhan transplants Mao to New York as an exotic imitation of the Statue of Liberty in 1996 (figure 13.4) or as a contrast between the symbol of freedom and political repression.

Li Shan and Liu Dahong set their visual deconstruction of Mao in a Chinese context. Li represents Mao as a double and gendered figure, relating the chairman to his wife, Jiang Qing, the leader of the Gang of Four (2005). Liu's critical engagement with Mao and the Cultural Revolution includes the transformation of the Mao mausoleum on Tiananmen Square into an inhospitable, ghostly building. In both cases, the artists attempt to bring Mao down "from his pedestal and expose the relationship that existed between him and the Chinese people as bizarre" (Erickson 2004, 22). All of these pop cultural designs also have a global political reading that seems to fuse formerly contrasting voices. The fact that these works by Chinese artists in exile are now exhibited in China, like Yu Youhan's "Mao and the Statue of Liberty" in the Shanghart Gallery in Shanghai, shows to what extent the positions of the artist and Erickson, the curator, converge with the public perception in China of artistic circles. Tracing the transcultural travels of these exhibits will be part of future research that will lead to new insights into the potential acceptance of pop art by dissidents in contemporary China.

The current stage of transnational pop culture as a manifestation of ChinAmerica was reached in the presidency of Barack Obama, especially with his first visit to China in November 2009. Chinese society's fascination with the charismatic president, which one Chinese in Wuhan expressed by undergoing facial surgery to resemble Obama, was counterbalanced by the reservation of the Chinese politicians. In contrast to the visits by Presidents Bill Clinton and George W. Bush to Beijing in 1998 and 2002, respectively,

FIGURE 13.4. Yu Youhan, "Mao and
Statue of Liberty." © Courtesy
of Yu Youhan and Shanghart
Gallery, Shanghai (1996).

Obama's visit featured alleged students—actually officials in Communist
youth organizations—at a town hall meeting in Shanghai who asked relatively moderate questions. Obama's choice of Shanghai instead of Beijing
for his first programmatic speech in China was seen as an act of solidarity
with the common Chinese people, corroborated by the skin color of the first
nonwhite president of the United States of America, which created a bond
of nonwhite ethnicity.⁵ Obama's closeness to China and the Chinese people,
augmented by the residence of his half-brother Mark Ndesandjo in Shenzhen,
PRC, establishes a form of fraternization between Asia, Africa, and Latin
America—and hence all of America. The popular acclaim of the American
president is also the basis of the new popular culture that developed in the
context of his visit in China. Obviously, the commercial aspect of the pop
cultural use of Obama shows in many items on sale for tourists. Similar to
the Chinese pop artists in the United States, who create an Americanized
Mao, popular culture in China designs a sinicized image of the American
president. Similar to my coinage of the term "ChinAmerica," Chinese popular culture has coined the names "Maobama" and "Obamao" that are
visible on T-shirts, touristic paraphernalia, and the Internet and in cartoons.
However, what surpasses the commercial nature of pop art is Obama's portrait on a T-shirt with the inscription "serve the people" in the famous calligraphy of Mao Tse-tung, familiar to all Chinese people (figure 13.5).
The combination of the transnational mind-set of the American president

FIGURE 13.5. Mao, "Serve the People: Wearing the Red Army Suit Obama Turned Obamao." *Sing Tao Daily Online*. 25 Sep. 2009, 20 Apr. 2010.

with the ideological direction of the Chinese chairman suggests a revision of Mao's alleged role as the servant of the people—a position that, according to Kao-Yao, is derived from heaven. At the beginning of the twenty-first century some popular artists suggest (see, for example figure 13.6) that the transfer of power from Mao to a sinicized Obama is better than for the Chinese leaders to hold that position.

I read the pop cultural vision of Obamao or Maobama as an expression of transcultural convergence that replaces global competitiveness and ideological contrasts with the consensus of a transnational community. It is my assumption, supported by the history of political changes brought about through pop cultural work (see Ryback 1990), that the power of visual images plays an important role in the development of ChinAmerica in a transnational world. More research is required into the acceptance of these pop cultural images in Chinese society.

The coinage of the name Obamao or Maobama indicates a transnational amalgamation. It stands for the successive integration of the American president into the Chinese student and working world and seems to suggest the transnational realization of ChinAmerica as a vision for the twenty-first century.

In what way the visual power of pictures plays a role in this development of a transnational world, as demonstrated in Fishkin's "Asian Crossroads/

FIGURE 13.6. "Chairman Obamao."

Transnational American Studies" (2006), still needs further research. It re-connects us with Pound's fascination with Chinese ideograms and their influence on the international movement of imagism as well as the implicit relationship of Chinese characters to pictorial thinking.[6]

The transnational dimension of images will also contribute to the formation of a planetary community as part of a concern with ecology, which is simultaneously advanced by activists and political leaders. Although there were serious difficulties with the role of the Nobel Peace Prize laureate Barack Obama as an exemplary planetary citizen at the Copenhagen climate summit of 2009 (see Hornung 2011a), the apparent linkage of peace work and ecology in recent decisions of the Nobel Prize committee also promotes the raising of a planetary consciousness worldwide. Such a planetary vision is also the subject of a remarkable passage about two people walking on the Great Wall in Don DeLillo's *Mao II*. Over dinner Brita relates this story to her friend Karen:

> Brita said, "I've heard about a man and woman who are walking the length of the Great Wall of China, approaching each other from opposite directions. Every time I think of them, I see them from above, with the Wall twisting and winding through the landscape and two tiny human figures moving toward

each other from remote provinces, step by step. I think this is a story of reverence for the planet, of trying to understand how we belong to the planet in a new way. And it's strange how I construct an aerial view so naturally."

"Hikers in shaggy boots," Karen said.

"No, artists. And the Great Wall is supposedly the only man-made structure visible from space, so we see it as part of the total planet. And this man and woman walk and walk. They're artists. I don't know what nationality. But it's an art piece. It's not Nixon and Mao shaking hands. It's not nationality, not politics." (DeLillo 1991, 70)

This "story of reverence for the planet" of two artists with no specific national affiliation seen from an aerial position in outer space projects a vision of ChinAmerica inspired by transnational imagination. Hence the production and reception of popular culture can function as a forerunner—or, better, as an avant-garde—of political change. The realization of ChinAmerica in the twenty-first century hinges on the collaborative efforts of individuals and supporting agencies. Increasing cooperation between academic associations on a transnational scale, often initiated by national American studies associations, is a promising sign. The foundation of the Chinese Association of American Studies after Mao's death affirms the transnational direction of the field. Supported by the US-China Education Trust, founded in 1998, several conferences have taken place that implicitly promote the vision of ChinAmerica. Roberts's volume of papers given at the annual conference of the Chinese Association of American Studies in Hong Kong in 2006 has the significant title of *Bridging the Sino-American Divide* (2007). In spite of all the differences, the opinions expressed in these essays by American, Chinese, and European scholars and critics also indicate a transnational convergence and help counteract some of the contrasting aspects of the political realities in both China and the United States, especially with regard to human rights (see Wan 2001). But I am also acutely aware of counterarguments like those made by Fareed Zakaria, which proclaim the coming of *The Post-American World* (2011), or predict the rise of China, as Martin Jacques does in *When China Rules the World* (2009). Instead, my argument finds support in a more recent study by Ferguson, *Civilization* (2011), in which he describes periods of cultural and political dominance in world history. The dominance of Asian cultures up until 1500 has been succeeded by 500 years of dominance by the West (see also Schmidt 2013, 11). Rather than engaging in an unproductive battle of divergence, Ferguson advocates convergence for the twenty-first century. Transnational scholarship seems to chart the way, as is evident in increasing cooperative works by Chinese, European, and American researchers in the form of joint publications (Blair and McCormack 2010); recently founded journals like *Critical Zone: A Forum of Chinese and Western Knowledge* and the *Journal of Transnational American Studies*, which began publication in 2006 and 2009, respectively; and regular conferences (see Tong, Wang, and Kerr 2006; Huber and Zhao 2011). A very effective example of a transnational ChinAmerican vision is that of the late Steve Jobs, who used the commencement address at Stanford University in 2005 to tell students that he had dropped out of the regular courses at Reed College and subsequently used his spare time to study calligraphy, which in turn gave him the essential impulse for the Apple design: "I learned about serif and sans serif typefaces, about varying the amount of space between different letter combinations, about what makes great typography great. It was beautiful, historical, artistically subtle in a way that science can't capture, and I found it fascinating. . . . If I had never dropped in on that single course in college, the Mac would have never had multiple typefaces or proportionally spaced fonts. And since Windows just copied the Mac, it's likely that no personal computer would have them" (quoted in Isaacson 2011, 40–41).

Jobs's interrelation of Chinese calligraphy and American technology, which includes the economic fabrication of Apple products in Shenzhen, China, hopefully also prefigures the political realization of ChinAmerica.

Notes

This is an expanded version of an earlier essay: "ChinAmerica: Intercultural Relations for a Transnational World," in *Transnational American Studies*, edited by Udo J. Hebel (Heidelberg: Universitätsverlag Winter, 2012) 13–30.

1. Both Eastern and Western scholars have pointed to Pound's misreading of the Chinese writing system. Along with Fenollosa, he thought "that Chinese ideography was so pictographically transparent (as opposed to phonetic writing), that one could decipher the characters without even knowing Chinese" (Williams 2009, 150). Zhang Longxi argues that Chinese writing is not pictographic or ideographic "because the characters are linguistic signs of concepts and represent sound and meaning of words rather than pictographic representations of things themselves" (1999, 44). Pound's *Cathay* (1915), a volume of poems that he allegedly translated from the Chinese, are now considered "modernist scandals," for he was not proficient in the Chinese language (Williams 2009). Nevertheless, they document his serious engagement with Chinese tradition and its impact on Anglo-American modernism.

2. This translation from the Chinese is by Zheng Chunguang. James Legge provided a different translation: "Heaven hears and sees as our people hear and see; Heaven brightly approves and displays its terrors as our people brightly approve and would awe" (Mueller 1899, 56).

3. In his contribution to *ANDY WARHOL CHINA 1982*, the Chinese artist Ai Weiwei writes that the Mao portrait is the most famous of Warhol's portrait figures: "The ubiquitous portrait caused Mao Zedong to be looked upon as a god in China. However, in Andy's rendering, the allegorical force of Mao's portrait was made conventional, its enormity neutral, objectified, emptied of its moral value as well as its aesthetic intent" (Ai 2008, 5).

4. Peter Wise calls Warhol's Mao silk-screen prints "Ping-Pong Pop" (2008, 3).

5. During my seven-month guest professorship at Peking University in 2009, I could closely follow in many of the lectures I gave on Barack Obama's autobiography to capacity crowds of students at different Chinese universities the reception of the new American president among the young generation of Chinese. At the beginning of Obama's second term, the uninhibited fascination of young Chinese with him wore off.

6. Pointing to Zhaoming Qian's observation that Pound criticism has "ignored the crucial role of China in the development of Anglo-American modernism," John Williams recognizes the resurrection of Pound's Chineseness by the Misty Poets, a group of post–Cultural Revolution authors in China, "who turned to Pound as a radical model for their creation of a new transnational literary tradition" (2009, 156–57).

Bibliography

Ai, Weiwei. 2008. "Light as a Feather." In *ANDY WARHOL CHINA 1982*, edited by Peter Wise, 5. Hong Kong: Timezone 8.

Albee, Edward. 1971. *Tiny Alice, Box, and Quotations from Chairman Mao Tse-Tung.* Harmondsworth, UK: Penguin.

Banerjee, Mita, Carmen Birkle, and Wilfried Raussert, eds. 2006. "Asian American Studies in Europe." Special issue of *Amerikastudien/American Studies* 51 (3).

Bigsby, Chris. W. E. 1975. "*Box* and *Quotations from Chairman Mao Tse-Tung*: Albee's Diptych." In *Edward Albee: A Collection of Critical Essays*, edited by Chris W. E. Bigsby, 151–64. Englewood Cliffs, NJ: Prentice.

Blair, John G., and Jerusha Hull McCormack, eds. 2010. *Western Civilization with Chinese Comparisons.* Shanghai: Fudan University Press.

Bourne, Randolph. 1916. "Trans-National America." *Atlantic Monthly*, July, 86–97.

Capelle, Birgit. 2011. *TIME in American and East Asian Thinking: A Comparative Study of Temporality in American Transcendentalism, Pragmatism, and (Zen) Buddhist Thought.* Heidelberg: Universitätsverlag Winter.

———. 2013. "Asian Aspects of Temporal Experience in Transcendentalist Life Writing." In *Ecology and Life Writing*, edited by Alfred Hornung, 99–108. Heidelberg: Universitätsverlag Winter.

Chang, Gordon, and Shelley Fisher Fishkin. n.d. "Chinese Railroad Workers Project at Stanford University." http://web.stanford.edu/group/chineserailroad/cgi-bin/word press/. Accessed May 20, 2015.

Chang, Jung, and Jon Halliday. 2007. *Mao: The Unknown Story.* London: Vintage.

Clark, Paul. 2008. *The Chinese Cultural Revolution: A History*. New York: Cambridge University Press.

DeLillo, Don. 1991. *Mao II*. New York: Penguin.

DeLoughrey, Elizabeth, and George B. Handley, eds. 2011. *Postcolonial Ecologies: Literatures of the Environment*. Oxford: Oxford University Press.

Erickson, Britta. 2004. *On the Edge: Contemporary Chinese Artists Encounter the West*. Stanford, CA: Iris and B. Gerald Cantor Center for Visual Arts at Stanford University.

Fairbank, John King. 1983. *The United States and China*. 4th ed. Cambridge, MA: Harvard University Press.

Fenollosa, Ernest, and Ezra Pound. 2008. *The Chinese Written Character as a Medium for Poetry: A Critical Edition*, edited by Haun Saussy, Jonathan Stalling, and Lucas Klein. New York: Fordham University Press.

Ferguson, Niall. 2008. *The Ascent of Money: A Financial History of the World*. London: Allen Lane.

———. 2011. *Civilization: The West and the Rest*. London: Penguin.

——— and Moritz Schularick. 2007. "Chimerical? Think Again." *Wall Street Journal*, February 5.

Fishkin, Shelley Fisher. 2005. "Crossroads of Cultures: The Transnational Turn in American Studies—Presidential Address to the American Studies Association, November 12, 2004." *American Quarterly* 57 (1): 17–57.

———. 2006. "Asian Crossroads/Transnational American Studies." *Japanese Journal of American Studies* 17:5–52.

Fluck, Winfried, Stefan Brandt, and Ingrid Thaler, eds. 2007. *Transnational American Studies*. Vol. 23 of *REAL: Yearbook of Research in English and American Literature*. Tübingen: Gunter Narr Verlag.

Fluck, Winfried, Donald E. Pease, and John Carlos Rowe, eds. 2011. *Re-Framing the Transnational Turn in American Studies*. Hanover, NH: Dartmouth College Press.

Gao, Mobo. 2008. *The Battle for China's Past: Mao and the Cultural Revolution*. London: Pluto.

Gilroy, Paul. 2006. *Postcolonial Melancholia*. New York: Columbia University Press.

Hebel, Udo J., ed. 2012. *Transnational American Studies*. Heidelberg: Universitätsverlag Winter.

Heise, Ursula. 2008. *Sense of Place and Sense of Planet: The Environmental Imagination of the Global*. New York: Oxford University Press.

Hornung, Alfred. 1994. "'MAKE IT NEW': The Concept of Newness in American Studies." In *Anglistentag 1993 Eichstätt*, edited by Günther Blaicher, 307–19. Tübingen, Germany: Niemeyer.

———. 2005. "Transnational American Studies: Response to the Presidential Address." *American Quarterly* 57 (1): 67–73.

————. 2011a. "Planetary Citizenship." *Journal of Transnational American Studies* 3 (1): 39–46. https://escholarship.org/uc/item/8n55g7q6. Accessed May 20, 2015.

————. 2011b. "Transnationalism and American Studies: The View from Abroad." *Encyclopedia of American Studies Online*. http://www.theasa.net/project_eas_online/ page/project_eas_online_eas_featured_article/. Accessed on May 20, 2015.

————. 2012. "ChinAmerica: Intercultural Relations for a Transnational World." In *Transnational American Studies*, edited by Udo J. Hebel, 13–30. Heidelberg: Universitätsverlag Winter.

————. 2014. "The Planetary Vision of American Studies." In *Kültürötesi Bir Gezgin: Gönül Pultar'a Armağan Kitabı—A Transcultural Wanderer: A Festschrift for Gönül Pultar*, edited by Mustafa Pultar, 269–76. Istanbul: Tetragon Yayınları.

————. 2015. "Maoism and Postmodernism." *European Review* 23(2): 261–72.

Huber, Jörg, and Zhao Chuan, eds. 2011. *A New Thoughtfulness in Contemporary China: Critical Voices in Art and Aesthetics*. Bielefeld, Germany: Transcript.

Ickstadt, Heinz. 2002. "Bilder des Terrors und der Terror der Bilder in den Romanen Don DeLillos." In *Der 11. September 2001*, edited by Sabine Silke, 97–110. Frankfurt: Peter Lang.

Isaacson, Walter. 2011. *Steve Jobs*. London: Little.

Jacques, Martin. 2009. *When China Rules the World: The Rise of the Middle Kingdom and the End of the Western World*. London: Lane.

Karnicky, Jeffrey. 2001. "Wallpaper Mao: Don DeLillo, Andy Warhol, and Seriality." *Critique* 42 (1): 339–56.

Kearns, George. 1980. *Guide to Ezra Pound's Selected Cantos*. New Brunswick, NJ: Rutgers University Press.

Kissinger, Henry. 2011. *On China*. New York: Penguin.

Künnemann, Vanessa, and Ruth Mayer. 2009. "Transnational Nationalisms—China and the United States in a Pacific World: An Introduction." In *Trans-Pacific Interactions: The United States and China, 1880–1950*, edited by Vanessa Künnemann and Ruth Mayer, 1–17. New York: Palgrave.

————, eds. 2011. *Chinatowns in a Transnational World: Myths and Realities of an Urban Phenomenon*. New York: Routledge.

Lai, Him Mark, Genny Lim, and Judy Yung, eds. 1991. *Island: Poetry and History of Chinese Immigrants on Angel Island, 1910–1940*. Seattle: University of Washington Press.

Lee, Yan Phou. 1887. *When I Was a Boy in China*. Boston: D. Lothrop.

Lenz, Günter. 2002. "Toward a Dialogics of International American Culture Studies: Transnationality, Border Discourses, and Public Culture(s)." In *The Futures of American Studies*, edited by Donald E. Pease and Robyn Wiegman, 461–85. Durham, NC: Duke University Press.

Lim, Shirley Geok-lin, John Blair Gamber, Stephen Hong Sohn, and Gina Valentino, eds. 2006. *Transnational Asian American Literature: Sites and Transits*. Philadelphia: Temple University Press.

Lyotard, Jean-François. 1984. *The Postmodern Condition: A Report on Knowledge*. Translated by Geoff Bennington and Brian Massumi. Minneapolis: University of Minnesota Press.

Mao Tse-Tung. 1966. *Quotations from Chairman Mao Tse-Tung*. Beijing: Foreign Language Press.

Meissenburg, Karin. 1987. *The Writing on the Wall: Socio-Historical Aspects of Chinese American Literature in the English Language, 1900–1980*. Berlin: Iko-Verlag.

Mueller, Max F., ed. 1899. *The Sacred Books of China: The Texts of Confucianism*. Translated by James Legge. Vol. 5 of *The Sacred Books of the East*. Oxford: Clarendon Press of Oxford University Press.

Olster, Stacey, ed. 2011. *Don DeLillo: Mao II / Underworld / Falling Man*. London: Continuum.

Ostendorf, Berndt, ed. 2002. *Transnational America: The Fading of Borders in the Western Hemisphere*. Heidelberg: Universitätsverlag Winter.

Pease, Donald E. 2009. *The New American Exceptionalism*. Minneapolis: Minnesota University Press.

———. 2011. Frontmatter in *Re-Framing the Transnational Turn in American Studies*. Edited by Winfried Fluck, Donald E. Pease, and John Carlos Rowe. Hanover, NH: Dartmouth College Press.

Pound, Ezra. 1915. *Cathay*. London: Mathews.

———. 1935. *MAKE IT NEW*. New Haven, CT: Yale University Press.

———. 1957. *The Cantos of Ezra Pound*. London: Faber.

Qian, Zhaoming. 2009. "Against Anti-Confucianism: Ezra Pound's Encounter/Collision with a Chinese Modernist." In *Orient and Orientalism in US-American Poetry and Poetics*, edited by Sabine Sielke and Christian Kloeckner, 127–43. Frankfurt: Peter Lang.

Qu, Wanli, ed. 1969. *Book of History*. Taipei: Commercial.

Roberts, Priscilla, ed. 2007. *Bridging the Sino-American Divide: American Studies with Chinese Characteristics*. Newcastle, UK: Cambridge Scholars.

Robinson, Greg. 2011. "Transnationalism in American Studies." *Encyclopedia of American Studies Online*. http://www.theasa.net/project_eas_online/page/project_eas_on line_eas_featured_article/. Accessed on May 20, 2015.

Rowe, John Carlos. 2011. "Transnationalism and American Studies." *Encyclopedia of American Studies Online*. http://www.theasa.net/project_eas_online/page/project _eas_online_eas_featured_article/. Accessed on May 20, 2015.

Ryback, Timothy W. 1990. *Rock around the Bloc: A History of Rock Music in Eastern Europe and the Soviet Union*. New York: Oxford University Press.

Schiffrin, Harold Z. 1968. *Sun Yat-sen and the Origins of the Chinese Revolution*. Berkeley: University of California Press.

Schmidt, Helmut. 2013. *Ein letzter Besuch: Begegnungen mit der Weltmacht China*. Munich: Siedler Verlag.

Schneck, Peter. 2007. "'To See Things before Other People See Them': Don DeLillo's Visual Poetics." In "Transatlantic Perspectives on American Visual Culture," edited by Astrid Böger and Christof Decker. Special issue of *Amerikastudien/American Studies* 52 (1): 103–20.

Spivak, Gayatri Chakravorty. 2003. *Death of a Discipline*. New York: Columbia University Press.

Symons, Julian. 1987. *Makers of the New: The Revolution in Literature, 1912–1939*. New York: Random House.

Teng, Ssu-yü, and John K. Fairbank. 1972. *China's Response to the West: A Documentary Survey 1839–1923*. Cambridge, MA: Harvard University Press.

Tong, Q. S., Wang Shouren, and Douglas Kerr, eds. 2006. *Critical Zone: A Forum of Chinese and Western Knowledge*. Vol. 2. Hong Kong: Hong Kong University Press.

Tunc, Tanfer Emin, Elisabetta Marino, and Daniel Y. Kim, eds. 2012. "Redefining the American in Asian American Studies: Transnationalism, Diaspora, and Representation." *Journal of Transnational American Studies* 4 (1). http://www.escholarship.org/uc/item/53c6c1kp. Accessed February 18, 2015.

Vertovec, Steven. 2009. *Transnationalism*. London: Routledge.

Wan, Ming. 2001. *Human Rights in Chinese Foreign Relations: Defining and Defending National Interests*. Philadelphia: University of Pensylvania Press.

Wang, Jessica Ching-Sze. 2007. *John Dewey in China: To Teach and to Learn*. Albany: State University of New York Press.

Williams, R. John. 2009. "Modernist Scandals: Ezra Pound's Translations of 'the' Chinese Poem." In *Orient and Orientalism in US-American Poetry and Poetics*, edited by Sabine Sielke and Christian Kloeckner, 145–65. Frankfurt: Peter Lang.

Wise, Peter. 2008. "Ping-Pong Pop." In *ANDY WARHOL CHINA 1982*, edited by Peter Wise, 3. Hong Kong: Timezone 8.

Wolfe, Tom. 1970. *Radical Chic and Mau-Mauing the Flak Catchers*. New York: Farrar, Straus and Giroux.

Wong, Jan. 1996. *Red China Blues: My Long March from Mao to Now*. New York: Doubleday.

Wong, Sau-ling. 1993. *Reading Asian American Literature: From Necessity to Extravagance*. Princeton, NJ: Princeton University Press.

———. 2007. *Cong bixu dao shechi: Jiedu yayi meiguo wenxue*. Chinese translation of *Reading Asian American Literature: From Necessity to Extravagance*, by Zhan Qiao, Pu Ruoqian, and Li Yaping. Beijing: Zhongguo shehui kexue chubanshe.

Yan, Shanshan. 2010. "Americanization in China: An Analysis of General Motors and Its Strategies in China." PhD diss., Johannes Gutenberg University Mainz.

Yang, Jincai. 2013. "Ecocritical Dimensions in Contemporary Chinese Literary Criticism." In *Ecology and Life Writing*, edited by Alfred Hornung, 71–84. Heidelberg: Universitätsverlag Winter.

Yin, Xiao-huang. 2000. *Chinese American Literature since the 1850s*. Champaign: University of Illinois Press.

Yung Wing. 1909. *My Life in China and America*. New York: H. Holt.

Zakaria, Fareed. 2011. *The Post-American World*. New York: Norton.

Zhang, Longxi. 1999. *Mighty Opposites: From Dichotomies to Differences in the Comparative Study of China*. Stanford, CA: Stanford University Press.

14

YUAN SHU

NEGOTIATING THE TECHNOLOGICAL EMPIRE: COSMOPOLITICS, COLONIAL MODERNITY, AND EARLY CHINESE AMERICAN AUTOBIOGRAPHICAL WRITING

SINCE ASIAN AMERICAN STUDIES witnessed a paradigm shift from the domestic to the transnational in the mid-1990s,[1] the critical reconfiguration of the field has represented the transnational as a space of liberation and cultivation of ethnic identities from multiple locations and with diverse contacts. As the new critical interest extends to earlier periods, more attention has been focused on early Chinese American autobiographical writing, which was often associated with what Roger Daniels dubs "negative history" (1988, 4), an unusable past representing Chinese Americans as objects rather than subjects of US history. Because of their cultural background and transnational sensibilities, this corpus of texts either became ethnic documents for the dominant US historiographers or were scrutinized as politically suspect through the lens of Asian American identity politics, which during its peak in the 1970s accentuated masculine resistance, ethnic authenticity, and literary vernacular as central to the field imaginary.[2] In recent years, these texts—which include Wong Chin Foo's polemic essays (1883 and 1887), Yan Phou Lee's *When I Was a Boy in China* (1887a), and Yung Wing's *My Life in China and America* (1909)—have been remembered as the cultural legacy of early Asian America and reexamined together with African American versions of subjectivity and Euro-American models of masculinity from the same period.[3] These Chinese American authors have also been retooled from the "ambassadors of goodwill" (Kim 1982, 24) to "cultural defenders and brokers" for China in the late-nineteenth-century United States (K. Wong 1998, 3), a label change that reflects an increasing interest in exploring the Chinese dimension of the texts. However, as the scholarship continues to operate in the US national framework, it cannot fully capture the transnational dynamics of the texts, which would involve critical engagement with colonial modernity in China on the one hand and would entail vigorous critique of Western science and technology as well as Western discourses in the nineteenth-century United States on the other hand.

Meanwhile, in the Chinese world on the other side of the Pacific, early Chinese American autobiographical writing has received unprecedented attention since the 1980s.[4] As shown by the 1985 reissuing of Yung's *My Life in China and America* in Chinese translation in a book series titled Going to the World,[5] which featured the journal and travel writing on Western Europe and North America of the Chinese officials and intellectuals of the Qing Dynasty in the late nineteenth century, the early Chinese American authors have been rediscovered by the Chinese state media and academy as pioneering Chinese intellectuals and practitioners of what has now been officially established as the reformation and open-door policy. In the genealogy of this "post-socialist discourse" (X. Zhang 2008, 2), Yung and his Educational Mission students have figured as precursors of Chinese modernity, and their efforts in rebuilding a technologically advanced China have been construed as acts of patriotism by Chinese scholars in the humanities and social sciences.[6] With the rise of China as a global economic power in the twenty-first century, the interest in Yung and his Educational Mission has gradually changed its focus from learning and absorbing Western science and technology to the current concentration on the ways in which the early Chinese American authors negotiated Western discourses and articulated their Chinese imaginaries in the West.

In calling attention to these different framings and changing receptions of early Chinese American autobiographical texts in their US and Chinese contexts, I seek to move beyond the national frameworks and situate the primary texts in the transnational context of the nineteenth and twentieth centuries, which postcolonial critics in East Asian studies call "colonial modernity."[7] As the theorization of the fragmentary, multilayered, and multidirectional colonial formations in East Asia in the late nineteenth and early twentieth centuries, colonial modernity as a historical condition and a critical concept would connect the lived experiences of the authors in the United States to the changing reality in China and shed light on Chinese American approaches to engaging Western discourses and appropriating Western science and technology. Writing provocative essays for major magazines and newspapers in the United States and returning to China to rebuild its material culture, these authors not only confronted what Walter Mignolo theorizes as the "colonial difference"[8]—which had translated the nineteenth-century Western racial classification into hierarchical cultural values through the "coloniality of power" (2002, 60)—but also practiced what James Clifford describes as the "articulation theory" in rethinking the Chinese tradition in response to the Western military, economic, and cultural dominance.⁹ During this process, these Chinese American authors, I argue, developed different visions and strategies for Chinese America in relation to China and the Chinese modernization process.

Colonial Modernity, Enlightenment Cosmopolitanism, and Alternative Epistemology

Postcolonial critics theorize Western colonialism as inseparable from Western modernity, a structural relationship that constituted the evolution of industrial capitalism. Similarly, the notion of colonial modernity offers an interesting way to theorize the transnational dimension of the early Chinese American writing. In her remapping of East Asian studies in a changing context of global capitalism, Tani Barlow articulates "colonial modernity" in terms of "a speculative frame for investigating the infinitely pervasive discursive powers that increasingly connect at key points to the globalizing impulses of capitalism" (1997a, 6) and represents colonialism as a constituting moment that manifests the complex field of power relationships in the expansion of global capitalism. Barlow's loosely defined notion not only evokes a Foucauldian sense of power and self-reflexivity that addresses what she calls the "present deficiencies of criticism" (ibid., 3) but also points to a critical ontology that would foreground the production of geopolitical spaces under the effect of global capitalism. As a way to move beyond what she criticizes as the reified "India-England model" (ibid., 4–5) in postcolonial studies that privileges South Asian studies as its field imaginary, Barlow seeks to bridge the crucial gap between postcolonial theory and scholarship in East Asian studies, which resisted postcolonial theorization and—like US exceptionalism in a twisted sense—envisioned China as "an exception to all rules" on the ground that the Chinese nation-state had never been formally colonized by the Japanese or the Western imperialist powers (ibid., 8).

If colonial modernity serves as a framework for reconsidering colonial specifics in East Asia in the teleology of global capitalism, then its manifestation in China could be best captured by the term "semicolonialism." In Shu-mei Shih's theoretical repertoire, semicolonialism designates a complex formation derived from "the specific effects of multiple imperialist presences in China and their fragmentary colonial geography and control, as well as the resulting social and cultural formation" (2001, 31). To differentiate her usage of the term from that of Chinese Marxist historians and critics in their analyses of the semicolonial and semifeudal structures in China from 1840 to 1949, Shih accentuates the fragmentation and multiplicity of Chinese culture and society created through the less formal but more exploitative and destructive channels in the competing Western and Japanese spheres of influence during the same historical period. Semicolonialism thus rendered economic penetration, racial discrimination, and territorial jurisdiction closer to neocolonialism than to formal colonialism as practiced in India or in the Philippines. What this means for Shih is that Chinese intellectuals in the semicolonial space and time had been afforded "more varied ideological, political, and cultural positions than in formal colonies where the ordinary Manichean division of nationalists and collaborators held sway" (ibid., 35). In other words, precisely because the semicolonial structure lacked a formal institutional infrastructure, it did not present the Western and Japanese imperialist powers as "the unequivocal targets of cultural resistance" (ibid.) for Chinese intellectuals or provoke a sense of urgency among Chinese intellectuals to reconfigure Chinese culture as a locus of resistance. On the contrary, because Chinese intellectuals had been granted a limited and often illusionary sense of autonomy in their cultural representation, they readily embraced Western and Japanese cultures with an openness they construed and celebrated as "cosmopolitanism" (ibid., 373). Using cosmopolitanism in domestic and local politics, these intellectuals deconstructed traditional Chinese culture and showcased their own intellectual abilities in embracing Western and Japanese cultures in contrast with the behavior of the impoverished masses. Shih concludes that such "openness" to Western and Japanese cultures in the specific semicolonial context of China inevitably "undermined cultural nation-building projects and became the locus of the willing colonization of consciousness" (ibid., 374).

Though Shih's critical interest is focused primarily on Chinese modernist writing in the early twentieth century, her critique of colonial modernity in China and of the complicity of Chinese intellectuals with the colonizing powers offers a unique case study of the question of resistance and of the relationship between nationalism and cosmopolitanism in a semicolonial context. In other words, if Chinese culture was totally deconstructed in Chinese modernist writing, then what could be reconfigured as a locus of resistance to the colonizing powers and colonial regimes in the transnational context? In what political and cultural circumstances would nationalism and cosmopolitanism constitute a binary opposition? In contrast with Chinese modernist writers, I argue that early Chinese American authors employed cosmopolitanism as a legitimate means of critiquing Western imperialism and racism in the transnational context and offered three different approaches to Chinese culture as locus of resistance. Appropriating what Pheng Cheah recently reinscribed as Immanuel Kant's cosmopolitanism, which he interprets as a prenationalist formulation as well as in opposition to statism rather than nationalism,[10] the Chinese American authors vigorously fought anti-Chinese racism in US culture and society, reinvented Confucian humanism as an alternative epistemology and a new vision of cosmopolitanism in the transnational context, and articulated a China composed of new generations of subjects, who, I argue, would equally serve as ideal Chinese American subjects, equipped with Western scientific knowledge, humanistic sensitivity, and moral courage.

The first author I investigate here is Wong Chin Foo, author of the polemic essay "Why Am I a Heathen?" (1887). The publication of the essay had been occasioned by political and racial tensions in the United States as well as in China. On the US side, the Chinese Exclusion Act had been passed by Congress five years before, and the anti-Chinese movement and sentiment had become rampant, escalating from political debates to physical assaults with the aim of expelling Chinese laborers from the West Coast. On the Chinese side, with sporadic resistance and violence perpetuated against the Western missionary presence and establishment in China's heartland, US missionaries in the field had openly called for "an Anglo-Saxon armed assault" on China, which in their view "would create turmoil and weaken China's institutional resistance to Christianity" (Miller 1974, 269). In such circumstances, Wong's essay exemplified an educated Chinese American's response to the anti-Chinese movement in the United States and reaction to the Western civilizing mission in China.

Wong begins by explaining how he had been attracted to the Christian faith, how he had come to the United States for higher education at the age of seventeen, and why he had remained a "heathen." While he expresses confusion about the contradictory doctrines of different Christian denominations, he directs his attack at the commercial orientation of Christian organizations, the everyday practices of a technologically oriented capitalist society, and the imperialist theory underlying the Western civilizing mission in China. Publicly announcing himself as a heathen against the background of anti-Chinese sentiment, Wong dissociates himself from the missionary establishment and grounds his identity on the Confucian tradition. His enunciation of a heathen identity and cultural locality puts to the test what Kant articulated as enlightenment, which in its pure theoretical stance gave the individual freedom to question the dominant thought in a given culture and society and to present an alternative perspective on the subject matter to the general public for examination.[11] Through this process, Wong performs what Michel Foucault calls the "limit-attitude" in his own reading of Kant's enlightenment: "criticism is no longer going to be practiced in the search for formal structures with universal value, but rather as a historical investigation into the events that have led us to constitute ourselves and to recognize ourselves as subjects of what we are doing, thinking, saying."[12]

It is precisely in this spirit of cosmopolitanism that Wong critiques the

Protestant work ethic, relating its need for "ceaseless action" to the capitalist mode of production, which has revolved around profit making and labor saving. He gives a concrete example: "If my shoe factory employs 500 men, and gives me an annual profit of $10,000, why should I substitute therein machinery by the use of which I need only 100 men, thus not only throwing 400 contented, industrious men into misery, but making myself more miserable by heavier responsibilities, with possibly less profit?" (1887, 173). Speaking as someone from a self-contained agrarian society, Wong invokes the grand vision of Confucian humanism, which—in privileging "the happiness of a common humanity" (ibid.)—has played a pivotal role in maintaining social stability and cultural prosperity in China for centuries. In an extensive critique of the insatiable desire of Western capitalism for markets and profits, Wong moves to the Western civilizing mission in China and condemns British gunboat diplomacy and the opium trade for gaining access to China's port cities: "When the English wanted the Chinamen's gold and trade, they said they wanted to 'open China for their missionaries.' And opium was the chief, in fact, only, missionary they looked after, when they forced the ports open" (ibid., 176–77). Wong conflates Christianity with imperialism and comments on the devastating effects of the British military intervention in China: "And this infamous Christian introduction among Chinamen has done more injury, social and moral, in China than all the humanitarian agencies of Christianity could remedy in 200 years" (ibid., 177).

Reading the theory and praxis of US Protestant capitalism in relation to British imperialism, Wong assumes the high moral ground and boasts of his own heathenness. He sarcastically alludes to racial relations in the United States: "we are so far heathenish as to no longer persecute men simply on account of race, color, or previous condition of servitude, but treat them all according to their individual worth" (ibid., 175). Wong also presents himself as morally superior because of his observation of "the great Divine law," which varies from "Do unto others as you wish they would do unto you" to "Love your neighbor as yourself" in secular terms (ibid., 179). He ends his essay by calling on US Christians to accept his reasoning and embrace Confucian humanism as a new way of life: "This is what keeps me the heathen I am! And I earnestly invite the Christians of America to come to Confucius" (ibid.). Though often reductive and even essentialist, Wong's essay nevertheless offers an interesting and powerful comparison of Christian Americans and Confucian Chinese.

As Wong critiques the connection between the Protestant ethic and the capitalist spirit, he reinvents Confucian humanism as an alternative epistemology and grounds his own ethnic identity in the Chinese tradition. It is in this sense that Wong exemplifies what Mignolo calls "a critical awareness of the colonial difference," which points to the important role of "indigenous epistemology" in the decolonization process (2002, 67). To Mignolo, the coloniality of being cannot simply function as a continuation of Western subjectivity but rather should effect a "relocation of thinking and a critical awareness of the geopolitics of knowledge." In this light, "the densities of the colonial experience are the location of emerging epistemologies, such as the contribution of Franz [sic] Fanon, that do not overthrow existing ones but that build on the ground of the silence of history" (ibid.). What Mignolo suggests here is that the colonized should develop their own epistemologies as a locus of their identities and resistance and, in the process, negotiate and appropriate colonial modernity from these vantage points. The emphasis on indigenous epistemology marks a point of departure from Gayatri Spivak's notion of "strategic essentialism" (quoted in Ashcroft, Griffiths, and Tiffin 1998, 159–60) and makes possible a repositioning of Third World knowledge production vis-à-vis what Mary Louise Pratt calls "Europe's 'planetary consciousness,'" which had served as "a basic element in constructing modern Eurocentrism" (2008, 15).

As a matter of fact, Wong foregrounds this critical consciousness in his text: "Of course, we decline to admit all the advantages of your boasted civilization; or that the white race is the only civilized one. Its civilization is borrowed, adapted, and shaped from our older form" (1887, 174) In an earlier essay, "Political Honors in China," Wong lavishes praises on the Chinese political system: "In no other nation upon the earth are political honors based upon scientific attainments in all branches of study as they are in China, wherein are illustrated the true principles by which talent and wisdom are honored and rewarded, literature, science, morals, and philosophy encouraged, and a nation's happiness and prosperity secured" (1883, 300).

The hyperbolic description would not have made much sense in semicolonial and semifeudal China, the sovereignty of which had been constantly trampled on by the Japanese and Western imperialist powers, but it would have served the purpose of questioning and challenging the "colonial difference" in the transnational context.

Of course, what Wong did in the transpacific nineteenth century was not really to retrieve an original or authentic Confucian humanism or epistemology but, rather, to effect what Clifford redefines as "articulation theory" based on Stuart Hall's model of articulation for political and ideological changes. Clifford foregrounds two important implications from his reading of Hall's critical theory. First, articulation based on a specific ideology "offers a non-reductive way to think about cultural transformation and the apparent coming and going of 'traditional' forms" (Clifford 2001, 478). Second, the question of authenticity related to the object of articulation is secondary, and "the process of social and cultural persistence is political all the way back" (ibid., 479). If we follow Clifford's theorization, the invention of Confucian humanism in the transnational context as an alternative epistemology not only empowered Wong to challenge the anti-Chinese movement and the "colonial difference" but also enabled him to understand and articulate his Chinese identity and position in resistance to the colonial regimes and colonizing powers. Precisely because Wong's articulation of a Chinese identity and position had been conditioned by the transnational space and time of colonial modernity, he chose to stay in the United States to further his political visions and cultural pursuits, starting the first Chinese American newspaper, the *Chinese American Weekly*, in February 1883; organizing the first Chinese civil rights organization in the United States, the Chinese Equal Rights League in New York City, in September 1892; and authoring over twenty articles for mainstream US journals and magazines on topics from the Chinese in California to the translation of classic Chinese literature for the US readers. Though Hsuan Hsu interprets Wong's hyperbolic tone and contradictions in his polemic essays in terms of experimentation with a racial identity and a political position that characterized the flourishing periodical writing in the nineteenth-century United States, he nevertheless gives an adequate assessment of Wong's contribution to Chinese American identity formation: "Wong's periodical writings establish the groundwork for a Chinese American cultural identity by voicing indirect but insistent responses to leading discourses of racialization during the first, provisional decade of Chinese Exclusion."[13] Despite the fact that Wong's thought-provoking essays and coverage of his political activities and cultural views frequently appeared in national newspapers such as the *New York Times* and the *Chicago Daily Tribune* during that period, Wong's legacy has never been fully recovered by historians but remained what Qingsong Zhang calls "a forgotten chapter in the history of the American civil rights movement" (1998, 58).

A Cosmopolitan Imaginary, Colonial Difference, and the Reinvention of a Cultural China

When Wong's provocative essay on heathenness attracted attention and generated interest among US readers, Yan Phou Lee, a converted Christian and a graduate of Yale College who had been part of the Chinese Educational Mission, responded by writing an essay titled "Why I Am Not a Heathen" (1887b). Through logical reasoning and rhetorical reflection, Lee took advantage of the public sphere, which Jürgen Habermas concisely defines as "people's public use of their reason" (1989, 27), and created a critical forum through which different Chinese American voices would be heard and understood.

In his counterargument, Lee evokes his own personal journey from being a heathen to becoming a Christian and reduces Wong's critique of US racism and British imperialism to ethics at individual, institutional, and national levels. Redefining cosmopolitanism as an openness to all cultures, Lee downplays Wong's articulation of Confucian humanism as symptoms of what historians today call "sinocentrism" (K. Wong 1998, 20) and bases his own advocacy of cosmopolitanism on the premise that "other nations are superior to her [China] in science and the arts" (1887b, 311). In a different approach to fighting anti-Chinese racism, Lee calls for a "real" Christianity as opposed to its "false" representation and envisions a Christian humanism as solution to social injustice and racial inequality in the United States: "I fervently believe that if we could infuse more Christianity into politics and the judiciary, into the municipal government, the legislature and the executive, corruption and abuses would grow beautifully less" (ibid.).

Lee's invocation of cosmopolitanism in terms of Christian humanism and his critique of Confucianism as Sinocentrism should be interpreted differently in the Chinese and US contexts. On the one hand, in semifeudal and semicolonial China, Lee's advocacy of Christian humanism rather than Confucianism was directed toward the dominant Chinese state ideology, which had been challenged by Western military and political power, and reinforced the argument that Confucianism had become an obstacle in China's path to modernization and regeneration. On the other hand, against the anti-Chinese background of the nineteenth-century United States, Lee's questioning of Sinocentrism and appealing for a Christian humanism served as a gesture toward assimilation, which Amy Ling interpreted as an emerging "Asian American consciousness" (2002, 285). The consciousness, however, would be problematic and contradictory in two ways. First, understanding the huge material gap between China and the United States, Lee internalized the colonial difference by rejecting Chinese culture as a possible locus of resistance and resorting to an optimistic view of Christian humanism as a potential intervention in Western racist or imperialist theory and practice. Second, because cosmopolitanism defined a moment of idealism in Western intellectual history, Lee could not sustain such ideals in the racial reality of the United States or the colonial modernity of China. Instead, he constantly found himself caught in the contradiction of simultaneously employing self-Orientalizing strategies in cultural production and questioning Orientalist representation of China and Chinese Americans. In this process, Lee resorted to the strategy of reinventing a cultural China vis-à-vis a technological United States, a practice that would constitute what I call the second Chinese American approach to negotiating the technological empire of the United States in the late nineteenth century. It is precisely in this sense that I investigate Lee's autobiographical and ethnographical work, *When I Was a Boy in China* (1887a), which has been considered as the first major work in Asian American literary history.

Solicited by the D. Lothrop Publishing Company in Boston for its book series on "foreign cultures perceived by their own youths," Lee's *When I Was a Boy in China* was the first book published in the series (Kim 1982, 25). Though the topics in the work might have been dictated by its publisher or editor, as Ling convincingly argued, Lee reimagined a cultural China and represented its everyday practice in terms of what I call cultural difference in relation to the technological West. In his introductory chapter, "Infancy," Lee not only self-consciously addresses the privileged US reader as "you" but also describes the unpredictability of his own birthday in the Western calendar as "the uncanny" in the Freudian sense, because of its calculation based on the Chinese lunar calendar. Discussing the ritualistic practice related to the birth of a boy in a well-to-do Chinese family, Lee explains that the Chinese year was counted from the accession of the current emperor and that the Chinese month was reckoned by the movement of the moon around the earth. For that reason, he can identify his birthday only as on a certain day in the Third or Fourth Moon but cannot translate it into an exact date in a Western month. Humorous but self-Orientalizing, Lee establishes a pattern that constructs the West in terms of technological power, rationality, and individuality and articulates China in terms of traditionalism, mysticism, and collectivity.

When Lee describes the name-giving process in the same chapter, he continues to ground his narrative on points of difference: "The names given on those occasions are not like your 'Jack,' 'Harry,' or 'Dick,' but are usually words chosen from 'the dictionary' for their lucky import, or because they are supposed to possess the power of warding off evil influences in the child's horoscope" (1887a, 9). Subjecting Chinese practice to the gaze of the technological West, Lee exaggerates the difference between China and the United States: "American mothers have no idea what impositions Chinese mothers suffer from physicians and sellers of charms, on account of their superstitious fears concerning the health and welfare of their children" (ibid., 13).

Lee's depiction of the Chinese difference against the Western standard defines what Mignolo critiques as a "double bind" in his elaboration on the "colonial difference" (2002, 76). Following Robert Bernasconi's observation of African philosophy in its encounter with the West, Mignolo postulates that African philosophy is either too similar to Western philosophy to make any contribution to it, or too different from Western philosophy to qualify as philosophy per se. Mignolo's reading of this "double bind" cautions us against a possible colonization of the mind in subjecting ourselves to the Western standard and exemplifies the ways in which the coloniality of power functions and operates in its encounter with non-Western cultures and knowledge. Mignolo writes: "It is crucial for the ethics, politics, and epistemology of the future to recognize that the totality of Western epistemology, from either the right or the left, is no longer valid for the entire planet" (ibid., 86).

Interestingly enough, Lee was not only aware of the double bind, but he also tried to negotiate the Western frame of reference. In the chapter "Stories and Story-Tellers," Lee first describes Chinese legends as "really beautiful" and "as interesting as a good English novel" and then provides an actual sample story titled "Sold," through which he self-indulgently narrates the experience of a scholar involved in the annual imperial examination for would-be government officials and draws from an entirely different literary tradition and cultural sensibility. Moreover, Lee also buys into the dream that China would be regenerated through Western science and technology, a dream that he explicitly articulates in the last three chapters of his work. He describes Yung as a man "destined to exert a potent influence on the future of China": "Dr. Wing [sic], indignant at the wrongs which China had suffered and was suffering at the hands of so-called 'Christian' and 'enlightened' nations, sought for remedy, and conceived the brilliant project of educating a number of Chinese boys in America for future service at the government expense" (1887a, 93).

Lee concludes his work by commenting on his fascination with San Francisco as the showcase of the technological United States in the late nineteenth century and by reflecting on the violence in that technological culture, exemplified by a train robbery the Chinese Educational Mission students had experienced in their transcontinental journey from San Francisco to Springfield, Massachusetts: "Pistol-shots could be made out above the cries of frightened passengers. Women shrieked and babies cried. Our party, teachers and pupils, jumped from our seats in dismay and looked out through the windows for more light on the subject. What we saw was enough to make our hair stand on end. Two ruffianly men held a revolver in each hand and seemed to be taking aim at us from the short distance of forty feet or thereabouts. Our teachers told us to crouch down for our lives. We obeyed with trembling and fear" (ibid., 107–8).

Lee finishes his description with sarcasm: "One phase of American civilization was thus indelibly fixed upon our minds" (ibid., 108). In dramatizing such an event at the end of his work, Lee casts critical doubt on the value of the US material culture and leaves room for critical reflection on the colonial difference.

Lee's critical awareness is most clearly manifested in his critical essay,

"The Chinese Must Stay," written in response to the escalating anti-Chinese violence in the Western states and published in *North American Review* in 1889. Facing the increasing use of racist rhetoric that "the Chinese must go," Lee vigorously defends Chinese laborers and fights the anti-Chinese movement, which had escalated to physical violence and was dominating politics in the Western states. With the sweeping generalization that "no nation can afford to let go [of] its high ideals," Lee questions "this generation of Americans in their treatment of other races" and invokes the discourses of freedom, equality, and integrity in his intervention in the anti-Chinese movement (1889, 476). He details the laws passed by Congress against the Chinese and the anti-Chinese platform adopted by both political parties in "the Pacific states," and he decides that Americans have been more "dedicated to the proposition that all men are created to prey on one another" than to following the principle of equality articulated by the founding fathers of the American republic (ibid.). With official statistics, logical reasoning, and rhetorical eloquence, Lee dismisses all of the eleven charges leveled against the Chinese as contradictory, misconceived, and malicious.

Continuing to operate within the framework of cosmopolitanism, Lee defends Chinese laborers in terms of their potential for progress, assimilation, and citizenship. In response to the fourth charge—"That the Chinese have displaced white laborers by low wages and cheap living, and that their presence discourages and retards white immigration to the Pacific states" (ibid., 479)—Lee argues that it was precisely because of "the application of Chinese 'cheap labor' to the building of railroads, the reclamation of swamplands, to mining, fruit-culture, and manufacturing, that an immense vista of employment was opened up for Caucasians and that millions now are enabled to live in comfort and luxury" (ibid.). Now fully aware of the colonial difference that degraded Chinese laborers to the lowest position in the racial hierarchy, Lee cannot help asking rhetorically: "Machines live on nothing at all; they have displaced millions of laborers; why not do away with machines?" (ibid.). As if such bitter sarcasm is not enough to demonstrate his outrage at the unfair treatment of the Chinese in general and Chinese laborers in particular, Lee further challenges the racist reasoning: "Besides, are you sure that Chinese laborers would not ask more if they dared, or take more if they could get it?" (ibid., 480). At this emotional juncture, Lee the Christian almost sounds exactly like Wong the heathen in his language and emotional tone: "I maintain that a sober, industrious, and peaceable people, like the Chinese, who mind their own business and let others do the same, are as fit to be voters as the quarrelsome, ignorant, besotted, and priest-ridden hordes of Europe" (ibid.).

Though Lee endeavors to raise public awareness and dismiss the specific racist charges against Chinese abilities to "evolve" to be fit for Western civilization, he still works within the logical parameters of the colonial difference. His argument becomes a case of what Audre Lorde famously describes: "the master's tools will never dismantle the master's house" (1984, 110). Indeed, the colonial difference and the geopolitics of knowledge had played a crucial role in justifying and fueling the anti-Chinese movement in the United States in the late nineteenth century. Henry George, a well-known US economist of the period, had not only secured a reputation for his studies of the relationships between progress and poverty and between technology and corporate dominance, but he was also noted for his involvement in the research on the labor conflict between Euro-Americans and the Chinese on the West Coast. In his essays, from "The Chinese on the Pacific Coast" (1869) to "Chinese Immigration" (1883), the influential economist contended that China as a major Eastern civilization had historically achieved great material progress and cultural tradition, but it had fallen far behind the West in science and technology since the Industrial Revolution. George also argued that cheap labor had been the major factor in China's technological stagnation. In discussing Chinese laborers on the West Coast, George questioned their willingness to accept low wages and standards of living, which would not only result in their eventually replacing white laborers but would also destroy technological advancement in US culture and society: "It is certain that in a country where the Chinese standard of wages prevailed, no such machinery would ever have been developed, and that just as wages fall toward the Chinese standard so must the spirit of invention and adaption be checked, and stagnation take the place of progress" (1881, 412). In this seemingly scientific and objective study of the connections between low wages and Chinese labor, and between low wages and technological advancement, George does not factor in the racial dimension of labor and wages or critique the nature of the capitalist mode of production that always seeks to maximize profits and expand markets. Instead, he blames and victimizes Chinese labor in an essentialist way, which would replace the class conflict between white labor and capital with the racial tension between white and Chinese labor, and which would—intentionally or unintentionally—rationalize and reinforce the anti-Chinese movement.

Precisely because of the colonial difference and the geopolitics of knowledge, which Lee had paradoxically complied with and fought against at different moments, he finally found himself caught in what Ling calls "the Asian American frontier," which she defines as "a psychological and emotional state," "a between-worlds stance," and "the fluctuating double-consciousness of all racial minorities" (2002, 274). After fifty-two years of living in the United States and constantly struggling to find employment, Lee finally decided to leave his beloved family and country of adoption (the United States) for his country of origin (China) in 1931. And in 1937 Lee started referring to "we Cantonese" in his correspondence with the Yale Alumni Office (quoted in Ling 2002, 279). This identification with the Cantonese not only reflected Lee's deep disappointment with his experiences in the United States but also signified his final attempt to come to terms with his own culture and tradition—as a common Chinese expression has it, the fallen leaves always return to their roots of origin. Since his last correspondence with Yale University is dated March 29, 1938, Lee's family in the United States has presumed that he was killed by Japanese bombs in what he had described as an "inhuman, brutal, and savage war" (quoted in ibid.). Since Lee's autobiographical and ethnographical work and polemic essays represent the trajectory of an emerging Asian American consciousness, he certainly deserves what Ling describes as "an Asian American place of distinction" in literary history and cultural tradition (ibid., 285).

Negotiating Western Science and Discourse: A New Sense of Self, A New Vision of China

Yung Wing—whose autobiography, *My Life in China and America*, was published in 1909—was the first Chinese or Chinese American to graduate from Yale College, in 1854. He founded the Chinese Educational Mission, which officially started its operations in Hartford, Connecticut, in 1872. Unlike Wong (who sought to reinvent Confucian humanism as a Chinese American epistemology and an alternative to cosmopolitanism) or Lee (who recreated a cultural China vis-à-vis the technological West to negotiate the colonial difference), Yung developed a new sense of subjectivity with a thorough understanding of Western material culture and humanities. He envisioned a China rebuilt by future generations of Chinese subjects, equipped with Western scientific knowledge, intellectual abilities, and moral courage. As Western education was crucial to the new Chinese subject and the Chinese modernization process, Yung used his own experiences to exemplify and represent the performance of a Chinese subject, who would in fact represent the emerging Chinese American subjectivity.

While recent Asian American scholarship explores Yung's sense of self in terms of masculinity and in relation to the Anglo-American model,[14] scholars in China focus more on Yung's vision of a new modern China, situating his thoughts and practices in the broader spectrum of modern Chinese history, which encompasses topics from diasporic experiences to Chinese state policy on overseas Chinese, and from the impact of Western education on China's modernization process to the function of the Chinese imperial examination system.[15] Most Chinese scholarship defines Yung as a pioneering thinker in modern Chinese history, who persistently looked for a panacea to strengthen China and save it from feudal disintegration and Western colonization. Even the few Chinese scholars who do recognize Yung as a Chinese American intellectual still situate his work within what critics call China's postsocialist discourse on reform and open-door (X. Zhang 2008, 2), which has brought economic prosperity to China at the expense of social disparity and environmental devastation. I argue that Yung's advocacy of a new Chinese subject was based on his own experience as an emerging Chinese American subject, and that this subject—with a command of Western science and technology and the ability to reflect critically on Western and Chinese cultures—would be crucial to the regeneration of the Chinese nation-state. It is in this sense that Yung's work constitutes a third Chinese American approach to negotiating the technological United States in the late nineteenth century.

In the beginning chapters of his autobiography, Yung explains explicitly why and how Western education has enabled him to perceive and understand the injustice and humiliation that China has suffered in its encounters with Western powers since the First Opium War in 1840: "All through my college course, especially in the closing years, the lamentable condition of China was before my mind constantly and weighed on my spirits. In my despondency, I often wished I had never been educated, as education had unmistakably enlarged my mental and moral horizon, and revealed to me responsibilities which the sealed eye of ignorance can never see, and sufferings and wrongs of humanity to which an uncultivated and callous nature can never be made sensitive" (1909, 40).

Alluding to the early 1850s, when the joint forces of Britain, France, Germany, Japan, Russia, the United States, and other Western powers defeated China and forced it to sign humiliating treaties to consolidate their political and economic gains in the country, Yung argues that only Western-educated Chinese youths like himself could understand China's humiliation and shoulder the responsibility of regenerating China. Western education at this point meant two different things for Yung. To begin with, it offered him an understanding of the political, economic, and cultural logics under which the Western powers had established the colonial world order. Moreover, it enabled him to reflect critically on the possibilities of resistance, which would help China protect its national interests and survive Western colonial exploitation and oppression. In this light, Western education is instrumental rather than idealistic: "I was determined that the rising generation of China should enjoy the same educational advantages that I had enjoyed; that through western education China might be regenerated, become enlightened and powerful" (ibid., 41).

When Yung was looking for ways to fund his education at Yale, he was advised by his Anglo-American friends to apply for "the contingent fund provided for indigent students" and to sign a written pledge in which he would promise to "study for the ministry and afterwards become a missionary" (ibid., 34). Yung requested an exemption and presented his case before "the trustees of the academy" (ibid.) at Yale, arguing that missionary work in China would "handicap and circumscribe" his usefulness and that his goal was to have "the utmost freedom of action" to avail himself of "every opportunity to do the greatest good in China" (ibid., 35). He turned this hearing into a public forum, through which he articulated a vague sense of nationalism and enunciated a new Chinese American subject against the background of the Western civilizing mission in China.

When he wrote about the incident, Yung focused on his strong sense of critical reflexivity: "To be sure, I was poor, but I would not allow my poverty to gain the upper hand and compel me to barter away my inward convictions of duty for a temporary mess of pottage" (ibid., 36). His friend the Reverend Joseph Twichell called Yung's decision "a costly conclusion" (1909, 254), the effect of which was still be felt two decades later, after Yung returned to China in 1854 and was serving temporarily as a comprador for Western businesses in Shanghai. An article in *Scribner's Monthly* explained how Yung's "refusal to become a formal missionary acted strongly to his disadvantage" in Western business and religious circles in Shanghai, both of which had "somewhat naturally considered him a sort of hopeless convert after all."[16]

In addition to this critical reflexivity, Yung also dramatizes two experiences he had in Shanghai to emphasize the moral courage of the new emerging subject. In the first case, Yung stopped a group of Western sailors from insulting and harassing Chinese pedestrians on a Shanghai street and wrote a letter to the ship's captain to lodge a formal complaint, after which he received an apology. In the second case, when Yung was physically assaulted by a Scottish man at an auction in Shanghai, he fought back and defended himself. Asked by another European man if he was looking for trouble, Yung answered with dignity: "No, I was only defending myself. Your friend insulted me and added injury to insult. I took him for a gentleman, but he has proved himself a blackguard" (1909, 71). Yung devotes a good deal of space to the implications of the two incidents, from the physical to the intellectual and from the personal to the national:

> It was the chief topic of conversation for a short time among foreigners, while among Chinese I was looked upon with great respect, for since the foreign settlement on the extra-territorial basis was established close to the city of

Shanghai, no Chinese within its jurisdiction had ever been known to have the courage and pluck to defend his rights, point blank, when they had been violated or trampled upon by a foreigner. Their meek and mild disposition had allowed personal insults and affronts to pass un-resented and unchallenged, which naturally had the tendency to encourage arrogance and insolence on the part of ignorant foreigners. The time will soon come, however, when the people of China will be so educated and enlightened as to know what their rights are, public and private, and to have the moral courage to assert and defend them whenever they are invaded. The triumph of Japan over Russia in the recent war has opened the eyes of the Chinese world. (ibid., 72–73)

Teasing out the racial, political, and cultural implications of the two incidents, Yung demonstrates that only through understanding and appropriating Western knowledge could the Chinese defend their rights and confront Western colonial powers. In this case, Japan was an example to Yung in disrupting the colonial difference and fighting Western military powers.

In 1863, when Yung finally had the opportunity to discuss his vision of China's modernization with Viceroy Zheng Guo-fan, one of the most important political figures in modern Chinese history, he was authorized to build Jiangnan Arsenal, "a mother machine shop, capable of reproducing other machine shops of like character" (ibid., 151). After he successfully completed the task in 1865, Yung delineated his blueprint for China's modernization and presented four proposals to Zheng. In three of the four proposals, Yung sought to rebuild parts of the Chinese transportation infrastructure, such as the railroad and steamboat networks; to implement a system of joint ventures with Western transnational companies; and to protect Chinese sovereignty by prohibiting "missionaries of any religious sect or denomination from exercising any kind of jurisdiction over their converts" (ibid., 175). He even predicted that inexpensive resources and labor would make Chinese products more competitive on the global market.

It is in the second proposal that Yung explored the possibility of sending Chinese youths to the United States for Western education. During the nine years of the operation of the Chinese Educational Mission in Connecticut, Yung noted with delight the profound changes—both intellectual and physical—in the Chinese students: "Now in New England the heavy weight of repression and suppression was lifted from the minds of these young students; they exulted in their freedom and leaped for joy. No wonder they took to athletic sports with alacrity and delight" (ibid., 203). What ended the Chinese Educational Mission was precisely Yung's privileging of Western studies over Chinese studies for these students.

Yung's direct violation of the Chinese official code of "Chinese studies for the essentials and Western studies for practical applications" (Desnoyers 1997, 138) I argue, should not be construed simply as a negation of Chinese culture, but rather should be interpreted as a major step toward the cultivation of a Chinese American subject. In Yung's view, the new Chinese subject was identical to the emerging Chinese American subject, who would operate in the transnational space of colonial modernity and whose understanding of Western concepts of masculinity and nationalism would be far more important than any understanding of Confucianism, which had been used by the Chinese ruling class to regulate human relations in China for two thousand years. As Floyd Cheung observes, Yung's work had drawn on the "discursive traditions established by autobiographers like Benjamin Franklin, Frederick Douglass, and Booker T. Washington," and Yung had tried to appropriate "the rhetoric of individual and national manliness popularized by Theodore Roosevelt to perform a problematic yet bold personal and political resistance" (2005b, 79). Such a resistance, I would add, was not directed just toward institutional racism and cultural prejudices in the United States but also to Western colonialism and imperialism in China. Like most Chinese Americans at that time, Yung subscribed to the idea that prejudices against Chinese Americans had been closely related to the weakened status of China as a nation-state. It was for that reason that Yung was outraged when he heard that "there is no room provided for Chinese students" at the US Military Academy at West Point or the US Naval Academy in Annapolis (1909, 207). Yung finally lashed out at racism, bigotry, and prejudices directed at the Chinese in the United States:

> The race prejudice against the Chinese was so rampant and rank that not only my application for the students to gain entrance to Annapolis and West Point was treated with cold indifference and scornful hauteur, but the Burlington Treaty of 1868 was, without the least provocation, and contrary to all diplomatic precedents and common decency, trampled under foot unceremoniously and wantonly, and set aside as though no such treaty had ever existed, in order to make way for those acts of congressional discrimination against Chinese immigration which were pressed for immediate enactment. (ibid., 208)

Here Yung clearly related the incident to the Chinese Exclusion Act passed by Congress and denounced racist laws together with the US imperialist approach to China. This also became the last straw for the Qing government, which would finally decide to abandon the Chinese Educational Mission and withdrew all its sponsored students from the United States in 1881.

From a new Chinese subject to a new vision of China, Yung not only implicitly addressed racism in US society and Western imperialism in semi-colonial and semifeudal China, but he also related the well-being of Chinese

America to the status of China. What he sought was to create a new generation of Chinese subjects equipped with Western education, who would also serve as Chinese American intellectuals like himself. According to one Chinese historian,[17] Yung exchanged letters in 1900 with Sun Yat-sen, the founding father of the Republic of China, and volunteered to raise funds for Sun's revolutionary project called "Red Dragon"—his attempt to overthrow the Qing dynasty and establish a modern Chinese republic. Yung was overjoyed to learn in 1911 that his dream had come true. He was invited to the Sun's presidential inauguration, but his health deteriorated and he passed away on April 21, 1912.

Rereading China, Rethinking Asian America

By rereading early Chinese American autobiographical writing against the transnational background of colonial modernity in the late nineteenth and the early twentieth centuries, I suggest that Chinese Americans not only engaged the discourses of humanism and cosmopolitanism in the US context as a way to critique racism but also extended their critiques to semifeudal and semicolonial China as a way to save and modernize the Chinese nation-state. Such extended critiques of racism and imperialism marked the beginning of an Asian American consciousness as well as the emergence of Chinese American subjectivity in the transnational context. The political visions of Wong Chin Foo and Yan Phou Lee for a tolerant and multicultural US nation-state have gradually materialized as a result of the civil rights movements, including Asian American political activism, since the 1960s. Yung Wing's dream of a new China has also been partially fulfilled since 1978, when the Chinese government announced its "reformation and open-door" (X. Zhang 2008, 2) policy and introduced Western science and technology into China. With the implementation of a capitalist mode of production and the integration of its economy into the US-centered global order, China has started playing a more important economic role on the global stage. However, as Arif Dirlik rightly points out, China's modernity does not pose an alternative to global capitalism but rather serves as a hybrid model within the US-centered global order (2007, 144–45).

The recent paradigm shift in Asian American studies and the increasing Chinese interest in Yung and early Chinese American autobiographical writing both raise questions about how we should reconsider the interaction between the local and the global in Asian American literature and the transnational context of that interaction. Wai Chee Dimock and Lawrence Buell redefine "American literature as world literature" (2007), and similarly early Chinese American autobiographical writing might serve as an example of how ethnic American authors have tried since the late nineteenth century to negotiate Western discourses and to reinvent indigenous epistemologies as a locus of resistance to colonialism and capitalism on a planetary scale.

Notes

1. For essays on issues related to the paradigm shift, see Campomanes 1997; Koshy 1996; Mazumda 1991; S. Wong 1995.

2. See Chin 1985; Chin, Chan, Inada, and Wong 1974a and 1974b.

3. For more on Lee and Yung, see Cheung 2005a and 2005b; Ling 2002; K. Wong 1998.

4. At Yung Wing's suggestion, the Qing government established the Chinese Educational Mission at Hartford, Connecticut, in 1872 but recalled all the students in 1881. Yan Phou Lee was a student at the mission; Yung Wing served as its commissioner.

5. This book series was published by Yuelu Press in the 1980s.

6. At least ten books in Chinese have been published on Yung and his students by historians, critics, and journalists in mainland China, Taiwan, and Hong Kong.

7. Tani Barlow (1997a and 1997b) proposed the notion of "colonial modernity," and Shu-mei Shih (2001) further elaborated it as a critical concept to analyze the situation in China, roughly from 1840 to 1949.

8. See Mignolo 2002. He has now replaced the term "colonial difference" with a new one, "imperial difference."

9. See Clifford 2001, 477. He explores the theory mostly in relation to indigenous populations in Pacific island countries.

10. See Cheah 1998.

11. Kant wrote that "enlightenment is man's emergence from his self-incurred immaturity" (1970, 54). He also wrote: "For enlightenment of this kind, all that is needed is freedom. And the freedom in question is the most innocuous form of all—freedom to make public use of one's reason in all matters" (ibid., 55).

12. Foucault 1984, 46.

13. See Hsu 2006, 85.

14. See Cheung 2005b.

15. See Kong 2007; Li Huaxing 2005.

16. See Bowen 1875, 108.

17. See Li Huaxing 2005.

Bibliography

Adas, Michael. 1989. *Machines as the Measure of Men: Science, Technology, and Ideologies of Western Dominance.* Ithaca, NY: Cornell University Press.
Ashcroft, Bill, Gareth Griffiths, and Helen Tiffin. 1998. *Key Concepts in Post-Colonial Studies.* New York: Routledge.

Barlow, Tani. 1997a. "Introduction: On 'Colonial Modernity.'" In *Formations of Colonial Modernity in East Asia*, edited by Tani Barlow, 1–20. Durham, NC: Duke University Press.

———, ed. 1997b. *Formations of Colonial Modernity in East Asia*. Durham, NC: Duke University Press.

Bhabha, Homi. 1994. *The Location of Culture*. New York: Routledge.

Bowen, James L. 1875. "Yung Wing and His Work." *Scribner's Monthly Magazine*, May, 106–8.

Campomanes, Oscar V. 1997. "New Formations of Asian American Studies and the Question of U.S. Imperialism." *Positions* 5 (2): 523–50.

Chan, Sucheng. 1991. *Asian Americans: An Interpretive History*. Boston: Twayne.

Chatterjee, Partha. 1993. *The Nation and Its Fragments: Colonial and Postcolonial Histories*. Princeton, NJ: Princeton University Press.

Cheah, Pheng. 1998. "Introduction Part II: The Cosmopolitical—Today." In *Cosmopolitics: Thinking and Feeling beyond the Nation*, edited by Pheng Cheah and Bruce Robbins, 20–41. Minneapolis: University of Minnesota Press.

——— and Bruce Robbins, eds. 1998. *Cosmopolitics: Thinking and Feeling beyond the Nation*. Minneapolis: University of Minnesota Press.

Cheung, Floyd. 2005a. "Early Chinese American Autobiography: Reconsidering the Works of Yan Phou Lee and Yung Wing." In *Recovered Legacies: Authority and Identity in Early Asian American Literature*, edited by Keith Lawrence and Floyd Cheung, 24–40. Philadelphia: Temple University Press.

———. 2005b. "Political Resistance, Cultural Appropriation, and the Performance of Manhood in Yung Wing's *My Life in China and America*." In *Form and Transformation in Asian American Literature*, edited by Zhou Xiaojing and Samina Najmi, 77–100. Seattle: University of Washington Press.

Chin, Frank. 1985. "This Is Not an Autobiography." *Genre* 18 (summer): 109–30.

———, Jeffery Paul Chan, Lawson Fusao Inada, Shawn Hsu Wong. 1974a. "An Introduction to Chinese- and Japanese-American Literature." In *Aiiieeeee! An Anthology of Asian American Writers*, edited by Frank Chin, Jeffery Paul Chan, Lawson Fusao Inada, Shawn Hsu Wong, xxi–xlviii. Washington: Howard University Press.

———. 1974b. Preface in *Aiiieeeee! An Anthology of Asian American Writers*, edited by Frank Chin, Jeffery Paul Chan, Lawson Fusao Inada, Shawn Hsu Wong, vii–xvi. Washington: Howard University Press.

Clifford, James. 1986. "On Ethnographic Allegory." In *Writing Culture: The Poetics and Politics of Ethnography*, edited by James Clifford and George E. Marcus, 98–121. Berkeley: University of California Press.

Cohen, A. Paul. 1974. "Littoral and Hinterland in Nineteenth Century China: The 'Christian' Reformers." In *The Missionary Enterprise in China and America*, edited by John K. Fairbank, 197–225. Cambridge, MA: Harvard University Press.

Daniels, Roger. 1988. *Asian America: Chinese and Japanese in the United States since 1850*. Seattle: University of Washington Press.

Desnoyers, Charles. 1997. "Toward 'One Enlightened and Progressive Civilization': Discourses of Expansion and Nineteenth-Century Chinese Missions Abroad." *Journal of World History* 8 (1): 135–56.

Dimock, Wai Chee, and Lawrence Buell. 2007. *Shades of the Planet: American Literature as World Literature*. Princeton, NJ: Princeton University Press.

Dirlik, Arif. 2007. *Global Modernity: Modernity in the Age of Global Capitalism*. Boulder, CO: Paradigm.

Foucault, Michel. 1984. "What Is Enlightenment?," in *The Foucault Reader*, edited by Paul Rabinow, 32–50. New York: Pantheon Books.

Gaonkar, Dilip Parameshwar. 2001. "On Alternative Modernities." In *Alternative Modernities*, edited by Dilip Parameshwar Gaonkar, 1–23. Durham, NC: Duke University.

George, Henry. 1869. "The Chinese on the Pacific Coast." *New York Tribune*, May 1.

———. 1881. "Chinese Immigration." In *Cyclopedia of Political Science, Political Economy, and of the Political History of the United States*, edited by John Lalor, 409–14. New York: Maynard, Merrill.

Grimm, Henry. 1879. *"The Chinese Must Go": A Farce in Four Acts*. San Francisco: A. L. Bancroft.

Habermas, Jürgen. 1989. *The Structural Transformation of the Public Sphere: An Inquiry into a Category of Bourgeois Society*. Translated by Thomas Burger. Cambridge, MA: MIT Press.

Harte, Bret. 1870. "The Heathen Chinee." *Overland Monthly* 5 (September): 287.

Hsu, Hsuan L. 2006. "Wong Chin Foo's Periodical Writing and Chinese Exclusion." *Genre* 39 (fall): 83–105.

Jiang, Ming. 2002. *Long Qi Piao Yang De Jian Dui*. Beijing: Sanlian.

Kant, Immanuel. 1970. "An Answer to the Question: 'What Is Enlightenment?'" In *Kant's Political Writings*, edited with an introduction and notes by Hans Reiss and translated by H. B. Nisbet, 54–60. Cambridge: Cambridge University Press.

Kim, Elaine H. 1982. *Asian American Literature: An Introduction to the Writings and Their Social Context*. Philadelphia: Temple University Press.

Kong Xiang Jie. 2007. "Lue Lun Yong Wing Dui Mei Guo Jing Yan De Xuan Chuan Yu Tui Guang." *Guangdong Social Sciences*, no. 1, 91–99.

Koshy, Susan. 1996. "The Fiction of Asian American Literature." *Yale Journal of Criticism* 9 (2): 315–46.

La Fargue, Thomas E. 1942. *China's First Hundred*. Pullman: State College of Washington.

Lee, Yan Phou. 1887a. *When I Was a Boy in China*. Boston: Lothrop.

———. 1887b. "Why I Am Not a Heathen: A Rejoinder to Wong Chin Foo." *North American Review* 145 (September): 306–12.

———. 1889. "The Chinese Must Stay." *North American Review* 148 (April): 476–83.

Li, Huaxing. 2005. "Yung Wing: Zhong Guo Xian Dai Hua De Zhuo Yue Xian Qu." *Fudan Journal*, Social Sciences Issue 5: 46–52.

Li, Hung-chang. 1961. "Letters of Li Hung-chang Concerning the End of the Mission, 1880–1881." In *China's Response to the West: A Documentary Survey, 1839–1923*, edited by Ssu-yu Teng and John K Fairbank, 94–95. Cambridge, MA: Harvard University Press.

Lin, Hongxun, and Gao Zonglu. 1977. *Zhan Tianyou Yu Zhong Guo Tie Lu*. Taipei: Institute of Modern History, Academia Sinica.

Ling, Amy. 2002. "Yan Phou Lee on the Asian American Frontier." In *Re/collecting Early Asian America: Essays in Cultural History*, edited by Josephine Lee, Imogene L. Lim, and Yuko Matsukawa, 273–87. Philadelphia: Temple University Press.

Lorde, Audre. 1984. *Sister Outsider: Essays and Speeches*. Trumansburg, NY: Crossing Press.

Mazumda, Sucheta. 1991. "Asian American Studies and Asian Studies: Rethinking Roots." In *Asian Americans: Comparative and Global Perspectives*, edited by Shirley Hune, Stephen S. Fugita, and Amy Ling, 29–44. Pullman: Washington State University Press.

Mignolo, Walter D. 2000. *Local Histories/Global Designs: Coloniality, Subaltern Knowledges, and Border Thinking*. Princeton, NJ: Princeton University Press.

———. 2002. "The Geopolitics of Knowledge and the Colonial Difference." *South Atlantic Quarterly* 101 (1): 57–96.

Miller, Stuart Creighton. 1974. "Ends and Means: Missionary Justification of Force in Nineteenth Century China." In *The Missionary Enterprise in China and America*, edited by John K. Fairbank, 249–82. Cambridge, MA: Harvard University Press.

Pratt, Mary Louise. 2008. *Imperial Eyes: Travel Writing and Transculturation*. 2nd ed. New York: Routledge.

Shih, Shu-mei. 2001. *The Lure of the Modern: Writing Modernities in Semicolonial China, 1917–1937*. Berkeley: University of California Press.

Tseng, Kuo-fan, and Li Hung-chang. 1961. "The Proposal of Tseng and Li in 1871." In *China's Response to the West: A Documentary Survey, 1839–1923*, edited by Ssu-yu Teng and John K Fairbank, 91–94. Cambridge, MA: Harvard University Press.

Twichell, Joseph H. 1909. "Appendix." In Yung Wing, *My Life in China and America*, 247–73. New York: Henry Holt.

Wong, Chin Foo. 1883. "Political Honors in China." *Harper's New Monthly Magazine*, June–November, 298–303.

———. 1887. "Why Am I a Heathen?" *North American Review* 145 (August): 169–79.

Wong, K. Scott. 1998. "Cultural Defenders and Brokers: Chinese Responses to the Anti-Chinese Movement." In *Claiming America: Constructing Chinese American Identities during the Exclusion Era*, edited by K. Scott Wong and Sucheng Chan, 3–40. Philadelphia: Temple University Press.

Wong, Sau-ling C. 1995. "Denationalization Reconsidered: Asian American Cultural Criticism at a Theoretical Crossroads." *Amerasia Journal* 21 (1–2): 1–27.

Yung Wing. 1909. *My Life in China and America*. New York: Henry Holt.

Zhang, Qingsong. 1998. "The Origins of the Chinese Americanization Movement: Wong Chin Foo and the Chinese Equal Rights League." In *Claiming America: Constructing Chinese American Identities during the Exclusion Era*, edited by K. Scott Wong and Sucheng Chan, 41–63. Philadelphia: Temple University Press.

Zhang, Xudong. 2008. *Postsocialism and Cultural Politics: China in the Last Decade of the Twentieth Century*. Durham, NC: Duke University Press.

YUAN SHU

ACKNOWLEDGEMENTS

THIS VOLUME IS DERIVED from the 2010 Texas Tech University symposium "American Studies as Transnational Practice," which I organized as
the director of the Comparative Literature Program. Bringing leading and
rising scholars in American studies—Donald E. Pease, Eva Cherniavsky,
and Hsuan Hsu—into a critical dialogue with the leading scholar in Latin
American studies and decolonial studies, Walter Mignolo, the symposium
produced a synergy that would move beyond transatlantic studies and point
toward the transpacific. I invited Donald E. Pease to co-edit this volume
with me. I sincerely appreciate Donald E. Pease's generous guidance and
support, which have informed and reshaped the volume into a response as
well as a sequel to his *Re-framing the Transnational Turn in American Studies*. I am especially pleased at his reformulation of the account of the state
of the field that was laid out in the introduction to that precursor volume.
I am also grateful for the opportunities to speak at Dartmouth, first at the
Master of Arts in Liberal Studies Program in 2012, and then at the Futures
of American Studies Institute in 2014.

   To better understand transpacific American studies, I applied for and received a special initiative grant from the Henry Luce Foundation. With the
support of the foundation and its program director Li Ling, I was able to
bring many of the contributors to this volume to the "Oceanic Archives
and Transnational American Studies" symposium at Hong Kong University,
which was co-sponsored by Otto Heim and Kendall Johnson, and to the
"American Studies as Transnational Practice" symposium at Tsinghua University in Beijing, hosted by Wang Ning in 2012. I thank each collaborator
and participant for intellectual exchanges and wonderful friendships, which
furthered our objectives and sharpened our focus.

   I also want to express my gratitude to Texas Tech University, which
supported me when I was directing the Comparative Literature Program
and provided me with financial support and a developmental leave when

I was co-editing the volume. Lawrence Schovanec delivered the welcome speech at the 2010 symposium as dean of College of Arts and Sciences, and continued his support for the volume as provost. Juan Muñoz, senior vice president and vice provost, has generously supported the Comparative Literature Program and the Asian Studies Program philosophically and financially throughout the years. Associate dean David Roach has always been generous and supportive of me and the interdisciplinary programs. Department of English colleagues Kanika Batra, Ann Ransdell, Rich Rice, former chair Sam Dragga, and current chair Bruce Clarke all offered indispensable support during the symposium and beyond.

CONTRIBUTORS

Eva Cherniavsky is the Andrew R. Hilen Professor of American Literature and Culture at the University of Washington. She is the author of *That Pale Mother Rising: Sentimental Discourses and the Imitation of Motherhood in Nineteenth-Century America* (Indiana University Press, 1995) and of *Incorporations: Race, Nation, and the Body Politics of Capital* (University of Minnesota Press, 2006). Her current research considers the changing contours of the political in the context of neoliberal governance, with an emphasis on the reimagination of citizenship in popular culture.

Shelley Fisher Fishkin, the Joseph S. Atha Professor of Humanities, a professor of English, and the director of American studies at Stanford University, is the award-winning author, editor, or coeditor of over forty books and over a hundred articles, essays, columns, and reviews. She holds a PhD in American studies from Yale University and is a former president of the American Studies Association and a founding editor of the *Journal of Transnational American Studies*.

Paul Giles is the Challis Professor of English at the University of Sydney, in Australia. His most recent book is *Antipodean America: Australasia and the Constitution of U.S. Literature* (Oxford University Press, 2013).

Alfred Hornung is a research professor in the Institute of Transnational American Studies at the Johannes Gutenberg University of Mainz, Germany, and a specialist in postmodern American culture and transcultural life writing. He was a fellow at Harvard University, Yale University, and the National Humanities Center, and he is a member of the Center for Cross-Cultural Studies at Peking University. He received the Carl Bode-Norman Holmes Pearson Prize in 2013 and was elected a member of Academia Europaea: The Academy of Europe for Letters, the Humanities and Natural Sciences in 2014.

Walter D. Mignolo is the William H. Wannamaker Professor and director of the Center for Global Studies and the Humanities at Duke University. His work has been translated into Chinese, Korean, Indonesian, German, Italian, Rumanian, French, Swedish, Spanish, and Portuguese.

Viet Thanh Nguyen is an associate professor of English and American studies and ethnicity at the University of Southern California, as well as the coeditor of *Transpacific Studies: Framing an Emerging Field*. He is also the author of *Race and Resistance: Literature and Politics in Asian America* and a novel, *The Sympathizer*.

Donald E. Pease, a professor of English and comparative literature, the Ted and Helen Geisel Third Century Professor in the Humanities, and chair of the Master of Arts in Liberal Studies Program at Dartmouth College, is an authority on nineteenth- and twentieth-century American literature and literary theory and the founder and director of the Futures of American Studies Institute. He has authored numerous books, including *Theodor Seuss Geisel*, and over a hundred articles on figures in American and British literature. He serves as the editor of the New Americanist series at Duke University Press, which has transformed the field of American studies.

Rafael Pérez-Torres, a professor of English at UCLA, has authored three books: *Movements in Chicano Poetry: Against Myths, Against Margins* (Cambridge University Press, 1995); *Mestizaje: Critical Uses of Race in Chicano Culture* (University of Minnesota Press, 2006); and *To Alcatraz, Death Row, and Back: Memories of an East L.A. Outlaw*, written with Ernest B. López (University of Texas Press, 2005). Pérez-Torres's current work addresses the role of modernity and modernization in the shaping of Chicana/o culture.

John Carlos Rowe is the USC Associates' Professor of the Humanities and a professor of English and American studies and ethnicity at the University of Southern California, where he has served as chair of the Department of American Studies and Ethnicity. He is the author of nine books, more than 150 essays and reviews, and editor or coeditor of ten books, including *Literary Culture and U.S. Imperialism: From the Revolution to World War II* (2000), *A Concise Companion to American Studies* (2010), *Afterlives of Modernism: Liberalism, Transnationalism, and Political Critique* (2011), and *The Cultural Politics of the New American Studies* (2012).

Ramón Saldívar, a professor of English and comparative literature and the Hoagland Family Professor of Humanities and Sciences at Stanford University, was awarded the National Humanities Medal by President Barack Obama in 2012. A cowinner in 2006 of the Modern Language Association Prize in US Latina and Latino and Chicana and Chicano Literary and Cultural Studies for his book, *The Borderlands of Culture: Américo Paredes and the Transnational Imaginary* (Duke University Press, 2006), he is currently working on a new project, tentatively titled "The Racial Imaginary: Speculative Realism and Historical Fantasy in Contemporary Ethnic Fiction."

Yuan Shu is an associate professor of English and director of the Asian Studies Program at Texas Tech University. He has published in journals ranging from *Cultural Critique* to *MELUS* and is working on a book-length project on transnationalism and Asian American literature.

Etsuko Taketani is a professor of American literature at the University of Tsukuba. She is the author of *U.S. Women Writers and the Discourses of Colonialism, 1825–1861* (University of Tennessee Press, 2003) and *The Black Pacific Narrative: Geographic Imaginings of Race and Empire between the World Wars* (Dartmouth College Press, 2014).

Rob Wilson is a professor of literature and cultural studies at the University of California, Santa Cruz. His scholary books include *American Sublime: The Genealogy of a Poetic Genre, Reimagining the American Pacific: From "South Pacific" to Bamboo Ridge and Beyond*, and *Be Always Converting, Be Always Converted: An American Poetics*. He is at work on a new study called "Pacific beneath the Pavements: Toward an Ecopoetics of World Oceanic Becoming."

INDEX

Page numbers in italics refer to illustrations.

170, 172, 188, 348–351; post-9/11 economic ascendancy, 3–4, 8, 15, 18, 357–58, 383–84; sinocentrism, 101n12, 190, 373; Sino-Japanese War, 187–199, 201; Taiping Rebellion, 268–69; Western nationalism and, 297–98. *See also* ChinAmerica; Chinese Americans; Confucian political theory

ChinAmerica: Chinese Association of American Studies, 357; defined, 340; exceptionalism of, 29, 340–41; methodological approach to, 344; modern period, 344–48, 367–68, 378–383; neorealism period, 351–58; postmodern/Maoist period, 348–351

Chinese Americans: "agrarian dream" outlook of, 12; Chinese American epistemology, 96–97, 101n12; Chinese American studies, 342–43; Chinese labor history project, 343; Confucian epistemology and, 96–97, 101n12; racial discrimination against, 16, 265–66, 269, 341, 369–370, 372–383

civil rights movement, 26, 138, 158, 160, 372. *See also* human rights

Clifford, James, 94–95, 228–29, 366–67, 371–72

Clinton, Bill, 51, 353–54

Clinton, Hillary, 8, 17–18, 254

Cold War: American studies political role, 283–84; Asian-Pacific "de-Cold-Warization," 218–19; cinematic representations of Manchuria, 169–170; Mark Twain antiauthoritarianism and, 124–25, 135n88; "negro propaganda" agenda, 171, 173–76; Pacific Charter policies and, 5–6; post-WWII Asian communism, 11; transnational relationships and, 3–4, 48; U.S. exceptionalism and, 39–40, 51

colonial imperialism: colonial modernity, 13, 30, 366–69; deimperialization, 20, 100, 244–45, 286–88; "double bind" intellectual hegemony, 90, 374–75; imperialized subjectivity, 28, 287–88; Japan Westernization

initiative and, 14–15; legacy inequities in multicultural society, 52, 138–39; in Lowell's *Near the Ocean*, 249–253; Manchukuo as colonial state, 171–72, 177–78, 180–191, 201–2; Manifest Destiny paradigm, 12, 239–240, 263, 281; Mexico as paradigmatic conquest, 162; neoliberal imperialism, 3, 81, 87–88, 288; Oceania tourism and, 225–26, 234n43; Pacific island imperialist imaginary, 242–45, 267–69; Pacific neoimperialism, 3, 220, 260–61, 265, 267–69, 273; Pu Yi as puppet leader, 171; Roman Empire as model, 249–252, 263; semicolonialism, 367–69, 371; Theodore Roosevelt Pacific strategy, 4; totalitarian communism and, 15; transnational imperial structure and, 8–9, 298; U.S. imperialism emergence, 286–87; U.S. utopian/idealistic transpacific agenda, 239; Western neoimperialism, 261, 264–65. *See also* decolonization; postcolonialism

commemoration, 29, 312–15, 318–326

communism: anticolonialism and, 15, 26; CPUSA views of Japan, 187–88, 193, 195–96; Japanese "moral communism," 198–99; Maoist Cultural Revolution, 348–352; Mark Twain antiauthoritarianism and, 124–25, 135n88; post-Soviet transition economies, 67; post-WWII Asian communism, 11; Vietnam communism, 314, 317–321, 332–33, 335. *See also* socialism

Confucian political theory: antiwar advocacy and, 98–99; Chinese articulation of, 14–15, 19, 92–93; human rights and, 19; as neoliberalism alternative, 24–25, 85, 92–93; *qi* concept in, 95–96. *See also* China

Connery, Christopher, 220, 241–42

Cooper, James Fenimore, 159, 242

cosmopolitanism, 41, 71, 109, 298, 342, 367–370, 373–74

[402] Index

multiculturalism: conviviality as intercultural solidarity, 342; Manchukuo
ethnic diversity, 181–87; in post-
Soviet-bloc higher education, 72;
Randolph Bourne transnational
approach, 348; Western nationalism
and, 297–98. See also ethnicity
multinational corporations, 2, 6,
11–12, 173, 177–186, 190.
See also capitalism
Murayama, Milton, 229
Murdoch, Rupert, 241–42
Murray, Yxta Maya, 158–59
My Life in China and America (Yung),
29–30, 365–66, 378

Nakamura, Tameji, 118–19
Nancy, Jean-Luc, 235n56
Nanking Massacre, 191
nationalism: antinationalist memory art,
314–15; assimilative citizenship as
device of, 68; Cold War hyper-
nationalism, 1; denationalization,
22; European ethnonationalism, 69,
71; expansionist capital and, 70;
imperialized subjectivity in, 287–88;
New American postnationalism, 24;
post-WWII Japanese nationalism, 16.
See also nation-states
nation-states: enfranchisement/citizenship
in, 47–50, 148, 270–72, 298–300;
as European concept, 296–97;
exceptional spaces in, 52–53; failed
states, 50; globalization of markets
and, 44–46; interculturalism vs.
multiculturalism in, 299; Japan
as nation-state, 14–15; mandated
identities in, 56–57; New American
postnationalism, 24; popular sovereignty, 74–75, 78–80; sociology
as instrument of, 288–89; state as
educator, 73–74; systemic crises and,
44; territorial belonging and, 27; U.S.
as plurinational state, 25; welfare
state dismantling, 46, 51. See also
nationalism

Native American and Indigenous Studies
Association, 300–301
Native Americans, 21, 84, 222, 248,
264–66, 270–71, 298–300. See also
indigeneity
Ndesandjo, Mark, 354
Negri, Antonio, 20, 88
neoliberalism: contemporary U.S. Asia
policy and, 17; history of, 86–87;
imperial domination in, 3, 81, 87–88;
neo-citizenship, 74–81; neoliberal
rationality, 75–76; New American
studies and, 24; post-Soviet-bloc per-
spective on, 70–71; public diplomacy
and, 67–68; public welfare and, 46;
Western nationalism and, 298.
See also globalization
neorealism, 351–52
Nétillard, Susanne, 120–21
New American studies, 24
New Caledonia, 215, 228–29
New Zealand, 6, 240, 247–48
Nguyễn, Phú Cu'ò'ng, 318, 319
Nguyen, Viet Thana, 23, 29
9/11 terrorist attack, 3, 20, 51, 238
Nolan, Sidney, 249–253, 252
North Atlantic Treaty Organization
(NATO), 5, 238

Obama, Barack, 3–6, 8, 13, 29, 152,
156–57, 238–39, 341, 345, 353–56,
355–56, 359n5
Oceania ecumeme: as anti-imperial
discourse, 215–16, 240–41; Asian
mainland exclusion from, 221;
ecological solidarity and, 220–21,
272–73; ecumeme conceptual
foundation, 216–17; Oceanic
studies, 219. See also Pacific
transnational region
Ōe, Kenzaburō, 20, 114–15, 118–19
O'Gorman, Edmundo, 292–94, 307
Okinawa, 11, 213
Open Society Institute (OSI), 78
Orchid Islands, 222–23
Orientalism, 214–15, 244, 260